The Old
Chisholm
Trail

Nancy and Ted Paup Ranching Heritage Series

Paul H. Carlson & M. Scott Sosebee, General Editors

The Old Chisholm Trail

From Cow Path to Tourist Stop

Wayne Ludwig

Texas A&M
University
Press

College Station

This paper meets the requirements of
ANSI/NISO Z39.48–1992 (Permanence of Paper).
Binding materials have been chosen for durability.
Manufactured in the United States of America
∞♻

Library of Congress Cataloging-in-Publication Data

Names: Ludwig, Wayne, 1954– author.

Title: The old Chisholm Trail: from cow path to tourist stop / Wayne Ludwig.

Description: First edition. | College Station: Texas A&M University Press, [2018]

Series: Nancy and Ted Paup ranching heritage series | Includes bibliographical references and index.

Identifiers: LCCN 2018006344 (print) | LCCN 2018012655 (ebook) |
ISBN 9781623496722 (ebook) | ISBN 9781623496715 | ISBN 9781623496715 (cloth : alk. paper)

Subjects: LCSH: Chisholm Trail—History. | Cattle trails—West (U.S.)—History—19th century. | Cattle drives—West (U.S.)—History—19th century. | West (U.S.)—History, Local. | West (U.S.)—History—19th century. | Frontier and pioneer life—West (U.S.)

Classification: LCC F596 (ebook) | LCC F596 .L86 2018 (print) | DDC 978/.02—dc23

LC record available at https://lccn.loc.gov/2018006344

In memory of
GEORGE W. SAUNDERS,
founder of the
Old Time Trail Drivers' Association,
the trail drivers, and the
pioneers of Texas

Contents

Contents

A gallery of illustrations follows page 84

Series Editors'
Foreword

ASK ALMOST ANYONE TO "draw an American" and more likely than not the depiction you will get back is of a cowboy. The cowboy, the laborer of the ranch, has become the quintessential American hero, the nation's icon of record. Books, essays, personal narratives, and commentaries associated with ranching, cattlemen, cowboys, and related topics in the American West date from well over a century ago. Such an image remained popular as the twentieth century turned to the twenty-first and began to include works on cowboy poetry, music, fiction of the kind found in Beadle's dime novels, myth, films, television programs, diaries and journals, and serious discourses. Their themes were myriad and covered sheepherders and sheep raising, details of agricultural husbandry, range wars of various kinds, drovers and trail driving, rustling, lawmen, agricultural financing, and more other topics than one can imagine. Combined, they began to make the cowboy, the ranch, and the expanses of the "West" the equivalent of the American Camelot, the mythical ideal of what Americans saw in themselves, that "rugged individualist" who brought justice and order to a chaotic land and time.

The reality of the cowboy, and his profession of raising and tending cattle, is different than the myth. The cowboy, or a "hand" or "waddie," which is more accurate when you speak of the worker who tended cattle on a ranch, was anything but a lone individual. The hands on a ranch worked together in pursuit of a common goal. Their working days were long, twelve to fourteen hours, and they worked for meager pay, often for an absentee owner. Ranching, as a business, is not a romantic pursuit. The business is subject to the whims of Mother Nature, a fickle market, and an often unforgiving land. The old saying "the best way to make a small fortune raising stock is to begin with a large one" is not far from the truth.

The Nancy and Ted Paup Ranching Heritage Series carries forward the time-honored tradition of offering fresh but distinguished books in the respected genre. The series will strive to stress that new research and studies on the heritage of ranching, stock raising, and the men and women who toiled and struggled in establishing such a business is valuable and needed. The initial book in the series, *The Old Chisholm Trail: From Cow Path to Tourist Stop*, represents the first comprehensive examination of the famous Texas-to-Kansas cattle-driving route in more than half a century. In a broad, engaging narrative, it charts the evolution of major Texas cattle trails, explores the rise of the Chisholm in legend and lore, and analyzes the growth of cattle trail tourism associated with increasing automobile traffic and community leaders concomitantly seeking to promote economic benefits through modern highway travel.

The result of years of original and innovative research—often using documents and sources unavailable to previous generations of historians—Wayne Ludwig has produced a groundbreaking study that offers an original interpretation in an agreeable prose style. The book makes an important and modern contribution to the history of the American West.

Paul H. Carlson and M. Scott Sosebee
General Editors
Nancy and Ted Paup Ranching Heritage Series

Foreword

AS A MATTER OF INTRODUCTION, the Saunders family has been in the horse and cattle business since we came to Texas in 1850. My great-grandfather, W. D. H. Saunders, drove cattle east to Mississippi during the Civil War. Starting in 1871, my great-granduncle, George W. Saunders, drove cattle north to Kansas and other northern markets, to New Orleans and the Texas Gulf Coast, and south to Mexico. My grandfather, Thomas B. Saunders II, was the first cattle dealer in the Live Stock Exchange Building after it was built in the Fort Worth Stockyards in 1902. This office stayed open for business for seventy-five years. My dad, Thomas B. Saunders III, said that the cow business is more than just a business; it is a way of life. Having said that, the history of the cattle trails is more than just a bunch of stories about cowboys and cattle; it is part of our heritage.

Many stories have been told over the years about the trails. Fiction became mixed in and was often accepted as fact. This book, written by Wayne Ludwig and dedicated to George W. Saunders and the old trail drivers, will clear up many myths and untruths about the Chisholm Trail and the Great Western Trail that have developed over the years since 1915. This is the best and most well researched book of its kind. Wayne went to the actual sources for information, including the men who actually rode the trails and knew their names, and whose own histories were recorded either in their own personal documents or those of their descendants.

I am very honored to have the privilege to write the foreword for this book because Uncle George was adamant about correctness of the history of this time period—a period so important to the history of Texas. After the Civil War ended, all the Southern states were broke. The only thing Texas had were cowboys and a multitude of cattle.

These cattle were the only true American breed, and they evolved into what they are today. Over a period of three hundred years of running wild and natural selection, these cattle provided the foundation for Texas' economic survival after the war.

A while back, we at the Texas and Southwestern Cattle Raisers Association were fortunate to acquire a collection of papers that detail Captain John T. Lytle's involvement in the cattle business from the 1870s to the early 1900s. It is the use of sources like this, along with maps and other documents from the actual period of the cattle drives, that helps separate fact from fiction to set the record straight. This book documents the period in Texas history when Texas cowboys took millions of head of cattle north by way of various trails and saved the economy of Texas. As Berta Nance said in 1932, "Other states were carved or born; Texas grew from hide and horn."

Tom B. Saunders IV
Weatherford, Texas

Preface

IN JANUARY 2011 I was invited to a ceremony at the Sheraton Hotel, located at 1701 Commerce Street in downtown Fort Worth. The occasion was to rededicate a Chisholm Trail marker post that had been installed in 2000, had been removed during a remodeling project, and was being reinstalled. Being a native of Fort Worth with an interest in local history, a fan of the classic television Westerns and Western movies, and generally interested in the history of Texas and the American West, I asked what I thought was a perfectly logical question: Why is there a Chisholm Trail marker post in Fort Worth? I knew that Fort Worth was known as Cowtown, that herds passed through Fort Worth on their way north, and I knew about the 1960s-era monument to the "Eastern Cattle Trail . . . Chisholm Trail" on the bluff north of the Tarrant County courthouse, and I had read somewhere a long time ago that Jesse Chisholm's trail was a route between somewhere in Indian Territory and somewhere in Kansas. I was unaware at that time that the Chisholm Trail is the subject of a long-running debate (or argument, depending on who you ask) that might have started in the early 1900s, or maybe even earlier. We have a Chisholm Trail mural in Sundance Square in downtown Fort Worth, and we used to have Chisholm Trail Days in the Stockyards, but I always figured that was just for decoration or tourists and did not pay much attention at the time.

That question led to research that included interviews with people who have well over a hundred years of collective research experience on the subject. Soon I found that what I initially thought should be a simple question with a simple and direct answer prompted evasive or incomplete responses, which aroused my curiosity even more and led to more questions. Why were some folks so quick to embrace a map that had been drawn decades after the drives ended and was as likely as not based on opinion rather than fact? Why were some former trail drivers, who later stated that the trail in Texas was the Chisholm Trail, quoted as gospel, while other former trail men who contradicted that story ignored or discredited for some ambiguous reason? What was it that some folks seemed to want to avoid discussing? If the trail through Texas was actually known as the Chisholm, where was the supporting documentation from the historical period of the cattle drives? Why did the conversation end or folks seem to become irritated when the discussion turned from twentieth-century folklore to nineteenth-century documentation? What was it about the Chisholm Trail name that prompted reactions that defy logic, such as, "Yes, your facts are correct, but this is the Chisholm Trail, and that's that!"

I also learned very quickly that passions can run high on the subject of the names and routes of the old cattle trails in Texas. It was not uncommon to encounter situations in which research was apparently done in order to support a predetermined notion or conclusion. Upon further investigation, the parts of the story that did not fit the particular view that was being advanced were omitted. Omissions of this type cast an obvious shadow of doubt on the rest of the account being offered, because they tell only a selective story, and the narrative often changed considerably when all of the information was included. I encountered a variety of attitudes early in the process, and no shortage of opinions. I found that some opinions were based on nothing more than 1930s-era anecdotes, some seemed well thought out, and some folks simply were not interested in letting a few facts get in the way of their opinion.

After about a year of research, I was encouraged to write a book on the subject. I had never attempted a project of this size before and sought guidance. I was asked, "If you do it, how would you approach your project?" Knowing that the line between historical fact and folklore can become easily blurred, especially regarding the Chisholm Trail, I determined early on to approach this endeavor as an investigation. My approach was to avoid preconceived conclusions, seek the facts, follow the trail of evidence wherever it led, determine what can and cannot be corroborated by data from as close to the historical period of the event as possible, document findings, remain objective, and just let the chips fall where they may. I have tried to use a thorough, consistent approach and base conclusions on the evidence.

The story of the Chisholm Trail is much more involved than the tale of a single cattle trail and cannot be sufficiently told exclusive of the other major trails and related events. It is important to note that there was usually more than one way to get from one point to the next. Historical periods of use and transition from one trail to the next overlapped, and the histories of the trails are intertwined. Although the topic of the Chisholm Trail was the driving factor in my research, I included other major cattle trails because they are all a related part of the trails' history. The Chisholm Trail eventually became so famous that it overshadowed the others. While I explore other trails, I mainly trace the Chisholm Trail's progression from a trade route and simple cow path during the cattle trailing era through its transition into legend and tourist attractions.

I will not discuss the politics of the era to any extent except in the context of the cattle drives, since the often complex political issues of the period are not the primary focus of this work. Tales of cowboys, their adventures on the trails, and the Indian wars have been extensively covered in other works, are not the primary focus of this project, and are included only to the extent of illustrating appropriate examples. If any language is used herein that is not considered prudent or correct in today's world, it is used in the historical context of the period or in a direct quote and should not be interpreted as a derogatory remark toward anyone.

I have left a trail of sources and information for those who might be interested in following it. The name and route of the Chisholm Trail in Texas has been debated for more than one hundred years; whether any part of the old debate is settled within this volume is up to the reader. I have no control over what has been written in the past or handed down by oral history, only over my own research and writings. Statements from other selected literary works, reports, historical markers, and anecdotes have been compared to the historical record as found for the purpose of corroborating the information, and no critique or criticism of any individual or work is intended.

Information that may have been overlooked in the past or that has become available as a result of recent advances in technology combined with previously known information will provide a different view of the evolution of the cattle trails. From the first Spanish cattle trail in 1779 to the failed national cattle trail in 1887, the subsequent Chisholm Trail controversy, how the Chisholm name came to be applied to the Texas portion of the trail, and the transition of the Chisholm Trail from a simple path to a legend will be examined.

If I do not achieve any other result from this project, it has provided the opportunity to meet new people, make new friends, learn through discovery, and learn which historical cattle trails actually connect and which fictional paths are trails to nowhere. My purpose is to be as historically accurate as possible, to separate folklore from fact where feasible, and, I hope, to tell an interesting story along the way. The trip up this trail has taken approximately six years; I hope you enjoy the book, and be careful what you ask—you never know where it might lead.

Acknowledgments

THIS PROJECT WOULD NEVER HAVE HAPPENED without the involvement of others who share a common interest in our historical past. I would like to take this opportunity to thank Jay Dew, Katie Duelm, and the staff at Texas A&M University Press for their interest and assistance in publishing this manuscript. It was a pleasure to work with copyeditor Noel Parsons, and I appreciate his efforts and attention to detail. I am grateful to Clara and Bob Holmes for inviting me to the Chisholm Trail marker rededication ceremony that initially attracted my curiosity, for reading my first draft, and for providing feedback and encouragement. Thanks to Tom B. Saunders IV, Roland S. Jary, and Matthew S. Jary for sharing research, ideas, and family archive material. Debbie Liles and Rick Selcer, historians, authors, and teachers, endured my early drafts and mentored me throughout the writing process; thank you both for your patience, guidance, advice, and kindness. Thanks to R. W. Hewett for sharing his ancestor's letters telling of life on the trail. Actor and Western artist Buck Taylor was gracious in providing the cover art, evoking an image of another era; thanks, Buck.

Additional thanks are due to John Phillips, Gwyn Dominick, and Kevin Dyke of the Edmon Low Library at Oklahoma State University; Chad Williams of the Oklahoma Historical Society; Deanna Holderith and Hilary Baker of the Cattle Raisers Museum; Ellen Brisendine of *The Cattleman* magazine; Aaron Holt of the National Archives at Fort Worth; Will Cradduck, herd manager of the Official State of Texas Longhorn Herd; Debbie Davis, Frank Sharp, and D. Phillip Sponenberg of the Cattlemen's Texas Longhorn Conservancy; Brenda McClurkin, Cathy Spitzenberger, Betty Shankle, and Ben Huseman of Special Collections, University of Texas at Arlington Libraries;

Cynthia Smith and Ed Redmond of the Geography and Map Division, Library of Congress; and Roberta Sittel and Jace Klepper of University of North Texas Libraries.

I also thank Robin Carter, Commission Support, Texas Department of Transportation; Morex Arai, Lisa Caprino, Stephanie Arias, and Manuel Flores of the Huntington Library; Pat Halpin of the Old Trail Drivers' Association; Tom Weger, Montague County historian; authors Margaret and Gary Kraisinger; Nell Ann McBroom and the staff at Tales 'N' Trails Museum; Dawn Youngblood of the Tarrant County Archives; Kevin Mackey of the Grace Armantrout Museum; Barbara Morris Westbrook of the Atascosa County Historical Commission; author Dana S. Chisholm; and Tip Igou. I give special thanks to Andy Tewes, who rescued data when my computer hard drive crashed after a few months of research and writing.

Although research to satisfy my own curiosity was well underway, I initially had no intentions of writing a book. As the stacks of research material grew in my backroom office, my wife suggested that I put it to better use. To my wife, Martha, thank you for the encouragement to tackle this project and for enduring the long hours apart. To Martha, my daughters Amy and Emily, son-in-law Adam, brother Wes, and sister-in-law Holly, I appreciate your tolerance for the seemingly endless stream of cattle trails trivia and revelations. Wes, this project would not have been possible without your support, thank you. Thanks to my brother Warren for assistance with some of the images. Mom and Dad, Wanda and William, both passed away during this project yet were with me throughout. And once again, my eternal gratitude is due to my family, who supported, encouraged, and believed in me throughout this project.

The Old Chisholm Trail

1

The
Texas Cattle
Trails

SOMEWHERE ON THE PRAIRIE north of the Red River, within pistol shot of a cattle trail that led north toward the railhead at Abilene, Kansas, a small mound of recently turned dirt marked the grave of some unlucky drover. The poor soul's boots were left standing upright on the mound as a final tribute.[1] His name and the cause of his death are unknown; perhaps he was struck by lightning or killed in a stampede. The buffalo grass and grama grasses would soon reclaim their place in the prairie sod that covered the grave, and the boots would either be found in the grass by another drover or trampled by the next herd that passed over that particular patch of ground. This cattle trail, the main route to the railhead, would eventually become famous as the Chisholm Trail.

Cattle herds had been driven from Texas to various destinations since 1779. Less was written and therefore less is known of these drives, but enough information exists to provide a glimpse into that early period of trails history. The first longhorn herds were driven east across the Sabine River in 1779 by the Spanish.[2] The Comanches disrupted some of the early drives when they raided along the road between La Bahia and Nacogdoches, which was the route taken by the early cattle drives. After acquiring horses during the late 1600s, the Comanches had quickly become expert riders. The technology of the horse enabled them to roam from the plains of eastern Colorado and western Kansas into New Mexico and Texas, across the Rio Grande into Mexico, and conquer or displace any of the resident tribes that stood in their way. The horse gave them a tremendous range and advantage over an adversary afoot.[3]

After Anglo settlers arrived in Texas in the 1820s, the cattle trails evolved as the destination markets changed. The early drives went east to New Orleans. Later, during the 1840s, cattle markets were established in Missouri and the Midwest. Miners who flocked to California and Colorado during the gold rush were fed with Texas cattle. The population of Texas in 1850 was only 212,592,[4] and there were more wild cattle in Texas than people. Settlements were primarily located east of a line roughly drawn between the present locations of the cities of Gainesville, Fort Worth, Waco, Fredericksburg, and Laredo. A series of forts was located along or just to the west of that line to protect the frontier. West of the frontier line lay wilderness and prairie, opportunity mixed with danger.

The country west of the Mississippi River was sparsely settled by 1860, with 86 percent of the population concentrated east of the Mississippi. The total US population was roughly equivalent to the combined 2010 populations of New York, New Jersey, and Connecticut. The total population living in states and territories west of the Mississippi River in 1860 was only slightly greater than the combined 2010 populations of the Texas counties of Dallas, Tarrant, and Parker. The total population of Texas was slightly less than the 2010 population of Denton County, Texas.[5] There were only eight states in the continental United States west of the Mississippi River. Towns were few and far between.

In 1850 there was an average of less than one inhabitant per square mile and more than nine square miles of open land for every dwelling that existed in Texas. By 1860 the population grew to just over two inhabitants per square mile, with more than three square miles of open land for every dwelling.[6] Considering that most dwellings were clustered within settlements or towns, vast areas of Texas were open prairie and wilderness, where a traveler or drovers on the trail might go for days without seeing another person.

Texas had cattle but no means of interstate rail shipment at that time. Railroad construction had been concentrated among the population and industrial centers of the eastern United States. With few exceptions, rail travel was limited in 1860 to certain points generally east of a line drawn from Chicago to Cincinnati, Louisville, Chattanooga, Atlanta, and Savannah.[7] Top speed of a typical locomotive in 1860 was about twenty miles per hour. During the Civil War, limited numbers of cattle were driven west into New Mexico Territory; east into Arkansas, Louisiana, and Mississippi; and north to Missouri as wartime conditions permitted. After the Civil War, railroad construction resumed, and railheads were established in Missouri, central Kansas, and Nebraska. This meant that drovers could ship their herds to the beef markets by rail. Texas cattle were also driven north to stock the western and northern ranges of the United States.

Despite the fact that organized cattle drives from Texas had occurred for eighty-eight years by the time the first herd raised dust on the Chisholm Trail in 1867, the post–Civil War years are typically considered to be the golden age of the cattle driving period. Perhaps this is because the postwar drives had greater economic impact and occurred simultaneously with other landmark events in the history of the American West. Many veteran trail drivers from that period survived into the twentieth century to tell their stories and were living links to the frontier and a lifestyle that had vanished during their generation.

The US Bureau of Statistics estimated that 5,200,000 head of cattle were driven north from Texas between 1866 and 1884. This estimate includes beef cattle shipped from the Kansas markets and cattle used to stock the northern and western ranges. Stricter quarantine laws, overstocking, extreme weather, and poor range conditions combined to reduce the northbound flow of trail herds between 1885 and 1887. Approximately half of the range cattle died during the winter of 1886–87, when carcasses littered the ranges from Montana to central Texas. Although cattle drives from Texas still occurred, no official volume estimates were found for the three-year period 1885–87. By 1887 the last remaining northbound trail was being slowly choked by settlement and barbed-wire fences. Access to the Kansas and Nebraska railheads was cut off by quarantine laws. Drovers continued to trail smaller numbers of cattle north to Montana until the mid-1890s, but the failure to designate a national cattle trail in 1887 marked the beginning of the end of the trail driving era. Estimates of the total post–Civil War volume of cattle driven from Texas range from 6,000,000 to 10,000,000; the exact number is unknown. The larger estimates are often vague, and it is not clear whether the volume of cattle shipped via railroad from Texas during the later years of the period is included.[8]

Approximately 2,400,000 head of cattle were driven north from Texas during the Chisholm Trail's primary years of use, 1867–75.[9] Less than half of the volume of cattle driven from Texas traveled the Chisholm Trail. This trail was shorter in length than later trails that led to Nebraska, Colorado, Wyoming, Montana, and the Dakotas, and it was not the first cattle trail from Texas nor was it the last. Nevertheless, for some reason the Chisholm Trail has received more publicity since the early 1900s than all of the other cattle trails combined. It was certainly important and has its place in history; however, it was only one of several routes that were used by Texas drovers to move their herds to the railheads and livestock markets during the historical period of the post–Civil War cattle drives.

Accurate calculations of Texas cattle driven to the main cattle markets of Kansas City, Saint Louis, and Chicago cannot be performed, since the reported totals include cattle received from Texas as well as cattle received as a result of the natural herd increase of the western ranges.[10] Based on an assumed average sale price of $25 per head and the estimated number of cattle driven from the state, the sale of Texas cattle during the period raised an estimated $130 million, which is the equivalent of nearly $3.1 billion in 2016. In addition, an unknown number of horses used to drive the cattle were sold at the end of the trail, railroad freight revenue increased, stockyards were built, towns were founded and grew around the railheads, and salaries were paid. Other related industries such as tanneries, hatters, supply stores, and bootmakers flourished. The total economic impact is incalculable. Cattle sales provided the economic engine that rescued Texas from bankruptcy immediately after the war.

Texas cattle also benefited the national economy. In 1883 the United States exported more than $10 million worth of fresh beef to Great Britain. Exports of preserved beef grew from less than $1 million in 1864 to a peak of $7.9 million in 1880. Cattle exports to Great Britain and Ireland in 1884 totaled $17.3 million. The combined value of US cattle and beef products exported in 1884 alone totaled over $41 million. Cattle from Texas and the western ranges accounted for approximately 95 percent of the exports.[11]

The number of drovers who went up the trails is a matter of speculation. George W. Saunders, founder of the Old Time Trail Drivers' Association, estimated that thirty-five thousand men went up the trails during 1868–95. Historian T. C. Richardson estimated the number at forty thousand men. The ratio of non-Anglo drovers is also questionable; Saunders estimated that one-third of the men who went up the trails were black or Mexican. It is unknown whether Saunders based his estimate on his own experiences, observations, and interviews or whether he based it on data that have been lost to time. Charles Goodnight estimated an average of one man for every 150–200 head of cattle when he prepared for a drive. The estimates cannot be proven or disproven based on a ratio of drovers to cattle, since the total number of cattle is unknown, and each trail boss had his own ideas. A complete roster containing the name and race of every drover who went up the trail, along with the number who made multiple trips, does not exist.[12]

The first black cowhands who went up the trails generally learned their trade as slaves on ranches. The subject of slave ownership has usually been connected with farming or cotton production, and the connection to the livestock business has rarely been mentioned. Many slave owners who had their beginnings in the cattle business on the ranges of the northwestern frontier of Texas eventually became successful cattlemen, and some, such as John S. Chisum and Oliver Loving, became legendary. Although Chisum owned a small number of slaves, for the years 1859–64 the number of slaves he owned increased as his Denton County cattle herd increased. Tax records show that Chisum owned four slaves in 1859, six in 1860, seven in 1861–62, and thirteen in 1864. Chisum's cattle herd almost doubled in size during the same period. Loving's slaveholdings were similar; tax records show four slaves in 1856–58, five in 1859–60, seven in 1861, eight in 1862, seven in 1863, and thirteen in 1864. While only two names are mentioned here as examples, during the period of 1854–64 an average of 91 percent of the slave owners in seven of the northwestern frontier counties also owned livestock, mainly cattle and horses. Similar conditions likely existed along the frontier as new counties were created in sparsely settled areas with livestock as the primary economic engine. Slaves were an integral part of that growth prior to and during the war. Many former slaves, such as Bose Ikard and Daniel Webster "80 John" Wallace, used their acquired ranching skills to become drovers and ranchers after the war.[13]

The Trail Drivers of Texas contains many accounts of experiences on the trail by drovers, but only a few of those accounts make reference to drovers of a minority race. It is likely that many men who worked on the trails and ranches were illiterate, did not think that anyone would be interested in what they had to say, or simply were occupied with the pursuits and hardships of life and did not care to fool with recording their stories. It is also possible that a man's race was not considered as important on the trail as were his capabilities; therefore, there was no special recognition of race in the average trail outfit. Some have attempted to equate the number of articles and books that mentioned or were authored by minority drovers, or the lack thereof, to a measurement of the racial makeup of the drovers during the historical period. Rather than an accurate comparison, this is simply a reflection of the fact that many of their stories were untold. The exact number and racial makeup of the drovers remain unknown. There is no doubt that the drovers, regardless of race, depended upon one another, and they all faced the same risks, hardships, and dangers on the trails.

Notable among the few women who went up the trail was Amanda Burks, who accompanied her husband, William Franklin Burks, on a cattle drive from Nueces County, Texas, to Kansas during the spring of 1871. William Burks rounded up one thousand head of his best cattle and arranged to travel near the herd of Jasper "Jap" Clark, who was also taking a herd to Kansas. Burks and Clark left Nueces County "with about ten cowboys each, mostly Mexicans, and the cooks." Amanda Burks traveled in her buggy pulled by two horses and endured the same dangers of life on the trail as did the men. In an incident that was somewhat humorous in retrospect, Burks thought she would help the cook by starting a campfire while he was gone for water. The fire immediately spread to the prairie grass and burned a strip for fifty miles ahead until it burned out. When investigators learned the next day that the culprit was a woman, nothing was said except a remark by one of the men that "he was glad that he didn't strike that match." W. F. and Amanda Burks traveled back to Texas in December by rail to Saint Louis and New Orleans and by water from New Orleans to Corpus Christi. Amanda stated that she arrived home in better health than when she left. After the death of her husband in 1877, Amanda Burks remained in the ranching business. She continued to buy land, and at one time she owned a thirty-three-thousand-acre ranch in La Salle County, Texas, and a ten-thousand-acre ranch in neighboring Webb County. She eventually became known as Queen of the Old Trail Drivers.[14]

The establishment of cow towns at the end of the trail followed a typical pattern. As railroad construction progressed from east to west, a railhead was established at the end of the line. The capacity to hold large herds of cattle nearby and load them on freight cars for shipment meant that the site was a potential shipping point for Texas herds bound for market. As a town began to grow around the railhead, stockyards, saloons, banks, stores, houses, and hotels were built. The same combination of rich prairie land and proximity to a railroad that benefited the cattleman also attracted the farmer, who soon began the conversion of the prairie to farmland.

The cattle business brought prosperity to the new town, which attracted settlers and new businesses. Conflict arose between farmers and drovers as farmland encroached on the trail and fears increased concerning the spread of the infectious disease Texas fever to local domestic cattle. Townspeople eventually grew tired of dealing with the sometimes boisterous celebrations of drovers at the end of the trail. Local law enforcement officers, who often looked the other way because of the economic benefits of the cattle business, were compelled by local officials to deal with offenders in a stricter manner. Meanwhile, railroad construction continued, and a new railhead appeared to the west. Local opposition reached the point that if drovers did not voluntarily shift their destination to the new railhead, they were forced out by growth and local resistance, or revised quarantine laws forced them farther west to the next railhead. The cattle trade, which was once welcomed and was sometimes the main reason a town existed, became less desirable as towns grew and citizens became more "respectable." Drovers simply changed their route accordingly. This process was repeated at the next railhead, and the cycle continued for the duration of the trail driving period.

Toward the end of the lifetime of the trail drivers, books and articles were written about their experiences on the trails, and the Western genre was popular in both literature and film. Some of these accounts were given by the individuals themselves, or sometimes by a friend or descendant. These accounts were consistent in some respects, yet often inconsistent or contradictory in other ways. For example, several sources might have consistently described a certain trail route but offered conflicting information regarding whether the trail was known by a name. Inconsistencies eventually became reason for speculation and debate regarding topics such as the origin of the Texas longhorn and certain cattle trails. The name of the Chisholm Trail had become embedded in the public consciousness. This trail was a popular topic and therefore attracted much of the speculation and debate, and it is not unusual for fact to be obscured by legend.

In order to understand the history of the Chisholm Trail, it is necessary to understand the evolution of the cattle trails in general and a few of the events that affected them. The route of a cattle trail was influenced primarily by the lay of the land and the availability of good grass and water between the origin and the destination. These were primary considerations for the entire duration of the cattle driving period. Good grass and water meant that a herd could graze along the trail and arrive at a destination in better condition and likely bring a better price. Other factors such as the growing population density, westward expansion of the population, the Civil War and Reconstruction, construction of railroads across the Great Plains, quarantine laws against the spread of Texas fever, and US government Indian policies affected the location and duration of both the cattle markets and the cattle trails.

A popular misconception is that a cattle trail followed a straight, narrow course, much like a modern interstate highway. In reality, a trail followed the lay of the land and a path of least resistance. Where the cattle trails crossed the natural range of the American bison, they sometimes followed portions of the bison's annual migration route, as these paths tended to be the best way through the area. A cattle trail was not necessarily a single path but a network of trails that developed along a common general route. Range conditions varied as a result of weather and other factors. As herd traffic increased, the potential to overgraze near the best bed grounds increased. Lightning sparked grass fires that burned large areas of the prairie. River crossings occurred wherever a suitable spot was found. The course of travel was altered based on these and other conditions along the route. The more commonly used river crossings tended to be located where treeless riverbanks sloped gradually, the current was slowed due to an upstream bend in the river, and quicksand could be avoided. The Red River crossing at Preston, Texas, also featured rock bluffs that acted as a natural funnel for northbound herds.

Many traces of the old Texas cattle trails had disappeared by the 1930s, lost to the farmer's plow and development or reclaimed by nature. Some points along the trails are known, such as certain river crossings or landmarks. T. C. Richardson stated in 1937 that "trails originated wherever a herd was shaped up and ended wherever a market was found. A thousand minor trails fed the main routes."[15] The width of the trail varied from not much wider than an average rural highway to several miles or more when herds changed course as a result of any of these conditions. Because of the lack of reliable documentation, in many areas it is difficult to determine whether the main trail wandered into an adjacent county. Some counties or towns had not yet been organized at the time of a specific event during the cattle trailing period. For these reasons, the main trail routes will be discussed in subsequent chapters in terms of the present-day counties through which they passed, based upon the best information available.

The trails as we know them today were often known during their historical era by another name or by no name at all. Among the drovers, cattle trails did not seem to be commonly known during their historical period of use by a trail name other than the name of the destination or a landmark along the route, such as Opelousas, Sedalia, Abilene, Ellsworth, Dodge City, or Fort Griffin. Periods of trail use overlapped. Popular use of trail names such as the Chisum Trail, Goodnight-Loving Trail, or Chisholm Trail came along later, generally after the use of the names by writers. Application of trail names other than the destination name led to controversy that continues to this day. The Chisholm Trail name has been applied haphazardly to include almost any trail leading from Texas after the Civil War. Since the trails were still in use, acceptance of fiction as fact has skewed the public perception of the cattle trails. The current popular narrative of the Chisholm Trail is inconsistent and continues to cause spirited speculation and debate. New information will bring a new perspective to the Old Chisholm Trail.

2

Sea Lions
and Old
Texans

WILD LONG-HORNED CATTLE were plentiful in Texas after the Civil War, but they were not native fauna. How did they come to be in Texas? How could the longhorn cattle thrive in conditions that were detrimental to most domestic bovine breeds? The origin of the Texas longhorn is sometimes the subject of speculation. Some maintain that the longhorn developed from crosses between domestic breeds such as the English longhorn and Spanish cattle, while others hold that the pure Texas longhorn traces its roots to Spanish and Portuguese cattle. Early conclusions regarding the origin breeds of the wild Texas longhorn were based on the science at that particular time. Modern blood tests and genetic sampling reveal the answer.

Abel Head "Shanghai" Pierce came to Texas in 1853 and soon went to work as a ranch hand for W. B. Grimes on the prairies of the Gulf Coast. He accepted his first year's salary of two hundred dollars in cows and calves. His boss took advantage of Pierce's inexperience, and Pierce accepted older cows that ranged in age from ten to twenty-five years at a value that was roughly twice what they were worth. The cows all died the following winter. From this hard lesson in the beginning, Pierce learned the livestock business and became one of the most successful and respected cattlemen of the era.[1]

Pierce was later known to brag about the qualities of his "sea lions," which is what he called his longhorn cattle raised on the seas of prairie grasses along the Texas Gulf Coast. After the Civil War he drove a herd from his range along the coast to New Orleans. Later he stated that where a road existed in Louisiana, it was so wet that it "would have bogged a saddle blanket." He said that his steers, which were raised on the lush coastal prairie, were particular as to where they put their feet and were smart enough to walk on logs and roots to avoid the slimy Louisiana mud. He boasted that his steers were so smart and agile that they "would walk a cypress knee up to the stump, jump over it, land on a root, and walk it out for another jump." According to Pierce, his steers became such experts that when they encountered an especially bad bog hole, the steer would "hang his horns in a mustang grape vine, or maybe a wisteria, and swing across like a monkey. The way they balanced, jumped, and swung actually made my horse laugh."[2]

Exaggerations aside, longhorn cattle mean different things to different people. To a tourist, *Bos texanus*, or the Texas longhorn, might conjure up a vision of a street-side vendor in an Old West setting where one can climb into the saddle of a tame steer with an impressive set of horns and have a photograph taken to show the folks back home. To the average city dweller, it might remind them of last year's stock show or county fair, when they could not explain to their inquiring child why one cow's horns were so large and twisted or why its legs were longer than those of the cow in the next stall. Fans of the Hollywood Western might be reminded of the herd headed north in the classic movie *Red River*, of scenes from the great television miniseries *Lonesome Dove*. Others may see the longhorn as no more than a popular "head and horns" logo on a football helmet or numerous other products. However, some people still make their living raising longhorn cattle.

The longhorn of yesteryear, sometimes called the "Old Texan," was described as tall, flat-sided, and thin-flanked. It could move through the thickest brush with the agility of a panther or run like an antelope on the open prairie. It could fight off wolves and other predators, rustle its own food in any weather, and smell water from miles away. Its hard hooves and long legs enabled it to travel easily across rough ground.[3] The longhorn was as wild as the deer or antelope and required no assistance from man for its daily needs.

The longhorn is a descendant of cattle brought to the New World from the Iberian Peninsula by Spanish explorers. Christopher Columbus brought the first cattle to Santa Domingo during his second voyage in 1493. Gregorio de Villalobos brought cattle from Santa Domingo to Mexico in 1521. There were a number of logistical problems associated with shipping livestock across the ocean, and fewer than one hundred head of cattle were initially stocked at Hispaniola, which became the base for Spanish settlement of the New World. In addition to sufficient amounts of food and fresh water needed for the slow Atlantic crossing, the animals required protection of some sort against the pitching and rolling motion of the small ships on the high seas. Horses and cattle were placed into cramped stalls with a combination of padding and canvas slings to support them and help them endure the motion of the ship. Once they reached their destination, however, the vegetation was plentiful, the climate was ideal, and within a few years the initial herd had grown to the point that cattle were shipped from Hispaniola to Cuba, Puerto Rico, and Jamaica. Similar conditions on these islands led to rapid herd growth, and by 1521 these four islands were poised to provide the seed stock to the mainland. By the 1880s millions of the offspring of Spanish cattle ranged from Argentina to Canada.[4]

In a 1979 genetic study by representatives of the Yale University School of Medicine, University of Wisconsin–Madison Laboratory of Genetics, and University of Milan Institute of Zoology, blood samples were collected from more than one hundred animals in each of the following groups: Spanish Retinto and De Lidia, Portuguese Alentejana and Mertolenga, and American longhorn cattle. The resulting data analysis revealed close genetic relationships between these breeds and confirmed the Iberian, most likely Portuguese, origin of the longhorn.[5]

The Retinto, or Retinta, is the most common breed in Spain, where the animals originated in West Andalusia. Breed characteristics include dark red coloration with black nose and black hooves and lyre-shaped horns. Their size and development varied from region to region, and they were used as draft animals and for meat production. Mature cows might reach weights near twelve hundred pounds, and mature bulls can weigh in the range of two thousand pounds. The De Lidia, also known as the fighting bull or Ganado Bravo, is typically black or dark brown, although colors may include gray, brindled, roan, red, or chestnut. The De Lidia has an elegant stature and is noted for aggressiveness, strength, long legs, and agility. Mature bulls can weigh in the range of thirteen hundred to sixteen hundred pounds. The Alentejana, which originated in the region of Alentejo, Portugal, is also used as a draft animal and for meat production. Characteristics of this breed are similar to those of the Retinta from Spain, although the Alentejana has a typical golden red coloration and longer horns. Mertolenga cattle, and the Southern Crioulo from Brazil, descended from the Alentejana and were also used as draft animals and for meat production.[6] Characteristics of each of these breeds can be observed in the Texas longhorn.

Cattle appeared on the mainland of Mexico (New Spain) beginning in 1521 when Gregorio de Villalobos arrived with the first herd. In 1527 the area of Panuco on the mainland held a large population of Indians, and the Antilles islands of Hispaniola, Cuba, Puerto Rico, and Jamaica held large populations of cattle. In a ploy calculated to help overcome their poverty, Spanish inhabitants proposed a plan to Governor Beltrán Nuño de Guzmán to trade Indian slaves for cattle. The available workforce of the native population on the islands had been reduced because of losses from European incursion. This plan would satisfy the need for labor on the islands and for cattle on the mainland, and since it made economic sense, Guzmán approved it. Guzmán set the exchange rate at fifteen slaves per animal. Each ship's captain kept one-third of the slaves to pay for expenses, and Guzmán may have taken another third for himself. Based on ships' records, 5,861 slaves were taken by June 1530. Considering that only approximately one-third of the slaves taken were actually traded for cattle in the islands, and considering the exchange rate, and that some could have been traded for horses in lieu of cattle, approximately one hundred head of cattle had been brought to Panuco by 1530.[7]

The northeastern coastal areas of Mexico proved even more ideal for herd growth than did their previous island homes. By 1620 there were an estimated 176,000 cattle in the Panuco region. An observer, referring to the coastal zone from the Panuco River south to Vera Cruz, remarked, "Cattle are being born and multiplying unbelievably. You cannot exaggerate their numbers." Herd growth was phenomenal because of the ideal environmental conditions. Factor in mortality rates and losses from disease, natural occurrences such as floods, and predation by Indians, and it might be safe to assume a doubling rate of every four years with 30 percent loss. Under these assumptions it would seem possible to reach a population of approximately 176,000 in ninety years from a base population of 100.[8]

From the area north of Vera Cruz along the coastal regions north to the Río Bravo, and then west along a strip just south of that river toward the present site of Laredo, the feral cattle herds mingled, spread, and multiplied. Each new Spanish settlement established in the region brought with it a small herd of cattle and horses. Their custom was to castrate only a small number of males, and the practice of sterilizing females was unknown at that time, leaving most of their livestock fertile to breed.[9] The cattle were left to their own devices as they either escaped, the settlements and ranches failed, or they were simply abandoned for various reasons. These cattle reverted to their feral state quickly, mixed with other wild cattle, and continued to spread throughout the region. The animals sought out the deepest, densest thickets for refuge during the day. At night they ventured out to graze on nearby prairies, and they returned to their hideaway at dawn. As the herds grew and expanded their range, competition for grass forced them to range even further.

The Mexican state of Tamaulipas was a vast breeding ground where, through the process of natural selection and the laws of nature, the highest qualities of the Retinto, Alentejana, De Lidia (Ganado Bravo), and Mertolenga breeds were molded into what eventually became known as the Texas longhorn. Rivers and streams attracted cattle. Trees, brush, and vegetation that grew along the banks provided cover and forage. The Río Bravo provided a bit of a natural barrier to migration, but when a cow decides to move, it will move, and hell or high water will not deter it. Longhorns were no different, and they began to find their way across the river into south Texas. As more feral cattle migrated north of the Rio Grande, they continued their established habits of seeking out the densest, thickest, thorniest vegetation in which to remain hidden during the day and grazing on the open prairie only at night.

Wild herds that migrated north predated the introduction of cattle into Texas by the Spanish. With the establishment of mission San Francisco de los Tejas among the Tejas Indians on the Neches River in 1690, the first Spanish mission in Texas, Alonso de León drove what may have been the first cattle herd from Mexico into and across Texas. Out of two hundred head of cattle, only twenty were present at the consecration of the mission. This was likely the first herd intentionally established in Texas. According to the report of Domingo Terán de los Ríos in 1692, Terán left the mission San Francisco de los Tejas, and his meat supply ran out before he reached the Trinity River. He sent out scouts who returned five days later with cattle from an unidentified source. By 1714 French explorer Louis Juchereau de St. Denis reported that the lands of the Tejas Indians in east Texas were swarming with wild cattle and horses. In order to see this kind of substantial increase in only twenty-four years, it seems reasonable to assume that wild herds must have preceded the introduction of cattle into Texas by the Spanish, as it appears that they were already well established.[10]

Meanwhile, in Texas, as in Mexico, the process of natural selection that had begun on the islands of the Antilles continued as feral herds flourished on both sides of the Rio Grande. The bloodlines of mixed-breed American cattle were added to the equation, albeit in relatively small additions.[11] Although domestic breeds such as the English longhorn were later crossbred with the wild longhorn, by the time Anglo settlers began to arrive in Texas with these domestic cattle the longhorn had already evolved in the wild for nearly three centuries. The wild cattle were sometimes known to kill domestic cattle that attempted to enter their herds. Over a period of more than three hundred years, nature produced the Texas longhorn, a breed that was perfectly suited to its environment, had no peer in the bovine world, served as the foundation for the cattle industry in the western United States, and influenced Texas history and the history of the American West.

The longhorn developed a natural resistance to the disease called Spanish fever, which also became known as Texas fever, and the breed proved resistant to other bovine diseases as well. Domestic cattle raised by man had no such immunity to the fever, and fatality rates could run as high as 90 percent among infected herds with a high population of older animals.[12] In addition to the general inability of domestic cattle to rustle food for themselves in the wild or defend against predators, this disease would have been another limiting factor to the introduction of domestic bloodlines into the feral cattle herds.

Longhorns were lean, lanky, and long-legged. Their long legs and hard hooves and ability to do without water for longer periods than domestic cattle enabled them to travel long distances with relative ease. They could find food for themselves and could eat most anything, from the lush native prairie grasses to yucca and prickly pear, from which they obtained moisture during dry periods. A longhorn could smell water or rain from miles away; it knew that the scent of rain meant green grass. Famous cowman Charles Goodnight stated, "No animal of the cow kind will shift and take care of itself under all conditions as will the longhorns. They can go farther without water and endure more suffering than others."[13]

Life expectancy of a longhorn cow could be well into her twenties. A cow was capable of producing a calf each year throughout most of her life, and it was not unusual for cows well into their twenties to calve. Nature designed the longhorn to produce a calf with a lower average birth weight. The longhorn cow has a larger birth canal, and the calf has a narrow head and shoulders. These combined factors meant easier unassisted calving and an extremely high percentage of live births. A higher percentage of live, unassisted births meant a better chance of survival for cows and calves.[14]

A newborn calf on the ground, with all of the associated signs and scents of a recent birth, could easily become a convenient meal for wolves, coyotes, or other predators, no matter how well the cow hid her calf. A longhorn calf might remain hidden in brush or tall grass, without so much as blinking an eye, right up until the last instant of discovery, and when the alarm was raised, the mother, as well as any other cows in the immediate area, rushed to the calf's defense.[15] A cow might range a short distance while her calf stayed hidden, but she knew exactly where she had left her calf, and the calf knew to stay put. Mothers were fiercely protective of their calves, and many a lobo wolf was driven away by the horns and hooves of defensive longhorn cows. The longhorn calf could gain its feet and walk much quicker than domestic breeds, typically within thirty minutes of birth, which helped increase calf survival rates even more.

Longhorn cows were known to lick blowflies from themselves and their newborn calves and thus treat themselves with no veterinary assistance from man, and if worms infested an area it could not lick, the cow might stand in water for extended periods in an attempt to rid itself of the pests.[16] Along the Gulf Coast, longhorns might stand in salt water to evade mosquito swarms. The longhorn's ears contained extra-long hair to help deter flies and other pests. Its tail was longer than normal and built for swatting and swishing to repel pests. Its lines were generally clean, without a lot of loose skin that might get caught in the thick underbrush.

The longhorn's colors were widely varied, and unique: brindle, grulla, slate, dun, brown, black, white, red, solid, streaked, splotched, speckled, in so many various combinations of colors, shades, and patterns that no two were alike. The longhorn typically had a line along its back and coarse hair around its ears.[17] But the outstanding visual characteristic of Texas longhorn cattle is, of course, the horns. The horns are not shed and continue to grow for the life of the animal. Primary influences on horn development are genetics, diet, environmental conditions, and age.

Longhorn horns were forged by nature during three hundred years of natural selection. They were not simply for decoration but were used to brush aside thorny limbs, provided a means of defense against predators, and were used as tools for foraging. Horn size, shape, and spread were as unique and varied as color patterns in longhorns. Forward twist, lateral twist, wavy twist, corkscrew twist, hardly any twist, single-drop, double-drop, forward curl, backward curl, no curl, rolling dips, slight dips, no dips, black tips, ivory tips, brown tips, yellow-greenish tips, caramel-colored, black, white, greenish and all hues in between—factor horn length, circumference, keratin patterns, and the fact that horns were not necessarily always symmetrical into the equation, and the possible combinations are endless.

Humans used horns to make canteens, powder flasks, signal horns, and utensils. The longhorn's hide, whether tanned or untanned (rawhide) had many uses. The description "tough as rawhide" originated with the use of the longhorn's hide for everything from making shoes to repairing wagon wheels. The use of rawhide was limited only by the imagination. Rawhide stretches when wet and shrinks as it dries; it could be cut into strips, soaked with water, and wrapped around a separated wagon wheel, and after drying it would hold the iron tire securely to the wheel for many miles. It could be plaited into lariats or bullwhips, formed into utensils such as a bowl or spoon, or used for more serious purposes. Print Olive, a rancher in Williamson County, Texas, allegedly caught a rustler changing brands on an Olive cow, whereupon he killed the cow, forced the rustler to skin the cow, wrapped him in the green hide, stitched it closed, and left the would-be thief in the sun for the shrinking properties of the rawhide to do its work.[18]

By 1899 the longhorn breed was in serious decline. Examples of the Old Texan were scarce, and a steer with an impressive set of horns was rare. Longhorn cows had been bred with Durham bulls, along with other breeds, since the 1870s to improve the meat quality and provide better table fare for consumers. Crossbreeding increased during the 1880s as more ranches were established, and the pure longhorn was almost lost. Perhaps one of the most famous longhorn steers was Champion, a pale red and brown steer that was once owned by Jim Dobie, uncle of folklorist and author J. Frank Dobie. Entries were invited for the longhorn in the cattle shows at the 1899 International Fair in San Antonio, and only four contestants were entered. The contest was between two steers, Champion and a steer owned by George West. Both steers were from Live Oak County. Champion was declared the winner, and his picture soon appeared in newspapers and adorned advertising for the fair association. Champion's horn spread was reported in the *Chicago Tribune* as nine feet seven inches. Despite all of the hoopla, no official measurement was ever taken of Champion's horns. J. Frank Dobie stated: "When, in the 1920's, I used to ask Uncle Jim Dobie about the measurements, he would reply 'I am afraid to say.' Like the great majority of real cowmen, he disliked the popular exaggeration of so many factors pertaining to range life and was more given to under- rather than over-statement."[19]

Champion's horn spread was reported at various times by various sources to be anywhere from over six feet to over nine feet. The absence of a recorded measurement leaves plenty of room for speculation and myth. Undoubtedly Champion's horns were mounted and may still exist somewhere, but the actual size is lost to history. Or is it?

According to Alan Rogers of the National Texas Longhorn Museum in Kansas City, Missouri, Champion's spread can be calculated to an approximate degree. A mature steer's poll section (the width of the skull between the horns) measured an average of between ten and twelve inches, and the average distance between eye sockets is consistently ten and one-half to eleven inches. Allowing a twelve-inch poll section, and comparing that measurement against the total horn width in a head-on photo enlargement made from a cabinet card, the spread of Champion's horns can be calculated at approximately six feet six inches. Although the exact width may never be known, and although Champion was certainly an outstanding steer, in the interest of historical accuracy Champion's mythical nine-foot horn spread can be ruled out.[20]

J. Frank Dobie stated that the average horn spread of a longhorn steer headed up the trail during the 1880s was approximately four feet, with five-foot spreads on older steers common and six-footers being exceptional, with the occasional report of eight-foot mossy-horned steers.[21] Many reports of the huge eight-foot spreads come from the early days, when life on the range was more tenuous and the herders had other worries besides saving horns, so many of these examples were lost to time. Jim Dobie's steer Champion was an example of a wide spread with a Texas twist.

About 1916, Ira "Cap" Yates, son of trail driver I. G. Yates, began stocking his ranches in the Big Bend area of Texas with longhorns that exhibited the characteristics of the Old Texan cattle, of which comparatively few remained. Fayette Yates, Cap's son, continued the tradition, and by the late 1960s their herd had grown to approximately fifteen hundred head of the old-style Texas longhorns. Before he died in 2007, in addition to herd preservation Fayette Yates assembled a horn collection, which included head mounts and full body mounts that exhibit the wide variety of horn characteristics typical of the longhorn. Included in the collection is the head mount of the famous steer Amigo Yates, with a tip-to-tip spread measured eight feet, nine and one-half inches. The Yates Longhorn Collection is under private ownership and is currently on display in Lajitas, Texas.[22]

With newspaper headlines such as "Dogie Almost as Scarce as Dodo" and "Longhorn Cattle Almost Extinct," another effort was undertaken in 1927 to save the breed. Recognizing that the longhorn had been crossbred almost out of existence, officials of the Wichita Mountains Wildlife Refuge convinced the US Department of Agriculture to set aside funds for purchasing animals to stock a herd and thus preserve the best specimens that could be found. After traveling over five thousand miles and inspecting thousands of head of cattle, Will Barnes and John Hatton assembled a herd of twenty cows, three bulls, and three steers to reside at the wildlife preserve. Graves Peeler, brand inspector and cattleman, also worked to save the longhorn. He established a herd of the old-style longhorns and eventually helped others start their own herds. Peeler, along with assistance from J. Frank Dobie and businessman Sid Richardson, helped assemble a longhorn herd that was donated to the state of Texas in 1941. This herd became the Official State of Texas Longhorn Herd, which resides primarily at the Fort Griffin State Historic Site near Albany and at San Angelo State Park. The herd at the Wichita Mountains Wildlife Refuge in Oklahoma has served as the nucleus for other herds to perpetuate the breed. Bloodlines from the Peeler, Yates, and Wichita Mountains herds have been introduced into the Texas state herd over the years.[23]

Milby Butler, Graves Peeler, Cap Yates, M. P. Wright Jr., John Gayle Phillips, John Hatton and Will C. Barnes, and Emil Marks, whose herds are known as the Seven Families of Texas Longhorns, are generally credited with saving the Texas longhorn from extinction during the early 1900s. Some breeders, such as the Butlers, subsequently bred longhorns to emphasize specific qualities, such as horns, color, topline, and so on, to improve eye appeal or marketability. While these breeders certainly played a role in the preservation of the longhorn, the focus here is on the cattle that were left primarily to natural selection on the range with no manipulation to enhance specific characteristics. All longhorn lovers owe the Seven Families a huge debt of gratitude.[24]

There are cattle with long horns, there are cattle with a higher percentage of the indicine genome, which is indicative of cattle that spread from India into Africa and across the Iberian Peninsula, and there are genetically pure Texas longhorns. The modern Texas longhorn has been diluted by crossbreeding for various reasons, such as to produce longer tip-to-tip horn measurement, greater weight, certain qualities for livestock competition entries, or certain hide colors and patterns. The pure Texas longhorns, the cattle that are closest in appearance and genetics to the Old Texan that went up the trails, is more endangered today than at any time in the past. The Cattlemen's Texas Longhorn Registry estimates that only about three thousand historically correct longhorns remain (fig. 1). Purity is determined by a combination of three factors: physical appearance (phenotype), herd history, and genetics (genotype). These are standard criteria for inclusion in rare breed conservation programs. The first step, phenotype, is remarkably accurate; it is rare for an animal to pass visual inspection and fail genetic testing. The mission of the Cattlemen's Texas Longhorn Conservancy and Cattlemen's Texas Longhorn Registry is the preservation and perpetuation of the historically correct, genetically pure Texas longhorn, along with related research and education programs.[25]

Many prairie grasses, in their natural and undisturbed state, are naturally resistant to the spread of weeds, trees, and many types of dense brush. Naturally occurring fires helped keep woody plants from gaining a foothold on the prairie. In the years since the cattle trailing days, mesquite, huisache, and other species have spread across vast areas of Texas. Cattle and other animals played a small role in spreading seeds into the grasslands, but the eventual loss of the natural prairie grasses, lack of natural fires, and changes in ranching and farming practices had a far greater effect on the spread of woody species.[26] Despite occasional claims that the presence of mesquite trees indicates an old cattle trail, it is much more likely that the mesquite's presence is due to man's activities.

Through television, movies, art, and literature the longhorn is often presented in the setting of the wide-open spaces of the Great Plains; however, they adapted to their environment, and whether it was in the thickest and thorniest brush country, on the plateaus, on the coastal plains, or in the rolling hills of the Texas Hill Country, they adapted and flourished. Like the bison to the Comanche, the longhorn was important to the pioneers of Texas. Wild longhorn cattle were there when the first Anglo settlers set foot in Texas. They were trained as beasts of burden; used as a source of tallow, hides, and rawhide and of food; or driven to a cattle market and sold. After the Civil War, so many longhorn hooves beat paths into the ground on their way to railheads in Kansas and Nebraska that traces of their passing are still visible in a few places. Fortunes were made and lost, and Texas was carried from the brink of bankruptcy after the Civil War to become the leader in the US livestock industry, all on the back of the lean, lanky Texas longhorn.

3

Quarantines
and Cattle
Ticks

Before the Civil War, cattle markets in New Orleans and Missouri were the closest destinations for Texas drovers. Over the next few decades, expansion and organization of the railroad system, along with related changes in technology, brought great changes to the cattle business. Although railroad construction in the United States was in various stages of progress by 1860, little construction had occurred at that time west of the Mississippi River. By 1860 railroad tracks had been laid by the Tebo and Neosho Railroad Company as far west as the site that became Sedalia, Missouri, but railroad expansion to the west came to a halt as manpower and resources were diverted by the Civil War. Railroad construction resumed after the war, and for a time Sedalia became an important destination for Texas cattle, but the transmission of Spanish fever, or Texas fever, from Texas cattle to cattle in Missouri and Kansas gave rise to opposition, including armed resistance and legislation, and the combination of resistance to Texas herds, the beginning of the war in 1861, and a new railhead at Abilene, Kansas, in 1867 prevented Sedalia from becoming the major cattle shipping point that Abilene or Dodge City would become in the coming years.[1]

As more Texas cattle headed to Missouri cattle markets, the herds met increased resistance from farmers and stockmen in Missouri and Kansas. An understanding of the symptoms and impact of Spanish fever is critical to understanding the sometimes violent opposition that Texas drovers encountered. Herd losses in Missouri, Kansas, Arkansas, Virginia, Kentucky, Carolina, and Georgia had been attributed to Spanish fever. The disease did not discriminate between a farmer's milk cows or a stockman's beef cattle. The problem was so potentially devastating to domestic cattle that a letter to the *Prairie*

Farmer in 1868 stated, "Texas stock should not be allowed to cross the 35th parallel of north latitude alive."[2]

Many of the Missourians and other northern stock raisers were genuinely concerned with protecting their livestock and livelihoods. Violence or threat of violence usually produced instant results. Resistance might be in the form of a lone farmer with a shotgun or an armed mob. In the words of S. M. Welch of Waverly, Missouri: "Talk to a Missourian about moderation, when a drove of Texas cattle is coming, and he will call you a fool, while he coolly loads his gun, and joins his neighbors; and they intend no scare, either. They mean to kill, do kill, and will keep killing until the drove takes the back track; and the drovers must be careful not to get between their cattle and the citizens either, unless they are bullet-proof. No doubt this looks a good deal like border-ruffianism to you, but it is the way we keep clear of the Texas fever."[3]

Others took advantage of the situation to rob, steal, or stampede cattle and horses and murder those who resisted. J. M. Daugherty, along with five cowhands, drove a herd of 500 steers from Texas north along the Kansas-Missouri border as a teenager in 1866. About twenty miles south of Fort Scott, Kansas, they were attacked by a group of fifteen to twenty Jayhawkers. Daugherty and John Dobbins were riding in the lead and were the first to encounter the troublemakers. Dobbins drew his six-shooter and was promptly shot dead by the Jayhawkers. The herd stampeded at the sound of the shots. The Jayhawkers disarmed Daugherty and held a kangaroo court at a nearby creek, where Daugherty was declared guilty of driving tick-infested cattle into their country. Some wanted to hang Daugherty from the nearest tree, while others wanted to whip him to death. Daugherty's plea that he was ignorant of the dangers "ticky cattle" caused northern stock, along with his youth, was taken into consideration by a key Jayhawker, and Daugherty was finally released. After he caught up with the herd, he and two others returned to bury Dobbins. They cut down a small tree and carved out a headboard and footboard to mark the grave. They lost 150 head of cattle in the stampede, and the balance was sold a short time later at Fort Scott. The Jayhawkers were likely soldiers mustered out of the Union Army looking for an excuse to steal cattle or stampede herds.[4] This was only one example of the opposition faced by Texas drovers.

The exact cause of Spanish fever was unknown at the time. About all that was known was that within a short time after exposure to Texas cattle or to the route over which Texas cattle had traveled, domestic breeds soon became sick. The affected cattle exhibited symptoms of emaciation, high fever, bloody urine, and anemia. Death usually occurred within a few days. Calves and younger cattle sometimes survived and recovered; however, the disease was typically fatal to older cattle. Herd losses to the disease could be catastrophic, depending upon the age and overall health of the affected herd. It was also known that the Texas cattle did not exhibit any of these same symptoms, but they somehow imparted this disease to domestic cattle. To further complicate the matter, the disease was not consistent in its appearance after exposure; therefore not all Texas cattle were necessarily infected.[5]

After an outbreak in early June 1868, and amid concerns of a wider spread of the disease, the US commissioner of agriculture authorized an investigation by Professor John Gamgee. Gamgee was a noted authority and London veterinarian who had been prominent in investigations into bovine diseases in Europe. The observations and details of his investigation, assisted by H. D. Emery, editor of the *Prairie Farmer*, were recorded and their findings were subsequently published in *Report of the Commissioner of Agriculture on the Diseases of Cattle in the United States* in 1871. The first case in the report described an outbreak:

> About the middle of June, 1868, a disease broke out at Cairo, Illinois, at a point where large numbers of Texas cattle had been landed. It was the disease sometimes called "Spanish fever," but generally known as "Texas cattle disease." This epizootic, long known and dreaded by owners of herds in Missouri and Kansas, and to some extent, in Kentucky, Tennessee, and Virginia, became unusually serious in the track of Texas cattle beyond the Mississippi, in 1867 and 1868. While it was practically unknown in more eastern states, general interest in its manifestations was not aroused; but, when a new channel for the Texas cattle trade was opened, and the river steamboats landed their living freight in the heart of the West, the ravages of the strange disease extended rapidly, carrying infection along the pathway of transportation to the seaboard, filling the public mind with alarm for the safety of farm stock, and even exciting apprehensions that the public health might become involved in the future progress of the disease.[6]

Gamgee also enlisted botanist H. W. Ravenel of South Carolina to assist in the investigation. They visited infected areas in Illinois, Missouri, and the then-new cattle depot at Abilene, Kansas, and recorded the results of their observations, interviews, and pathological studies. They visited the Texas coastal region in the spring of 1869 and examined vegetation, soil, management practices, and other conditions at the origin points of the cattle. They soon narrowed the scope of the possible source of the disease to cattle that were born and raised in areas of Texas bordering the Gulf of Mexico.[7]

The mysterious disease did not seem to occur on the home ranges in the Gulf region. Some longhorns were infected with a deadly disease of which they exhibited no symptoms, yet they somehow transmitted this disease to other cattle. Longhorns north of the coastal regions were affected in the same deadly manner as were domestic cattle. The disease was almost always fatal in a sick animal, yet the survivors did not suffer from symptoms again. The disease did not seem to be transmitted by cattle that were obviously sick. Could this deadly disease be transmitted from cattle to humans, or did farmers unnecessarily fear for their own safety and that of their surviving stock?

The incubation period of the disease was thought to be a period of five to six weeks. The first visible indications of the disease included droopiness about the head and ears, an arched back, listlessness, and reluctance to rise or move. By the time symptoms were visible, the body temperature had already risen. Urine and feces were retained for hours, and when released, were considerable and bloody. The pulse and respiration rates increased as tremors and paralysis of the hindquarters, forequarters, or both commenced. Blindness was typical in animals that became comatose, while other animals developed a delirium that was accompanied by a wild gaze and extreme restlessness. It was a mystery why a few certain animals from the south recovered, yet the disease was almost always fatal to northern stock. Death typically occurred in ten to twelve days from the time the body temperature began to increase and within three or four days after the appearance of visible symptoms. The animal's liver and gall bladder were often affected. The spleen was consistently observed to swell two to five times its normal size, with the internal structure of the spleen disintegrated along with extensive hemorrhaging. Gamgee proposed that the disease should be called splenic fever, due to the fact that the spleen of an infected animal was so obviously and consistently affected.[8]

Gamgee's study took into consideration the hardships of cattle driven to market, along with the hardships of the drovers that drove them to their destinations, searching for possible causes or contributing factors. Some early conclusions were that cattle from the south, and especially from the Gulf Coast, were affected with an apparent or latent form of the disease as a consequence of the water, soil, and vegetation that they consumed. The system of infected animals was contaminated, but they themselves were immune to the effects. It was theorized that southern cattle driven for periods of several weeks or more improved in condition and excreted the poisons, which in turn poisoned the cattle of the states or regions through which they were driven. All breeds of cattle in states north of the Gulf Coast states that fed on grass contaminated by southern cattle were attacked by the disease, but the disease was rarely transmitted by the feeding of hay. The disease mainly occurred during the hot months of summer and autumn, and it never occurred after frosts had killed the wild grass. It also occurred in spring after a southern herd had passed over that patch of prairie. Heat and drought could aggravate the disease in an animal. The view was that the flesh, blood, or other tissues from a diseased animal could not transmit or cause the disease in man or in other animals.[9]

Gamgee noted that Texas cattle were usually covered with ticks, but he eliminated them as a possible means of transmission. The tick theory held generally that the tick, *Ixodes indentatus*, attached itself to the body of the native host animal in Texas. As the ticks reproduced, young ticks dropped off the host animal to "poison" the grasses as the host animal was driven to market. This theory assumed that the disease was spread when cattle ingested the young ticks. Cattle that fed upon or passed over the same grasses were therefore infected. The tick theory acquired some advocates but was dismissed for the following reasons: no relationship was found between the abundance of ticks and the severity of the disease; no ticks were found in the alimentary canal, stomachs, or intestines; and ticks were commonly found in other areas of Texas, yet those cattle did not transmit the disease.[10]

The investigation concluded that the disease was caused by southern cattle. Cattle that transmitted the disease appeared well and increased in weight under the proper grazing conditions yet showed internal signs of the disease when slaughtered. The disease was not transmitted during the winter and was not transmitted by cattle that were infected by southern cattle. The disease was not transmitted to local cattle in similar latitudes or locations where climatic conditions were the same as those of the Texas Gulf Coast. The disease was thought to be eliminated from the system and was not transmitted after a stay of a few months in a northern climate. Whole herds were decimated by the disease, yet just beyond the line of exposure to southern cattle no cattle were harmed. The incubation period was inconsistent, medication was of little use, and the disease was fatal nine times out of ten. Losses could not be accurately stated but were undoubtedly at least several million dollars, with the greatest losses in Kansas and Missouri. The study concluded that it was likely that the disease was transmitted through the excrements of southern cattle because of the frequency with which local cattle became infected after grazing where southern cattle had recently passed.[11]

Throughout the duration of the Civil War, northbound herds from Texas were interrupted, and there was a noticeable absence of the disease. In areas where the disease had previously destroyed local herds, cattle exhibited no symptoms during the war. After the war, where entry was denied to Texas cattle there was no Texas fever, but where droves of cattle were permitted, outbreaks of the disease began to occur in Missouri and Kansas. The appearance of the disease seemed to be in proportion to the movement of Texas cattle.[12]

Restrictive laws against importing Texas cattle into Missouri were largely ineffective, as drovers attempted to pass into and through the state anyway, and citizens took it upon themselves to stop them by any means necessary. To stampede or to shoot Texas cattle before they entered certain areas was considered an acceptable alternative means of control. Payment of cash or bonds by Texas stockmen were an unfortunate and unwanted price of doing business. Many Texans believed the restrictions and opposition to both them and their cattle to be unconstitutional. Prevention and control of Texas fever was linked to the general preservation of the peace.[13] The realities, harsh consequences, and public perception associated with Texas fever continued to plague Texas stockmen as they drove herds to Kansas and Missouri markets to satisfy the nation's postwar hunger for beef.

By 1875 the slaughter of the bison on the Great Plains and subsequent defeat and removal of Indians from their tribal lands were making it somewhat safer to venture out onto the plains and opened the area to westward expansion of settlements and extension of railroad lines. Where railroad traffic had been confined mainly east of the Mississippi River before 1860, by 1875 some railroad trunk lines had been completed into south Texas, from Texas north into Kansas, and across the states of Kansas and Nebraska west into the territories of Colorado and Wyoming.[14] Through the combination of trunk lines and associated branch lines, it was now possible to travel, and to ship cattle, north from Texas. From there, herds could be either driven to stock the ranges of the northern territories or shipped east to slaughter. At the speed of fifteen to twenty miles per hour, compared to eight to fifteen miles per day, which was the typical rate of travel of a herd on the trail, the railroad opened new possibilities to the stockmen. Beef contracts to supply the military and to supply Indian reservations, along with stocking the ranges of the northern and northwestern territories, opened new lands and new opportunities later during the 1870s and 1880s. However, as with most things in life, new opportunities can often bring unexpected drawbacks, and railroad transit also opened new areas to potential exposure to Texas fever, the name by which it was now almost universally called.

The alarming effects of the fever in the Texas Panhandle led stockmen to meet at Mobeetie, Texas on July 23, 1880. While they discussed other items of business, their main concern was protecting their herds from the disease. The men passed resolutions requiring herds that originated in the south and the east to follow one of three prescribed routes through the Texas Panhandle: the eastern route across the Red River at Doan's Store, the middle route along the Rath Trail north across the Red River, or the western route past Blanco Canyon, Tule Canyon, Palo Duro Canyon, and Tascosa, then to Colorado.[15] The terms "eastern" and "western" as used in these resolutions should be taken in the context of Panhandle geography and should not be confused with the terms *eastern* and *western* used by drovers to describe the trail that crossed the Red River at Red River Station (the Eastern) and the trail that crossed the Red at Doan's (the Western).

The Rath Trail was a route laid out by Charles Rath in 1876 for freight wagons leading from Dodge City past Fort Supply in Indian Territory, past Mobeetie in Wheeler County, past Matador in Motley County, and ending at Rath City on the Double Mountain Fork of the Brazos River in Stonewall County, Texas. A distance of one and one-half miles on either side of the Rath and Western Trails were set aside for use by drovers using those routes; the Panhandle stockmen pleaded, "We do most earnestly request all cattle men to respect these established limits." The Panhandle stockmen requested all drovers to call on local stockmen for information regarding these trails, agreed to assist when called upon, and required cattle that had not been wintered north of the Brazos River and west of the Wichita Mountains to be held in place and separated from range cattle until after the first frost. As enforcement they pledged to withhold all assistance from those who ignored their requests.[16]

The subsequent placing of armed riders by Charles Goodnight and Orville Nelson at intervals between Goodnight's JA Ranch and Nelson's Shoe Bar Ranch to assist drovers in following the recommendations gave rise to the so-called Winchester Quarantine. Efforts to obtain a legal quarantine were unsuccessful, but the Winchester Quarantine was kept in place until the fencing of the Panhandle range in 1886.[17] The gist of the Winchester Quarantine is made plain in a letter of August 20, 1881, from Charles Goodnight to his friend George T. Reynolds:

Dear Sir:

I send Mr. Smith to turn your cattle so they will not pass through our range. He will show you around and guide you until you strike the head of this stream and then you will have a road. The way he will show you is nearer and there are shorter drives to water than any route you can take. Should you come by here you will have a drive of 35 miles to make.

I hope you will take this advice as yourselves and I have always been good friends, but even friendship will not protect you in the drive through here, and should you attempt to pass through, be kind enough to tell your men what they will have to face as I do not wish to hurt men that do not understand what they will be very sure to meet.

I hope you will not treat this as idle talk, for I mean every word of this, and if you have any feeling for me as a friend or acquaintance, you will not put me to any desperate actions. I will not perhaps see you myself, but take this advice from one that is and always has been your friend.

My cattle are now dying of the fever contracted from cattle driven from Fort Worth, therefore do not have any hope that you can convince me that your cattle will not give mine the fever, this we will not speak of. I simply say to you that you will never pass through here in good health.

Yours Truly,
C. Goodnight[18]

Stockmen in the Texas Panhandle suffered similar consequences as their counterparts had suffered farther to the north. In some cases these Panhandle stockmen had faced armed resistance to their northbound herds in years past in Kansas and Missouri. They employed similar, if not stronger, tactics to protect their Panhandle herds.

In 1884, about half a million head of cattle were driven from Texas to the northern territories over the trail and by rail. Rail traffic was increasing, and more cattle were moved to the territories that year by rail than in any previous year. Herds were sold at Caldwell for distribution in Indian Territory. Herds were sold in greater quantity at Dodge City for distribution in Colorado and New Mexico Territory, and the remaining herds were sold at Ogallala to supply range stock in Wyoming and Montana Territories, or shipped east on the Union Pacific Railroad.[19]

Cattle herds from southern Texas that were driven north over the trail at a slower pace were much less likely to transmit Texas fever, and the farther north they went the less likely they were to transmit the disease. A result of the investigation of 1868 was the assumption that the disease was limited by latitude and elevation, as there were no reported incidents north of the South Platte River or in Colorado. That assumption was challenged by the cattle drives of 1884, when cattle reached the northern terminals in a matter of days by rail instead of weeks or months on the trail, and the fever hit areas where it was previously unknown. The actual means of transmission was still unknown; however, it was still generally accepted that the disease was spread through inhalation or ingestion over grasses that had been contaminated by the excrement of Texas cattle.[20]

Since it was already known that a slower pace over the trail somehow diminished the threat of the disease, cattle shipped by railroad were suspected in this outbreak. The inconsistency of the disease led to differences of opinion. The territorial veterinarian of Wyoming stated in 1884 that "experience has taught us that transporting Texas cattle north of a certain latitude by railroad has been followed by the spread of Texas fever among northern cattle." A railroad traffic manager, reasoning that if cattle contaminated the ground with the disease as they walk slowly along the trail, stated in 1885, "My judgment would be that it is altogether the safest plan of transportation of Texas cattle by rail." Railroads instituted cattle car cleaning and sanitizing procedures at shipping points and at destination stockyards, and traffic managers tended to proclaim the railroad to be the safest method of transport. At the same time, many trail men tended to favor the long drives, which allowed the cattle to graze and gain weight along the route.[21]

The potential for destructive outbreaks of Texas fever caused several states and territories to pass legislation to control the importation of Texas cattle. Some laws were more restrictive than others, and the level of limitation placed on Texas herds seemed to be proportionate to the sufferings of the people of the respective state or territory. The strictest laws might have been in Missouri, where the legislature passed an act in 1872 that prohibited cattle from Texas, Mexico, or Indian Territory from being driven into any county of the state between March 1 and November 1 of each year. Cattle from these sources were also prohibited from remaining in any county during the same time period. Cattle that had spent the previous winter in the state were exempted. Texas cattle could be shipped via railroad or steamboat through the state but could not be unloaded within the borders of the state, and railroad or steamboat companies could be held liable for all damages that resulted from an outbreak of Texas fever along the transport route. This law was challenged, and the US Supreme Court ruled in the case of *Railroad Company v. Husen* that the law did not provide for inspection or quarantine, did not differentiate between sick animals and well animals, effectively banned interstate commerce for eight months out of the year, and was therefore "a plain intrusion upon the exclusive domain of Congress." The judgment of the lower court was reversed, and a new trial was awarded in the case.[22]

The quarantine law of Wyoming Territory authorized the governor to appoint a veterinary surgeon, based upon the recommendation of the Stock Growers' Association, to serve as territorial veterinarian in 1882. The territorial veterinarian had the authority to quarantine infected areas and to require that a certificate be issued to healthy animals before they could be moved from an infected area. He could also make recommendations to the governor, and the governor had the authority to prohibit the importation of livestock into the territory at discretion.[23]

In 1884 the legislature of New Mexico Territory approved an act to prevent the entry of diseased cattle. This act empowered the governor to appoint cattle inspectors, whose duty it was to inspect herds entering the territory for disease or exposure to or signs of contagious disease. The inspector issued a certificate to the person in charge of the cattle if the animals were found to be free of disease, which allowed them to proceed. A certificate was not issued if disease was observed or suspected, and the herd was therefore denied entry. Inspectors were entitled to collect one dollar per head of high-grade or thoroughbred cattle inspected, twenty cents per head of all other cattle inspected, up to one thousand head, and ten cents per head in excess of one thousand cattle in the same herd. Inspectors were also entitled to collect a fee of ten cents per mile traveled from their usual place of abode to the place of inspection. The inspection and mileage fees were payable by the owner of the cattle prior to delivery of the inspection certificate. If a certificate was not issued, the fees could be recovered by the owner in a civil action. Inspectors also had the power to administer an oath regarding affidavits, and anyone who swore falsely in an affidavit was guilty of perjury. A subsequent act passed on April 3, 1884, empowered the governor to suspend enforcement, using discretion and judgment of the public interest and circumstances.[24]

The Kansas legislature approved House Bill No. 116, to protect cattle against Texas fever and to repeal earlier laws passed for the same purpose in 1884, on March 7, 1885. This law prohibited the importation of cattle capable of communicating or liable to communicate the disease known as Texas, Spanish, or splenic fever between March 31 and December 1 of any year. Enforcement was the duty of the sheriff, deputy sheriff, undersheriff, or constable, who had the authority to impound and quarantine cattle that were in violation until a release order was obtained by the Live Stock Sanitary Commission. The officers could not be held liable for damages by the owner of the cattle for performing their duty. Cattle that came from south of the thirty-seventh parallel were automatically assumed to be capable of communicating contagious disease, and the owners or persons in charge of those cattle were assumed to have full knowledge at the time of the alleged offense. These provisions did not apply if the owner or person in charge produced a certificate that the cattle had been kept since December 1 of the previous year west of the east line of the Indian Territory and north of the thirty-sixth parallel or west of the twenty-first meridian west from Washington DC and north of the thirty-fourth parallel.[25]

The Texas Fever Law was approved by the general assembly of the state of Colorado on March 21, 1885. This law prohibited cattle or horses that had an infection or contagious disease, or that had been herded or been in contact with an infected animal in the ninety days previous, from being imported into Colorado. It prohibited the importation of cattle or horses from any state, territory, or country south of the thirty-sixth parallel of north latitude, between April 1 and November 30, unless the owner of the stock possessed a bill of health issued by the state.[26]

The restrictions during spring, summer, and fall reflected the knowledge that outbreaks of Texas fever were not likely to occur during the winter months in latitudes north of Texas. Penalties for violations could be substantial, and persons found guilty of violating the statutes were subject to varying degrees of civil and criminal penalties. Winters were harsh and not conducive to trailing cattle, and the general feeling of Texas cattlemen was that these seasonal restrictions violated the constitutional principle of interstate commerce.

In May 1885, *Report in Regard to the Range and Ranch Cattle Business of the United States* was published by the US Department of the Treasury. With regards to Texas fever, the report included information learned from the 1868 investigation as well as more recent observations and information. At the time of publication, the cause of Texas fever still was unknown, and a cure was a mystery. By then, though, it had been confirmed that cattle that originated from the Texas Fever District, which encompassed all of east Texas, the coastal plains along the Gulf of Mexico, the brush country of south Texas, and the Big Bend, were capable of transmitting the disease to Texas cattle that originated north of the Texas Fever District and to the domestic cattle of other states and territories (fig. 2).[27] Whether transportation was by trail or by rail, cattle from the southern areas of Texas that were transported during the traditional warm-weather months were known to transmit the disease unless kept in quarantine for a period of at least several weeks after reaching their destination (fig. 3). Restriction, sometimes by any means legal or otherwise, and quarantine of Texas cattle were common methods to attempt to control the disease.

Continued outbreaks of the disease prompted the US Department of Agriculture to create the Bureau of Animal Industry in 1884 to investigate the disease further. Another study of the disease was begun in 1888, and in 1891 Theobald Smith, a bacteriologist and pathologist working with veterinarians Fred L. Kilborne and Cooper Curtice at the bureau, described a protozoon that they found in the bodies of infected cattle. It was named *Piroplasma bigeminum*, later renamed *Babesia bigemina*. Through continued research and field experiments, they determined that the protozoon was transmitted by the common cattle tick, and they published their findings in *BAI Bulletin No. 1 (1893)*. Scientific advances since the earlier study in 1868 undoubtedly influenced the outcome of the later investigation.[28]

The discovery that Texas fever was transmitted by the common cattle tick, *Margaropus annulatas*, confirmed the suspicions of many Texas stockmen who had long suspected a link between ticks and the disease. The longhorn developed a natural immunity through the bite of infected ticks, much like being vaccinated, and passed this immunity to each successive generation. Many of the mysteries regarding transmission of the disease related to the life cycle of the tick. After feeding on the host animal, ticks mate while on the host, and the female drops off the host to the ground, where she deposits up to several thousand eggs over a period of approximately a week, and then dies. The male drops off the host and dies. Depending on weather conditions, the eggs hatch in three to four weeks, and the larvae, called seed ticks, crawl up on grass tips and other vegetation seeking a new host. Seed ticks usually crawl to a portion of the host's anatomy where the skin is thinner, such as the softer skin inside the flanks, and attach to the host.[29] The disease was transmitted though the bite of infected seed ticks, and the protozoan parasite that caused the infection thrived in tropical and subtropical climates. This explained how only ticks from certain regions carried the disease, and how longhorn cattle from the specified Texas Fever District could transmit the disease, while longhorn cattle outside the Texas Fever District did not transmit and were susceptible to the disease.

The life cycle of the cattle tick accounted for the mysterious transmission of the disease by direct contact or when northern cattle grazed on grassland over which Texas herds had passed. It was also clear how the disease was transmitted by rail despite rail car cleaning and sanitizing procedures. A herd shipped by rail reached the destination much faster than did a slow-moving herd on the trail; ticks remained attached to the host animal while the car was cleaned and sanitized and remained unaffected. The rapid rail transit of the cattle did not allow the life cycle of the cattle tick to run its course before reaching the destination, and rail transport was therefore a major contributing factor to the fever outbreak north of the South Platte River in 1884.

Attempts at tick eradication began soon after the cause was discovered. In 1894, rancher Robert J. Kleberg designed and built what may have been the first cattle dipping vat in the world on the King Ranch. Early concoctions of a combination of crude oil, water, and sulfur achieved limited success. In 1909 the arsenic bath mixture that became a common method of treatment was used in conjunction with the dipping vat successfully for the first time. The typical vat was a concrete-lined pit approximately thirty feet long, three feet wide, and seven feet deep. During the dipping process the animal was driven through a chute into the vat, where it was immersed in dip solution as it swam the length of the vat. The dip killed any ticks carried by the animal, and with repeated treatments at prescribed intervals the life cycle of the diseased ticks could be broken. In September 1917 there were 21,095 public or private vats available for use. Later it was discovered that Texas fever and other diseases can also be transmitted by several different species of ticks, and tick eradication and control efforts continue today.[30]

Although no longer in use, some of these old vats still exist. Periodically, a claim may surface that one of these vats is a historic relic of the Chisholm Trail and might even be cited as proof that the historic old trail traversed a particular area.[31] But the days of the long trail drives were all but over and the Chisholm Trail had been closed well before the tick was officially linked to Texas fever in 1893. Therefore, although a vat might be considered a relic of ranching heritage, the dates involved preclude these vats from being directly connected to the Chisholm Trail.

4

Life
on the Trail

REGARDLESS OF THE LOCATION of a cattle market or which trail was traveled, certain things had to happen before a herd was put on the trail. The cattle were not tame domestic bovines grazing peacefully in a pasture, but wild, long-horned cattle that lived in some of the most rugged areas of Texas. It was dangerous work catching wild cattle that were accustomed to defending themselves against all manner of predators and also holding them long enough for their herding instincts to overcome their desire to escape. If a cowhand managed to survive the cow hunt uninjured, there were plenty of other hazards waiting up the trail.

When a cattle herd was driven up the trail to a market, much more was involved than just rounding them up and pointing them in the right direction. A crew had to be hired, horses had to be obtained, supplies and equipment had to be purchased, and a cattle herd had to be gathered. Horses that were already saddle-broke and trained could be purchased. Wild mustangs, descendants of horses introduced to the Southwest by the Spanish, and noted for their endurance on the range, were hunted, captured, and trained by the settlers and stockmen. The purchase of trail-ready horses was more expedient but also more expensive. More preparation and planning was required to capture, break, and train wild mustangs, but it required minimum initial investment, and the horses could be sold for a nice profit at the end of the trail. Demand for good horses increased as more wild cattle were gathered and more ranches were established (fig. 4).

Horses and cattle were hunted or gathered; the term *roundup* came into use later. Several methods were used to catch wild horses. In one method of horse hunting, pens were built around water holes, with V-shaped extensions that formed a chute. A man who had concealed himself near the pen opening closed the gate after a group of horses passed on the way to water, trapping them inside. In another method, a group of men carrying enough provisions for several days located a small horse herd and followed them. If the men could stay close enough to keep the horses from taking the time to graze, water, or rest, the horses tired to the extent that they could be captured or driven to holding pens.[1]

In a third method, pens were built in thickets along the edge of a prairie using posts, brush, and rawhide thongs. Wings built of brush funneled the horses toward the pen, which had a narrow opening that no more than three horses could pass through at a time. Riders located a herd and used a relay system to keep the horses moving toward the pen. Once trapped, the horses were roped by the feet and hobbled to restrict their movement. Many horses were maimed or killed in their panic to escape the pens. After a few days to a few weeks, depending on the individual animal, the hobbles were removed and the horses driven with fewer problems.[2]

Whether purchased or gathered from the range, a wild horse had to be broken to accept a saddle, hackamore or bit, and rider before it was of much use. Different bronc busters had different methods of breaking a horse. Common methods were to tie down the horse until it was saddled, release the horse, and then jump into the saddle as the horse rose, or to blindfold the horse with a jacket or other such item, saddle the horse, and mount as the blindfold was removed. In either case the rider attempted to stay in the saddle until the horse tired itself out from bucking and running. An account from 1857 described one or more riders giving chase as the horse began to tire to ensure that it was "thoroughly fatigued" and to test its wind and endurance.[3] This often occurred on the open prairie, with no pens or obstructions to get in the way.

The plains tribes of Native Americans used similar methods to train a horse to accept a rider, except that they sometimes maneuvered the subject horse into water, sand, or swampy ground. The extra resistance of the water or soft ground tired the horse quicker. As the horse became too tired to resist, it learned to accept the rider and could then be ridden and trained. One session in shoulder-deep water often played out the horse to such an extent that it could be ridden out of the water onto dry land and it would not make any further attempts to buck. Water and soft ground also reduced the risk if the rider was thrown.[4]

A common misconception is that horses and cattle just naturally mix together. Movies and television tend to portray the ranch hand riding the wild, bucking bronc in one or two scenes and using the same horse to rope or cut cattle from a herd in the next. Horses have different characteristics—different levels of alertness, curiosity, strength, speed, endurance, and quickness. Some horses possess better night vision and a greater sense of their surroundings. Other horses have a natural capacity to develop "cow sense"—to almost know what the cattle will do before they do it. After a horse learned the basics of stop and go, if it was to be used to work cattle it had to be introduced and learn to accept the presence of the cattle. Then it could be trained to trail, track, hold, and control the movement of cattle more on its own and with less direction from the rider. Some horses were so intelligent that once an individual cow had been indicated by the rider, the horse proceeded to cut it from the herd without further direction or influence from the rider. This trait can be observed in current cutting horse competitions.

In those days there were no fences, and livestock grazed on the open range. Neighbors from up to thirty or forty miles away assembled for a cow hunt to gather, sort, and brand the increase. The men met at a predetermined place on the proper date. Prior to the invention of the chuck wagon, each man brought his own supplies, including bedding; coffee pot; tin cup; a wallet containing biscuits, salt, and sugar, if it was available; and four or five horses. A wallet was a sack with the mouth in the middle and both ends sewn shut. The contents might differ slightly to include bacon, cornbread, or other basics. If desired, fresh meat could be had by killing a yearling. A man's bedding generally consisted of his saddle blanket, his saddle for a pillow, and perhaps a tarp, if one was available.[5]

Methods varied, and techniques were adapted according to necessity. Cow hunts were held in the spring and fall. After meeting at a prearranged place, the men split into small groups, spread out so that they formed something of a net, and drove back towards the starting point. They worked so that cattle that drifted out of the path of one group drifted into the path of another group. Both branded and unbranded cattle were captured. As a herd was formed, men rode slowly around the herd in shifts around the clock to hold them on the open prairie. Singing to the cattle, especially at night, had a calming effect on the herd and served to reduce the chance of a stampede caused by the sudden appearance or noise of a rider. When the wild cattle broke from the herd and ran, they were pursued and either driven back or roped and dragged back to the herd.[6]

Cattle might be considered gentle if they did not immediately charge a rider on horseback or spook at the sight of one and could be controlled to an extent by riders. In brushy country, cattle were roped at night by moonlight when they went out on the prairie to graze, or pursued during daylight and dragged out of some of the thickest, thorniest fortresses concocted by nature. James H. Cook described chasing wild cattle through the Texas brush:

> Suddenly I heard a crash ahead, and in less than two seconds every rider in advance of me was riding as if the devil were after him. My horse knew the work, and plunged after the riders ahead. I held up for a moment; then the thought struck me that, if I did not keep those ahead of me in sight, I might never get back to camp. I did not know in which direction we had been riding, and one acre of ground looked just like all the rest—everywhere brush, timber, cactus. I gave my horse the reins, trailing the ones ahead by the crashing of limbs and dead brush. I was kept pretty busy dodging the limbs which were large enough to knock me from the saddle and warding the smaller limbs and brush from my face with my arms. I think I rode all over that pony—first on one side, then on the other; then, as he dived under some big live oak limb, almost under his neck. We crossed several prickly-pear patches where the clumps grew from two to ten feet high and about as close together as they could stand. My pony would jump over, knock down, or run through any of them. He was a cow-catcher by trade. He certainly made me pull leather, and I clung to his mane as well in order to keep in close touch with him. I had a very strong desire for this chase to end.[7]

If the brush was too thick to lasso the cattle, the rider was faced with a choice of either losing the quarry or using a method called tailing. In this method, the rider maneuvered alongside the animal, reached out and caught it by the tail, and took a quick turn around the saddle horn or gave it a good yank, causing the animal to trip or somersault. The rider dismounted quickly and hog-tied the feet of the tailed animal before it recovered, gained its feet, and charged. Tailed cattle were left for several hours to calm down and then released near gentle cattle that were brought to act as a decoy herd for the wild cattle. Once among the decoys, the wild cattle could be driven with the decoys. If one escaped, the capture process was repeated and the offender tied to a tree or to another steer with a short rope so that its movement was severely restricted until it had settled; this was called necking.[8]

Ownership was determined by brand and other marks. Prior to 1848, Texas had provisions for brands, but they were loosely enforced.

Brands, marks, and earmarks were registered at the county clerk's office of the county in which the livestock was kept beginning in 1848. The brand was an identifying mark burned into the hide of the animal with a hot iron. The hide on the neck or around the jaw was sometimes cut in a particular place and manner to leave a flap of skin hanging when the wound healed; this was called a wattle. The earmark was a notch or design cut into one or both ears of the animal.[9]

After the owners were satisfied that all of the cattle had been gathered from an area, each proceeded to cut out his cattle and determine ownership of unbranded calves. A calf was branded according to the brand of its mother. Ownership of unbranded cattle was determined by earmarks or wattles, and ownership of cattle lacking a brand or mark was settled among the owners. Cattle were branded and marked, and the group moved to another location and repeated the entire process until they agreed that they had covered their range. Unbranded, unmarked cattle were called mavericks. The term likely had its origins in one of several story variations that involved Samuel Maverick of Matagorda County, later of San Antonio. Maverick reportedly accepted a herd as settlement on a debt, but he neglected to brand the cattle along with the increase, and the local residents referred to unbranded cattle as belonging to Mr. Maverick, or Maverick's. Maverick gathered his herd and moved near San Antonio in 1854 and again left the increase unbranded. When he sold his cattle and brand in 1856, unbranded cattle in the vicinity were regarded as Maverick's, gathered, and branded as part of the herd.[10]

If the cattle were to be turned back out on the range, they were branded, calves were castrated, the count was tallied, and they were either turned out or driven to their home range and turned out. If a herd was gathered to be trailed to a market, the cattle were sorted according to the requirement: steers of certain ages comprised most of a herd intended for beef, while a herd intended to stock a ranch included more cows and bulls. Cattle that did not meet requirements were turned out or driven to their home range and turned out. Smaller herds from different stockmen were often combined into a larger trail herd. The Texas legislature passed a law in 1871 that required the use of road brands for herds driven across the northern limits of the state (figs. 5, 6).[11]

The individual brands and tally of cattle bearing each brand were recorded. The cattle were branded with a common road brand to indicate ownership while on the trail. Brands, earmarks, and counts were recorded in a Stockman's Mark and Brand Book or in a small pocket notebook, either of which fit handily in a coat or vest pocket (figs. 7, 8). The county, names of the parties involved in the transaction, count, description or age, and drawings of the brands, wattles, and earmarks were documented (fig. 9). The totals were listed along with the appropriate legal statements. The documents were signed by the inspector of hides and animals and/or by the county clerk and embossed with the official seals (fig. 10).[12] The documents were carried as proof of ownership while the herd was on the trail.

After the crew was hired, suitable horses obtained, the herd assembled and road-branded, and provisions acquired, the outfit was ready for the trail. The size of the crew varied depending on the size of the herd. Charles Goodnight stated that he preferred a crew of sixteen to eighteen men to handle a herd of 3,000 cattle, while another foreman preferred one drover for every 250 head of cattle.[13]

The owner, foreman, or trail boss sometimes rode twenty miles or more ahead to scout for water or scout the route. The cook drove the mess wagon, later called the chuck wagon. The wrangler was in charge of the spare horses, called the cavvieyard, later called the remuda. The mess wagon typically drove ahead of the herd and to one side, with the cavvieyard also ahead and to one side of the herd. The two most skillful men were designated as the point men, or pointers, and rode at the front of the herd to keep it on the correct course. The point men rode on either side of the herd near the front, but not directly in front. The cattle were guided rather than led; the steers in the lead were more apt to go in the desired direction if they did not feel forced to do so. Some steers had stronger personalities than others, such as Charles Goodnight's Old Blue, and took their place at the front of the herd each day. The swing and flank riders were spaced out on both sides of the herd between the pointers and the drags, and the drags brought up the rear. The drag riders kept the stronger cattle forward and the weaker cattle, the drags, moving at a steady pace.[14]

A herd on trail was usually fifty to sixty feet wide, and strung out for half a mile or more, depending on herd size. If the cattle were allowed to stay too close together, the body heat produced by the animals affected their endurance, and they could overheat; if allowed to string out too far, they might trot to fill the gaps, which could also affect their endurance and condition. A herd fresh on the trail was pushed harder at first in order to settle the cattle and get them accustomed to the trail. After about the first two weeks on the trail, the herd was considered to be "trail broke."[15]

Some preferred to stay clear of settlements; these might attract Indians, or something such as the sudden appearance of a barking dog might spark a stampede. A good trail man knew when to water or graze the herd, and for how long. Sometimes diversions of half a mile or more from the trail were necessary to find suitable grazing or bed grounds. At least two men, depending on conditions, rode in slow circles around the herd all night on guard duty. These were the night herders, or nighthawks. Guard duty was split into several shifts. If conditions were ripe for a stampede, all hands were on duty. The cattle were moved off of the bed ground at dawn to graze while the crew finished breakfast.[16] When all was ready, the herd was started up the trail.

Every animal leaves a track or a trace of its passing as it moves over the ground. As a route becomes more heavily used, it progresses from a single set of tracks to a faintly defined path to a clearly defined path. A lone longhorn cow in the brushy thickets of south Texas might not leave any obvious trail to an untrained eye, but when a herd was gathered and moved to a market it was quite different. Thousands of hooves pounded a path across the ground over which a herd traveled. By the time a herd passed, vegetation was trampled and the soil was compacted, leaving a trail that could easily be followed.

Drovers navigated by the sun, the stars, and the compass. The North Star provided an unerring nightly reference. The tongue of the chuck wagon could be pointed toward the North Star at night for a reference the next morning. The night watch shifts were timed by the movement of the Dippers in the night sky. Knowing how to read the stars was a useful skill. There is a story of an unnamed tenderfoot on his first night duty who was told to ride in and wake his relief man when the North Star set. He rode in the next morning, exhausted from the night's work, and found his relief drinking coffee after a good night's sleep. The tenderfoot complained that he had watched that star all night and it never moved.[17] (The North Star, of course, remains in a fixed position in the night sky.) Sometimes a lesson learned the hard way is better remembered, and it will also provide a learning opportunity for another tenderfoot at a later date. The ability to navigate by the stars was essential, especially if one traveled alone at night. A good trail man did not necessarily need a map to find his way.

While it might have been a relatively simple matter to follow an obvious trail, comfort and survival along the way were quite another matter. A drover might have had an extra set or two of clothes and a blanket or tarp in addition to his saddle blanket for bedding. His saddle served as a pillow. Tents or any other type of shelter were not typically carried. Food and cooking utensils were basically the same as those used on the cow hunts. No provision was made for medical care. James H. Cook stated, "Should anyone become injured, wounded, or sick, he would be strictly out of luck. A quick recovery and a sudden death were the only desirable alternatives in such cases, for much of the time the outfit would be far from the settlements and from medical or surgical aid."[18]

Meals on the trail consisted of little more than bacon, stew, beans, biscuits, and an occasional pie or cobbler. A beef might have been killed occasionally to feed the crew. A good cook used ingredients picked up along the trail to supplement the supplies bought to prepare meals. Kindling for the cook fire was carried in a canvas or cowhide slung underneath the wagon, called a possum belly or caboose. On the open plains where there were no trees, kindling and fuel for the fire consisted of dried bison manure, called buffalo chips. An invoice dated May 14, 1881, from Frank E. Conrad & Co. at Fort Griffin, Texas, to "Mess[rs]. Schreiner & Lytle" (the partnership of John T. Lytle and Charles A. Schreiner), provides insight regarding trail fare: "300 lbs. Flour, 252 ½ lbs. Bacon, 50 lbs. Coffee, 40 lbs. Dried Peaches, 25 lbs. Grits, 25 lbs. Hominy, 40 lbs. Beans, 6 gall [gallons] Molasses, 50 lbs. Salt, 6 gall Pickles, 5 gall Syrup, 1 can Yeast Powder, 1 gall Cider Vinegar, and 2 cans Black Pepper."[19] Items such as overalls, boots, ammunition, and so on, were purchased as needed. The name of the drover who required the items was listed on the invoice, and the cost of these items was deducted from his pay at the end of the trail when the herd was sold and the crew was paid (fig. 11).

The same basics were found on other invoices from stores in Dodge City and Ogallala. The quantities and items varied based on availability and the distance to be traveled, and sometimes items such as canned tomatoes or sugar were purchased. The invoice dates of May 14, 1881, at Fort Griffin; June 19, 1881, at Dodge City; and July 20, 1881 at Ogallala for the same Lytle herds indicate an average rate of travel of just over ten miles per day.[20] It is possible that they actually made better time but were delayed at river crossings or perhaps for some other reason.

Fresh water came from creeks, rivers, and springs along the trail. Hazards of the trail included sickness caused by bad water, lack of vegetables or fruit in the diet, or poor food preservation and preparation techniques. Other dangers were plentiful on the trail. J. C. Davis wrote in a letter to his sweetheart that they had experienced a string of bad luck during the spring: "1 Killed, 1 with his Back Broke, 1 leg Broke, 1 Colar [*sic*] Bone Broke, & i came very near geting [*sic*] Drowning in the Canadian River ystday." A few weeks later Davis wrote that the cattle had been sold for $30 per head, and "I will start for the washataw [Washita] to buy a few fat cattel to Ship or Sell to the Butcher then i will come to see you." The loneliness of the trail life was apparent in Davis's letters to his beloved Dicy Clark of Parker County, Texas. Jack Bailey wrote in his journal, kept during a trail drive in 1868, of being so sick and lonely that he "was such a fool to come on this trip," and "one consolation is that I am not afraid to die."[21]

Besides the potential accidents that were common to working around large numbers of horses and cattle, drovers contended with all manner of weather extremes: rain, wind, sleet, hail, drought, snow, heat, cold, storms, and lightning. G. W. Mills told of several experiences in storms on the plains. On a drive near Taylor, Texas, in April 1879, a rainstorm hit late one afternoon. It rained all night as the temperature dropped. Several head of horses and cattle died from the sudden cold, and the drovers nearly froze to death. The cold was so severe that the horses that were ridden that night were unfit for service for the rest of the trip.[22] The cattle drifted approximately eight miles during the night. Each man was expected to hold his own and stay with the herd. After having spent all night in the saddle in the rain and cold, Mills and the rest of the crew arrived in camp, looking forward to "coffee and hot grub of some kind." Instead, they found no fire, no coffee, and the cook asleep in the wagon. The cook protested that it was too wet to build a fire, but the boss promptly relieved him of his duties and hired a new cook the next day.[23]

In another occurrence, a hailstorm struck on the plains near Fort Dodge early in the afternoon on the Fourth of July, 1880. The storm was so severe that it killed jackrabbits, antelopes, and a few yearlings. It became so dark in the afternoon that a man ten feet away could not be seen and so cold that the trail hands nearly froze to death on the Fourth of July. Their hands and backs were covered with knots and welts from the hailstones, which were piled nearly four inches deep on the prairie the next morning. Mills stated, "We had no supper nor breakfast; getting back to camp next morning at ten, we found the cook fixing to leave, thinking surely that all the men had been killed."[24]

Lightning was especially dangerous, as it can strike from miles away, and a rider on horseback was likely the tallest object on the treeless plains. Lightning strikes killed many a horse, steer, and drover on the trails. While it may be enjoyable to observe a thunderstorm and lightning from the relative safety of a porch or other shelter, it is quite another thing to be caught outside in the open when lightning streaks across the skies. The duration between the flash of lightning and the sound of thunder depends upon the distance to the lightning; sound travels at approximately one-fifth of a mile per second, and the distance can be estimated by counting the seconds between the flash and the sound. Lightning directly overhead is another matter. In an instant these events take place: the flash of lightning and the crash of thunder are practically simultaneous; the thunder is felt as well as heard, much like the muzzle blast and report of a giant cannon; a person's hair stands up on end; and the air sizzles like bacon grease in a hot skillet. J. B. Connor described a lightning storm that occurred while on night herd with the horses near the Salt Fork of the Red River in 1885:

> The lightning was continuous, so was the thunder, which was most terrific. While the storm was in progress the horses bunched together around me, stuck their heads between their knees and moaned and groaned till I became frightened and decided that the end of time had come. I was only nineteen years old, and thought I was as brave as any man, but the action of the horses was too much for me, so I got down off my horse and lay flat down on the ground and tried to die, but could not. The storm passed on and I found myself unhurt, so after that fearful experience I did not mind other storms.[25]

River crossings were especially dangerous for drovers. When a herd on trail approached a river or creek, the trail boss either rode ahead or sent a rider ahead to flush waterfowl or wild game; the sudden rise of a flock of ducks or geese might startle the herd and start a stampede. The herders also scouted the area for conditions or hazards; the presence of quicksand along a riverbank indicated the need for extra caution, or perhaps to locate another, more desirable crossing. Heavy rainfall could cause high water, swift currents, muddy banks, and conditions that were more dangerous than usual. In extreme conditions drovers held the herd until the waters receded enough to proceed. River crossings could be as routine as wading through shallow water on a good gravel riverbed, but swimming a herd across a river was one of the most dangerous events, next to stampedes, that occurred on the trail.[26]

The drovers typically took a herd across a river in small groups. The main herd was held back while a group of fifty to a hundred or so head was started across, then the next group crossed, and so on. The trick was to get the cattle to cross without milling, or swimming in circles. The drovers had to keep them moving and have enough men present across the river to control the cattle that had crossed, in the river to prevent milling and keep the animals on the move, and in the rear to control those that had not yet crossed and keep them moving forward. Depending on conditions, sometimes they kept the herd moving across a river in a continuous line until they were all across. There was no standard procedure that fit every situation. Horses were not as prone to milling as were cattle. Cattle were also watered in groups and were not watered at every crossing. Depending on the condition of the herd, and the size and topography of the river or creek, a herd of two thousand to three thousand head could create a jam or be otherwise hard to handle if allowed to water all at once. There was a science to watering a herd on the trail; too little water and the cattle might be restless during the night or try to return to water, while too much water could be fatal to the cattle.[27]

J. M. Nance told of several river crossings while on a drive from Hays County, Texas, to Cheyenne, Wyoming, during the spring of 1877. While crossing the Brazos upstream from Waco, the river was high and the entire herd of twenty-one hundred head of cattle was swimming the river at the same time. "It looked as if I had no cattle at all, for all we could see were the horns." The chuck wagon was floated across with the aid of a boat. The herd then crossed the Red River at Red River Station and encountered high water at the Washita River. Another herd had crossed just ahead of Nance's herd and had built a raft to get their equipment across. Nance traded some ropes for the raft and used it to move his equipment across, then swam the cattle across in small groups of seventy-five to one hundred the next day. The cattle tried to mill and turn back, but the drovers were able to get them across. They had little trouble swimming the horses across. When they reached the North Canadian River, it was flooded, and other herds were approaching. After they waited for several days with no change in river conditions, to avoid the likely mixing of cattle with other herds Nance decided to cross in a similar manner as they had done at the Washita. They built a raft to cross the equipment and began to swim the herd. In Nance's words:

> The cattle were started across and were going fine, when it came up a terrific hailstorm, which interrupted the proceedings. One man was across on the other side of the river, naked, with his horse and saddle and about half of the herd and the balance of us were on this side with the other half of the herd and all the supplies. There was no timber on our side of the river, and when the hail began pelting the boys and myself made a break for the

wagon for shelter. We were all naked, and the hail came down so furiously that within a short time it was about two inches deep on the ground. It must have hailed considerably up the river, for the water was so cold we could not get any more of the herd across that day. . . . The water was so cold that neither horse nor man could endure it, and in trying to cross over several of them came near drowning and were forced to turn back, so the man on the other side had to stay over there all night alone and naked. . . . Next morning everything was lovely and our absent man swam back to us after he had put the cattle in shape. He had a good saddle blanket which he said had kept him comfortable enough during the night.[28]

The remainder of this herd and outfit crossed the next day but lost a man to injury when his horse fell, causing three broken ribs and a broken collarbone. While that man survived his fall, many drovers drowned during similar tasks. Mounds of dirt near the crossings, often covered with rocks or marked with a stick shoved into the ground for some remembrance, served as silent testimony to the dangers encountered at river crossings.

A stampede could occur at any time and for almost any reason, or for no discernible reason. Charles Goodnight told of a stampede that occurred near the Pecos River as a herd of bison, which stretched for miles, approached from the northwest while on their annual fall migration. The cattle were headed southwest and he thought that they had time to get the herd through, but the bison stampeded at the sight or scent of the cattle and split the cattle herd, causing them also to stampede. The bison ran for forty-five minutes before they passed and left Goodnight and his hands to round up the cattle. Half of the herd had run toward Horsehead Crossing, and the remainder had reversed their course and run back along their back trail.[29]

Many stampedes occurred in the dead of night. Imagine a landscape broken by ravines of various widths and depths, the herd bedded for the night, the nighthawks singing softly as they rode guard around the herd, the crew asleep with their horses saddled and staked nearby, and a night so dark that a horse's head could not be seen by the rider. Add a sudden storm with a flash of lightning, thunderclap, rain, and hail, and a stampede was almost assured.[30] The herd might appear to rest peacefully, or they might show signs of nervousness; either way, a stampede started in the span of a moment, and the herd was up and running.

Night horses were chosen for their intelligence, night vision, and sure-footedness. A good horse reacted to a stampede immediately and raced through the darkness for the lead, and hopefully the rider was able to stay aboard. Although the rider might not see the cattle in the darkness, he put his trust in his horse. The goal was to pull alongside the leaders and turn them so that they ran in an arc back into the rest of the herd and cause them to mill, eventually slowing the herd to a halt. If the riders were unable to turn the runaway herd into a mill, the cattle might scatter to all points of the compass. It was a dangerous race for man, horse, and cattle. Goodnight described the experience of helplessness as the rider held on and blindly charged through and across unseen obstacles: "It was an unforgettable, elemental experience that weaklings could not relish nor timid men endure."[31]

Prairie dog holes, ravines, and other unexpected hazards took their toll in the darkness. Near Ellsworth in 1875, a loud thunderclap triggered a stampede. The cattle and landscape were only visible during flashes of lightning every few seconds. James H. Cook later stated, "Between the flashes of lightning the darkness was so intense that I could not even see the horse I was riding." As Cook and another rider raced to head off the lead cattle, a bolt of lightning lit the scene for a brief second, and Cook's horse braced its forefeet suddenly and stopped while the other horse and rider appeared in midair, along with several steers. Cook's horse had seen or sensed the edge of a high creek bank and stopped a few feet short, while the other horse and rider sailed over the edge at a full gallop. The stampede was stopped eventually, and the next morning the unfortunate rider and his horse were found dead at the foot of the drop-off among a small heap of dead cattle. The rider had been crushed beneath his horse.[32]

When a stampede was over a head count was taken. If any men were missing, a search began. During the mad rush in the dark a horse could step in a prairie dog hole or lose its footing in a number of ways, leaving its rider injured or afoot. The search often ended as in this instance, when the missing man was found dead, killed from a fall or trampled by the stampeding herd.

Regardless of the cause of death, funerals on the trail were simple yet sincere affairs. After the grave was dug, a small group gathered around. The body of the unfortunate soul was wrapped in a saddle blanket and lowered into the grave. This was the time for an appropriate statement to be made about the deceased or a supplication of some sort to the Almighty, but each felt unequal to the task. If no one spoke, the awkward silence was broken by the sound of the shovel as it was jabbed into the dirt to fill the grave. If rocks were available, the filled-in grave was overlaid as well as possible to discourage marauding animals. Sometimes a memento was left or a headboard was fashioned from whatever material was handy. Men who were prone to such thoughts silently wondered if they would be the next to be wrapped in a saddle blanket for eternal rest in some lonely place upon the plains. Philip A. Rollins described the end of the ceremony: "The silence was usually ended by an expression spontaneously emitted from overwrought nerves, and often profane in form though not in intent. Speech broke the tension, horses were remounted, and the world was faced again."[33] The drive resumed, and the herd continued on toward its destination.

During the Civil War the exodus of men from their home counties in Texas to serve the Confederate cause left many areas without adequate protection. Accordingly, Indian depredations increased during the course of the war. Raids, especially from the Comanches and Kiowas, took an increasing toll in lives and lost livestock on the northwestern and western frontier. Cattlemen often operated in remote areas on the fringes of the frontier and consequently bore the brunt of Indian depredations after the war. Due to the great distance between military outposts, it was often left to the cowhands or Texas Rangers to respond to attacks. Indian encounters on the trail sometimes consisted of attacks, attempts to steal horses, or demands for supplies such as tobacco or a few head of cattle. If the demand was not met or negotiations did not produce an agreeable result, the Indians might return and cause a stampede. Weaker cattle or extras that had been brought along for the purpose were usually cut out of the herd and given to the Indians in return for peaceful passage.[34]

Sometimes a herd was wintered in the northern part of Indian Territory due to quarantine laws in the destination state. Winters in that country were more severe than in southern Texas, where many of the drives had originated (fig. 12). The cattle could drift south in the face of strong winter storms approaching from the north. When a winter storm approached, driven by a strong north wind, cattle turned their tails to the wind. If the storm was bad enough, the cattle walked, or drifted, in the direction that the wind blew until they either walked over the edge of a drop-off or encountered an obstacle of some sort that blocked the drift. Although the buffalo grass that grew on the prairie retained high nutrition value during the winter, snow and ice covered both the grass and the cattle. Coupled with extreme cold, under these circumstances the cattle starved, if they did not freeze to death first. A blizzard made these bad conditions even worse. The winter of 1871–72 was especially hard, when approximately a quarter of a million head of cattle and several hundred horses died within a week in Kansas during blizzard conditions.[35]

Occasionally a herd was sold along the trail, but more often it continued to its destination, where it was sold and the hands paid off (fig. 13). The pay rate averaged twenty-five to thirty dollars per month, depending on experience; a top hand or a good cook might make slightly more, and the trail boss made about ninety dollars per month.[36] If the horses were not sold at trail's end, the boss assigned a few of the hands to return the cavvieyard to the home ranch in Texas. Some turned and headed back to Texas at the first opportunity, while others took the time for a bath and haircut and to purchase new clothes before returning. Many availed themselves of the numerous distractions, in the form of saloons, women, and gambling, that were designed to contribute to the local economy and part the drover from his hard-earned money. After several months on the trail and with money in their pocket, the men, many of whom were still in their teens or early twenties, were usually ready to let off a little steam.

The average trail hand was likely no more prone to drunkenness than the average man of any other profession. While there was an initial outburst of exuberance after lonely months on the trail with little sleep, the tendency to pack as much action into a short amount of time, repeated by almost every trail crew that came to town during the trailing season, contributed to the false notion that all drovers were habitual drunks. Their arrival increased a cow town's population several times over and therefore increased the business at saloons and gaming houses. However, most of the trail men knew that drunkenness was incompatible with their chosen profession.[37] This temporary situation also caused problems with local law enforcement, who often had to walk a line between keeping the peace and maintaining a working relationship with the stockmen whose herds and employees sustained the local economy.

Some went on to greater success in the livestock business. Some made a trip or two up the trail and then found another vocation, while others continued in the trailing business. Years later, G. O. Burrows summed up his trail experiences riding sore-backed horses, getting wet and cold, going without sleep, and many other hardships that were forgotten when the herd was sold and he started back to Texas:

Have often stopped a few days in Chicago, St. Louis, and Kansas City, but always had the "big time" when I arrived in good old Santone [San Antonio] rigged out with a pair of high-heeled boots and striped breeches, and about $6.30 worth of other clothes. Along about sundown you could find me at Jack Harris' show occupying a front seat and clamoring for the next performance. This "big time" would last but a few days, however, for I would soon be "busted" and have to borrow money to get out to the ranch, where I would put in the fall and winter telling about the big things I had seen up North. The next spring I would have the same old trip, the same old things would happen in the same old way, and with the same old wind-up. I put in eighteen or twenty years on the trail, and all I had in the final outcome was the high-heeled boots, the striped pants, and about $4.80 worth of other clothes, so there you are.[38]

Many trail drivers grew up on the frontier. They were accustomed to the hardships of everyday life such as sleeping outside on the ground in all weathers with nothing more than a saddle blanket for cover. An unknown number served in the Confederate Army during the war. Others protected the frontier, where they patrolled between stations established about a day's journey apart along the frontier line from Cooke County through Wise, Parker, Johnson, Bosque, Coryell, Lampasas, Burnet, Blanco, Bandera, Medina, Kendall, Atascosa, Live Oak, McMullen, La Salle, Dimmit, and Maverick Counties. They lived in an often violent world where the howl of a wolf, the yip of a coyote, or the hoot of an owl might be the natural result of a nearby animal, or it might signal impending danger from attack. They were products of their time; their character was shaped by forces that are difficult to comprehend by modern standards. Despite the risks and privations, their days on the trail were often considered, as Historian of the Plains William E. Hawks stated, "the good old days, when men were men, and would offer you everything they had, even to their lives, and they thought it was right."[39]

5

The Earliest
Trails

THE EARLIEST CATTLE TRAILS leading east from Texas developed
between 1690 and 1821, during the Spanish colonization of Texas.
New Orleans, founded in 1718, grew to be an important trade center
and was the closest major port to Texas. The details of the establishment of a cattle market or the first cattle drive from Texas to New
Orleans are unknown. Although it was likely established earlier, the
first indication of a cattle market at New Orleans that was found
in newspapers appeared in 1837. The firm of Tourne and Beckwith
advertised shipping rates of ten dollars per head for cattle and twelve
dollars per head for horses. By February 1839, traffic in cattle had
apparently grown to the point that the Louisiana House of Representatives considered "an appropriation for the keeping of an office for
the recording of brands of cattle" in Lafayette Parish. This is interesting because one of the eastbound cattle trails crossed the Mermentau River, passed through Lafayette Parish, and crossed Bayou Teche
near the present site of Breaux Bridge. The first northbound cattle
trails developed in response to the flood of settlers into Missouri and
the upper Midwest during the 1840s and 1850s. The network of trails
led from southern Texas to the northeast corner of Indian Territory
and on to Missouri and beyond. These were the predecessors; the
dust along Chisholm's Trail was not stirred by Texas cattle until 1867.[1]

Texas once served as a buffer zone between northern New Spain
and the English colonies. Before 1779 the export of cattle from the
Spanish province of Texas was illegal. In 1778 Teodoro de Croix,
commandant-general of the interior provinces of New Spain, realized the revenue potential of the cattle herds in the Bexar–La Bahia
region and declared that all unbranded cattle in the region were
the property of the king. A four-month grace period was allowed for

cattle and horses to be gathered and branded and for brands to be registered. After the grace period expired, a license was required to round up wild, unbranded, or stray livestock, and a tax was levied on each animal so captured.[2]

Spain declared war against Great Britain on June 21, 1779, at the request of France and to repay French assistance in recovering possession of Florida and Gibraltar. Spain did not formally recognize the United States; however, Spanish joint operations with the French provided welcome assistance to the Americans during their revolution. Louisiana governor Bernardo de Gálvez, *who* had been appointed by King Carlos III to raise a force and conduct military operations against the British along the Gulf Coast, anticipated the declaration of war and sent a messenger to Texas governor Domingo Cabello asking for two thousand head of cattle to be delivered to his force in Louisiana. Gálvez had once led Spanish troops from the province of Chihuahua against the Apaches in the province of Texas, where he had encountered large herds of wild cattle, and he recognized that this resource could provide a traveling commissary. Since the export of cattle was illegal at the time, Cabello waited for approval from Commandant-General Croix, then ordered a herd of sufficient size to be gathered from the Bexar–La Bahia region. Due to potential disputes over unbranded cattle in the Bexar region, most of the herd was gathered in the area between La Bahia and the coast. Several smaller herds were driven from the general vicinity of the present site of Goliad County to Opelousas, Louisiana, in late summer of 1779. They traveled along the La Bahia–Nacogdoches Road to Nacogdoches, from there to Natchitoches, and on toward Opelousas, where the herds were delivered to Gálvez.[3]

Another route led from the same region past the present site of Beaumont, Texas, where the trail crossed the Neches River and then the Sabine River east of Beaumont. Both routes led to Opelousas and New Orleans, and both were later referenced as the Beef Trail or Opelousas Trail. This network of trails, which evolved from east-west Indian trails between Louisiana and Texas, became known as the La Bahia or Opelousas Road and constituted the earliest cattle trails used to move herds from Texas. The beeves that were driven along these trails over the next few years fed the troops that Gálvez led to defeat the British at Manchac, Baton Rouge, Natchez, Mobile, Pensacola, and New Providence in the Bahamas from 1779 to 1782, thus aiding the colonists during the American Revolution.[4]

Liberty County cattleman James Taylor White drove cattle to New Orleans for profit as early as the late 1830s or early 1840s. Newspaper advertisements for the New Orleans cattle market appeared as early as 1848, when a price of four to five cents per pound for beef cattle was published in the September 14 edition of the *Daily Crescent*. Prices fluctuated based on availability and grade, or quality, of the cattle. In January 1849 beef cattle prices were advertised in the same publication at eight cents per pound.[5]

Cattle were bought and sold by the head (each individual animal) or by weight. Cattle were either weighed or their weight was estimated, as agreed by the buyer and seller. Net weight, or carcass weight, was calculated based on a percentage of live weight, or estimated live weight. The average weight of a well-fed, four-year-old longhorn steer was 950–1,050 pounds. If the average weight was determined to be 950 pounds and net weight was determined at 50 percent of live weight, at $0.05 per pound each animal was worth $23.75. Texas cattle did not necessarily command the same price as domestic beef cattle, as the Texas breed was lean and rangy.[6]

An article in the *Houston Telegraph and Texas Register* in 1842 described four land routes from Louisiana to Texas: the lower route that passed by Opelousas, the route that passed by Alexandria, the middle route that passed Natchitoches on the old San Antonio Road, and the upper route past Shreveport. Stockmen could take their droves overland east from Texas to any of these points along or near the Red River but had to deal with swampland south to New Orleans. The swamps and bayous along the Atchafalaya River were a formidable obstacle. The Atchafalaya Rafts were formed, possibly during the late 1700s, when logs and limbs clogged massive areas of the river and bayou system and blocked navigation through the area. The raft was a series of logjams that extended for several hundred yards to several miles in length and blocked navigation for approximately forty miles of the Atchafalaya River. The raft was reported cleared in 1842, which opened up navigation from "all the country within eighty miles of Opelousas" all the way to New Orleans. This allowed trailed cattle to be transported by boat more easily to New Orleans.[7]

William B. Duncan drove cattle from the vicinity of Refugio County east to New Orleans during the 1850s. The size of the droves that were moved east from Texas during that period tended to be smaller, numbering about 250 head of cattle or less. According to Duncan's observations recorded in his diary, the average drove encountered on the trails to New Orleans numbered 185 head of cattle.[8] The topography of east Texas and the country east of the Sabine River was not conducive to moving large herds. The lay of the land, the use of cow boats to navigate the Atchafalaya, and the limited staging and grazing areas around New Orleans made it difficult to move a larger herd like those that were later driven to northern markets.

Duncan traveled a route from Refugio County to Liberty County and crossed the Trinity River at the Atascosito Crossing between the present sites of Liberty and Kenefick. He hired extra hands at certain river crossings to help get the drove across; the number of drovers that made the entire trip is unknown. Four extra hands were hired at a cost of $3.00 each to cross the Neches River near Beaumont. Duncan also paid four extra hands $4.00 each in addition to $13.00 in ferry charges to get across the Sabine River near Nibletts Bluff, Louisiana. It cost $11.25 in ferry charges to cross the Calcasieu River at the Bagdad Ferry. He crossed the Mermentau River near the current site of Jennings and then proceeded to Butte la Rose on the Atchafalaya. From there cattle were transported by boat across the Atchafalaya Swamp to Plaquemine. The cattle were unloaded and penned until they could be transported by another boat downriver to New Orleans, where they were penned until the herd was sold.[9]

Cow boats that operated between Plaquemine and the stock landing at Jefferson City, such as the steamer *Post-Boy*, carried 200–250 head of cattle per trip. A guide was furnished to help drovers reach Bayou la Rose; freight rates from there to Jefferson City cost up to $2.50 per head, depending upon the class of cattle. Extra charges were assessed to take a small drove to New Orleans without waiting for a full load. Another trail led from the vicinity of Vermillionville, later renamed Lafayette, south along Bayou Teche, crossed the Atchafalaya River near Berwick, then went east to Vacherie. From Vacherie the cattle were shipped by steamboat to New Orleans. Drovers typically retraced their route, traveling by boat back to Butte la Rose and then overland back to Texas.[10]

Along the way Duncan purchased horse feed, meals, and lodging at local residences or establishments, paid for penning and pasturage for the cattle, hired additional hands to assist in river crossings, paid for ferry crossings, and paid shipping charges on the cow boats. If additional horses were required, he must have hired them along the way, as he did not mention taking extra horses or hiring the services of a wrangler. Because of the lay of the land, the degree to which it was settled, and the size of the droves, it was more economical to pay for penning and pasturage than to hire additional hands to guard the cattle at night. Duncan received from eleven to twenty-two dollars per head for his cattle at New Orleans over the course of several years. His profits, after expenses, ranged from about sixty-eight dollars to just over two thousand dollars per trip.[11]

The drovers faced storms, lightning, stampedes, river crossings, and weather extremes. There were also the hazards of working with livestock, the discomfort caused by insects in the coastal regions and bayous, and the difficulties of recovering escaped stock. Hired hands sometimes did not report as expected. Cattle were typically penned during nights on the trail; sometimes the pens were already occupied by another drove, and an alternate had to be found. If penned cattle decided to stampede, they simply broke down the pen. Drovers also had to deal with ailments that are not usually mentioned in books or movies. On a trip in 1854, after enduring lost cattle and delays due to torrential coastal rains, Duncan developed a toothache. Near "Breau's" (likely the present site of Breaux Bridge, Louisiana) he helped another drover get his herd across Bayou Teche. The next day he was so sore and stiff he could hardly walk, with "bowels very much deranged." After he spent a day suffering in bed, he rode into town to mail a letter to his wife and find a dentist. The dentist, named Dr. Kills, filled one tooth and pulled two teeth. After about a day and a half of rest and some medicine to stop the bleeding, he finally got his cattle loaded on a cow boat. After taking cholera medicine for the continuing bowel problem, he "could not sleep for the musketoes."[12]

The driving season was usually relatively long because of the milder coastal climate, from February until December. In addition to the route that Duncan took, cattle were also driven from Texas past Nacogdoches, Natchitoches, and Opelousas to the Mississippi River, past Alexandria to the Mississippi, or to Shreveport on the Red River, where the cattle were shipped downstream to New Orleans. As more droves headed for New Orleans, the potential existed for oversupply and depressed prices. During the 1850s market prices for Texas or western beef cattle fluctuated from three and one-half cents to twelve cents per pound and from six dollars to forty dollars per head, depending on availability and the grade of cattle.[13]

Although the routes east to New Orleans were later called the Opelousas Trail, Beef Trail, or Beef Road, no examples of these trail names are found in newsprint during the trails' historical period of use. Duncan used the names of destinations to describe his routes. When a road name was used, it contained the origin or destination as a reference, such as San Antonio Road. The beef, hide, and tallow market at New Orleans supported a localized network of related businesses and services along the trails. It provided economic opportunity for early Texas cattlemen, but the trails that led east to New Orleans were soon overshadowed by the trails to northern markets, where the ability to drive larger herds meant potentially larger profits.

The oldest of the major trails over which longhorn herds were driven north from Texas is often ignored by researchers and writers, perhaps because that network of trails was also overshadowed later by the Chisholm Trail. This route was essentially the reverse of the Texas Road, also known as the Texas Emigrant Road. Many people traveled the Texas Road from the Ohio, Mississippi, and Missouri River valleys to settle in Texas. The Texas Road passed the present sites of Baxter Springs, Kansas, and the Oklahoma sites of Vinita, Pryor, Wagoner, Fort Gibson, Checotah, Eufaula, McAlester, and Durant; crossed the Red River near Colbert; and entered Texas. A portion of the road followed the old Osage Trace, which led from the Grand, or Neosho, River in Kansas to the vicinity of Fort Gibson in Indian Territory and from there to the vicinity of Fort Smith in Arkansas.[14] This route provided a way for traders to reach the Osage people and for the Osages to travel to and from their homelands to the plains.

About the time that the Old Three Hundred received land grants to settle Stephen F. Austin's Texas colony, the western edge of Anglo settlement in America was basically along the Mississippi River to a point slightly north of the Missouri River. Narrow fingers of settlements extended west along the Missouri to Independence, along the Arkansas River to Fort Smith, and along the Red River to a point northwest of Natchitoches. After Louisiana was admitted to the Union in 1812 as a state, the remaining Louisiana Territory was renamed Missouri Territory. Missouri Territory included the lands that would become all or a portion of the states of Missouri, Arkansas, Texas, Iowa, Minnesota, Kansas, Nebraska, Colorado, North Dakota, South Dakota, Montana, Wyoming, Oklahoma, and New Mexico.[15]

The southernmost strip of Missouri Territory, located from the Mississippi River west to the one-hundredth meridian, south of 36° 30′ north and north of the Red River, became Arkansas Territory in 1819. The southeastern portion of Missouri Territory was admitted to the Union as the state of Missouri in 1821. Most of the western portion of Arkansas Territory was removed in 1824, with another section removed in 1828, and the remainder was admitted into the Union as the state of Arkansas in 1836. The sections removed in 1824 and 1828 became part of Indian Territory, through which the northbound cattle trails from Texas later passed.[16]

Subsequent to the War of 1812, the area within the vast remaining lands of Missouri Territory bordered on the south by the Red River, on the north by the Great Bend of the Missouri River, and between the 95th and 101st meridians west had been envisioned by some in the US government as a "Permanent Indian Frontier." Under this concept, Indian tribes that were removed from the path of advancing settlements from the east could be relocated to this designated permanent frontier. This idea was based on the European concept of the right of preemption as it pertains to landownership, which basically gave white settlers the chance to occupy and own Indian lands after the native inhabitants sold their land, were conquered, or abandoned their land. White traders were to be granted access by permit only, and no white settlements would be established within the designated area. The land was thought to be fertile enough to support both agriculture and game. The concept of the Permanent Indian Frontier would have opened valuable land to settlement east of the Mississippi River and provided separation between the settlements and the Indians that would theoretically have removed friction between the races. At least that was the prevailing thought within the government at that time.[17]

The tribes that had not already been forced out became subject to the Indian Removal Act of 1830. This act basically gave the president of the United States the authority to grant unsettled lands west of the Mississippi River in exchange for Indian lands within the borders of existing states. Some lands west of the ninety-fifth meridian were already occupied by the Plains Indians, who resented the intrusions by the eastern tribes into their traditional lands. Between 1825 and 1840, a complex chain of events, which included land negotiations, sales, trades, and military force, resulted in the forced relocation of tribes from east of the Mississippi River. Tribes in the northern and eastern United States were given a choice between ceding their lands in exchange for annuities, presents, and new land to the west, or facing extermination. Cherokee tribal leaders in Georgia, Alabama, and Mississippi unwillingly agreed that resistance was futile. They ceded their land in the eastern United States in exchange for land west of the Mississippi River. The removal of approximately seventeen thousand members of the Cherokee Nation that remained in the southeastern United States and their relocation to Indian Territory occurred in 1838–39. Approximately four thousand men, women, and children died along the way from exposure, disease, and starvation. The Cherokees, Choctaws, Chickasaws, Creeks, and Seminoles, called the Five Civilized Tribes because of their adoption of certain Anglo cultural practices, were relocated to Indian Territory. This forced removal of eastern Indians became known as the "Trail of Tears" and placed them between the cattle ranges in Texas and the future cattle markets in Missouri.[18]

US government policies placed the eastern tribes into environments to which they were not accustomed and helped set the stage for future conflicts with drovers. However well planned the removal policies might have been, the relocated tribes from the east found life in the west difficult. Methods of farming and hunting there were different than in their homelands. The plains tribes viewed the easterners as intruders and were themselves viewed by the newcomers as barbarians because of their lifestyle. The Osages blamed the newer arrivals for the loss of hunting grounds. The Comanches, Kiowas, and Wichitas disputed the territory assigned to the Five Civilized Tribes. Between 1824 and 1827 Fort Towson was built on the Red River, Fort Gibson on the Arkansas River, and Fort Leavenworth on the Missouri River for the purpose of keeping the peace among the Indian tribes that found themselves in relatively close proximity to one another.[19] By the early 1840s the lure of cheap land brought settlers, farmers, and adventurers west of the Mississippi into Arkansas, Missouri, Iowa, and Texas. The influx of settlers created a market for Texas beeves, and the relocated tribes soon found themselves being crowded out again by encroaching settlement.

About 1818, when settlers first arrived in what became western Missouri, the emigrants encountered "Indians and half-breed Spanish and French." They described the cattle that were possessed by these early inhabitants as "cattle of Spanish breed, tall, lithe, sinewy, with horns of immense size and length. They were as swift of foot as the native deer and antelope, but their flesh had the flavor of wild game." They declared the cattle unsuitable for food but valuable for their hide, horns, and tallow.[20] It is not known how or when the longhorn was first driven to Missouri, but the description of the longhorn given by early settlers is unmistakable.

Lands that lay immediately west of the borders of Arkansas and Missouri and from the Red River north past Fort Leavenworth had been granted to various tribes by the US government.[21] Settlers continued to immigrate into Arkansas and Missouri, and demand for supplies and foodstuffs in the trans-Mississippi region increased along with new settlements. A few enterprising Texans recognized the potential profits if a cattle herd could be driven from Texas to a market in Arkansas, Missouri, or Illinois. The route that led emigrants south into Texas also pointed north toward and through part of the lands granted as a permanent frontier. The tribes that had been relocated to the Permanent Indian Frontier soon found themselves in the path of incursions from south of the Red River in the form of cattle drives headed north.

Longhorns were driven north from Texas on a more regular basis beginning sometime in the early to mid-1840s. Edward Piper is sometimes credited as driving the first sizable herd north from Texas to Ohio in 1846. The exact origin of the trail leading from southern Texas is unknown, and the route is partially dependent on the origin. A cattle drive could potentially have originated anywhere within an area that covered thousands of square miles. A map of Texas published in 1855 by J. H. Colton and Company shows wagon roads from near Brownsville and from Rio Grande City to San Patricio and on to San Antonio, and wagon roads from Laredo, Presidio del Rio Grande, Eagle Pass, and Uvalde to San Antonio. Only seven north-south roads were mapped in 1855 from these points, and all led either directly or indirectly to San Antonio. Just as all roads from the Rio Grande led to San Antonio, it makes logical sense that the cattle trails would generally parallel these wagon roads through the sparsely settled country and also lead toward San Antonio.[22]

The cattle trails out of south Texas most likely converged in the vicinity of or between San Antonio and Austin. Not only would these have been supply points, but this also reflects the travel pattern of the period and makes sense from a topographical perspective. The prairie from Bexar County to the Brazos River crossings in McLennan, Hill, and Bosque Counties, and on to the Red River crossings in Grayson County, lay east of the Edwards Plateau and the Cross Timbers and west of the Post Oak Savannah and the Piney Woods. This was a natural migration or travel route with abundant grass and water.

From San Antonio a wagon road led north to Austin and Georgetown and passed west of Belton and to Waco Village in McLennan County. Good crossing points at the Brazos River were found at Waco Village, near Towash Village and Fort Graham upstream in Hill County, and at the site that became known as Kimball Bend slightly farther upstream in Bosque County. From Waco Village the road continued through Hill and Navarro Counties to Waxahachie and on to Dallas. A road continued north from Dallas along a route, only partially shown on the 1855 Colton map, through Collin and Grayson Counties to Preston on the Red River or to Shawneetown, just downstream from Preston.[23] This route from San Antonio to Preston was twenty to forty miles inside the line of organized counties in 1855 and just inside the western edge of the settled area.

North of the Red River, the trail diverged in several places through Indian Territory, providing alternate routes that might be taken (fig. 14). From the Red River the route led toward Boggy Depot, where another trail led in a more easterly direction to Fort Smith. From Boggy Depot the most direct route led past Fort Gibson and followed the Neosho River north (fig. 15). Another route led from the Preston/Colbert area in a more northerly direction toward Fort Washita, where a branch angled toward Boggy Depot and another branch continued north past the Shawnee Hills, near Shawnee Town on the Canadian River, and toward the general vicinity of the site that became Arkansas City, Kansas. This trail branch is marked as Shawnee Cattle Trail on an 1879 map of the Indian Territory (fig. 16). It was more likely used after the destinations had shifted west to the vicinity of Abilene or Wichita. This section of trail was out of the way to reach Baxter Springs, Saint Louis, Independence, or any of the other established markets, but it led directly to the vicinity of the site that became Wichita, Kansas.[24]

When the herds reached the vicinity of Horse Creek, north of the Neosho River, additional trails forked off in different directions toward the railheads and markets of Baxter Springs, Kansas City, Sedalia, and Saint Louis.[25] Although the route from Preston to Baxter Springs is not named on the 1879 Roeser map, the various trails between these points follow the routes and landmarks given in descriptions of the Shawnee Trail, showing that "The Trail" was not a single path, but a network of trails. By 1879 the eastern part of Kansas was closed by quarantine law, and herd traffic had been shifted west to central Kansas for nearly twelve years.

Maps of Texas from this historical period tend to display roads, postal routes, railroads, topographic features, and an occasional Indian trail, but cattle trails are not typically indicated as such. Using modern-day references, from the southernmost point in Texas in Cameron County the main trail route most likely passed through the present counties of Willacy, Hidalgo, Brooks, Kenedy, Kleberg, Nueces, Jim Wells, San Patricio, Live Oak, Bee, Goliad, Karnes, Wilson, Gonzales, Guadalupe, Caldwell, Hays, and Travis. San Antonio in Bexar County would have been a supply point; herds that passed through Bexar County might also have passed through Comal County. The route continued north through the counties of Williamson, Bell, and Falls to the Brazos River crossings in McLennan or Bosque County. The trail then led through the counties of Hill, Navarro, Ellis, Dallas, Collin, and Grayson, which was the most direct route to the main crossing on the Red River at Preston. Herds that originated east or west of this line of counties funneled into the main trail at various points generally south of the Colorado River.[26]

There were no natural lakes in Texas that were of sufficient size to pose a barrier to herd travel; however, numerous creeks and rivers lay between the Rio Grande and the Red River. The rivers to be crossed would, of course, depend upon the origin point of a herd. Along the route described, the Nueces, San Antonio, Guadalupe, San Marcos, Colorado, San Gabriel, Leon or Little (the Leon becomes the Little below the confluence of the Leon and Lampasas Rivers), Bosque (to reach Kimball's Bend, Fort Graham, or Towash Village on the Brazos), Brazos, Trinity, and Red Rivers were encountered.[27] Some commonly used crossings were downstream of Austin on the Colorado River; downstream of Round Rock on Brushy Creek; Waco; Fort Graham; Towash Village or Kimball Bend on the Brazos River; near Dallas on the Trinity River; and Preston on the Red River.

North of the Red River the main route passed through the present Oklahoma counties of Bryan, Atoka, Pittsburg, McIntosh, Muskogee, Wagoner, Mayes, Craig, Delaware, and Ottawa, with various trails leading through the counties of Pushmataha, Latimer, Le Flore, Sequoyah, and Cherokee. Rivers that were crossed included the Blue, Clear Boggy, Middle Boggy, Muddy Boggy, Canadian, North Canadian, Arkansas, and Neosho or Grand Rivers, along with numerous creeks.[28] This list includes some, but by no means all, of the water crossings and helps to understand the general route. The trail undoubtedly veered at times into adjoining counties, and river crossings might have occurred several miles upstream or downstream from the usual points, depending upon conditions at the particular time. The main route carried the bulk of the herd traffic. Some herds also traveled northwest along the Brazos, avoided the Piney Woods of east Texas, and funneled into the main trail at one of the Brazos crossings.

The trail led toward various cattle markets in the Midwest. The extension of the railroad to Sedalia provided a closer destination from which Texas cattlemen could ship their herds to eastern markets. The town of Sedalia, Missouri, was founded November 30, 1857, as Sedville. General George R. Smith filed a plat that consisted of approximately sixteen acres of prairie land and named the town after his youngest daughter, Sarah, whose nickname was Sed. Smith foresaw the coming of civilization and the railroad to central Missouri. On October 16, 1860, a plat for the town of Sedalia was filed, which included the former site of Sedville, which had actually existed only on paper. Lots in Sedalia were offered for sale to the public in October 1860. Within a matter of weeks after the Missouri Pacific Railroad reached Sedalia in January 1861, the Civil War began. The much-anticipated business boom that usually went hand-in-hand with the arrival of the railroad was delayed. Construction of new buildings halted; however, a cattle yard, or corral, covering approximately five acres was built in the summer of 1861 after troops arrived in town. The war also stopped new rail construction, and Sedalia remained the railroad terminus for the duration of the war. The delay provided time for those that were already there to establish trades and to plan for growth after the war ended. Many Federal troops that were stationed at Sedalia liked it so well that they remained to settle after the war.[29]

As a railroad terminus, Sedalia was an important supply point for the region. Wagons traveled from as far away as Texas to trade, sell, or purchase goods. "Great droves of Indian ponies and cattle" were brought to Sedalia, along with huge quantities of hides, for trade or shipment to the east in 1863. Although a risky proposition during the war, big risk reaped big profits, and the traders' camps dotted the prairie around the town as long as the weather cooperated.[30] Many Texas drovers were now either engaged in the war or in the protection of the frontier counties in Texas. Sedalia was in Union territory, and many Missouri farmers still remembered the outbreaks of Spanish fever during the 1850s. Due to these and other wartime conditions, the number of herds that were taken north during the war slowed tremendously.

The town of Sedalia existed only for a few weeks as a railhead prior to the outbreak of war. Within two years of the war's end, the main cattle trail moved to the west, reducing the postwar flow of herd traffic. Railroad construction, which had been suspended during the war, resumed. Sedalia's life as a cattle town was short-lived. Baxter Springs, which was incorporated in 1869, served the cattle trade as a staging area of sorts, where buyers congregated to meet northbound herds as they exited Indian Territory. The railroad reached Baxter Springs in 1870, with the arrival of the Kansas City, Fort Scott & Gulf Railroad. The combination of the extension of this railroad south of Baxter Springs, construction of the Missouri, Kansas & Texas Railway into Indian Territory, and increased settlement in the area soon cut the town off from the Texas cattle trade.[31]

It is unknown exactly how or when the name Shawnee Trail came into use. The route passed by Shawneetown on the Texas side of the Red River, the Shawnee Hills in Indian Territory, the land in Indian Territory to which the Shawnees had been relocated, and it eventually led toward the land in Ohio from which the Shawnees had been pushed to the west. According to the 1879 Roeser map of Indian Territory, there was also a Shawnee Town located on the North Canadian

River, where a trail branch labeled as Shawnee Cattle Trail passed nearby.[32] The term *Shawnee trail* was used in print as early as 1850 in a report from Captain Randolph B. Marcy, who surveyed a route from Fort Smith to Santa Fe in 1849. Marcy described their position and route in this manner:

> From here to the Shawnee trail, our route runs 15° south of west; from thence to the second ford of Coal creek, 30° 30′ south of west; thence to little Cedar mountain, 100 miles from Fort Smith, the course is 22° south of west; here the road runs 18° north of west to Stony Point, 5° north of west to the Shawnee village, and 26° south of west to Shawneetown, 125 miles from Fort Smith. At this place the road forks; the right going to Edwards' trading house, (eight miles off,) and the left is our trail. Should travelers desire to purchase supplies, this is the last point where they can be obtained, as the road here leaves the settlements.[33]

The trail was later called the Shawnee Trail, Sedalia Trail, Baxter Springs Trail, Beef Trail, Texas Trail, or simply the trail. The Sedalia name could not have been associated with the trail until at least 1860 and most likely not until the spring of 1861, after the arrival of the railroad and the spring cattle driving season. The war intervened shortly thereafter. The Baxter Springs connection was also short-lived. Most of these terms correspond with the custom of using an origin, destination, or landmark to describe or designate a trail. There seems to be no common usage in newspapers between 1845 and 1866 of any of the trail names that were later associated with this trail. The few relevant newspaper articles used generic terms such as "drove[s] of cattle bound for northern markets." The earliest use of the name Shawnee Trail in newsprint occurred in January 1870. The article referred to the Shawnee Trail "below the mouth of the Walnut" (the mouth of the Walnut River at the Arkansas River in Kansas) leading toward "Abilene, on the Kansas Pacific, where the cattle are shipped to the eastern market" (fig. 16).[34] The Shawnee Trail as a trail name is documented in Captain Marcy's 1850 notes and on the 1879 Roeser map of Indian Territory. These references are specific to two separate trails leading different directions, with both trails located north of the Red River. There is no documentation to indicate that drovers or the general public used a trail name to describe the Texas portion of this trail. There are no maps that date to this historical period that shows this cattle trail designated either by route or by name in Texas.

The road north from Dallas later became Preston Road, so named because of the destination of Preston, or Preston's Crossing. Shaw-neetown was located on the south side of the Red River approximately where US Highway 75 currently crosses the river, and Colbert's Ferry was located approximately half a mile downstream from the bridge (fig. 14). The actual location of Preston Crossing is now covered by Lake Texoma. The original site of Fort Graham, on the east side of the Brazos River at Little Bear Creek, was flooded with the construction of Lake Whitney, and the fort barracks were reconstructed at Old Fort Park on the eastern shore of Lake Whitney. Towash Village, named after a leader of the Ioni Indians who lived in that area, was just downstream of Fort Graham on the east side of the Brazos along Towash Creek; this site was also flooded with the construction of Lake Whitney.[35]

A suspension bridge across the Brazos, built in 1870, now stands at Waco. Kimball Bend is located upstream of Fort Graham, where Highway 174 crosses the Brazos. The trail likely crossed the Colorado just east of Austin, between Onion Creek and Webberville. North of the Red River, the main trail crossed Muddy Boggy Creek in the vicinity of Atoka; crossed the Canadian River just below the conflu-ence of the Canadian and North Canadian, where the site is covered by Lake Eufaula; and crossed the Arkansas near the mouths of the Verdigris and Neosho, near Muskogee. Years later, in 1871–72, the Missouri, Kansas & Texas Railroad laid tracks from Parsons, Kansas, southward through Indian Territory across the Red River and into Denison, Texas. Throughout much of the route, the tracks were laid alongside the path of the Texas Cattle Trail, also known as the Gibson (for Fort Gibson) or Kansas trail. US Highway 69 currently parallels this route through Oklahoma from the railroad bridge on the Red River at Colbert northeast to Vinita.[36]

The end of the war in 1865 brought a renewal in railroad construc-tion, extending lines farther west across the plains. Coupled with westward expansion of the settlements and quarantine laws against Texas cattle, the trail destinations were pushed farther to the west. New cattle markets soon arrived in central Kansas, and in 1867 the portion of the cattle trail that lay between the Brazos and Red Rivers shifted to the west toward these new destinations. The oldest portion of the trail south of the Brazos continued to be used and provided the foundation for the newer trails to the newer markets. A relatively short stretch of trail in Indian Territory and southern Kansas, known locally as Chisholm's Trail, was about to enter its historical period of use.

Two
Chisholms
and a Chisum

THE NAMESAKE OF THE Chisholm Trail has been debated since the cattle trailing era. At some point since the heyday of the post–Civil War cattle drives, Thornton Chisholm, John S. Chisum, and Jesse Chisholm have each been credited with blazing the famous Chisholm Trail that led to Abilene, Kansas. That honor has also been claimed to extend to other men with the last name of Chisholm, Chisum, Chism, Chissum, Chisolm, or Chissm. The only connection that most of the subjects had to the trail that led toward the new railhead at Abilene was that their last names are pronounced phonetically the same as the trail name.

In April 1866 a cattle drive began at Cardwell Flats near Cuero in DeWitt County, Texas. Thornton Chisholm left DeWitt County with his crew and a herd of eighteen hundred head of cattle, split into two smaller herds of nine hundred head each, bound for the cattle market at Saint Joseph, Missouri. Chisholm took a route from DeWitt County past Gonzales, San Marcos, Austin, Glen Rose, Mineral Wells, Seymour, and Vernon; crossed the Red River near the North Fork at Doan's Crossing in Wilbarger County; passed the Oklahoma sites of Frederick, Lawton, Oklahoma City, and Tulsa; passed the Kansas sites of Parsons and Topeka; and drove on to Saint Joseph, Missouri.[1] Doan's Crossing, along with many other of these towns, did not exist in 1866 but is included to illustrate the route.

The most direct route from DeWitt County to Saint Joseph followed Thornton Chisholm's route as far as the Brazos River. From the Brazos the usual trail led slightly northeast toward Dallas County, crossed the Red River at Preston in Grayson County, led towards the northeast corner of Indian Territory, and went on to Saint Joseph. This is the route that was commonly used until the new cattle market opened at Abilene, Kansas. Instead, Chisholm apparently followed the Brazos upstream and continued northwest toward the confluence of the North Fork and Prairie Dog Town Fork of the Red River, then back to the northeast across Indian Territory, and finally north to Saint Joseph.

The destinations for what became known as the Chisholm Trail were mainly the Kansas cow towns of Abilene, Newton, Wichita, Ellsworth, and Caldwell. Thornton Chisholm's 1866 route swung approximately one hundred miles west of the trail that developed in 1867 to these destinations. Cattle had been trailed over much of the route between DeWitt County and the Brazos River for approximately twenty years by 1866. His route, as given in family accounts, passed near Jesse Chisholm's trail in Indian Territory, as the Thornton Chisholm route led northeast from the crossing near the North Fork of the Red River past the sites of Yukon and Council Grove, but it did not follow Jesse Chisholm's trail.

The reason that Thornton Chisholm chose a route to Saint Joseph by way of the North Fork of the Red River, well out of the way and far to the west of the established trail toward Missouri, was a mystery to many. Sometimes the simplest answer is the correct answer; according to a letter from Chisholm's son, the reason they went so far out of the way was simply that "no one knew for sure just where to go, only that they must head north and east, hoping eventually to reach the railroad, which they had heard about." Instead, they headed north and northwest and then doubled back to the northeast. The drive took over seven months, and the herds were sold at Saint Joseph in the fall. The drive would have taken slightly more than two months on the established trail, considering an average travel rate of twelve miles per day. Thornton Chisholm was killed in a freight hauling accident in Burnet County in 1868.[2]

The Four State Chisholm Trail, written by a descendant of Thornton Chisholm and published in 1966, stated that Jesse Chisholm's "only relation to the Trail was that he did have a store where some of the first riders could have bought supplies," but he "did not deal with cattle but was primarily interested in trading and his relationship with the Indian tribes," and he has been "erroneously mentioned as the one for whom the Trail was named." The claim was made that the last names are spelled the same, and the naming of the trail after Jesse Chisholm rather than Thornton Chisholm was due to confusion and misconception.[3]

There is no doubt that Thornton Chisholm and his crew made a long and dangerous drive, and although parts of it were over new

ground, no accounts were found of any subsequent herds that followed Chisholm's seven-month route from DeWitt County to Saint
Joseph. By the summer of 1867 the Kansas quarantine law prohibited herd traffic along Thornton Chisholm's route through eastern
Kansas, as that country was being settled and the cattle markets
had shifted to the west. There is no map or other documentation
from the historical period of the event to support the Chisholm Trail
name to the destination of Saint Joseph, Missouri. Although Thornton Chisholm's name might be applied to his singular route from
DeWitt County to Wilbarger County to Saint Joseph, it should not
be confused with the Chisholm Trail that led to the cattle markets of
central Kansas beginning in 1867.

An article that appeared in an 1892 edition of *Scribner's Magazine*
stated that the Chisholm Trail was named for John Chisholm, a bachelor from Paris, Texas. It claimed that Chisholm was the first to drive
over this trail, later moved to New Mexico, and died a few years before
the time the article was written, leaving uncounted droves of cattle on
his ranches.[4] The article described the new cattle market at Abilene,
Kansas, in 1867, along with other details. While other statements in
the article can be verified by other documentation and sources, it
is clear that this is a reference to John Simpson Chisum, a bachelor
who once lived at Paris, Texas, ranched in Denton County and later in
Coleman County, relocated to New Mexico Territory, and died in 1884,
leaving a cattle herd estimated at thirty thousand head on the ranges.

This article in *Scribner's* may have been the earliest article available to a widespread audience to make the claim that John Chisum
blazed the Chisholm Trail. The idea that John "Chisholm" (actually
Chisum) drove the first herd north from Texas over the Chisholm
Trail contained in this *Scribner's* article was subsequently published
in the *Wichita Daily Eagle* and several other newspapers and eventually found its way into books that were written later. This notion can
likely be traced to a succession of newspaper notices that were published in various publications following Chisum's death in December
1884. A notice that appeared in a newspaper in Lincoln County, New
Mexico, where he had established his ranch, described Chisum as
"eccentric in many ways and bruff [*sic*] in manner, yet he was always
a warm friend and no man ever looked closer after the pleasure and
comfort of the men under his employ during his long experience as
a cattle man." A subsequent notice in another publication described
Chisum as "New Mexico's pioneer cattle king." In 1885, the *National
Live-Stock Journal* published a notice of Chisum's death that quoted
the *Silver City Enterprise*: "Chisum's trail, through the Indian Terri-

tory, was named after him. . . . At the time of his death he was, perhaps, the largest individual owner of cows in the Territory." These articles were likely sources for the *Scribner's* article, which in turn was a likely source for later articles.[5]

An article in the 1916 edition of the *Southwestern Historical Quarterly* stated, "The Chisholm Trail is named for John Chisholm. He was an eccentric old bachelor who resided in Paris, Texas, and engaged extensively in the cattle business." The article went on to include other details from the *Scribner's* article, and *Scribner's* is listed in the footnotes as the source. *History and Reminiscences of Denton County*, published in 1918, stated, "We had what was called the Chisum Trail, leading from here to the northern markets. It was made by John Chisum of Denton County." No footnote or other reference was given by the author, so the basis for this statement is unknown. It is just as likely as not that its source was the *Scribner's* 1892 article or the 1916 *Southwestern Historical Quarterly* article, and the author changed the spelling from Chisholm to the correct spelling of John Chisum's name. In a 1936 edition of *Geography of Denton County*, the trail from Fort Worth through part of Denton County past Red River Station to northern markets was described as the Chisum Trail, "named for John S. Chisum, a most successful cattleman of Denton County, who built for himself the title of America's Greatest Cattle King." There is no footnote in support of this statement; however, *History and Reminiscences of Denton County* is listed in the bibliography. The similarity of these articles within a relatively short time frame indicates that they were all based upon the same source data.[6]

Variations on the story that appeared in *Scribner's* were published in other works or repeated by others. Some mixed the names, such as "John Chisholm" or "Jesse Chisum." Some mixed the occupations, such as implying that Jesse Chisholm was a famous cattleman. Some mixed both name and occupation, implying that John Chisholm was an Indian trader and interpreter and maintained trading posts in Indian Territory. To further confuse the issue, there is a possibility that Jesse Chisholm had a second wife after Eliza, his first wife, died and before his marriage to Sahkahkee McQueen, and it is possible that Chisholm had a son named John by this union. Jesse Chisholm's daughter, Jennie, referred to a John Chisholm who had drifted into New Mexico in a 1911 letter; she later referred to him as Frank or Jepee, but he was allegedly never heard from again, and nothing is known about him. There is therefore nothing to indicate that John or Jepee Chisholm ever drove cattle to Kansas during the summer of 1867 or engaged in the cattle business. This could be another contributing factor to the John/Jesse Chisum/Chisholm muddle.[7] No mention of a John, Frank, or Jepee Chisholm is found in relation to the opening of the trail or cattle market at Abilene, Kansas.

Various spellings of Chisholm can be found in trails lore, all pronounced exactly the same. Newspaper articles can be found in which the writer either used a variety of spellings of the name to correct the spelling of another in an attempt to identify the "correct" Chisholm/Chisum/Chism/Chissum/Chisolm or Chissm, or applied the name incorrectly to the Western Trail route. These articles, as in most other cases, tended to reflect the writer's opinion regarding identification of the correct Chisholm, as no other proof or documentation was typically offered.[8]

Within a month of John S. Chisum's death, an Arizona newspaper reported that sensational accounts of Chisum and a connection with Billy the Kid had already been widely circulated.[9] While Chisum was well known within the livestock business, the sensationalized links with Billy the Kid expanded recognition of the Chisum name to a national audience. The combination of phonetic similarity, opinion, and assumptions was unavoidable. Over the years, assumptions have been made such as those exhibited in this example from the Pickens County Cowpunchers Association:

> The old cattlemen of southern Oklahoma and northern Texas do not agree with Dr. Thoburn that this trail was named for Jesse Chisholm. They claim that it was named for John Chisum, who had a large ranch at Bolivar, Denton County, Texas, and through which the trail passed. They claim that there was a Chisum Trail in Texas prior to its crossing Oklahoma. John Chisum at that time was reputed to be the largest open range cattleman in the world, and these old timers claim that it is much more probable that this great cattle trail was named for a cattleman rather than for a trader who only traveled this route through northern Oklahoma, from Wichita, Kansas, to Anadarko.[10]

It is also possible that others assumed that there was a link to the famous trail based on nothing more than the phonetic similarity in last names. It might have been a natural assumption that the Chisholm Trail was named for John Chisum, and it might seem to be a correct assumption that a famous cattle trail should be named for a famous cattleman. After all, Chisum's Denton County ranch was located near the route of a major trail that led north to Kansas, and his jinglebob earmark and Long Rail brand were very well known by the time of his death in 1884. However, John Chisum moved his ranching operation from Denton County to Coleman County in 1863 and established his ranch in New Mexico Territory during the spring and summer of 1867.[11] Joseph McCoy made no mention of Chisum's presence or the presence of Chisum cattle in Abilene when the first herds arrived in the summer of 1867. There is no evidence that John Chisum drove any herds from Denton County, Coleman County, or New Mexico Territory to Abilene, Kansas, during the summer of 1867. Even if Chisum cattle appeared at Kansas markets later, the trail had already been blazed, and no evidence has been cited in support of claims that Chisum cattle were the first to travel a trail to Kansas.

The name Chisum Trail was likely applied later to Chisum's 1863 route from Denton County to Coleman County and from Coleman County up the Pecos River into New Mexico Territory in 1864. The claim that John Chisum was connected to the trail that led to Abilene, Kansas can most likely be traced to the phonetic similarities between Chisum and Chisholm; later confusion between the Chisum Trail that led west into New Mexico Territory and the Chisholm Trail that came into use a few years later that led north to Abilene, Kansas; and incorrect assumptions that were accepted as fact. There is no documentation from the period of the event to support claims that John S. Chisum or John Chisholm had any involvement in the establishment of the Chisholm Trail to Abilene, Kansas, during the summer of 1867.

The most probable namesake for the trail was Jesse Chisholm, a trader and translator who operated several trading posts in Indian Territory and southern Kansas. In 1847 Chisholm established a home and trading post on the Canadian River approximately twenty-five miles west of Fort Holmes, near the present site of Asher, Oklahoma. He spoke at least fourteen Indian languages and was often called upon to act as a translator. By the late 1850s Chisholm had opened another trading post at Council Grove on the North Canadian River, along the western edge of what is now Oklahoma County, and roamed over much of the western half of the Indian Territory.[12]

There was a route that followed the natural topography of the country from the Wichita Mountains northward—one used by the bison during migrations between the northern and southern ranges and traveled by the Indians. Between 1849 and 1852 Captain R. B. Marcy surveyed west from Fort Smith across the Indian Territory to establish the best route to New Mexico and California. He hired a Delaware Indian named Black Beaver as guide and interpreter. Marcy noted existing trails leading north from the vicinity of the Wichita Mountains. Although he did not follow these trails all the way north into Kansas Territory, it was apparent that the trails followed the natural lay of the land in the easiest route northward. The route of Captain Marcy can be seen on an 1858 map commissioned by Jefferson Davis, who, as secretary of war, ordered surveys to determine the best potential route for a transcontinental railroad. The 1855 route of Major Hamilton W. Merrill can also be seen on this map leading from Fort Belknap in Texas north across the Red River; passing east of the Wichita Mountains and east of Fort Cobb; continuing north across the Canadian, North Canadian, and Cimarron Rivers; entering Kansas Territory; and passing just west of the mouth of the Little Arkansas River.[13]

At the outbreak of the Civil War, Colonel William Emory was ordered to consolidate the troops from the forts in Indian Territory. He was subsequently ordered to withdraw to Fort Leavenworth in Kansas. Guided by Black Beaver, Emory's column traveled north along some of the same trails that Marcy had noted while guided by Black Beaver. The trails provided a natural route north into Kansas.[14]

Jesse Chisholm established another trading post at the mouth of the Little Arkansas River in 1864. Chisholm's route between his trading posts followed along much of the same route as Merrill and Emory had previously traveled. This route from the mouth of the Little Arkansas to Council Grove became known locally as Chisholm's wagon road, or Chisholm's trail. The route appeared on maps of Indian Territory as Chisholm's Trail beginning in 1875.[15] The town of Wichita, Kansas, was established at the north end of this trail. After the railhead and cattle market opened at Abilene, Kansas, in 1867, a route was surveyed to guide drovers from the end of Chisholm's Trail at the Little Arkansas over the plains to Abilene. Chisholm's trail eventually became famous as the Chisholm Trail.

7

Jesse Chisholm
Blazes a Trail

THE TERM *blaze a trail* means to do something no one else has done before; to mark a trail or pave the way for others. Marks made on trees by removing a small section of bark with an axe or similar tool to indicate a route were called blaze marks. This method of marking a trail worked fine in wooded areas, but trees tended to be scarce along the cattle trails across the prairies. Jesse Chisholm is often said to have blazed the Chisholm Trail, but others traveled much of the route before Chisholm. The Delaware Indian Black Beaver guided at least two expeditions along part of the route that became famous later as a cattle trail.

Jesse Chisholm's grandfather, John Chisholm, emigrated from Scotland to South Carolina in 1777. Both John Chisholm and Ignatius Chisholm, Jesse's father, were, among other occupations, dealers in the slave trade. Ignatius Chisholm left Knoxville, Tennessee, under questionable circumstances and married a Cherokee woman near Hiwassee. They lived among the Cherokees, where Ignatius made a living as a trader. The woman was identified as a sister of a chief named Corn Tassel, and no other name was apparently recorded. She gave birth to Jesse in 1805 or 1806 and later to his two younger brothers, John and William. In 1810 Jesse was brought west into what became Arkansas Territory. By 1828, when the Cherokees began to settle in the vicinity of Fort Gibson in Indian Territory, Jesse Chisholm was already living near the fort, where he engaged in trading. Chisholm learned to speak up to fourteen Indian languages, in addition to his knowledge of the universal sign language of the plains.[1]

Because Chisholm spoke so many Indian languages, he was often called upon to act as interpreter during negotiations. His language skills and rapport with most tribes or bands took him as far away as

Washington, DC, California, and Mexico, but Indian Territory was his backyard. Sam Houston enlisted his assistance as interpreter during the Tehuacana Creek councils of 1843–45. The councils resulted in "a treaty of peace and friendship between the Republic of Texas and the Delaware, Chickasaw, Waco, Tah-woc-cany [*sic*], Keechi, Caddo, Ana dah-kah [*sic*], Ionie [*sic*], Biloxi, and Cherokee tribes of Indians." Chisholm was also present at the Comanche Peak council in 1845. Whether Chisholm and Houston were somehow related by marriage has been the subject of speculation. There is a possibility that Houston's second wife, who was Cherokee, and Ignatius Chisholm's second wife were sisters, but this has not been proven. It is likely that Houston and Jesse Chisholm met while both were in the Fort Gibson area.[2]

In 1847 Chisholm remarried after his first wife died. He and his second wife, Sahkahkee, then moved west and established a home at what would become known as Chisholm Springs, near the current site of Asher, Oklahoma, where he also maintained a small trading post. Later, during the 1850s, Chisholm established a trading post at Council Grove on the North Canadian River. By 1858 he operated from Chisholm Springs to Fort Arbuckle to the Wichita Mountains to the Cimarron River, over much of what is now western Oklahoma.[3]

In 1860 Chisholm owned six slaves in the Creek Nation; five females ranging in age from two to thirty-eight and one male age six. Sahkahkee Chisholm owned two females ages two and twenty, and William Chisholm owned one female age eighteen. Presumably the slaves were used in support of the trading business. Jesse Chisholm also may have operated a salt works northwest of Council Grove, in a location where the salt could be picked up in chunks. Despite the rumors in some circles, there is no evidence to indicate that Chisholm mistreated or abused his slaves, as Ignatius had done and as many had done during that period.[4]

Chisholm is sometimes said to have been a slave trader or slave hunter who made his living from the sufferings of others. Although he was a slave owner, and as such may have bought, sold, or traded slaves as any other owner might have legally done during that period, there is no evidence to indicate that he was a slave trader who bought and sold slaves on a large scale. Chisholm was, however, in frequent contact with various Indian tribes and sometimes encountered slaves or captives who had been stolen during raids on the settlements and held in various camps. It was not uncommon for children and young girls to be taken during a raid and, if the captive lived long enough, ransomed back sometime later.

Chisholm was also known to have rescued some of these captives and returned them to civilization. The usual method was to purchase or trade for the captive; the price depended upon the captors. American and Mexican captives were often kidnapped at a very young age and raised as an Indian. Some captives bonded with their captors and as a result had no desire to be "rescued." American captives who had been rescued were often returned to relatives. Rescued Mexican captives were more difficult to resolve, and Chisholm took in and raised some of them until they could fend for themselves.[5]

Black captives were considered valuable property, and a higher price was usually demanded by their captors. Chisholm is known to have purchased a "captive Negro boy, ten years or so of age," for goods worth approximately $150 at a Comanche camp on the San Saba River in 1839. The boy, Aaron, had been taken along with his brother, Manuel, from Dr. Joseph Robertson in Bastrop County. Manuel was purchased by a Creek Indian at another camp on the Colorado River. Both boys were eventually taken to Edwards's Trading Post on the Little River in Indian Territory, where Chisholm sold Aaron to his sister-in-law for $400. Robertson learned the whereabouts of his two slaves and, after a failed attempt to recover them himself, petitioned the Republic of Texas to recover the boys. The boys were eventually returned in 1844. There were occasional instances in which Chisholm was involved in similar circumstances with captive slaves. During an investigation into the matter of Aaron and Manuel, General Ethan Allen Hitchcock stated, "This man Chisholm is very intelligent, and is, I believe, a man of sterling integrity."[6]

Chisholm continued to occasionally purchase or trade for Indian captives who were kidnapped during raids. During the winter of 1849–50 he traded "a good horse and a pile of goods" about fifteen inches high for a Mexican boy in his teens. The goods included a blanket, knives, red flannel, calico, tobacco, and brass wire. The boy, Vincente de Huersus, had been taken after his parents were killed during a Comanche raid in Mexico. He had been held as a slave during the six or seven years since his capture. Chisholm took the boy to Chisholm Springs, where, Vincente later recalled, there were nine other adopted captives. He was also adopted by Chisholm and named George. Vincente George Chisholm later served as a civilian scout and interpreter at Fort Sill. Before he died in 1917, he provided some details of his life with Jesse to historian J. B. Thoburn.[7]

Jesse Chisholm left Texas and returned to Indian Territory after participating in negotiation of the San Saba Treaty of 1850–51. This treaty did little to quell the unrest on the Texas frontier. Tensions also rose as the Comanches and Kiowas resented the presence of the Five Civilized Tribes on what they felt was their land in Indian Territory. Chisholm acted as interpreter and ambassador in negotiations between the US government and various tribes and between the tribes themselves in the territory through most of the 1850s. His trading business grew as he traveled throughout Indian Territory. Chisholm took his wagons to the tribal camps scattered from the Wichita Mountains to the Antelope Hills. Where no road or trail existed, he made his own way out of necessity.[8] Meanwhile, tensions of another type were nudging the United States toward war.

As the prospect of civil war grew imminent, Colonel William Emory was ordered on March 18, 1861 to consolidate forces from Fort Cobb and Fort Arbuckle to Fort Washita. The order stressed that safety of the troops and the interests of the United States were "paramount to those of the friendly Indians on the reservation near Fort Cobb, but good faith requires that notice shall be given them of the withdrawal of the troops, that they may have a chance to move temporarily to the vicinity of the posts to be occupied." On March 21 an order approving Emory's request to keep two companies at Fort Cobb further added, "If asked by the commander of Fort Smith for aid in guarding the post and depot, give it. If the State [of Arkansas] secedes, march all the troops beyond its limits." Emory ordered two of the four companies at Fort Cobb to remain at the fort at the request of the Indian agent at the Wichita Agency, where there was a supply of corn too large to move handily, while the other two companies proceeded to Fort Washita. Chisholm remained at Council Grove for the time being, where his counsel was sought by the Creeks.[9]

Before Emory's expedition could reach Fort Washita, a superior Confederate force was moving toward the forts in Indian Territory. Part of Fort Cobb's mission was to restrain incursions from the territory into Texas by hostile Indians, but Texas had already seceded from the Union. The fort was located so that it could easily be cut off without supplies or reinforcements, and an order issued on April 17, 1861, directed Emory to take all troops in Indian Territory north: "SIR: On receipt of this communication, you will, by order of the General-in-Chief, with all the troops in the Indian country west of Arkansas, march to Fort Leavenworth [*sic*], Kans., taking such useful public property as your means of transportation will permit. The troops may or may not be replaced by Arkansas volunteers. The action of that State will not affect your movement."[10]

Emory's column traveled west along the Washita River valley by the same route that Black Beaver and Captain Randolph B. Marcy had traveled between 1849 and 1852 toward the Wichita Mountains. The last troops left Fort Cobb and met Emory's column near the present site of Minco. Guided by Black Beaver, the column of approximately nine hundred soldiers and civilians headed north along the same route that Major Hamilton W. Merrill had taken toward Cottonwood Creek above the confluence of the Arkansas and Little Arkansas Rivers, near the present site of Wichita, and continued to Fort Leavenworth, where they arrived on May 31, 1861.[11] Chisholm traveled south from Leavenworth over much of this same route a few years later with supplies bound for Council Grove.

When the war broke out in 1861, Chisholm had many friends on both sides of the conflict, both Indian and white, military and civilian. He had ties to every tribe in Indian Territory. From the Arkansas River to the Red River, the tribes were also split by the conflict. The Cherokees tried to remain neutral, but it was impossible. The Cherokees, Creeks, Seminoles, Choctaws, Chickasaws—all were divided by the war. Colonel Emory's withdrawal of Union troops from Indian Territory to Fort Leavenworth left the Comanches, Wichitas, and other refugee tribes from Texas abandoned and dependent on their hated enemies, the Texans, for protection and supplies.[12]

On May 5, 1861, it was reported that Confederate forces had occupied Fort Arbuckle. Later that month, Albert Pike, commissioner of the Confederate states to the Indian nations and tribes west of Arkansas; William Quesenbury, who had been appointed as agent to the Creeks; and a few others left Fort Smith in two wagons and traveled up the Arkansas River to make treaties with the tribes of Indian Territory. By August 1, 1861, treaties had been signed with the Creeks, Choctaws, Chickasaws, and Seminoles. A treaty was signed on August 12 at the Wichita Agency near Fort Cobb with leaders of the "Pen-e-tegh-ca band of the Ne-um or Comanches, and the tribes and bands of Wichitas, Cado-Ha-da-chos, Hue-cos, Ta-hua-ca-ros, A-na-dagh-cos, Ton-ca-wes, Ai-o-nais, Ki-chais, Shawnees, and Delawares."[13]

Among other things, this treaty stated that the Confederate States would be friends and protectors; that the tribes might continue to occupy their present lands "as long as grass shall grow and water run" and to hunt and live without molestation; and that the Confederate States would provide rations, provisions, and farming implements as long as the tribes remained peaceful. The treaty also stated that the Confederacy would employ at the agency an interpreter, blacksmith, gunsmith, physician, and medicine for the benefit of the tribes; would furnish each warrior a flintlock rifle and ammunition;

and would indemnify livestock and property that might be killed or stolen. It also declared that "the life of every person belonging to said tribes and bands shall be of the same value as the life of a white man; and any Indian or white man who kills one of them without cause shall be hung by the neck until he is dead." Jesse Chisholm acted as translator and witnessed the treaty. Chisholm was also present when the Cherokees were eventually convinced to sign. However, because of the Confederacy's unwillingness or inability to fulfill their promises, the Wichitas, Delawares, and a few others soon left the area and traveled north into Kansas for the duration of the war. The Wichitas settled near the mouth of the Little Arkansas River, while the others continued farther north.[14]

According to letters, vouchers, and other records it is apparent that Chisholm was active in Indian Territory on behalf of the Confederacy throughout most of 1862. He purchased knives, hats, blankets, and a wide variety of goods intended for trade or gifts to the tribal leaders. Violence exploded in October 1862 when nearly one hundred Delawares and Shawnees arrived at camps just outside the reserve on the Washita River. The Tonkawas there were hated by others because of their reputation as cannibals and their loyalty to the Texans. According to the Delawares and Shawnees, the Tonkawas had killed a Caddo boy and were preparing a feast, which prompted the Delawares and Shawnees to attack. The primitive weapons of the Tonkawas were no match for the guns of the well-armed raiders, and more than two hundred Tonkawas were killed that night. The survivors fled east to Fort Arbuckle. When it was heard that a large group of Texans and Creeks were headed to Fort Cobb, the Wichitas and those remaining fled the Wichita Agency north into Kansas, which was controlled by the Union. Jesse Chisholm's whereabouts during that time are unknown, but it is likely that he left the area and went north into Kansas to escape the violence. Chisholm and Black Beaver were reported to have been with this group of reserve Indians in September 1863.[15]

During the winter of 1864–65, Chisholm served as ambassador on behalf of his old friend Jesse Leavenworth, then a newly appointed Union Comanche-Kiowa agent. Chisholm reported to Leavenworth that the Arapahos, Kiowas, plains Apaches, and Wichitas were willing to make peace when the US Army stopped fighting them. By the end of 1864, Chisholm had established a trading post near the mouth of the Little Arkansas River in Kansas, where the Wichita village was located. A letter from Chapeyanechis, second chief of the Comanches, described a council held early in 1865 among the Comanches,

Kiowas, Arapahos, Creeks, Chickasaws, Cherokees, and Seminoles to discuss making war against the South. Some made strong war speeches. A Comanche chief reminded them of their friends and relatives in that area and stated that "he did not think that sober men would propose to war on their friends and brothers." Jesse Chisholm was present and advised against war. Sometime after this council, the Comanches, Kiowas, and other prairie tribes were summoned to another council by Union officers. Jesse Chisholm again acted as interpreter. The Indians were offered a large amount of trade goods, guns, and ammunition if they would go into Texas and make war on the Texans, with the intent of disrupting the war effort. The plan was to kill men and boys and steal horses, mules, and cattle. Women and children were to be taken prisoner but must be returned. Stolen cattle would be purchased by the Union. They could keep Indian women, horses, and mules. Chisholm advised against this proposition, and the Union offer was rejected.[16]

In March 1865 it was reported to the headquarters district of the Upper Arkansas that a "Cherokee half-breed by the name of Chishem" had been trading with the tribes hostile to the Union all during the previous winter, and his loyalty to the Union was doubted. Leavenworth reported in May 1865 that "a Caddo chief sent word to Chisholm that all the Indians wished for peace except the Cheyennes." After the war ended, and despite reports of disloyalty to the Union, Chisholm's talents and standing with the tribes were such that he was retained by Leavenworth to contact the plains tribes in pursuit of peace. Chisholm continued his efforts, and was, for the most part, successful, albeit temporarily. Leavenworth reported to his superiors on December 1, 1865, "Mr. Chisholm, a half-Cherokee and a man of good character and who has always lived with or near the Comanche Indians, has rendered me, and the Government, the greatest service in bringing about peace on the frontier."[17]

Chisholm continued his trading activities and was occasionally called into service as a translator in peace or other negotiations. During July 1867 he attended the National Creek Council, where he acted as interpreter to help settle a dispute between the Creeks and the Caddos. From there he went to Fort Gibson, then to the vicinity of Fort Cobb, where he was requested to attempt to negotiate the release of some white captives held by the Cheyennes and Arapahos. Meanwhile, a cholera epidemic spread through camps in Kansas. A large group of more than four hundred men, women, and children from the Shawnee, Delaware, Caddo, and Ioni tribes left the Little Arkansas River and headed south down the trail that Chisholm had traveled between the Little Arkansas and the North Canadian. Nearly one hundred Indians died of cholera while camped at Ephraim Creek, where the dead lay out in the open. The creek was renamed Skeleton Creek in memory of those that perished.[18]

Jesse Chisholm was reportedly present but sick during the Medicine Lodge Creek Council in October. He was in Leavenworth a short time later to purchase trade goods, where he still felt the effects of illness. According to a later account given by James Mead, while in Leavenworth Chisholm had his photograph taken "in his soiled and travel-worn clothes, just as he came into town with his train from the plains, and after he was much broken in health from a long spell of sickness. The picture conveys a poor idea of the man when in his prime." Chisholm returned to Council Grove and was called upon in spring of 1868 to aid a group of surveyors who had been surrounded by hostile Comanches, Kiowas, and Cheyennes on the North Canadian River. Chisholm successfully delayed action by the hostiles, and the surveyors fled to safety at the Seminole Agency.[19]

Chisholm died a short time later near Council Grove, reportedly after eating a meal of bear grease. James Mead recalled later that a board driven into the ground at the head of Chisholm's grave was inscribed, "Jesse Chisholm, Died, March 4th, 1868"; however, the date of Chisholm's death was recorded in a Chisholm family Bible as April 4, 1868.[20] Regardless of this discrepancy, Chisholm could not have known that his name would soon be connected with what is perhaps the most famous period in the history of the American West.

8

A New Outlet

AS MORE PEOPLE SETTLED in Missouri and eastern Kansas, fears of Texas fever and resistance to Texas cattle herds increased. Railroad construction, which had slowed during the Civil War, resumed afterwards, and rails were laid toward the west through Kansas. Most of the eastern third of Kansas was closed to Texas herds by quarantine law in 1867. Joseph G. McCoy, an Illinois businessman, recognized a need for an outlet for Texas cattle. The new outlet had to be located west of settled areas at a railhead where appropriate facilities could be built, and it had to have plenty of good grazing and water and be accessible to drovers. McCoy saw business opportunities for Texas drovers, the railroad, and himself if he could negotiate a deal with railroad executives. The site McCoy selected that met the requirements was a lonely place on the plains that became the town of Abilene, Kansas.

During the period between 1850 and 1860, Missourians' resistance to Texas cattle herds increased along with the state's population. The Missouri population grew from 682,044 inhabitants in 1850 to 1,182,012 in 1860.[1] The Indian Intercourse Act of 1834 required traders to possess a special license issued by the Bureau of Indian Affairs, the War Department, or the commander of the nearest frontier military post in order to travel and conduct business within the territory west of Missouri. A special passport issued by any of the same agencies was required for all foreigners to be present within that country. Any attempt to survey, mark boundaries, or make any other attempt to create a settlement there was prohibited.[2] However, as Missouri became more populated, settlers looked to the west and trickled into these lands designated as the Permanent Indian Frontier.

This "permanent" frontier was rather short-lived and effectively ended with the Kansas-Nebraska Act of 1854, which created Kansas and Nebraska Territories. That act also repealed the Missouri Compromise, which outlawed slavery within the region, and provided for the issue of slavery to be decided by residents of the new territories.[3] The floodgates opened, and both proslavery and antislavery factions rushed to create settlements in the newly established Kansas Territory and to influence elections to favor their particular point of view. On election day in March 1855 at Lawrence, Kansas Territory, the *Kansas Herald of Freedom* reported:

> It is probably needless to say that the election will be contested, and no doubt set aside, for reasons which will appear elsewhere. . . . During the whole of the day Friday, until about 3 o'clock in the afternoon, the mercenaries from Missouri had possession of the ballot-box and the passage to it, and controlled it as far as they were disposed. Mr. Abbott, one of the judges of the election, who desired to see the law enforced to the letter, felt compelled to vacate his seat, when it was readily filled by a pro-slavery person—whether one of the imported ones from Missouri we are not informed.

A voter whose intentions were apparently known was ejected, forced to flee, and jumped down a riverbank "when a revolver was discharged at him, and a ball narrowly escaped his head." Another voter was threatened with a revolver, "but a friend at his left with a pair of similar instruments gave tone to the circumstance, and caused the mercenary to cower, and finally leave the premises." After the contingent from Missouri left, another group moved in to threaten and intimidate voters. Because of threats, newspapermen waited until later in the day to approach the polling place and did so only with an assortment of friends, Bowie knives, and revolvers.[4]

Violent clashes between the Jayhawkers, who were Union sympathizers, and the Bushwhackers or Border Ruffians, who were Confederate guerrillas, escalated into the Kansas-Missouri Border War. The Kansas-Nebraska Act aggravated the division in the United States over the issue of slavery, and the nation moved closer to the brink of war. The Kansas legislature passed an amnesty act in February 1859 which stated that no criminal offense committed in certain counties that arose from political differences of opinion would be prosecuted, and any pending charges were to be dismissed. While some believed that if bygones were bygones it might bring some peace to the territory, others held that crimes such as murder should not go unpunished. If last year's criminals are excused, will another amnesty law be needed the next year?[5] The Jayhawkers and Bushwhackers continued to fight throughout the Civil War. Because of the murderous, thieving, and guerrilla tactics used by both groups, the term *Jayhawker* came to be used during the Civil War, and afterward during Reconstruction, to generically describe anyone from Kansas, or specifically to describe murderers and thieves.

By 1860, 107,206 inhabitants had taken up residence in Kansas Territory, formerly part of the Permanent Indian Frontier. The settled areas were concentrated in the northeastern part of the territory and along the Missouri border. As Texas drovers skirted west of the Missouri border, they faced increased opposition from the new residents. Some tried to protect their farms from the ravages of Spanish fever borne by the Texas beeves, and others objected to herds trampling through their fields. There was also the ever present danger from rustlers, Jayhawkers, and Bushwhackers. The Kansas-Missouri Border War continued, and violence was not a stranger to the area. In April 1861 the simmering tensions between North and South exploded, and the United States was divided by war. For the next four years railroad construction stopped and the march of westward migration slowed considerably as efforts and resources were diverted by the war. Railroad construction had, with a few exceptions, stopped within a relatively short distance west of the Mississippi River when the war began. Construction efforts were renewed after the war, and the rails once again crept westward.[6]

The cattle driving season of 1866 found the country around Baxter Springs, Kansas, thick with herds for sale. In addition to the violence inherent along the Missouri border, thieves and con men took advantage of the fact that conditions at the time were too dangerous to allow buyers to carry large amounts of cash, and they sought to purchase cattle using drafts. After striking a deal with the Texas drovers, the con man would sell the cattle to another buyer for cash and then disappear, leaving the drovers with an often worthless draft. Some drovers avoided these schemes and financial ruin by wintering herds in southwestern Missouri or in the Cherokee Strip, or by traveling west of the settlements and taking their herd on to Illinois or Iowa and selling it directly.[7]

The generally accepted estimate of the number of cattle driven north from Texas during the season of 1866 is 260,000 head. This estimate is attributed to Joseph G. McCoy in interviews reported in 1867 and 1871 and is mentioned in his 1874 book, *Historic Sketches of the Cattle Trade of the West and Southwest*. The Kansas City Board of Trade reported the same number for the year 1866. A result of the renewed herd traffic was fresh outbreaks of Spanish or Texas fever. During the war, incidence of the disease diminished in proportion to the reduction of herd traffic.[8] The estimate of 260,000 head translates to somewhere between 130 and 174 different herds, depending on herd size, all traveling the same routes toward the same handful of destinations during the same season (the cattle driving season was generally considered to be March through October or November, depending on latitude and weather conditions). As the herd traffic and fears of Texas fever increased, resistance to the Texas cattle grew in both intensity and violence in Missouri and eastern Kansas. Farmers appealed to their legislators for additional and stricter quarantine regulations in the hope of protecting their domestic cattle from the killer disease carried by the wild Texas longhorns. Texas drovers circled farther west in attempts to avoid trouble on their route to the Midwestern markets.

Joseph G. McCoy operated a thriving business in Illinois, under the name J. G. McCoy and Company, that involved the purchase, feeding, and transport of livestock to various packing facilities. In 1867 he joined his brothers, William and James, at William K. McCoy and Brothers, where they engaged in similar activities. McCoy knew of the seemingly endless supply of cattle at depressed prices in Texas and the growing demand in the northern and eastern part of the country. Long-horned cattle were worth as little as two or three dollars per head in Texas but could fetch many times that amount in the markets of Saint Louis or Chicago. It was during this period that McCoy conceived the idea to provide a destination for Texas drovers that kept them west of the settlements in order to avoid conflict and from which their herds could be shipped to the northern and eastern markets.[9]

In February 1867 a Kansas law was passed that restricted the movement of Texas cattle within the state east of the sixth principal meridian and north of township nineteen. The law allowed cattle to be driven "from some point in southwest Kansas, west of the sixth principal meridian, and south of township eighteen, to some point on the U. P. R. E. D., west of the first guide meridian west of the sixth principal meridian, where such cattle may be shipped out of the State, but in no case unloaded within the State." (The sixth principal meridian intersects the southern boundary of Kansas east of the present site of Hunnewell, in the general vicinity of the intersection of I-35 and the southern boundary of Kansas. The first guide meridian west from the sixth principal meridian lies near the west side of the present site of Ellsworth. The northern boundary of township nineteen lies about twenty-one miles south of Ellsworth, and the southern boundary of township eighteen lies approximately four miles north of the present site of McPherson.) Upon payment of a bond of ten thousand dollars, and with approval of the governor of Kansas, cattle could be driven during any season through certain areas to a shipping point on the railroad. By June 1867, Nebraska, Missouri, Kentucky, Illinois, and Colorado Territory had also passed or revised similar laws that restricted the movement of Texas cattle within their boundaries.[10]

In spring of 1867, McCoy began searching for a suitable location that would be accessible to drovers and meet the strict quarantine requirements. He held a series of meetings with railroad officials and eventually selected a site on the open prairie. He reached a verbal agreement with officials at the Union Pacific Railroad, Eastern Division, to be paid "about five dollars for each carload of cattle sent from his proposed stock depot to the eastern markets." Abilene, Kansas, which in 1867 consisted of little more than a few log huts, was selected as the site of this new venture, and McCoy purchased land on which to build a hotel, offices, and stockyards. The country was practically unsettled, had excellent grass and water, and was perfect for staging herds of cattle.[11]

Abilene was about sixty miles east of Ellsworth; however, the aforementioned law established a point approximately one mile west of Ellsworth as the easternmost point on the railroad to which cattle could be trailed. Therefore, it was illegal to drive cattle to Abilene. McCoy obviously knew about this provision because of his research and discussions with railroad officials and had to have known that his chosen site was well inside the quarantine boundary. If convicted of a violation, penalties included a fine of one hundred to one thousand dollars and thirty to sixty days in jail. If convicted of a subsequent offense, the penalty of the first offense was doubled. It was also illegal to drive cattle along any public road or highway or to pass within five miles of a settler without their written consent. The owner of the cattle was responsible for all damages that occurred, including an outbreak of Spanish fever. Continuing to drive the same cattle through the state after conviction of a first offense was considered a subsequent offense. For reasons unknown, this portion of the law was apparently never enforced regarding Abilene.[12]

Lumber and materials were brought in from Missouri and other areas. By summer's end, offices and a stockyard that could accommodate three thousand head of cattle had been built, and construction was well under way on a three-story hotel, which became known as the Drover's Cottage. Although there were a few farmers east of Abilene, the new depot was well west of the settlements, with plenty of open country, a new hundred-car siding, a stockyard, and a brand new Fairbanks scale that was capable of weighing a carload at a time. McCoy was instrumental in the construction of a new transfer station and feed yard at Leavenworth, Kansas.[13] Now all they needed at Abilene were cattle.

About the time construction on the new facilities in Abilene began, McCoy sent a man who was familiar with the country to spread the word about the new depot at Abilene. W. W. Sugg saddled up and rode southwest from Junction City to the approximate present site of Wichita, continued south into Indian Territory, turned east, and rode until he either encountered a herd or crossed the trail of a herd headed toward the southeastern corner of Kansas. When he cut the trail of a herd, he followed until he caught up with the drovers. In that way he spread the news among drovers already on the trail that there was a new destination available—one that was free from the threat of armed mobs, enraged farmers, robbers, and swindlers, where northern buyers and Texas sellers could meet. This seemed too good to be true for the Texas drovers, and although many at first believed that they would ride into some sort of a trap, conditions were so dangerous along the Missouri-Kansas border that they began to take the risk and to divert their herds toward Abilene. The first to reach Abilene in the summer of 1867 was a herd that had been driven from Texas and sold in Indian Territory to Smith, McCord, and Chandler.[14] Thousands of cattle followed a new path from the Red River north through the central part of Indian Territory toward the new railhead at Abilene.

Fig. 1. Cattle of the Fort Griffin herd. Cattle of the Official State of Texas Longhorn Herd exhibit qualities typical of the Old Texans that went up the trails. Note the variety of coloration and horn types. The steers in the foreground show some examples of horns with a Texas twist; small to medium-size ears set horizontally directly under the horns; a straight, rectangular facial profile from the poll to the muzzle; medium-sized body; long legs; and clean lines with little or no loose skin. The quality of the range influences size and weight; these cattle forage on the natural range in Shackelford and Stephens Counties. Cattle of the Official State of Texas Longhorn Herd are as close as possible in appearance and genetics to the cattle that went up the trails prior to the extensive cross-breeding efforts of the 1880s and 1890s. The herd is located at Fort Griffin State Historic Site, Albany, Texas. (Photo by the author)

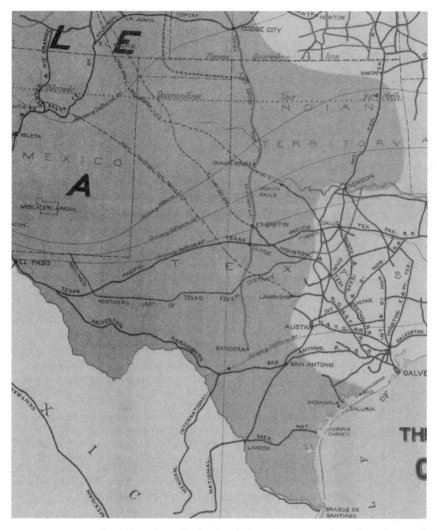

Fig. 2. Texas fever district. Detail from *The Range and Ranch Cattle Area of the United States, 1884*. This map accompanied a report of the same name published by the US Treasury Department in 1885. Note the "Assumed Northern Limit of Texas Fever District" that extends from a point east of El Paso to a point east of Denison. Cattle from south of that line were assumed to be capable of transmitting Texas, splenic, or Spanish fever. The shaded area is included in what was defined as the range and ranch cattle area of the United States, which extended north to the Canadian border and from the Dakotas west into California, Oregon, and Washington. Also note that the cattle trail to Dodge City is designated as the Fort Griffin and Dodge City Trail. (Courtesy of Geography and Map Division, Library of Congress, Washington, DC)

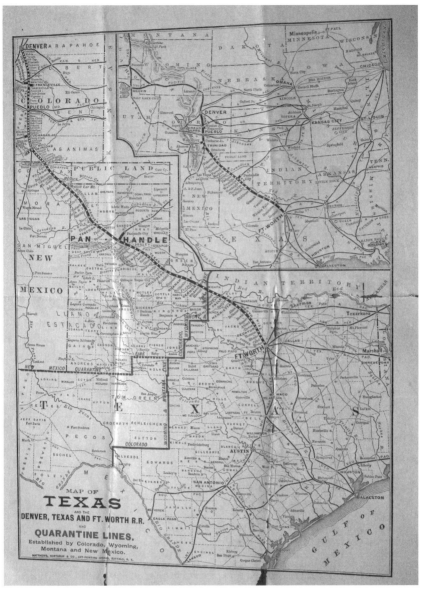

Fig. 3. Quarantine lines. *Map of Texas and the Denver, Texas, and Ft. Worth R.R. and Quarantine Lines Established by Colorado, Wyoming, Montana, and New Mexico.* This map accompanied the 1889 brochure *Regulations Governing the Admission of Southern Cattle into Colorado, Wyoming, and Montana, for 1889* (Denver: Denver, Texas, and Fort Worth Railroad Co., 1889). Without proof in the form of an affidavit that cattle were held north of the thirty-sixth parallel or west of quarantine lines indicated on the map, the cattle were deemed capable of transmitting Texas, splenic, or Spanish fever and were subject to quarantine for at least ninety days at the owner's risk and expense. The affidavit was certified by the county clerk or clerk of the district court nearest the range where the cattle were held. (Photo by the author, courtesy of the John T. Lytle Collection, Cattle Raisers Museum, Fort Worth, Texas)

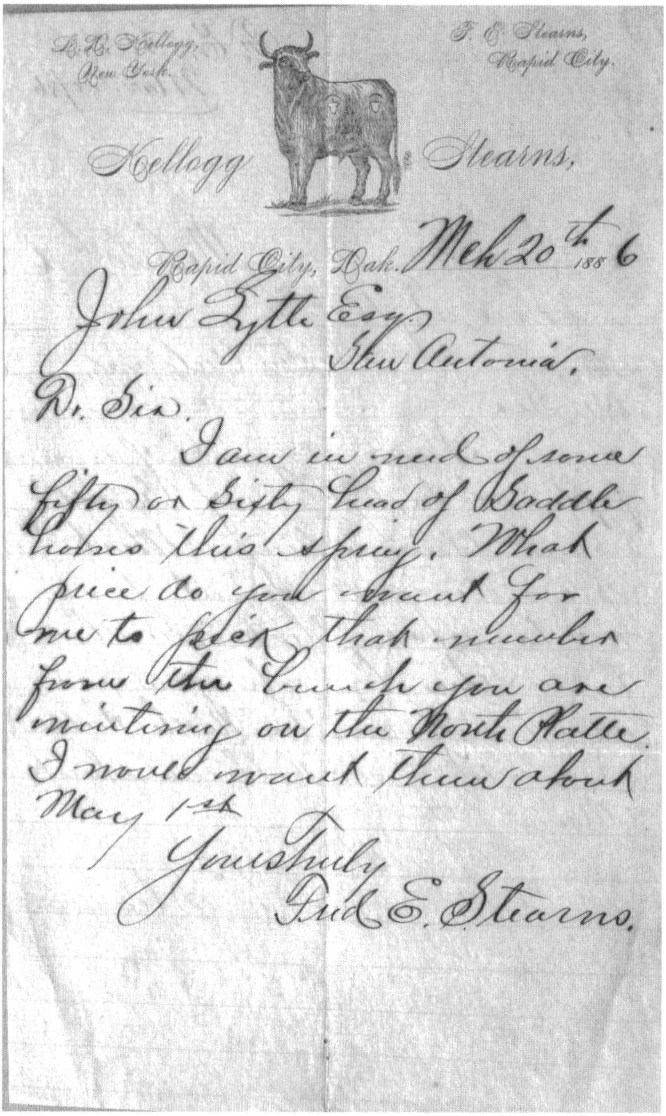

L. H. Kellogg,
New York.

F. E. Stearns,
Rapid City.

Kellogg & Stearns,

Rapid City, Dak. Mch 20th 1886

John Lytle Esq.
San Antonia.

Dr. Sir.

I am in need of some fifty or sixty head of Saddle horses this spring. What price do you want for me to pick that number from the bunch you are wintering on the North Platte. I would want them about May 1st.

Yours Truly
Fred E. Stearns.

Fig. 4. Letter from Fred E. Stearns to John Lytle, March 20, 1886. Price requests and orders for horses and cattle were often sent by mail. In this example, Fred E. Stearns of Rapid City, Dakota Territory, requested a price to pick fifty or sixty head of saddle horses from a herd that John Lytle was wintering on the North Platte River. (Photo by the author, courtesy of the John T. Lytle Collection, Cattle Raisers Museum, Fort Worth, Texas)

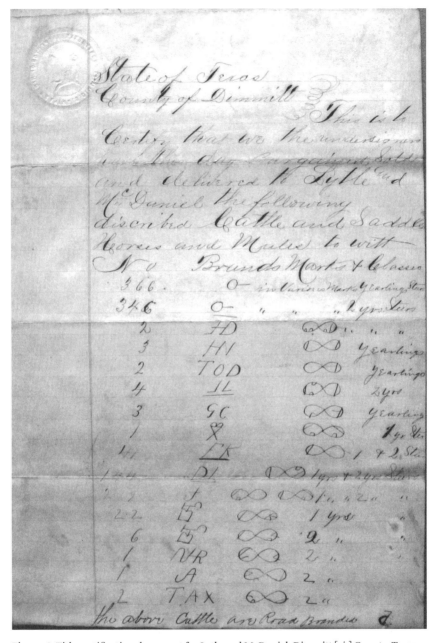

Figs. 5, 6. Title certification document for Lytle and McDaniel, Dimmitt [*sic*] County, Texas, May 19, 1885. This document shows that transactions were not always recorded in a formal mark and brand book. This example shows the quantity, class or description, earmarks, and brands of cattle, horses, and mules sold and delivered to the firm of Lytle and McDaniel. The road brand is also indicated on each page. (Photo by the author, courtesy of the John T. Lytle Collection, Cattle Raisers Museum, Fort Worth, Texas)

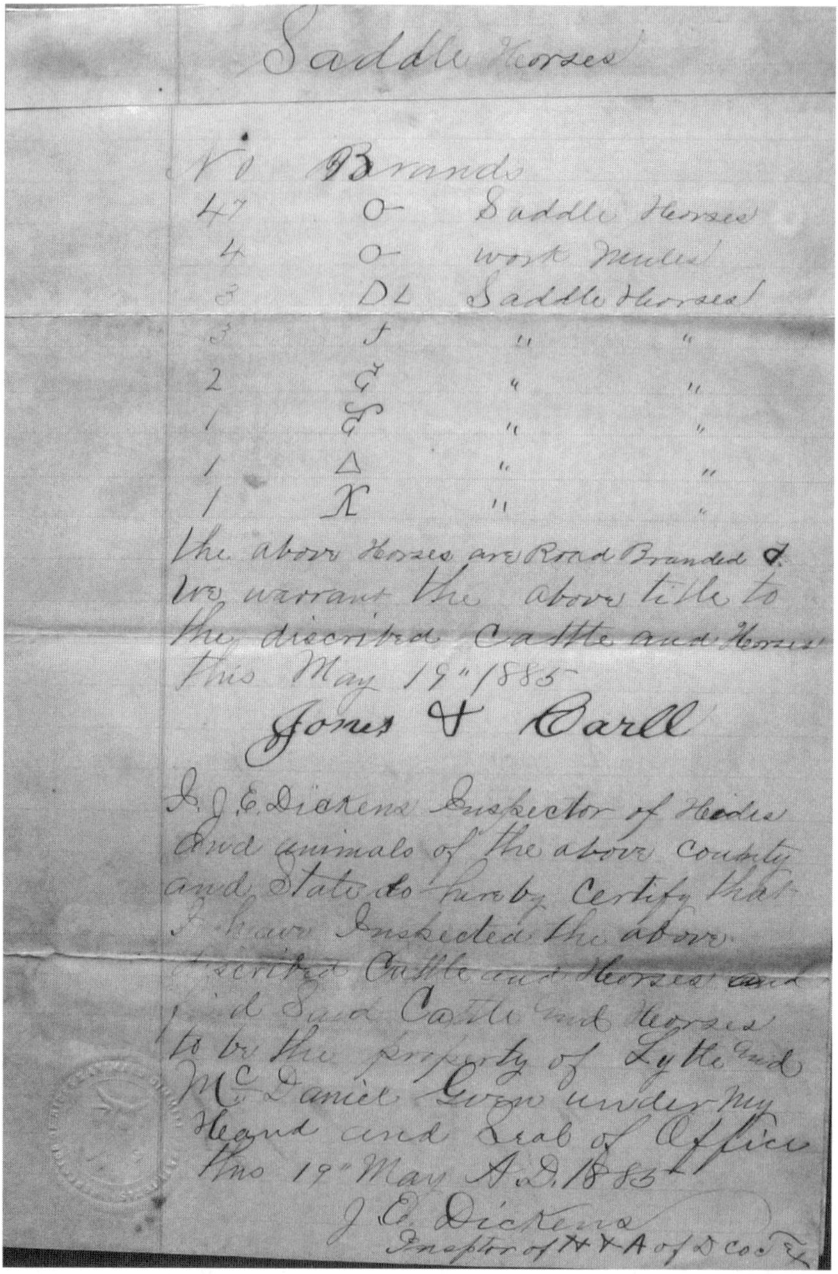

Saddle Horses

No	Brands	
47	o	Saddle Horses
4	o	Work Mules
8	DL	Saddle Horses
3	f	" "
2	GG	" "
1	GG	" "
1	△	" "
1	X	" "

the above Horses are Road Branded ♂.
We warrant the above title to
the discribed Cattle and Horses
this May 19" 1885

Jones & Carll

I. J. E. Dickens Inspector of Hides
and animals of the above county
and State do hereby Certify that
I have Inspected the above
discribed Cattle and Horses and
find Said Cattle and Horses
to be the property of Lythe and
McDaniel Gorow under my
Hand and Seal of Office
this 19" May A.D. 1885

J. E. Dickens
Inspector of H & A of D Co.

Fig. 6.

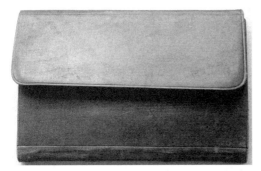

Fig. 7. Stockman's mark and brand book. This example was used in 1883. Brands, earmarks, and relevant information were recorded in the book as proof of ownership. (Photo by the author, courtesy of the John T. Lytle Collection, Cattle Raisers Museum, Fort Worth, Texas)

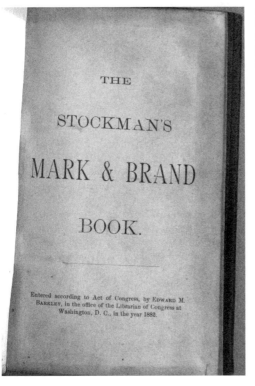

Fig. 8. Stockman's mark and brand book title page. (Photo by the author, courtesy of the John T. Lytle Collection, Cattle Raisers Museum, Fort Worth, Texas)

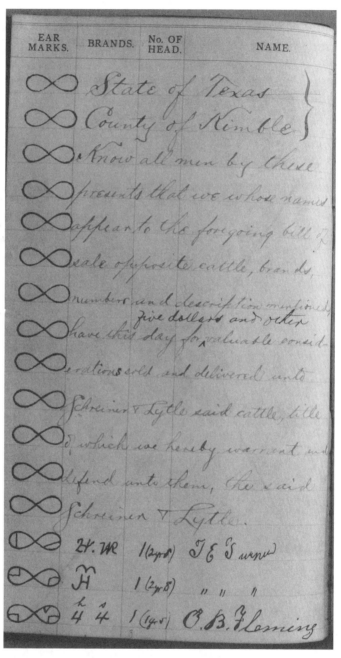

EAR MARKS.	BRANDS.	No. OF HEAD.	NAME.

State of Texas

County of Kimble

Know all men by these

presents that we whose names

appear to the foregoing bill of

sale opposite cattle, brands,

numbers and description mentioned,
five dollars and other

have this day for valuable consid-

erations sold and delivered unto

Schreiner & Lytle said cattle, title

of which we hereby warrant and

defend unto them, the said

Schreiner & Lytle.

	24. WR	1 (2yr)	J E S urns
	H	1 (2yr s)	" " "
	4 4	1 (4yr)	C. B. Fleming

Fig. 9. Page from stockman's mark and brand book. This example shows the county of issue, a general description, and the first page of diagrams of the specific earmarks, wattles, brands, quantities, and descriptions of the livestock. (Photo by the author, courtesy of the John T. Lytle Collection, Cattle Raisers Museum, Fort Worth, Texas)

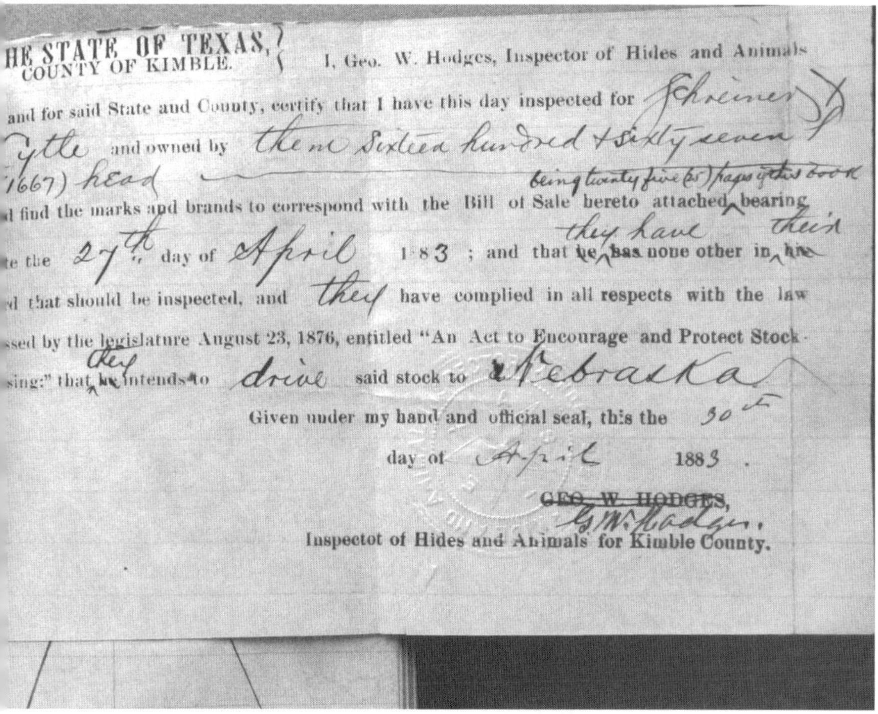

HE STATE OF TEXAS, }
COUNTY OF KIMBLE.   I, Geo. W. Hodges, Inspector of Hides and Animals

and for said State and County, certify that I have this day inspected for *Schreiner*

ytle and owned by *them Sixteen hundred + Sixty seven*
1667) head
                                                being twenty five (25) pages of this book
d find the marks and brands to correspond with the Bill of Sale hereto attached, bearing
                                                they have   their
te the *27th* day of *April* 1·83 ; and that *he* has none other in his

d that should be inspected, and *they* have complied in all respects with the law

ssed by the legislature August 23, 1876, entitled "An Act to Encourage and Protect Stock-
        they
sing:" that he intends to *drive* said stock to *Nebraska*

        Given under my hand and official seal, this the *30th*

        day of *April* 1883 .

                GEO. W. HODGES,
                G. W. Hodges,
        Inspector of Hides and Animals for Kimble County.

Fig. 10. Certification Page from stockman's mark and brand book. This page, bearing the signature and official seal of the county clerk or the inspector of hides and animals, documents the quantity of animals, ownership, and intended destination and certifies that the parties have complied with the relevant law. (Photo by the author, courtesy of the John T. Lytle Collection, Cattle Raisers Museum, Fort Worth, Texas)

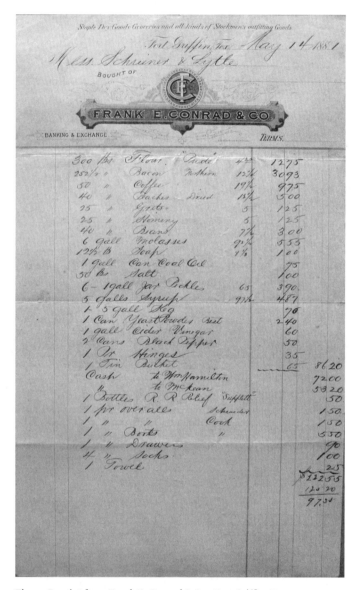

Fig. 11. Receipt from Frank E. Conrad & Co., Fort Griffin, Texas, to Mess[rs]. Schreiner & Lytle, May 14, 1881. This receipt shows a list of supplies purchased and carried in the mess wagon, later called the chuck wagon, for meal preparation on the trail. Coal oil was used in lanterns and as a general-purpose treatment for wounds and ailments; since medical help was scarce, the cook often served as a doctor. Other items, in this case overalls, boots, drawers, and socks, were purchased as needed and deducted from the drover's pay when the crew was paid. The store was located in the settlement known as The Flat adjacent to Fort Griffin. (Photo by the author, courtesy of the John T. Lytle Collection, Cattle Raisers Museum, Fort Worth, Texas)

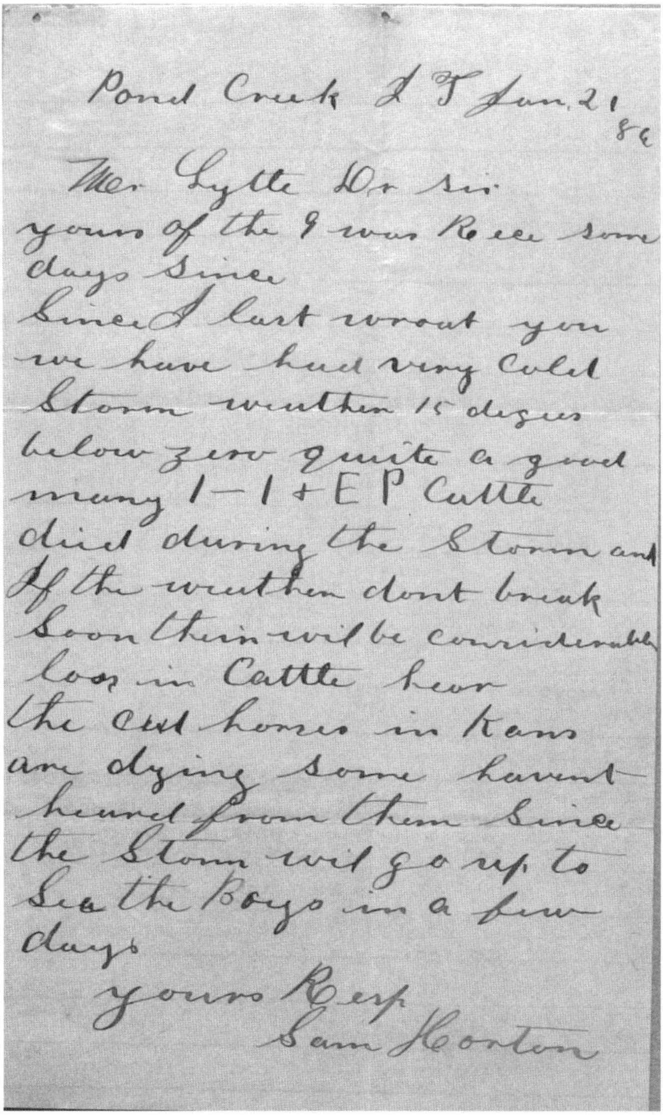

Pond Creek I T Jan. 21
86

Mr Lytle Dr sir
yours of the 9 was Rec some
days since
Since I last wrote you
we have had very cold
Storm weather 15 degres
below zero quite a good
many I—I + E P Cattle
died during the Storm and
If the weather dont break
soon there wil be considerable
loss in Cattle hear
the out horses in Kans
are dying some havent
heard from them Since
the Storm wil go up to
See the Boys in a few
days
yours Resp
Sam Horton

Fig. 12. Letter from Sam Horton to John Lytle, Pond Creek, Indian Territory, January 21, 1886. In this letter Horton reports harsh winter storms and bitterly cold temperatures of fifteen degrees below zero. He reports the loss of "quite a good many" head of cattle, with a warning of considerable losses "if the weather don't break." His trip to Kansas to "See the Boys" undoubtedly occurred on horseback in harsh winter conditions. (Photo by the author, courtesy of the John T. Lytle Collection, Cattle Raisers Museum, Fort Worth, Texas)

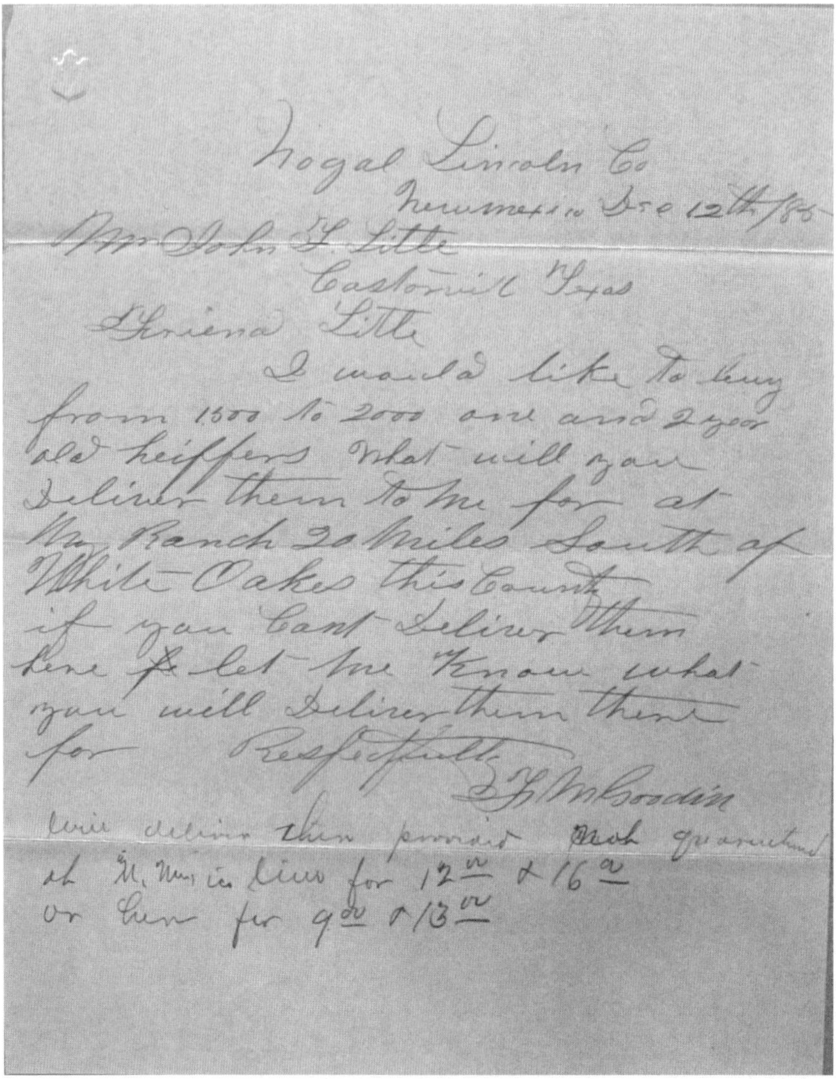

Fig. 13. Letter to John Lytle from Nogal, Lincoln County, New Mexico, 1885. The destination might have been a railhead or another ranch. In this letter Lytle is asked for a price for fifteen hundred to two thousand one- and two-year-old heifers either delivered to the buyer's ranch or picked up at Lytle's ranch. Lytle's response is written at the bottom of the page: delivered to buyer's ranch, provided they were not quarantined at the New Mexico line, for twelve and sixteen dollars per head, or delivered at Lytle's ranch for nine and thirteen dollars per head. (Photo by the author, courtesy of the John T. Lytle Collection, Cattle Raisers Museum, Fort Worth, Texas)

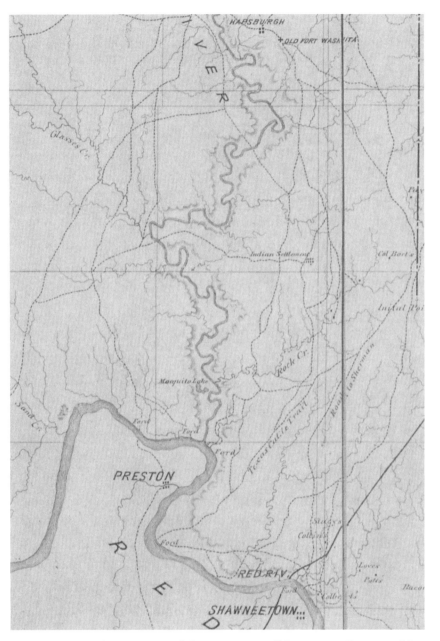

Fig. 14. Preston and Shawneetown. Detail from E. H. Ruffner, *Map of the Chickasaw Country and Contiguous Portions of the Indian Territory* (1872). Note multiple fords on the Red River with a network of trails. One route is designated "Texas Cattle Trail." Many routes were unnamed, and a named cattle trail was only one option to reach a destination. Shawneetown was located north of the present site of Denison, Texas. (Courtesy of Geography and Map Division, Library of Congress, Washington, DC)

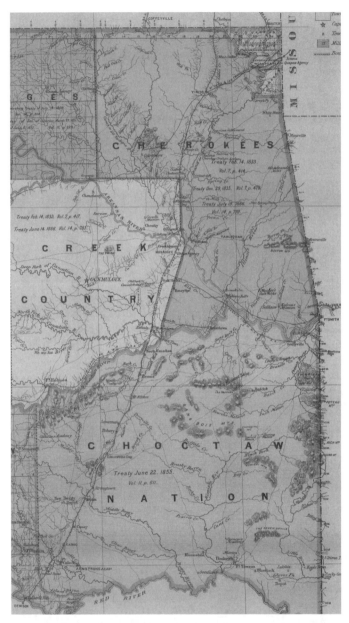

Fig. 15. Denison to Baxter. Detail from C. Roeser, *Indian Territory*, Serial Set 1885 (1879). Note the network of trails between Denison (*lower left*), Fort Smith (*right center*), and Baxter (*upper right*). The Missouri, Kansas &Texas Railroad laid tracks along much of the trail along the most direct route from Denison through Vinita (diagonally from lower left to upper right). (Courtesy of Oklahoma Digital Maps Collection, McCasland Collection, Edmon Low Library, Oklahoma State University, Stillwater)

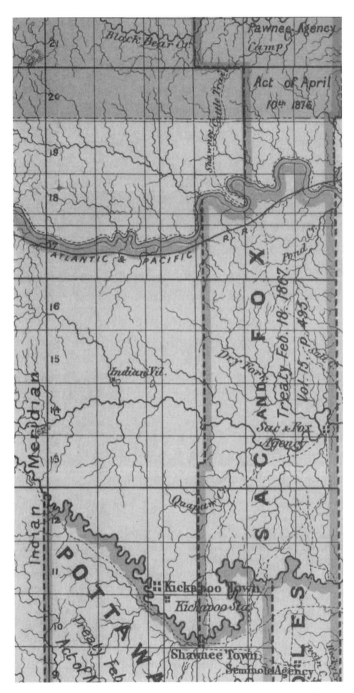

Fig. 16. Shawnee Trail. Detail from C. Roeser, *Indian Territory*, Serial Set 1885 (1879). A trail led north past Shawnee Town on the North Canadian River toward Arkansas City, Kansas. This trail is marked "Shawnee Cattle Trail" north of the Cimarron River and was likely used after the railheads shifted to central Kansas. Shawnee Town is south of the present site of Shawnee, Oklahoma. This trail may have been referenced later as the Western Shawnee Trail. (Courtesy of Oklahoma Digital Maps Collection, McCasland Collection, Edmon Low Library, Oklahoma State University, Stillwater)

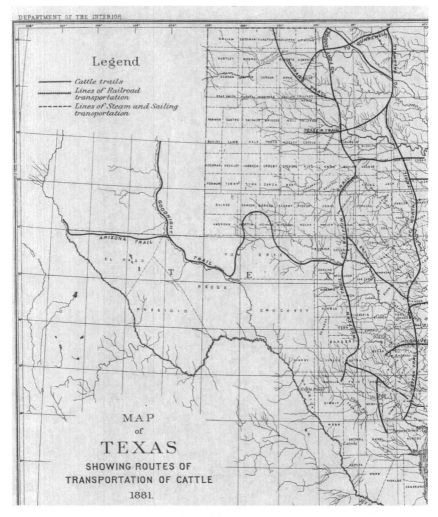

Fig. 17. Texas cattle trails, 1881. Detail from Julius Bien, *Map of Texas Showing Routes of Transportation of Cattle, 1881*. This rare Department of the Interior map, prepared to accompany a report in the Tenth Census of the United States, shows the approximate routes of the Eastern and Western Trails. These trails are also designated the Fort Worth Trail and Fort Griffin Trail, respectively. A trail from the Western Trail west along the Pecos River into New Mexico is shown as the Goodnight Trail. This might reflect contemporary traffic patterns, but this route differs from the route that Charles Goodnight described from the Concho River area to Horsehead Crossing on the Pecos River. (Courtesy of Geography and Map Division, Library of Congress, Washington, DC)

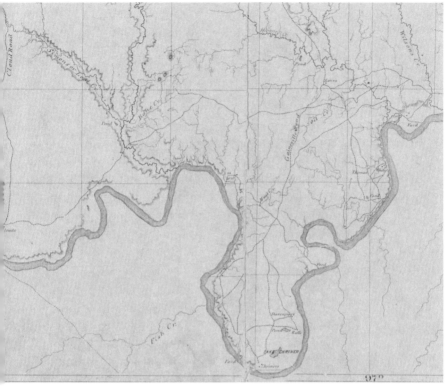

Fig. 18. Red River fords near Gainesville. Detail from E. H. Ruffner, *Map of the Chickasaw Country and Contiguous Portions of the Indian Territory* (1872). This map shows several fords on the Red River that were accessible from Cooke County, Texas. Cloud Road and the Gainesville Road both led toward Fort Arbuckle, where other trails led toward Council Grove on the North Canadian River. Lake Chriner is also known as Leeper Lake and is located south of the present site of Thackerville, Oklahoma. (Courtesy of Geography and Map Division, Library of Congress, Washington, DC)

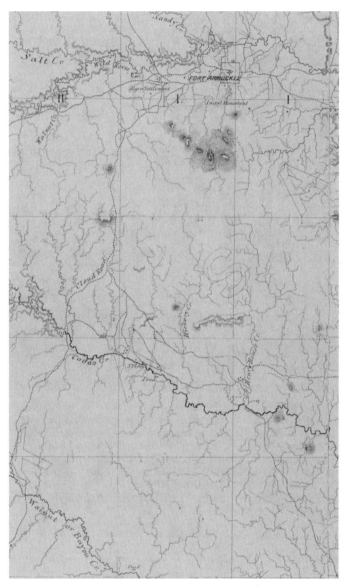

Fig. 19. Cloud Road to Fort Arbuckle. Detail from E. H. Ruffner, *Map of the Chickasaw Country and Contiguous Portions of the Indian Territory* (1872). The road from Love's, which joined the Gainesville Road, leads from the bottom right of the detail and joins Cloud Road north of Caddo Creek. Fort Arbuckle was located near the confluence of Sandy and Wild Horse Creeks about eight miles west of the present site of Davis, Oklahoma. (Courtesy of Geography and Map Division, Library of Congress, Washington, DC)

Fig. 20. Fort Arbuckle to Smith Paul's. Detail from E. H. Ruffner, *Map of the Chickasaw Country and Contiguous Portions of the Indian Territory* (1872). The trail led north from Fort Arbuckle to Smith Paul's, which later became the site of Pauls Valley. (Courtesy of Geography and Map Division, Library of Congress, Washington, DC)

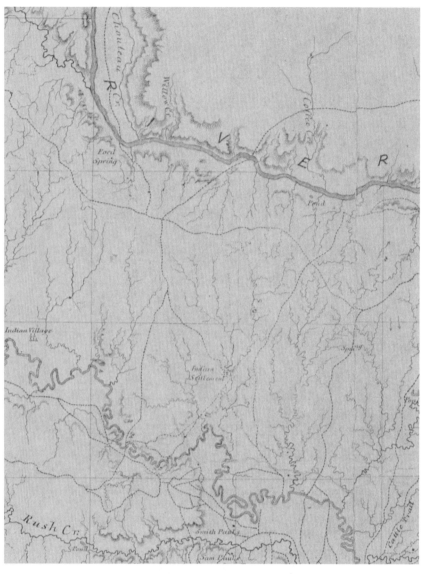

Fig. 21. Smith Paul's to Chouteau Creek. Detail from E. H. Ruffner, *Map of the Chickasaw Country and Contiguous Portions of the Indian Territory* (1872). From Smith Paul's the trail led to a ford on the Canadian River near the mouth of Chouteau Creek, then to the North Canadian River near Council Grove, where it merged with Chisholm's Cattle Trail. The trail marked "Cattle Trail" at lower right leads from near Cherokee Town to the Canadian River, then toward Fort Gibson. Later maps show a network of trails that merge with this trail near the Canadian River and lead north toward Arkansas City, Kansas. (Courtesy of Geography and Map Division, Library of Congress, Washington, DC)

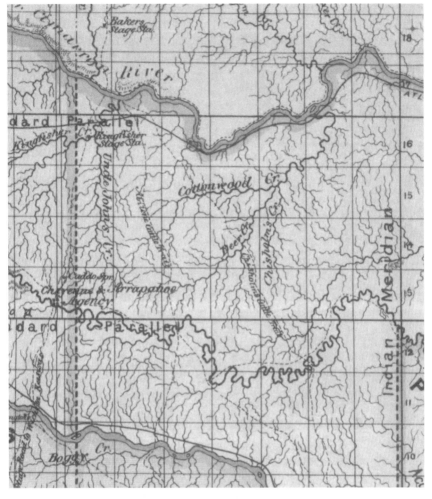

Fig. 22. Chisholm's Cattle Trail. Detail from C. Roeser, *Indian Territory*, Serial Set 1885 (1879). Chisholm's Cattle Trail lay between the North Canadian and Cimarron Rivers. The trail that leads into Chisholm's Cattle Trail from the south is the trail from the confluence of Chouteau Creek and the Canadian River. The Chisholm name is not extended to any interconnecting trails. (Courtesy of Oklahoma Digital Maps Collection, McCasland Collection, Edmon Low Library, Oklahoma State University, Stillwater)

Fig. 23. Abilene Cattle Trail from the Red River. Detail from E. H. Ruffner, *Map of the Chickasaw Country and Contiguous Portions of the Indian Territory* (1872). The fords on the Red River indicate the crossing point near Red River Station. The cattle trail in Texas, which is not shown, approached the fords from the east across Farmers Creek. The Abilene Cattle Trail intersected the Fort Sill and Texas Road a few miles northwest of Red River Station. The road indicated to Fort Richardson was a military road. The crossing at Farmers Creek is presently covered by Lake Nocona. (Courtesy of Geography and Map Division, Library of Congress, Washington, DC)

Fig. 24. Abilene Cattle Trail north of the Cimarron. Detail from C. Roeser, *Indian Territory*, Serial Set 1885 (1879). The trail north of the Cimarron River is indicated as the Abilene Cattle Trail and Stage Road. Chisholm's Cattle Trail merged with the Abilene Cattle Trail north of the Kingfisher stage station (present site of Kingfisher, Oklahoma), which is visible south of the Cimarron River at bottom left. The Chisholm name does not extend north of the Cimarron. (Courtesy of Oklahoma Digital Maps Collection, McCasland Collection, Edmon Low Library, Oklahoma State University, Stillwater)

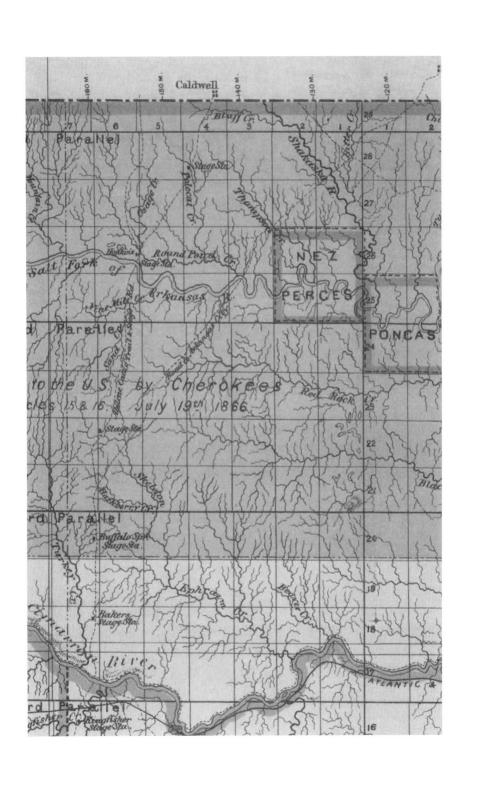

Fig. 25. Abilene and Chisholm Cattle Trails. Detail from G. P. Strum, *Indian Territory*, Serial Set 2261 (1883). The Abilene Cattle Trail is designated three times along most of its length through Indian Territory. Chisholm's Cattle Trail is designated once between the North Canadian and Cimarron Rivers. This nomenclature, which does not extend the trail names to interconnecting trails, is consistent on multiple maps from this era. The Kingfisher stage station (present site of Kingfisher, Oklahoma) is visible near Uncle John's Creek south of the Cimarron River at left center. (Courtesy of Oklahoma Digital Maps Collection, McCasland Collection, Edmon Low Library, Oklahoma State University, Stillwater)

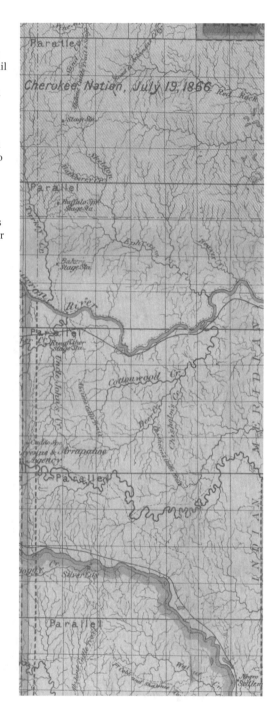

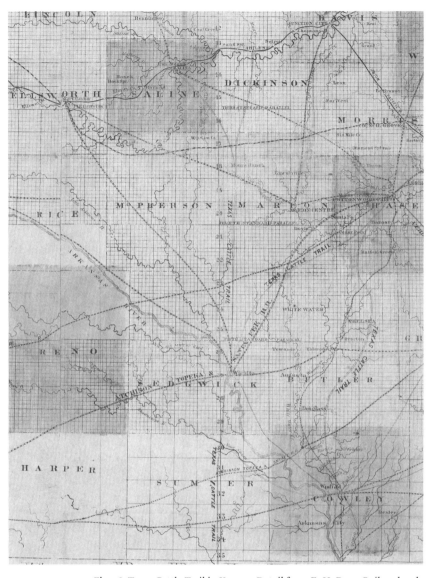

Fig. 26. Texas Cattle Trail in Kansas. Detail from E. H. Ross, *Railroad and Sectional Map of Kansas* (1871). The detail from this rare map shows the cattle trail leading from Indian Territory past Wichita and Arkansas City to Abilene, Salina, and Cottonwood Falls as the Texas Cattle Trail. The route of the Texas Cattle Trail past Wichita later came to be called the Chisholm Trail. The cattle trail goes no farther north than Abilene in Dickinson County and Salina in Saline County. Note that neither Newton nor Caldwell yet appear on the map, the cattle trail does not yet extend to Ellsworth, and railroad construction to Wichita is still in progress (as indicated by the broken lines). (Courtesy of Digital Maps Collection, Huntington Library)

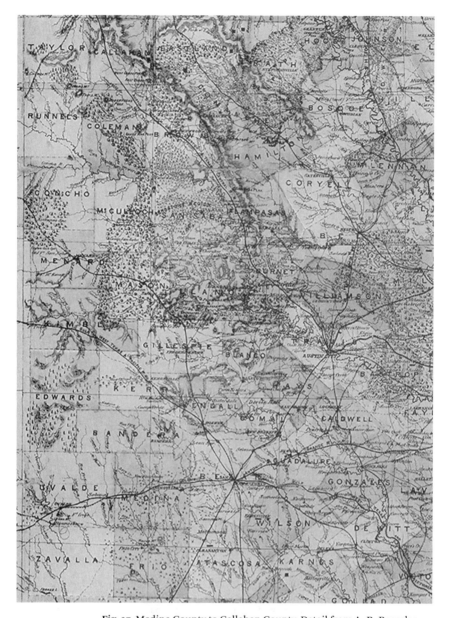

Fig. 27. Medina County to Callahan County. Detail from A. R. Roessler, *New Map of Texas Prepared and Published for the Bureau of Immigration of the State of Texas* (1874). The trail route developed generally west of the timbered belt through Kimble, Menard, McCulloch, and Coleman Counties through Callahan County. Timbered areas and other topographic features made it difficult, if not impossible, to drive herds through certain areas. (Courtesy of Special Collections, University of Texas at Arlington Libraries)

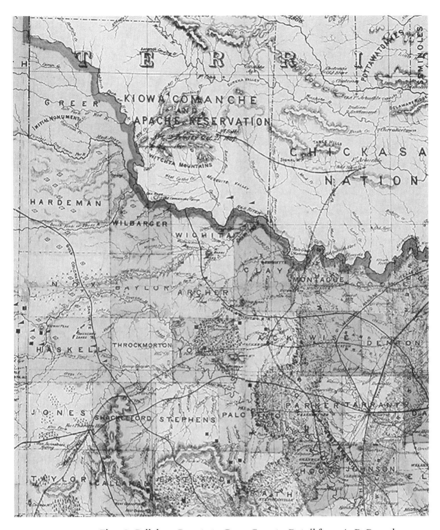

Fig. 28. Callahan County to Greer County. Detail from A. R. Roessler, *New Map of Texas Prepared and Published for the Bureau of Immigration of the State of Texas* (1874). Doan's Store is located in Wilbarger County near the Prairie Dog Town Fork of the Red River upstream (west) of the mouth of the North Fork of the Red. Northbound herds that crossed the Red River at Doan's entered Greer County, Texas, and did not enter Indian Territory until they crossed the North Fork of the Red River. Also note the open prairie between the Eastern and Western Cross Timbers from the Brazos River south of Johnson County north to the Red River; this was a natural travel route to the cattle trail crossings in Cooke and Montague Counties. (Courtesy of Special Collections, University of Texas at Arlington Libraries)

Fig. 29. Overview of the state of Texas in 1874. A. R. Roessler, *New Map of Texas Prepared and Published for the Bureau of Immigration of the State of Texas* (1874). The counties west of the one-hundredth meridian (eastern border of the Texas Panhandle) are mostly unorganized; many of these counties would be formed in 1876 and later. Greer County is visible at the southeastern corner of the Panhandle. (Courtesy of Special Collections, University of Texas at Arlington Libraries)

Fig. 30. Cheyenne Agency to Fort Supply. Detail from G. P. Strum, *Indian Territory*, Serial Set 2261 (1883). A road leads from the Abilene Cattle Trail past the Cheyenne Agency and Fort Reno along the north side of the North Canadian River to Fort Supply. This road, designated on the map as "Road from Cheyenne Agy to Camp Supply," was later claimed to be the Western Chisholm Trail. Chisholm's Cattle Trail is visible between the North Canadian and Cimarron Rivers near the lower right. The two routes are indirectly connected by a network of trails. This detail also shows leases that eventually impeded herd traffic. Most of the Cherokee Outlet, leased by the Cherokee Strip Live Stock Association, is shown across the top of the map. (Courtesy of Oklahoma Digital Maps Collection, McCasland Collection, Edmon Low Library, Oklahoma State University, Stillwater)

Fig. 31. Proposed National Cattle Trail. Detail from Julius Bien, *The Range and Ranch Cattle Area of the United States, 1884* (1885). This detail shows the route of the proposed national cattle trail from Doan's Store (bottom right) to the northern US border. The existing Dodge City Trail is represented by a double line; the proposed trail is represented by a double-dotted line. Although this route was never officially designated as a national cattle trail, some herds undoubtedly used parts of it to reach Wyoming, Montana, and Dakota. (Courtesy of Geography and Map Division, Library of Congress, Washington, DC)

Fig. 32. Chisholm name applied south of the North Canadian River. Detail from *Map of the Oklahoma Country in the Indian Territory* (1892). This is the first map that applied the Chisholm name to a trail south of the North Canadian River. The section of trail between the Canadian and North Canadian Rivers appeared on previous military and Department of the Interior maps but was unnamed. This map shows, from top to bottom, the Cimarron, North Canadian, and Canadian Rivers. Chisholm's Cattle Trail was designated on previous maps only between the North Canadian and Cimarron Rivers. Also visible at left is the Abilene Cattle Trail. The citation for this map dates it from 1892; however, it may have appeared as early as 1889. In either case, the Chisholm Trail's historical period of use was over by the time this map appeared. (Courtesy of Oklahoma Digital Maps Collection, Russal Brawley Collection, Edmon Low Library, Oklahoma State University, Stillwater)

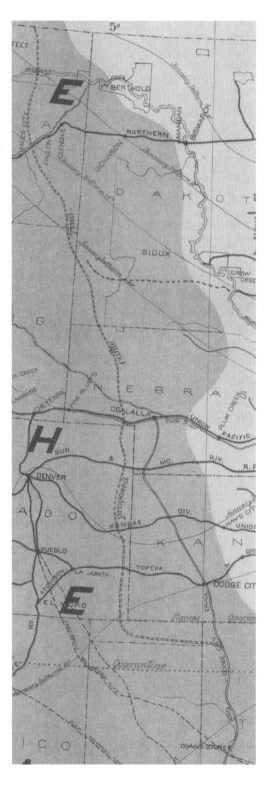

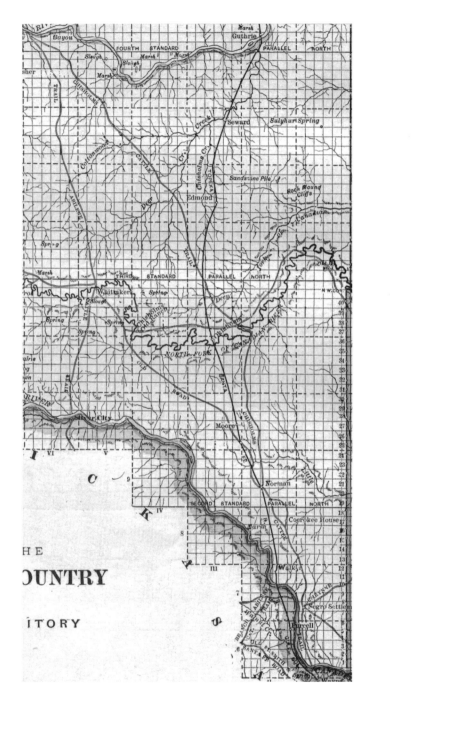

Bayou

RIV

Marsh
Guthrie

FOURTH STANDARD   PARALLEL   NORTH

Slough
Sleugh
Marsh   Marsh
Slough
Marsh

sher

TRAIL

Chisholm

Cottonwood

Seward   Creek

Deer   Cr.   Sulphur Spring

CATTLE   Chisholma Cty.

Hasting   TOPEKA

Sandstone Pile

Rock Mound
Cliffs

Edmond

Canadian

Spring

Marsh   THIRD   STANDARD   PARALLEL   NORTH

Whittakers   Spring

N.W. COR.

Spring
Slough
Deep   40

Spring   Spring   Chisholm   39
Old Ranch

Spring   NORTH FORK OF CAN.   38
37
36

airie
og
wn   35
OLD   34
33
32

ROAD
31
30
29

Sil
r City   28
27
26
25
24

I   VI   V   23
22

C   9   21

Moore   CHISHOLM

SANTA FE

Norman

K   IV   SECOND   STANDARD   PARALLEL   NORTH   20
18

8   Cherokee House   16
Marsh   15
14

HE   III   I   Walkr   13
12
11

OUNTRY   7

CHEYENNE

Negro Settlem

ITORY   Purcell

BRANCH   OLD   FT. SMITH

6   OLD
SANTA FE   RD.

A   CAN.
Spring

Fig. 33. Abilene Cattle Trail, 1902. Detail from *Map of Oklahoma Territory* (1902). The Abilene Cattle Trail was still identified multiple times along its length, while the Chisholm Trail, or Chisholm's Cattle Trail, was not marked on the 1898 and 1902 maps. This detail shows the Abilene Cattle Trail, indicated by a double line and designated north of Duncan and Marlow. The route of Chisholm's Cattle Trail from the North Canadian River near Council Grove is indicated by a single dotted line past Chisholm Creek to the Cimarron River north of Kingfisher, but the route is unnamed. (Courtesy of Oklahoma Digital Maps Collection, McCasland Collection, Edmon Low Library, Oklahoma State University, Stillwater)

Fig. 34. Chisholm Trail, Addington Quadrangle, 1901. Detail from *Indian Territory*, *Chickasaw Nation*, *Addington Quadrangle* (1901). The Chisholm Trail name appeared for the first time along the trail route past Monument Hill in 1901. This trail, which led from near Red River Station, had appeared on military and Department of the Interior maps as the Abilene Cattle Trail since 1872. The route still appeared on some maps as the Abilene Cattle Trail. The reason for the sudden change from Abilene Cattle Trail to Chisholm Trail is unknown; however, it coincides with the beginnings of the Good Roads movement. Addington can be seen at top left, Monument Hill at top center, and Ryan at bottom left. (Courtesy of US Geological Survey and University of North Texas Libraries, Government Documents Department)

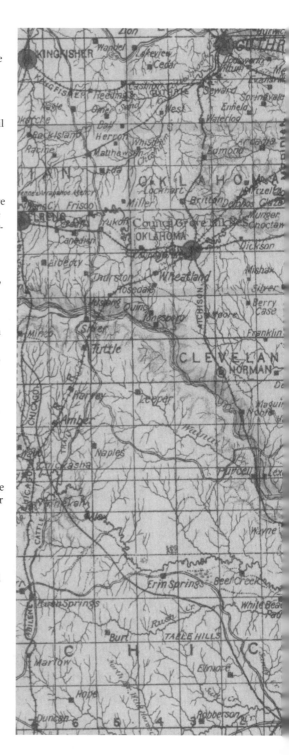

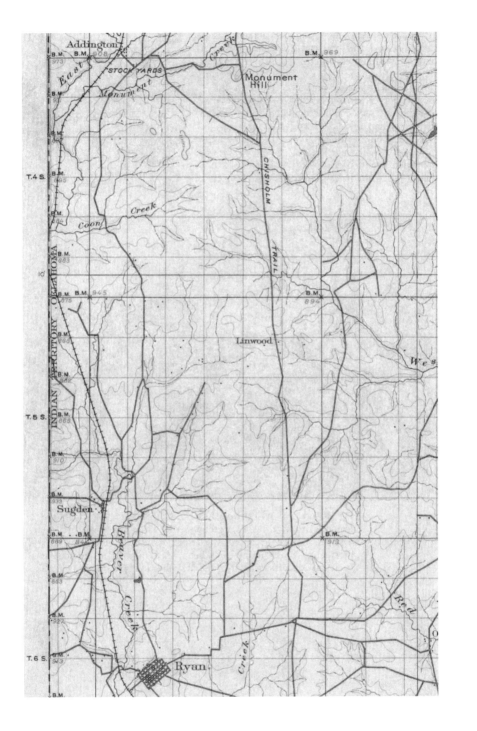

Fig. 35. George Washington Saunders about 1925. George W. Saunders drove cattle to Kansas and other northern destinations beginning in 1871. He was subsequently successful in the ranching and livestock commission business. Saunders is credited as the founder of the Old Time Trail Drivers' Association in 1915 and later served as president of the organization for many years. He solicited written accounts of experiences on the cattle trails and the frontier, and through his persistence *The Trail Drivers of Texas* was published. Saunders died in 1933. (Courtesy of Matthew S. Jary, from the collection of Roland S. Jary)

Fig. 36. Old Time Trail Drivers' Association, March 1915. This photo is from the first meeting of the group. George W. Saunders, vice president, is seated front center, apparently holding his watch; John R. Blocker, president, is seated immediately behind Saunders's right shoulder. (Courtesy of Matthew S. Jary, from the collection of Roland S. Jary)

Fig. 37. Monument at Doan's Store, *The Cattleman*, December 1931. This photo shows the original inscription that included "The Longhorn Chisholm Trail and the Western Trail." P. P. Ackley, who was in charge of the inscription, included "Longhorn Chisholm Trail" over the objections of the Doans, George W. Saunders, and the Trail Drivers' Association. The monument is located on the Western Trail, a long way from the Chisholm Trail. The incorrect inscription was later removed and changed to "THE WESTERN TEXAS—KANSAS TRAIL 1876—1895 / THIS MONUMENT ERECTED BY TEXANS." It is believed that this change occurred within a few years after the monument was erected. (Courtesy of Texas and Southwestern Cattle Raisers Association, *The Cattleman*)

Fig. 38. Chisholm Trail markers, Wise County Courthouse. The round, cast metal marker in the foreground is an example of the markers installed by P. P. Ackley from 1932 to 1938. Some markers have been painted, while others, such as this example at the courthouse in Wise County, Texas, were unpainted. This is believed to be one of the few remaining original markers. An unknown number of these markers were installed between the southern border of Texas and Canada, generally along the route of the Meridian Highway, or US 81, and along the route of the Western Trail. The markers remain controversial because of the trail name, their placement, and apparent lack of supporting documentation from the trailing era. Many of these markers have been replaced in Texas during 2016 by the Texas Department of Transportation, likely because of the Chisholm Trail's sesquicentennial and the effort to obtain a national historic trail designation. The white marker post in the background is an example of the markers that have appeared in Texas since about 1999. Although some have been placed adjacent to the Ackley markers, as in this example, this is not always the case. The marker posts are placed by a private group and are not subject to Texas Historical Commission review or guidelines. Several requests regarding documentation to support either type of marker were not answered. (Photo by the author)

Fig. 39. Monument at Doan's Store. This photo shows the monument as it presently appears with the newer inscription: "THE WESTERN TEXAS–KANSAS TRAIL 1876–1895 / THIS MONUMENT ERECTED BY TEXANS." A closer inspection of the bronze relief reveals P. P. Ackley's name engraved directly under the figure on horseback in the foreground. The resemblance of the figure to Ackley along with the engraved name contributed to the statements that Ackley seemed more interested in commemorating himself than the cattle trail. (Photo by the author)

Fig. 40. Chisholm Trail, 1933. *Map of a Portion of Oklahoma Showing the Location of the Chisholm Trail* (1933). This map of the Chisholm Trail was produced in 1933 by the Engineering Department of the Oklahoma State Highway Commission as a result of H.B. 149. Evidence of the old trail was still visible in some places. This route past Monument Hill north to Caldwell is the same route that was indicated as the Abilene Cattle Trail on military and Department of the Interior maps for at least thirty years, from 1872 to 1902. The Chisholm Trail name did not appear in this mapped location past Addington, Duncan, and Kingfisher until 1901. (Courtesy of the Oklahoma Historical Society and Oklahoma Digital Maps Collection, McCasland Collection, Edmon Low Library, Oklahoma State University, Stillwater)

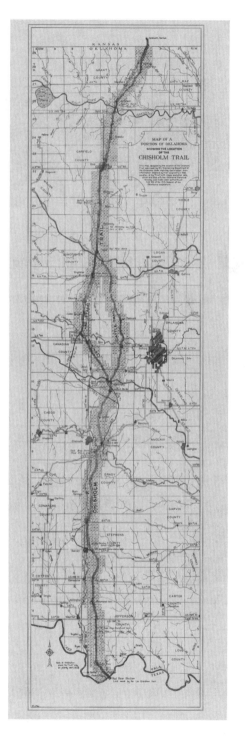

Fig. 41. Texas Cattle Trail, 1933. *Map of a Portion of Oklahoma Showing the Location of the Old Texas Cattle Trail* (1933). This map of the Texas Cattle Trail, or Western Trail, was produced in 1933 by the Engineering Department of the Oklahoma State Highway Commission as a result of H.B. 149. Evidence of the old trail was still visible in some places. Doan's crossing is located upstream of the mouth of the North Fork of the Red River. Herds that crossed here prior to 1896 were in Greer County, Texas, until they crossed the North Fork. The area between the North Fork and the one-hundredth meridian was made a part of Oklahoma Territory as a result of a Supreme Court decision in 1896. (Courtesy of the Oklahoma Historical Society and Oklahoma Digital Maps Collection, McCasland Collection, Edmon Low Library, Oklahoma State University, Stillwater)

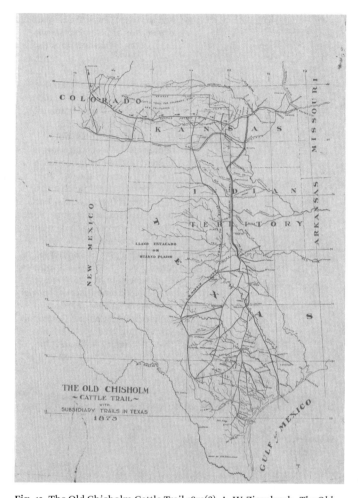

Fig. 42. The Old Chisholm Cattle Trail 1873(?). A. W. Ziegelasch, *The Old Chisholm Cattle Trail, with Subsidiary Trails in Texas, 1873* (date unknown). This map is often thought to be authentic to 1873, but its author, A. W. Ziegelasch, was born in 1893; therefore, the map cannot date to 1873. Adrian W. Ziegelasch worked as a draftsman for the state of Kansas during the 1920s, during the same time that the Meridian Highway project was gathering momentum and P. P. Ackley was campaigning to name the entire new road the Chisholm Trail. This map appears to be copied from *The Best and Shortest Cattle Trail from Texas* map published in 1873 by the Kansas Pacific Railway Company. The "Ellsworth Cattle Trail" led to Ellsworth, Kansas, on the original 1873 K-P map. The designation was changed to "Chisholm Trail" and rerouted from Ellsworth to Abilene on the Ziegelasch map. The timing of the likely appearance of this map during the 1920s and the changes from "Ellsworth Cattle Trail" to "Chisholm Trail" indicate that it is likely linked to the effort to apply the Chisholm Trail name to the Meridian Highway. (Courtesy of the Oklahoma Historical Society)

Chisholm's Trail

THE TRAIL NORTH to the new railhead at Abilene, Kansas, was more than thirty miles west of Preston, where herds had crossed the Red River since the 1840s. Because thirty miles was a two- or three-day trip for a trail herd, drovers found new places to cross the Red on a more direct route through Cooke County. A few years later, herd traffic shifted to a crossing point still farther west in Montague County. A network of trails, some along ancient buffalo migration routes, developed to the north through Indian Territory. One of those trails was used by Jesse Chisholm to travel between his trading posts. Cattle trails sometimes led along or near a military or other road or trail. A military road led from one fort to the next and meant the possibility of military protection, if needed. An existing road or trail might simply be the path of least resistance. But trails did not always lead where drovers needed to go, and when necessary they made their own trails. By chance, Chisholm's trade route happened to be located in the right place and was the best option to travel from the North Canadian River to the mouth of the Little Arkansas River and then north to Abilene. Chisholm's Trail was an important link in connecting the seemingly endless cattle supply in Texas with the railheads of central Kansas.

The exact date of Jesse Chisholm's first trip over the trail that bore his name is unknown. Chisholm's business associate, James R. Mead, seems to be the primary source regarding that first trip, but Mead gave slightly differing accounts over the years. In various historical group papers, newspapers, and interviews between 1890 and 1907, Mead placed that event at times ranging from the fall of 1864 to the spring of 1866. Whether Mead actually accompanied Chisholm on his first trip from the Little Arkansas River to Council Grove on the North Canadian River is not known, as Mead claimed to be with Chisholm in some accounts but made no mention of his presence in other accounts.[1] Mead described the trail in a 1900 letter to the editor of the *Wichita Daily Eagle*: "There already existed a trail and wagon road as plain as the road to market from the mouth of the Little Arkansas south to the vicinity of Fort Cobb, made in the fall of 1864 by a train of wagons of Jesse Chisholm, and two heavy four-mule wagons loaded by the writer and in charge of Henry Donnell, now living in Butler County, and which road was known as the 'Chisholm Trail' and was a great highway of travel at the first settling of Wichita."[2]

Chisholm had been traveling between his trading post at Council Grove, Fort Cobb, and the nearby Wichita Agency since some time in the late 1850s. This explains the portion of the road from Council Grove southward toward Fort Cobb mentioned by Mead in the article. According to Vincente George Chisholm, an adopted son of Jesse, Jesse's first trip over the route from the Little Arkansas to Council Grove was in the spring of 1865. The path that Chisholm followed from the Little Arkansas River to the North Canadian River had been traveled previously by Black Beaver, Major Hamilton W. Merrill, and Colonel William H. Emory, but it became known by the Chisholm name. About two years after Chisholm's wagons rolled south across the plains, the first cattle herds appeared headed north over his wagon tracks. By then, Chisholm had traveled this route between his trading posts often enough that the route between Council Grove and the Little Arkansas River became known as Chisholm's wagon road, or Chisholm's trail. Philip McCusker, a Comanche interpreter, used the name Chisholm's Trail to describe the route in a letter to Thomas Murphy, superintendent of Indian affairs for Kansas, in November 1867.[3]

Vincente George Chisholm stated that Jesse Chisholm did not establish his road for use as a cattle trail. Decades after the fact, Mead wrote that "on one occasion Chisholm brought up 400 head of cattle from his home place on the Canadian river." This account by Mead is contradicted by Vincente George Chisholm's claim that the herd was not driven by Jesse Chisholm but by a Delaware named Red Blanket. During the summer of 1864, members of some of the refugee tribes raided south of the Kansas border and moved cattle from Indian Territory north into Kansas. Chisholm's ranch on the Little Arkansas River in Kansas became a holding point for some of those cattle. Ownership was difficult to prove, as the prewar herds had been mostly abandoned when the tribes fled north into Kansas a few years before these events. To add to the confusion, Indians were paid by white men to rustle cattle while certain military officers looked the other way, and Indians loyal to the Union threatened to replenish their prewar herds by raiding in Kansas.[4]

According to Mead, the herd at Chisholm's ranch numbered approximately three thousand head. Some were driven to New Mexico to fill government contracts, while others were driven to the Sac and Fox agency, which was still located in Kansas. Chisholm was not known to be a cattleman, and Mead did not claim that Chisholm owned or drove the cattle, but he offered no other details.[5] Despite occasional claims to the contrary, there does not appear to be any evidence to support the notion that Jesse Chisholm drove any cattle herds to any destination. It seems unlikely that he would have had the time to do so, since he was involved in trading activities and peace negotiations during this same time frame.

The new outlet at Abilene, Kansas, was almost due north of the existing Brazos River crossings in McLennan, Bosque, and Hill Counties on the northbound cattle trail. The trail south of the Brazos had already been in use for at least twenty years. The treacherous Red River made sharp bends, which slowed the current and allowed for more suitable crossing conditions, at several sites in Cooke and Montague Counties. Chisholm's Trail happened to be situated on a good route between Abilene and these crossings on the Red River. Drovers headed north out of south Texas on the old, long-established cattle trail could follow the same route until they reached the crossings on the Brazos, then instead of a slight northeasterly direction toward Dallas County on the old trail, they would shift their direction slightly to the west of north and proceed toward Tarrant County and then on to the Red River in a more direct route toward Abilene.

Since the cattle trailing period ended, this trail route has been more contested than others. Resolution of this issue has been complicated by the fact that the cattle trails in Texas were not mapped or surveyed as they were in Indian Territory and Oklahoma. This left the subject of the main trail route through Texas open for many different interpretations. The most direct route from the southernmost county in Texas to the Brazos River remained the same, as there was no reason to alter the route until the Brazos was crossed. This main route remained from Cameron County through the present counties of Willacy, Hidalgo, Brooks, Kenedy, Kleberg, Nueces, Jim Wells, San Patricio, Live Oak, Bee, Goliad, Karnes, Wilson, Gonzales, Guadalupe, Caldwell, Hays, Travis, Williamson, Bell, and Falls to the Brazos River fords in McLennan, Hill, and Bosque Counties. Herds that passed through Bexar County could pick up the main trail in Hays or

Caldwell County. From the Brazos, the trail led through the counties of Johnson, Tarrant, Denton, Wise, Cooke, and Montague.[6] The route followed the prairie from north of Bexar County to the Red River in Cooke and Montague Counties, east of the Edwards Plateau and west of the Eastern Cross Timbers, with deviations for grass, water, and topographic features.

The main route indicated on *Map of Texas Showing Routes of Transportation of Cattle*, an 1881 Department of the Interior map, is generally the same or parallels the described route. The map shows that the main route began at the Nueces River in San Patricio County and passed through the counties of Bee, Goliad, DeWitt, Gonzales, Caldwell, Bastrop, Travis, Williamson, Bell, McLennan, Bosque, Johnson, Tarrant, Wise, and Montague to Red River Station. This trail crossed the Brazos River near Kimball in northern Bosque County. If a herd crossed upstream of Kimball Bend, it likely bypassed Hill County and entered Johnson County; if it crossed at Kimball Bend, it likely passed through the extreme northwestern corner of Hill County. On the map this trail is designated as the Eastern Trail or Fort Worth Trail. This is the only known map that shows the cattle trail that led from south Texas and crossed the Red River in Montague County that has provenance to the historical period of the cattle drives (fig. 17).[7]

The main crossing point on the Red River for herds, up until the railhead opened at Abilene in 1867 and the trail shifted to the west, was in Grayson County. The new trail crossed the Red River at several places, including near Gainesville and Sivells Bend in Cooke County and at Salt Creek, also known as Red River Station, in Montague County. Some herds may have crossed the Red River near Spanish Fort Bend; however, the closest northbound road or trail shown on 1872–85 maps of Indian Territory was located about nine miles east of the Red River, and the Spanish Fort crossing would have been out of the way. Trails were shown on the same maps leading from the more desirable fords near Gainesville and Salt Creek, which indicates that those routes were more commonly used. The fords in Cooke County were likely used for the first few years after Abilene became a destination for drovers (fig. 18). The vicinity of Gainesville was given as a crossing point in nearly all of the accounts in *Trail Drivers of Texas* that referred to a crossing point on the Red River on cattle drives that occurred between 1867 and 1871. An 1867 newspaper article referred to the cattle trail past Fort Arbuckle to the mouth of the Little Arkansas.[8]

North of the Red River, Chisholm's Trail lay between Council Grove on the North Canadian River and the mouth of the Little Arkansas River. The 1869 military map *Indian Territory with Parts of*

Neighboring States and Territories shows an unnamed trail that led from Chouteau's trading post on the Canadian River, a few miles upstream of Old Fort Arbuckle, to the north, where it crossed the North Canadian River in the vicinity of Council Grove downstream from Chisholm's Ranch. From there the trail led northwest, crossed the Red Fork of the Arkansas River near Uncle John's or King Fisher Creek, turned north past Pond Creek, Skunk Creek, and Bluff Creek, and went on to Wichita City at the confluence of the Arkansas and Little Arkansas Rivers. The Red Fork was also known as the Cimarron River and appeared on maps under both names. The point marked as Chisholm's Ranch is a few miles upstream of his trading post on the North Canadian River, where Chisholm maintained a cabin. Although it is unnamed, this is most likely Jesse Chisholm's old route between trading posts on the Little Arkansas and the North Canadian Rivers. The fact that the trail was mapped a year after Chisholm died indicates that the route was of sufficient significance to be included. The portion of the route between the North Canadian and the Red Fork was marked on subsequent Department of the Interior and military maps as Chisholm's Trail or Chisholm's Cattle Trail.[9]

Cloud Road led north from a ford at Sadler Bend on the Red River, located north of the present town of Muenster in Cooke County. The road was likely named for Ike Cloud, who had settled near the present site of Leon, Oklahoma, about 1860. Cloud Road was located about halfway between Spanish Fort Bend and Sivells Bend and was accessible from both locations. The road led north around the west side of the Arbuckle Mountains to Fort Arbuckle. The Gainesville Road led north from a ford on the Red River north of Gainesville past Sivells Bend to Love's, then slightly northwest, and merged with Cloud Road north of Caddo Creek (figs. 18, 19). From the vicinity of Fort Arbuckle a network of trails led north. A trail led to Smith Paul's farm located between Rush Creek and the Washita River (fig. 20), later the site of Pauls Valley. From Smith Paul's homestead a trail led north to a ford near the confluence of Chouteau Creek and the Canadian River, then slightly northwest to the North Canadian River, where it merged with Chisholm's Cattle Trail. The trail continued to the northwest and merged with the Abilene Cattle Trail near a ford at the Cimarron River near Uncle John's Creek (figs. 21, 22). From there the trail continued north and crossed into Kansas above Bluff Creek.[10]

Another trail led from the vicinity of Cherokee Town, a few miles east of Smith Paul's farm, to a ford at the Canadian River near Pond Creek. The trail led past Shawnee Town on the North Canadian River, crossed the Cimarron River about twelve miles upstream from Pond

Creek, and entered Kansas near the present site of Arkansas City. This trail is marked as "Cattle Trail" on the 1872 *Map of the Chickasaw Country* and as "Shawnee Cattle Trail" on the 1879 map *Indian Territory* (figs. 16, 21).[11] It was likely named due to its proximity to Shawnee Town on the North Canadian River.

The legislature of the Chickasaw Nation approved a law on September 21, 1869, that authorized a fee for all livestock driven north from Texas into the nation. The fee was payable to the nearest county clerk to the point of entry. Persons were required to appear and "pay over to said Clerk the sum of fifty cents per head for all cattle, horses, or mules he, she, or they wish to drive through this Nation." A certificate was issued upon payment. Violators were subject to arrest, and penalties were determined by the governor at his discretion. The law provided one exception: "That any person or persons driving stock through the Nation West of the waters of Walnut Bayou shall not be ameaniable [*sic*] to this act." The law took effect October 20, 1869.[12] Drovers who continued to cross the Red River at Sivells Bend or near Gainesville faced a potentially expensive proposition unless they found an alternative.

Red River Station, along Salt Creek in Montague County, was west of Walnut Bayou, and drovers could travel north along a different route to avoid the Chickasaw fee. Herd traffic likely shifted to Red River Station as a result of the 1869 Chickasaw fee and the closing of Fort Arbuckle in 1870. The fords at Red River Station and Salt Creek continued to be commonly used as herd crossings until the cattle market opened at Dodge City in 1876 and traffic began to slow. The trail entered Montague County southeast of Saint Jo, which was then known as Head of Elm. It passed west of Saint Jo, led north-northwest, turned west and crossed Farmer's Creek near Eagle Point, and continued west to Red River Station. The crossing at Farmer's Creek is now covered by Lake Nocona. Herds that approached Red River Station from the southwest passed west of Victoria Peak, later changed to Queen's Peak, and continued north along the west side of Salt Creek to Red River Station.[13]

Beginning in 1870, parts of Indian Territory were surveyed under the supervision of the commissioner of the US General Land Office using the Public Land Survey System, which divides land into divisions of township, range, and section. Several maps that date to the postbellum cattle drive period were located that are relevant, and the township lines that resulted from those surveys can be seen on the cited maps. The first occurrence of the Abilene Cattle Trail as a mapped, named route is found on the 1872 *Map of the Chickasaw*

Country and Contiguous Portions of the Indian Territory. The Abilene Cattle Trail led north from the Fort Sill and Texas Road about eight miles northwest of the fords on the Red River near Salt Creek. The trail stayed generally within six to eight miles east of the ninety-eighth meridian until it crossed the Little Washita River, then angled a little farther to the northeast as it approached the upper limit of the map at the Canadian River (fig. 23).[14]

Both the Abilene Cattle Trail and Chisholm's Trail appeared on the 1875 *Military Map of the Indian Territory*. This is the first appearance of Chisholm's Trail as a mapped, named route. Chisholm's Trail was designated on a segment of a trail that led northwest from the approximate location of Council Grove, a few miles downstream of Chisholm's Old Ranch. The trail led to the northwest and merged with the Abilene Cattle Trail near the Cimarron River downstream from Uncle John's Creek, near the present site of Kingfisher. The Abilene Cattle Trail led along the route described previously on the 1872 *Map of the Chickasaw Country and Contiguous Portions of the Indian Territory* north to the Canadian River. From the Canadian, the trail led north and crossed the North Canadian River in the vicinity of the present site of Yukon, merged with Chisholm's Cattle Trail, and crossed the Cimarron near Uncle John's Creek. The trail led past Turkey Creek, Skeleton Creek, and Nine Mile Creek; crossed the Salt Fork upstream of Nine Mile Creek; and then went on toward Caldwell (fig. 24).[15]

The designation of Chisholm's Trail was changed to Chisholm's Cattle Trail on the 1879 Department of the Interior map *Indian Territory*. The designated route of this trail remained the same: from the North Canadian River near Council Grove it headed northwest to the Cimarron River downstream of Uncle John's Creek, where it merged with the Abilene Cattle Trail. The route of the Abilene Cattle Trail also remained the same, from about eight miles northwest of the crossing at Red River Station north toward Caldwell. The name designation north of the Cimarron changed from the previous designation of Abilene Cattle Trail to Abilene Cattle Trail and Stage Road. These routes and name designations remained unchanged on subsequent Department of the Interior maps in 1883 and 1887.[16]

According to the 1879, 1883, and 1887 *Indian Territory* maps, a trail led north from the vicinity of Sivells Bend and Gainesville (the Gainesville Road) and split into two trails north of the Canadian River near the present site of Norman. One trail crossed the North Canadian River in the vicinity of Council Grove and merged with Chisholm's Cattle Trail, while the other merged with the Abilene Cattle Trail near the present site of Yukon. Chisholm's and the Abilene Cattle Trail then merged at the Cimarron. The Abilene Cattle Trail is designated by name multiple times along its length through Indian Territory, but Chisholm's Trail or Chisholm's Cattle Trail is designated only once, and only between the North Canadian and Cimarron Rivers (fig. 25). The Chisholm name was not extended to any of the network of trails south of the North Canadian River. The 1875, 1879, 1883, and 1887 maps were all compiled from military or US General Land Office surveys and records, and all are consistent regarding the name, route, and location of the Abilene Cattle Trail and Chisholm's Cattle Trail.

On an Oklahoma highway map, the route from Cooke County, Texas, passed through the present counties of Love, Carter, Murray, Garvin, McClain, Cleveland, Oklahoma, Canadian, Logan, and King-fisher. From the point that the Abilene Cattle Trail and Chisholm's Cattle Trail merged in Kingfisher County, the trail led through Garfield and Grant Counties, where the trail split into two separate legs, and entered Kansas in the vicinity of Caldwell. The route from the vicinity of Red River Station in Montague County passed through the present counties of Jefferson, Stephens, Grady, Canadian (where it merged with the western leg of the unnamed trail near Yukon), and Kingfisher, where it merged with Chisholm's Cattle Trail, and through Garfield and Grant Counties toward Caldwell. The route from Red River Station is generally along or parallel to US Highway 81 from near the Red River all the way to the Kansas border.[17]

The route north from Red River Station is also documented in a series of guide booklets published by the Kansas Pacific Railway from 1871 to 1875. These booklets were "For Gratuitous Distribution" to Texas cattlemen as an aid to navigation to the railheads in Kansas.[18] The booklets contained a detailed description of the route, including notations regarding streams, crossings, availability of wood and water, and other pertinent information. They also included a general map that showed a network of trails in Texas that converged at Red River Station and proceeded north. The descriptions of the route can be traced using landmarks on the 1879, 1883, or 1887 Department of the Interior maps. The 1874 version of *Guide Map of the Great Texas Cattle Trail from Red River Crossing to the Old Reliable Kansas Pacific Railway* listed landmarks that included Beaver Creek, Monument Rocks, Stinking Creek, Rush Creek, Little Washita River, Washita River, Walnut Creek, Canadian River, North Fork of the Canadian, Deer Creek, King Fisher Creek, Turkey Creek, Hackberry Creek, Skeleton Creek, Nine Mile Creek, Salt Fork, Pond Creek, and Bluff Creek.

Examples of notations in the guide books are:

Beaver Creek, Branch of, Total Distance [in miles from Red River]
15, Trail from Red River follows the divide through an open prairie, with an abundance of wood and water on the tributaries of
the Beaver. The stream being small, the crossing is always good
and safe. Good camping ground. Monument Rocks or Stinking Cr'k, Total Distance 30, Trail from Beaver Creek over high
rolling prairie; supply of wood and water abundant for camping
purposes; small stream with good crossing. Good camping
ground. . . . Little Washita, Distance 73, Trail from Rush Creek
greater part of the way through an old burnt Jack oak country.
No water for nine miles after leaving Rush Creek. Good road
and plenty of grass on north side of Little Washita. Good ford
and camping ground. . . . North Fork, Distance 116, Trail from
Canadian over a high rolling prairie. Camping grounds on north
side of river, with plenty wood and water. Good ford. . . . Turkey
Creek, Distance 149, Trail from Red Fork over rolling prairie, with
timber skirting east side. Small stream. Good camping ground,
with plenty wood and water. Take wood from here for camping
purposes. No wood at Hackberry. Supply store at this point.[19]

These landmarks follow the route of the trail marked on the *Indian
Territory* maps as the Abilene Cattle Trail. The trail exited Indian Territory in the vicinity of the present site of Caldwell, Kansas, in Sumner
County. A crew under the direction of Timothy Fletcher Hersey,
a civil engineer from Abilene, set out in the summer of 1867 to mark
a trail south from Abilene to the mouth of the Little Arkansas River.[20]
Drovers could easily follow the mounds of earth constructed by the
crew north across the plains to their destination at Abilene. After the
first herd followed the tracks of Black Beaver, Merrill, Emory, and
Chisholm, the trail would have been easy enough for subsequent
drovers to follow to intersect the route laid out by Hersey. They
intersected Hersey's extension at a crossing on the Arkansas River at
the present site of Wichita in Sedgwick County, passed through the
counties of Harvey and Marion, and ended at Abilene in Dickinson
County.

Competition between towns for herd traffic began rather quickly
after the initial surge of herds to Abilene during the summer of 1867.
An article appeared in the *Austin Republican* on April 28, 1868, that
encouraged the trade at Abilene, noting that Abilene was the location of "where the celebrated McCoy & Brothers have their superior
shipping and grazing arrangements." The citizens of Dickinson
County held a meeting on April 4, 1868, at Humbarger's Ford. They

resolved that farmers and citizens who objected to the cattle trade should withdraw their objection—that the trade was "beneficial to every permanent interest of our people"—and allow those engaged in the cattle trade "peaceable and undisturbed entry" into Dickinson County.[21]

Meanwhile, as the people of Dickinson County advertised the virtues of Abilene as a cattle destination, a letter appeared from a resident of Junction City in the *Dallas Herald* on May 16, 1868. The letter advised drovers to "avoid driving to Abilene, as the people are opposed to it in a measure," with an added note that "Abilene is a small place west, on the railroad." Indeed, less than a year earlier and prior to the arrival of the first Texas cattle herds Abilene was described as "a very small, dead place, consisting of about one dozen log huts—low, small, rude affairs, four-fifths of which were covered with dirt for roofing." The 1860 population of Dickinson County was only 378. With no major towns or business enterprise before the opening of Abilene as a transportation center, it is likely that the population of the county had increased only slightly prior to the summer of 1867. However, with a growing economy as a result of the railroad, the cattle business, and plenty of available land for grazing or farming, Dickinson County soon grew to a population of 3,043 people in 1870.[22]

Junction City, Kansas, also had railroad access in the summer of 1867, and in July it was reported that there were five thousand head of cattle within twenty miles of the town waiting on eastern buyers. Railroad construction across the southern plains of Kansas fueled competition between towns to attract cattle business as new shipping points were opened. As the railroads opened new opportunities for potential markets, herd destinations grew to include Newton, Wichita, Ellsworth, and Caldwell. The town of Newton grew around a site selected by the Atchison, Topeka, and Santa Fe Railway in the summer of 1870 near the terminus of their track and the nearby cattle trail. Settlers began to arrive at the new site approximately sixty-five miles south of Abilene by the spring of 1871. On June 2, 1871, the *Emporia News* reported that twenty houses were almost finished, lumber was available for more construction, and large numbers of Texas cattle were grazing on the prairie outside of town awaiting shipment on the AT & SF Railroad.[23]

Since Newton was, for all practical purposes, located on the trail, herds were diverted easily. By mid-July an estimated fifty thousand head of Texas cattle awaited shipment on daily trains from Newton to Topeka en route to Chicago. The AT & SF extended a branch south from Newton to Wichita in 1872 and another branch from Newton to the west. The Wichita stockyards were completed early in June. Eighteen carloads of cattle were shipped from Wichita on June 8, 1872, bound for Chicago, this being the first rail shipment of cattle from Wichita. As of June 21, 1872, eighteen thousand head of Texas cattle had been sold at Wichita and 110 carloads of cattle had been shipped. On October 24, 1872, the *Wichita City Eagle* reported that Abilene and Newton had previously been the main shipping points for Texas cattle; Wichita was poised to become the main cattle market.[24]

Another article described how Joseph G. McCoy, who had engineered the cattle trade at Abilene, and a Mr. Bryden were hired to divert the cattle business to Wichita. This may have been a reference to James Bryden, a cattle dealer from Corpus Christi, Texas. By that time the cattle trade at Abilene was all but dead, and the famous Drover's Cottage was in the process of being relocated to Ellsworth. During the week preceding November 14, 1872, twenty-five carloads of Texas cattle were shipped daily, and more than 125,000 head of cattle had been shipped or driven from Wichita over the summer season.[25]

The *White Cloud Kansas Chief* reported on September 14, 1871, that Texas cattlemen were driving to Ellsworth and buying large ranches in order to keep the farmers out of the prime grazing land around Ellsworth. The arrival of the first herd of Texas cattle in the 1872 season in Ellsworth was reported on May 23, 1872, by the *Leavenworth Weekly Times*. J. V. Vinton, W. B. McCullam, and G. Mathias arrived with one thousand head of cattle each. The arrival of these herds signaled another shift in herd traffic patterns. A lengthy article that appeared in the March 20, 1873, edition of the *Wichita City Eagle* suggested that Ellsworth would be the destination of the largest number of herds in the coming season.[26]

The first settlers arrived in the vicinity of the present site of Caldwell in 1870. The town had its beginnings as a trading post near the cattle trail. As traffic on the trail increased, local commerce increased. The citizens of Caldwell held a meeting on February 20, 1875, in order to "protect their interest derived from their trade with drovers driving over the Texas cattle trail." They adopted resolutions to condemn the action of parties who attempted to discourage drovers from driving Texas cattle through Sumner County and encouraged the driving of Texas cattle through Sumner County on the Texas and Wichita Trail (fig. 26). They asked the city of Wichita to exert influence on the Texas drovers to use said trail and to publicize the resulting resolution in certain newspapers. A few years later, the Atchison, Topeka, and Santa Fe Railway extended the Wichita branch south to Caldwell, and the road was completed on May 31, 1880.[27]

New railheads brought new business opportunities and growth in local economies, which, in turn, attracted more people. More farmers settled on the open plains around the railheads, and drovers had to contend with the "nesters" as well as the changing quarantine laws. Each new cow town was dependent upon the railroad and followed the same cycle: they sprouted, bloomed, prospered, faded, and were replaced by a new bloom elsewhere just like the prairie wildflowers. There was more than one way to navigate through Indian Territory, and with each new shipping point for Texas cattle or obstacle that arose, drovers simply diverted their herds toward the new destination and a new trail appeared or another branch was added to the trail. Chisholm's Trail as mapped by the US Army and the Department of the Interior during its historical period of use was less than one hundred miles in length, yet the name later became famous and arbitrarily applied to other cattle trails.

10

Chisum's Trail

ABOUT THE SAME TIME that Chisholm's Trail came into being north of the Red River, other events were happening south of the Red in Texas. John Simpson Chisum began to move cattle from his ranch in Denton County southwest to another ranch in Coleman County. While Jesse Chisholm was conducting business between his trading posts in the northern part of Indian Territory and southern Kansas, John Chisum, Charles Goodnight, and Oliver Loving were driving cattle from Chisum's ranch in Coleman County into New Mexico Territory.

John S. Chisum was born in Hardeman County, Tennessee, in 1824. He came with his family to Red River County, Texas, at the age of thirteen in 1837. His father, Claiborne Chisum, bought some land west of the present site of Paris, Texas, and moved the family west in 1838 to what became Lamar County. Claiborne Chisum was involved in an expedition to pursue and punish Indians for a series of raids in what became known as the Battle of Village Creek in 1841. John stayed behind to guard the family home. The nickname Cow John had been bestowed on John as a child; it seems that he had a cousin and an uncle with the same name, and the nickname was given to reduce confusion. While the nickname had nothing to do at the time with Chisum's abilities with cattle, it proved to be prophetic.[1]

Chisum worked at several occupations and was elected county clerk of Lamar County in 1852. He looked to something more profitable, however, and began to acquire land in Denton County in 1853. In 1854, at the age of thirty, he took on a partner and went into the cattle business. He reportedly built up a herd of about twelve hundred head of cattle by the end of 1854 and located his operation along Clear Creek in northwestern Denton County. Chisum was exempted from

Confederate service during the Civil War, likely because his services were needed as a cattle raiser and for protection on the frontier. He returned to Denton County from a cattle drive to Vicksburg in 1862 to find the prairie burned and his horses gone. Shortly after that he turned his attention southwest toward the Concho River and New Mexico Territory.[2]

One of Chisum's future business associates arrived in Texas in 1845. After coming to Texas as a child, Charles Goodnight eventually settled in Palo Pinto County. Goodnight and his stepbrother, Wes Sheek, formed a partnership in 1856 and kept a herd of 430 head of cattle on shares. Every fourth calf was their pay, and they understood that it would be several years before they realized a profit. The cattle, gathered from central Texas, were as wild as the cattle along the Rio Grande and would not hesitate to attack a mounted rider. Most were captured at night or early in the morning after they ventured out of the heavily timbered bottomlands. In spring of 1857, Goodnight and Sheek drove their herd from the present site of Somervell County up the Brazos to Black Springs in the Keechi Valley in Palo Pinto County, where they established a more permanent camp. The following year they built a cabin, and Goodnight moved his mother and stepfather to their ranch. Goodnight also worked as a freighter, then kept to the cattle business after Sheek married.[3]

Another of Chisum's future acquaintances, Oliver Loving, brought his family from Kentucky to Texas in 1843. They settled for a short time in Lamar County, where Loving worked as a farmer and freight hauler. By 1855 they had moved farther west, where Loving established a ranch in the Keechi Valley in what was to become Palo Pinto County. Goodnight and Loving met sometime in 1857 or 1858. Loving had driven several herds to Louisiana and was already known in the Keechi Valley area as a knowledgeable cowman when he and John Durkee drove a herd from Palo Pinto County to Illinois in 1858. The Colorado Gold Rush began in 1859, and in 1860 Loving and John Dawson left the Keechi with one thousand steers bound for Denver, Colorado. According to Goodnight, he went along with Loving, Dawson, and their crew as far as the Red River. Loving and Dawson crossed Indian Territory, struck the Arkansas River near the Great Bend, and followed the Arkansas to the Pueblo area, where they wintered the herd. War erupted in April 1861 while Loving was in Denver selling his cattle. Union authorities refused to let him leave Colorado; however, friends such as Kit Carson interceded on his behalf, and he was eventually allowed to leave. He returned to Palo Pinto County in August 1861.[4]

The exact route of Loving's drive to Colorado is unknown. Based on Goodnight's description, it seems likely that the herd headed north from the Keechi along the western edge of the Cross Timbers through Jack County, crossed the Red River somewhere between Salt Creek and the Little Wichita River, continued north toward the Great Bend, and followed the Arkansas River into Colorado. Depending upon where they crossed the Red and where they struck the Arkansas, it is possible that Loving and Dawson drove this herd over a portion of the trail that appeared on the 1872 *Map of the Chickasaw Country and Contiguous Portions of the Indian Territory* as the Abilene Cattle Trail.[5]

Loving and Chisum joined forces during the summer of 1862 to recover stolen horses. Loving had reason to believe that Union troops in Colorado had paid Indians to cross the Red River and steal horses to disrupt the war effort. Both men had lost their horse herds to thieves, and Loving approached Chisum with his suspicions. The two men, along with a dozen of Chisum's ranch hands, located the Comanche camp where their horses were held and recovered them. Loving told Chisum that he and Goodnight planned to drive their cattle herd west, cross the Pecos River, and then go north into New Mexico Territory. Chisum scouted a route, began moving cattle from his Denton County ranch to an area near Mukewater Creek in Coleman County in 1863, and made his first drive into New Mexico in 1864. Also in 1864, Goodnight moved cattle to a new range along Elm Creek in Throckmorton County.[6]

Goodnight gathered cattle from the Elm Creek range and prepared to leave in the spring of 1866 to drive a herd to Fort Sumner by way of Horsehead Crossing on the Pecos. During preparations for this drive, Goodnight had the idea to convert a heavy-duty wagon into a mobile kitchen. He bought a government freight wagon, took it to a carpenter in Parker County, and had it rebuilt with seasoned bois d' arc, which was tougher than any other wood that was available. He replaced the wooden axles with iron axles and included a bucket of tallow for greasing. His design was successful, and the mess wagon, later called the chuck wagon, was copied by others and became a familiar sight along the trails. Goodnight designed the first chuck box, which had a hinged lid and folding leg that lowered to form the cook's table. His design is still in use.[7]

Goodnight passed Loving's camp while traveling to Weatherford to purchase supplies. The two men discussed the drive and decided to combine their herds. They left from a point approximately twenty-five miles southwest of Fort Belknap with two thousand head of cattle and eighteen well-armed men. To travel on a direct route northwest to Colorado would have meant crossing the Comancheria, where there was a high risk of losing the herd, and perhaps their lives, to the Comanches and Kiowas. Instead, they traveled southwest, generally along the route of the Butterfield Overland Mail route, to Horsehead Crossing. They passed Camp Cooper, Fort Phantom Hill, Buffalo Gap, and Fort Chadbourne; crossed the North Concho River approximately twenty miles above the present site of San Angelo; watered at the headwaters of the Middle Concho River; passed through Castle Gap; traveled along the Butterfield route to Horsehead Crossing on the Pecos River; then followed the general route of the Pecos north into New Mexico Territory. They found a ready market for their cattle at Fort Sumner, where the Navajos and Mescalero Apaches on the reservation were on the brink of starvation. The stock contractors at Fort Sumner bought the steers but were not interested in the stock cattle, so Goodnight and Loving drove the remainder of the herd—about seven hundred to eight hundred head of cows and calves—farther up the Pecos. After they reached good grass and rested for a few days, they decided that Loving would take the herd north into Colorado, while Goodnight would return to Texas to make another drive before winter.[8]

In August of that year Chisum, Goodnight, and Loving left Trickham in Coleman County with a herd bound for the Bosque Redondo Reservation near Fort Sumner. Chisum continued to run cattle between his Trickham ranch and Bosque Grande, approximately forty miles south of Fort Sumner. In summer of 1867, while Chisum was establishing his ranch at Bosque Grande, Goodnight and Loving prepared for their third drive together. Loving gathered his herd from the Keechi, Goodnight gathered his herd from the Elm Creek range, and they arranged to meet at Cribb's Station, which was located on the Butterfield Trail southwest of Fort Belknap near Elm Creek. It was on this trip that Oliver Loving died of wounds received when he and "One-Armed" Bill Wilson, whom Goodnight described as "the clearest headed man in the outfit," were ambushed on the Pecos south of Fort Sumner.[9]

This trip was plagued with bad luck almost from the start—or, as Goodnight later said, "the sign just wasn't right." The cattle were exceptionally spooky and stampeded nearly every night. From the vicinity of Camp Cooper to Horsehead Crossing, they endured several Indian attacks. One drover was struck behind the ear with an arrow during an attack on the Clear Fork of the Brazos River. The arrow point, made of hoop iron, embedded almost up to the shaft in his skull. The wound would have been fatal if left alone; however, Goodnight was able to remove the arrow with a pair of shoe pinchers while two men held the victim down. The injured man made a full recovery.[10]

Loving and Wilson left the herd after they reached the Pecos River to ride ahead to arrange the sale of the herd at Santa Fe. Loving's impatience to reach Santa Fe proved fatal when the two men were attacked by Comanches on the tableland north of the Black River, and Loving suffered bullet wounds in his arm and side. At Loving's insistence, Wilson escaped, made his way back toward the herd, and was found by Goodnight three days later. Unknown to Wilson, Loving also escaped and was taken by travelers to Fort Sumner. When told of the events, Goodnight found the ambush site and located Loving in Fort Sumner. Loving's wounded arm was infected with gangrene, and the arm was amputated. Two nights later, the artery ruptured and could not be tied off as before. Loving told Goodnight, "I regret that I have to be laid away in a foreign country," and he was assured that he would be laid to rest near his home. Twenty-two days after he was wounded, Loving died on September 25, 1867. He was buried temporarily at Fort Sumner. In February 1868, escorted by Goodnight and other Texas cowmen, Loving's remains were hauled in a mule-drawn wagon back up their trail to Weatherford, Texas. A Masonic funeral service was held, and Loving was buried on a hilltop overlooking the town. While it is not known for certain, the circumstances of Loving's death and the lonely funeral procession back to Parker County likely influenced the Goodnight-Loving name for that trail.[11]

From its origin near Fort Belknap in Young County, the Goodnight-Loving route passed through the present Texas counties of Throckmorton, Stephens, Shackelford, Jones, Taylor, Nolan, Runnels, Coke, Tom Green, Schleicher, Crockett, Irion, Reagan, Upton, Crane, Ward, Loving, and Reeves. Goodnight described traveling up the east bank of the Pecos River and crossing to the west bank at Pope's Crossing, approximately one mile south of the Texas–New Mexico border.[12] The Pecos could also be crossed at Horsehead Crossing, which would place a portion of the trail along the west bank of the river in Pecos County.

Chisum's exact route from his ranch in Denton County is unknown. He reportedly scouted a route between Fort Belknap and Fort Mason before moving his cattle from Denton County to Trickham in Coleman County in 1863.[13] It is likely that Chisum's route passed west from Denton County, intersected the Butterfield Trail in Wise County, and followed or paralleled the Butterfield through the counties of Jack, Young, Throckmorton, Shackelford, and Jones through Buffalo Gap in Taylor County and into Coleman County. From Chisum's Coleman County ranch, Horsehead Crossing could be reached by following the Middle Concho or the South Concho through Castle Gap.

From Pope's Crossing the trail led through the present New Mexico counties of Eddy, Chaves, and De Baca and ended at Fort Sumner. Loving's route north from Fort Sumner passed Las Vegas and Raton, crossed the Arkansas River near Pueblo, Colorado, and ended in the vicinity of Denver.[14] This route passed through the present New Mexico counties of Guadalupe, San Miguel, Mora, and Colfax and likely passed through the present Colorado counties of Las Animas, Pueblo, El Paso, Elbert, Arapahoe, and Denver.

Although Charles Goodnight and Oliver Loving were later credited with blazing the trail that carried their name, it was John S. Chisum who drove a herd of Texas longhorns along much of this route into New Mexico Territory two years before Goodnight and Loving. James Patterson, one of the stock contractors who bought the steers from Goodnight and Loving during their first drive in 1866, also drove cattle to Fort Sumner before Goodnight and Loving. According to a letter dated September 2, 1865, from Brigadier General James H. Carleton to Captain William R. Shoemaker, Patterson was a stock contractor furnishing Texas cattle to Forts Sumner and Stanton. The letter states, "It is desirable to encourage the introduction of cattle from Texas to New Mexico now partly reduced in stock from Indian depredations—and this enterprise of getting cattle across the plains from that state which has already been twice successfully accomplished by Mr. Patterson, is the beginning only, it is hoped, of a great and profitable trade." Patterson had already driven herds from Texas to the Fort Sumner area twice by September 1865, at least nine months ahead of Goodnight and Loving. He presumably used the same route along the Pecos for the same reasons that Chisum, Goodnight, and Loving chose it.[15]

The route from Denton County, Texas, into New Mexico has also been referred to as Chisum's Trail, the Chisum Trail, or Chisum's Western Trail. The similarity of the names led to confusion between this trail and Chisholm's Trail, later called the Chisholm Trail, which led to the railheads of central Kansas. Loving's route north from Fort Sumner to Denver has sometimes been called the Loving Trail. Goodnight later extended that trail to the Platte River and beyond. An 1886 newspaper article referenced a short trail called the Goodnight Trail from Floyd County, Texas, to Deaf Smith County. The entire route from around Fort Belknap to the Pecos River and north into New Mexico and Colorado eventually came to be called the Goodnight-Loving Trail (fig. 17). Patterson's role in the development of the trail and the expansion of the cattle business into New Mexico has been mostly overlooked.[16]

11

The Fort Griffin
or Dodge City
Trail

DURING THE 1930S Chisholm Trail markers were installed along the route of the cattle trail that passed Fort Griffin, crossed the Red River in Wilbarger County, Texas, and led to Dodge City, Kansas. These markers were erected by an individual who had his own ideas about the cattle trails, financed his own trail marking projects, and laid out his markers with no additional historical oversight. The problem is that this trail was known as the Fort Griffin, Dodge City, or Western Trail and was located over one hundred miles west of Chisholm's Trail. The Chisholm Trail name became so famous that some later applied the term to any cattle trail, and these markers are examples of the incorrect application of the name to another trail. The two trails were distinctly different. Although their historical periods of use overlapped, the Fort Griffin Trail was used for a longer duration, was greater in length, and carried a larger volume of cattle than did the Chisholm Trail. From around Bexar County, Texas, the routes were separate, and each trail led to Kansas destinations that were more than 150 miles apart.[1]

Anglo settlement continued to creep westward during the 1860s and 1870s. Livestock quarantine laws changed amid fears of Texas fever as new areas were settled. The army attempted to keep emigrants out of Indian lands, but the flood of settlers was overwhelming. Treaties were negotiated—and usually broken in short order. The Plains Indians fought to keep their traditional way of life, and for their survival, but they faced superior technology and overwhelming odds. When a warrior fell in battle, that was a generation lost, but when a soldier fell, he was simply replaced by more soldiers. The army employed tactics learned during the Civil War to defeat the elusive enemy on the plains and eventually cleared the way for more settlement. Increased military presence meant an increased demand for beef to feed the troops. Destruction of the bison and restriction of the Indians to reservations also increased the demand for beef. When the bison disappeared, the fight was over. The introduction to the public of a successful design for two-strand barbed wire placed a new obstacle on the cattle trails. All of these factors played a part in the location and timing of the railheads and the movement of cattle to these destinations.

By 1860, settlements had pushed west of the 97th meridian in Kansas, just a few miles east of the present site of Abilene. The western edge of the frontier line of the country lay about thirty-nine miles east of the present site of Dodge City. Between 1860 and 1870, the population of Kansas almost tripled to 364,399, and the frontier line crept a few miles farther to about twenty-five miles east of the present site of Dodge City. This was well into the lands between the 95th and 101st meridians, which had been envisioned a few decades earlier as a Permanent Indian Frontier, where "Indians would be forever removed from the path of the advancing settlements" and where "all white men except properly licensed traders" would be forbidden. But the settlers kept coming, and the frontier line of the country edged further westward.[2]

Conflicts with the Plains Indians slowed the formation of new settlements in northern and western Kansas and Nebraska. The Sioux, Cheyennes, and Arapahos still roamed the plains of northern and western Kansas, much of western Nebraska, the Dakota and Montana Territories, and north into Canada. Their resistance was fueled by incidents such as the massacre at Sand Creek in November 1864, repeated incursions by white settlers into tribal territory, and the establishment of a road from Fort Laramie to the gold fields of Idaho and Montana with military outposts for protection. This route was to pass through the Powder River country, which was considered by the Sioux to be their "best hunting ground and the last one yet free from the encroachments of the white man." The Comanches and Kiowas still controlled much of the Comancheria, which included eastern Colorado, southwestern Nebraska, western Kansas, south through western Indian Territory and deep into Texas. Travel was possible in relative safety from the cattle towns of central Kansas east toward Leavenworth and Kansas City, but the cattle trail north initially went no farther than Abilene because of two factors: danger of attack and absence of a cattle market north of Abilene for several years (fig. 26). By December 1867 the Union Pacific Railroad had laid rails from Omaha west along the Platte River valley across the state of Nebraska. The Nebraska cattle markets followed a few years later.[3]

General William T. Sherman proposed to restrict the Plains Indians to either north of the Platte River or south of the Arkansas River in order to provide a wide corridor for railroad construction to the west coast. Sherman knew that the plains tribes were dependent on the bison. He also knew that the strategy to interrupt supply lines and destroy commissaries had been successful in the 1864 Savannah Campaign to compromise the Confederates' ability and will to fight. Sherman wrote, "As long as these Indians can hunt the buffalo and antelope within the described limits we will have the depredations of last Summer and worse yet, the exaggerations of danger raised by our own people, often for a very base purpose." General Philip H. Sheridan wrote that the vast herds of buffalo that covered the plains provided hostiles with a ready food supply, and they were not hampered by the usual problems of feeding an army on the move. Sheridan decided to confine military operations during the grazing and hunting seasons to protection of overland travel routes and settlements, and "then, when winter came, to fall upon the savages relentlessly, for in that season their ponies would be thin, and weak from lack of food, and in the cold and snow, without strong ponies to transport their villages and plunder, their movements would be so much impeded that the troops could overtake them."[4]

Over the next few years the combination of military campaigns, railroad construction, and encroaching settlement reduced the range of the bison, upon which the Plains Indians depended for sustenance. These conditions in turn resulted in crowded reservation lands, especially where the army could not keep the settlers out. The range of the once free-roaming people was reduced by Anglo migration and industrialization. The army's mission was to protect the reservation lands from encroachment by settlers and to protect the settlers from violence. Sheridan complained to Sherman:

> We cannot avoid being abused by one side or the other. If we allow the defenseless people of the frontier to be scalped and ravished, we are burnt in effigy and execrated as soulless monsters, insensitive to the sufferings of humanity. If the Indians are punished to give security to these people, we are the same soulless monsters from the other side. . . . During the last year, as soon as I withdrew the troops from the Sac and Fox reservation, the emigrants took possession. A flood of emigration, almost ten thousand strong, moved in solid mass and occupied the Osage

reservation because there were no troops there to keep them off. All the other reservations on which the Indian may yet be placed will be lost in the same manner unless guarded by the military.[5]

Sherman acknowledged the situation and responded: "The army cannot resist the tide of emigration that is flowing toward those Indian lands, nor is it in our province to determine the question of boundaries. When called upon, we must, to the extent of our power, protect the settlers, and on proper demand we have also to protect the Indian lands against the intrusion of the settlers. Thus we are placed between two fires—a most unpleasant dilemma from which we cannot escape—and we must sustain the officers on the spot who fulfill their orders."[6]

As a result of increased depredations during the early 1870s, the army grew less dependent on peaceful methods to resolve these problems. Trouble was more frequent when hunting parties left the reservations to hunt bison. On one hand, the presence of the railroads threatened the hunting grounds and must be opposed, while on the other hand, the railroads were the link between the eastern and western states and must be defended. Sherman reportedly proposed to "shoot buffaloes until they become too scarce to support the redskins."[7] Sheridan echoed a similar opinion. The army did not pursue an official policy of exterminating the buffalo; written orders to that effect were apparently never issued. However, certain officers did not enforce treaty provisions to prohibit access to hunting grounds and sometimes organized civilian hunts.

During one such accommodation in 1871, a party of civilian businessmen guided by William F. Cody left Fort McPherson and killed over six hundred bison. The tongues, which were considered a delicacy, and a few choice cuts of meat were kept, and the rest of the carcasses were left to rot on the plains. In another, perhaps more famous instance, Sheridan hosted the Grand Duke Alexis of Russia for a hunt on the plains in the vicinity of North Platte, Nebraska. The Union Pacific Railroad provided a special train from Omaha to North Platte for the event. The group included Alexis and his entourage, Sheridan and his entourage, two companies of infantry, two companies of cavalry, a regimental band, and supporting staff. "Hundreds of buffalo" were killed during the five-day hunt.[8]

Sherman toured the military outposts in Texas in spring of 1871. His small traveling party was observed in Young County by a party of Kiowas, who, seeing nothing of interest, let them pass unmolested. The next day several teamsters were killed when their wagon train was ambushed by the same party near the present site of Graham, Texas. Henry Warren, who was killed in the raid, was the freight contractor, and this incident became known as the Warren Wagon Train Raid. A teamster who managed to escape reported the news to Sherman at Fort Richardson. An enraged Sherman immediately ordered Colonel Ranald S. Mackenzie to take the Fourth Cavalry and bring order to the area.[9]

That same year, a commercial market for buffalo hides was born when a method for converting them into commercial leather was discovered. Suddenly hides became worth a price of one dollar to three dollars each. The same railroad companies that carried Texas cattle to eastern markets now carried loads of buffalo hides east from the plains. Hide hunters swarmed western Kansas, and Sheridan found that he had an unanticipated ally to end the war on the plains. Within two years Lieutenant Colonel Richard I. Dodge noted: "Where there were myriads of buffalo the year before, there were now myriads of carcasses. The air was foul with a sickening stench, and the vast plain, which only a short twelvemonth before teemed with animal life, was a dead, solitary, putrid desert." With the herds of the central plains decimated, the hide hunters looked south toward the herds of the southern plains. The Medicine Lodge Treaty of 1867 had reserved the right to hunt on lands south of the Arkansas River for the Arapahos, Cheyennes, Comanches, and Kiowas. The hide hunters encountered no resistance from the army in southwestern Kansas but were hesitant to cross the Cimarron River. Like Sheridan, Dodge believed that the state of war on the plains would exist only as long as the buffalo existed, and he offered no resistance to the hide hunters.[10]

A group of hide hunters was attacked in June 1874 by several hundred Cheyennes, Comanches, and Kiowas at Adobe Walls, located on the North Canadian River in the Texas Panhandle. The hide men knew that, being south of the Arkansas River, they were in violation of the Medicine Lodge Treaty; however, when the hunting party left Fort Dodge the army did nothing to stop them. A rider was sent for help, and the governor of Kansas appealed to General John Pope to send relief troops. Pope refused, later justifying his actions by stating that the trading post at Adobe Walls "was put there to enable the white hunters to invade unlawfully the Indian reservation." On the third afternoon of the battle a group of warriors appeared on a bluff east of Adobe Walls Creek. William "Billy" Dixon took aim with a .50-caliber Sharps rifle, squeezed off a shot, and one of the group fell from his horse, apparently dead. Dixon later stated that two other Indians rushed out from cover and recovered the body. The range of this famous shot has been variously estimated at distances up to a mile, but Dixon himself estimated the range at "not far from three-fourths of a mile."[11] Dixon's shot effectively ended the battle, for the Indians withdrew shortly thereafter.

This battle, known as the Second Battle of Adobe Walls, marked the beginning of the Red River War of 1874–75. Mackenzie's troops later fought a running battle in Tule Canyon and Palo Duro Canyon in which the Comanche horse herd was captured (to be subsequently slaughtered) and their abandoned camps and supplies were burned. With no horses and no supplies other than what they might have carried during the battle, there was little choice for the Kiowas and Cheyennes but to surrender and go to the reservation. This series of conflicts ended with the surrender at Fort Sill of Quanah Parker and the Quahadi band of Comanches in 1875; they were the last holdouts on the southern plains. The Texas Panhandle, along with the rest of the Comancheria, was now safer for Texas cattlemen.

The army required supplies to sustain the troops stationed on the plains, and in May 1870 advertisements appeared that solicited sealed-bid proposals to supply "beef cattle on the hoof" to troops under the jurisdiction of the headquarters, Department of the Platte, located at Forts Kearney, McPherson, Sedgwick, Russell, Laramie, Fetterman, Sanders, Steele, and Bridger; Camps Douglas and Brown; North Platte Station; and Miner's Delight. In July 1870 a cattle market opened in Colfax County at Schuyler, Nebraska. The *Nebraska Advertiser* reported that Schuyler would be the Nebraska headquarters of the Texas cattle trade. Sixteen carloads of cattle were shipped on July 16 to Chicago on the Union Pacific Railroad, with sixteen thousand head of cattle reported on the plains near Schuyler. During the cattle driving season of 1870, it was reported that twenty-seven thousand head of cattle were sold at Schuyler and that forty thousand more could have been sold if available.[12] The market at Schuyler could be reached by keeping to a route between Abilene and Ellsworth, through or around Smith County, Kansas, which was the western edge of the quarantine line in Kansas at that time, and on to Colfax County. This route would have been feasible until the quarantine line in Kansas shifted west in 1876.

The railroads continued to push west across southern Kansas. In July 1875 the *Wichita City Eagle* reported that the cattle trade had been forced out of Wichita. The town's population had grown to three thousand people. Despite its advantages and status as the headquarters of the Texas cattle trade, Wichita would soon be the former headquarters. The industry that had put Wichita on the map was forced to move to a new location because the town had grown. The new location was Dodge City, located on the Arkansas River near Fort Dodge in Ford County, well west of the quarantine line that had been set by the Kansas legislature in 1872.[13]

By the end of 1872, track had been laid by the Atchison, Topeka and Santa Fe Railroad from Newton west to the Colorado border. This brought the railroad to the small settlement that had developed near Fort Dodge. In May 1876 the *Leavenworth Weekly Times* reported the expected arrival of the first herds at Dodge City, followed by the prospects of an estimated three hundred thousand head of cattle by summer's end. The AT & SF charged the same rates to transport cattle from Dodge City as from Wichita. The cattle trade was anticipated to be a boon to Dodge: "The grazing being better and the distance to drive less from Western Texas, it is altogether reasonable to suppose that nearly all the cattle, for the next two years, will be shipped from Dodge City." The new destination of Dodge City was about 150 miles west of the previous destination of Wichita. As the destination moved to the west, drovers seeking a more direct route from their origin points in Texas shifted the trails to the west. As the herd traffic patterns changed, the prairie around Wichita was quickly taken up by farmers, and the sight of thousands of grazing cattle was soon replaced by grain fields, which brought a prosperous grain trade to Wichita.[14]

In March 1876 the Kansas legislature approved an act to amend Section 2, Chapter 195 of the 1872 law, further restricting the movement of Texas cattle within the state. The 1872 quarantine boundary had been set generally along a zigzag line from southern Sumner County north along the sixth principal meridian to the Arkansas River, along the Arkansas to the west line of Rice County, to the southwest corner of Osborne County, and to the northwest corner of Smith County. The 1876 amendment changed the boundary to a line from the southwest corner of Sumner County north to a line between Township 27 and Township 28 in Sedgwick County to the western line of Kiowa County; north along the western boundaries of Kiowa, Edwards, Pawnee, Rush, Ellis, and Rooks Counties to the southern line of Phillips County; along the southern line of the counties of Phillips and Norton to Decatur County; and to the northeastern corner of Decatur County. This action closed most of the state to Texas cattle. The area between these boundary lines west to the state line was specified as the quarantine grounds for cattle from Texas and Indian Territory. It was illegal to drive cattle from Texas or Indian Territory east of the quarantine line unless requirements for quarantine had been satisfied. Texas cattle could be shipped in rail cars from a point west of the quarantine, or dead line, through restricted counties.[15]

By 1874 taxes and tolls for passage through Indian Territory had apparently become such a nuisance to cattlemen that the secretary of the interior was called upon by John J. Ingalls to designate a strip of land dedicated to the driving of livestock. The proposal was to authorize a strip one and one-half miles wide from the mouth of Cache Creek in Baylor County, Texas, past Fort Sill and Fort Cobb to the mouth of the Walnut River for military, commercial, and postal purposes. The road was "to be kept open to driving stock and transit of merchandise free from any charge forever."[16] No action was taken, and the road was never officially designated.

The Indian reservation populations grew as the bison herds of the central plains were wiped out and more Indians became dependent on the federal government for sustenance. John T. Lytle contracted to supply a herd of thirty-five hundred steers to the Red Cloud Agency in Nebraska during the summer of 1874. According to Frank Collinson, a drover who worked for Lytle, they left Medina County, Texas, on March 16, 1874, with eighteen men, twenty-five hundred steers, and approximately one hundred horses. They acquired more cattle in Mason County, and set out for Fort Griffin with over thirty-six hundred steers. From Medina County they passed Camp Verde in Kerr County and Comanche Creek in Mason County, resupplied at Fort Griffin, and rested for a few days nearby. Since this was the first herd to travel this route, and the country between Fort Griffin and Camp Supply was basically unknown to cattlemen, General Ranald S. Mackenzie furnished a scout to guide Lytle to Camp Supply in Indian Territory. From Camp Supply there was a marked trail to Fort Dodge. They crossed the South Platte River near Sterling, Colorado, and the North Platte River near Camp Clarke. From Camp Clarke another marked government trail led to the Red Cloud Agency near Camp Robinson. The herd was delivered by August 1, and Lytle received an average of thirty-six dollars per head. No bison were seen between the Arkansas River and the Red Cloud Agency.[17]

Another development occurred in November 1874 that had a profound effect on the trail drives and livestock business. Joseph Glidden was awarded a patent for two-strand barbed wire. His design became the most successful of many barbed wire designs. By the spring of 1875 advertisements for Glidden's Barbed Wire Fence began to appear in newspapers throughout the country.[18] Within the next ten years, Texas cattlemen felt the effects of Glidden's invention as

Glidden's barbed wire fence played a major role in the demise of the cattle trailing business.

Lytle continued to drive herds along the same route. In spring of 1876, other herds followed much of this route to reach the new railhead at Dodge City. On June 1, 1876, the *Leavenworth Weekly Times* reported that six or eight large herds had traveled the new cattle trail, with word of an additional herd arriving almost daily. Later that same month, the Atchison, Topeka and Santa Fe began construction on the stockyards at Dodge City, which were described as the largest and best in the state. The new stockyards included feed pens, watering pens, branding pens, windmill, tank, watering system, barn, stables, and offices, "affording every accommodation the most fastidious stock man could ask."[19]

The most direct trail route from the southernmost Texas county remained basically unchanged: through the present counties of Cameron, Willacy, Hidalgo, Brooks, Kenedy, Kleberg, Nueces, Jim Wells, San Patricio, Live Oak, Bee, Goliad, Karnes, Wilson, and Bexar. From Bexar County the main route led through the present counties of Kendall, Kerr, Kimble, Menard, Concho, McCulloch, Coleman, Callahan, Shackelford, Throckmorton, Baylor, and Wilbarger. Within a few years the trail route diverged in Live Oak County and led through the present counties of McMullen, La Salle, Dimmit, Zavala, Uvalde, and Edwards, joining the main route in Kimble County. Watering stops have been reported that also place a trail route in the present counties of Gillespie, Llano, Mason, San Saba, and Taylor. According to Roessler's 1874 map of Texas, the route through the counties of Kimble, Menard, McCulloch, and Coleman was generally in open country just to the west of a dense belt of blackjack and post oaks that once covered most of Mason County and extended in a narrow belt to the north into McCulloch and Coleman Counties, along where the Cross Timbers and Rolling Plains ecosystems converge. This route would have avoided the mesquite that covered most of San Saba County and extended north into southern Brown County (fig. 27). Trails also led through adjacent counties as herds funneled from their origin points toward their destinations.[20]

According to the 1881 *Map of Texas Showing Routes of Transportation of Cattle*, a Department of the Interior map, the Western or Fort Griffin Trail to Fort Dodge is indicated generally along or parallel to the route described in the previous paragraph (fig. 17). This map shows the main trail's southernmost point in Duval County, with the route passing through the counties of McMullen, Atascosa, Medina, Bandera, Kerr, Gillespie, Mason, McCulloch, Coleman, Callahan,

Shackelford, Throckmorton, Baylor, and Wilbarger. Another origin point is indicated in Refugio County, and that branch passed through Bee County to join the main route in Atascosa County. A third trail leg is indicated in Zavala County, which passed through the northwest corner of Frio County and joined the main route in Medina County. The 1885 Bureau of Statistics map, *The Range and Ranch Cattle Area of the United States, 1884,* indicates the Fort Griffin and Dodge City Trail to Dodge City and Ogallala from Bandera north generally along the same route to Doan's Store in Wilbarger County (fig. 2). These two maps are the only known maps that show designated cattle trails in Texas with provenance to the historical period of the cattle drives.[21]

During the historical period of the postwar cattle drives, the North Fork of the Red River was considered to be the Texas border. Briefly, Texas claimed ownership of the area between the North Fork of the Red River and the one-hundredth meridian based on the Adams-Onís Treaty of 1819. A map compiled by John Melish in 1818 was considered at the time to accurately delineate the US borders and was specified as a supporting document in Article 3 of the treaty. The map described the northern border of Spanish territory along the Red River, and thus the northern border of Texas. The Prairie Dog Town Fork of the Red River was undiscovered at the time of the Melish map and was not delineated on it. Texas therefore claimed the area between the Prairie Dog Town Fork and the North Fork west to the hundredth meridian. The Texas legislature approved the formation of this area as Greer County in 1860, but the county was not formally organized until 1886. The subsequent dispute with the United States over the boundary was settled in 1896 by the US Supreme Court, which ruled that the South Fork, or Prairie Dog Town Fork, was the boundary because of its greater length, width, and continuation from east to west. Greer County became a US territory and later a part of the state of Oklahoma. The present Oklahoma counties of Jackson, Harmon, Greer, and the southern part of Beckham County comprise what was once Greer County, Texas. During the time of the cattle drives, however, herds that crossed the Red River at Doan's Store in Wilbarger County did not enter Indian Territory until they crossed the North Fork of the Red River (figs. 28, 29).[22]

From the crossing at Doan's on the Prairie Dog Town Fork, the trail led generally north and northwest through the present Oklahoma counties of Jackson, Greer, Kiowa, Washita, Custer, Dewey, Woodward, Ellis, and Harper. The trail passed east of the present sites of Altus, Warren, and Canute; near Camargo, southwest of Woodward; and west of Fort Supply (renamed from Camp Supply in 1878).

The trail entered Kansas near the former site of Yelton, Oklahoma, a few miles west of US Highway 183, and led through the present Clark County past Ashland to Fort Dodge and Dodge City in Ford County.[23]

From Dodge City a trail led north through the present counties of Hodgeman, Ness, and Trego to Ellis and Fort Hays in Ellis County. By 1874 the Nebraska market was shifting west along the route of the Union Pacific Railroad to Ogallala; holding pens and loading chutes were built by the Union Pacific in 1874 to attract the cattle trade to Ogallala. A separate trail led north through the present counties of Hodgeman, Ness, Gove, Sheridan, and Decatur to the Nebraska border.[24]

The trail was not restricted to a single route, as it shifted slightly to the west to avoid the ever-moving quarantine deadline. The trail shifted to include the present counties of Finney, Lane, Thomas, and Rawlins, and it entered Nebraska in the present counties of Red Willow and Hitchcock and passed through Hayes, Chase, and Perkins Counties en route to Ogallala. Later, the trail shifted yet again to include the present Kansas counties of Scott, Logan, Wallace, Sherman, and Cheyenne; entered Nebraska at Dundy County; then passed through Chase and Perkins Counties to the terminus at Ogallala in Keith County.[25] From Ogallala, herds could be shipped to eastern markets via the Union Pacific Railroad or continue across the prairies to stock the northern and northwestern ranges.

The L. B. Harris New Trail to Ellis appeared on the 1873 map *The Best and Shortest Cattle Trail from Texas*, published by the Kansas Pacific Railway. Little is known about Harris. He was from San Antonio and owned several ranches, one of which was located in Tom Green County. He trailed cattle to Wichita in 1872 and to Ellsworth in 1873 and 1874. His route, as indicated on the 1873 Kansas Pacific map, led from Camp Concho, near where he is known to have ranched a few years later, past Fort Chadbourne, Fort Phantom Hill, Fort Griffin, Camp Cooper, Fort Belknap, Fort Sill, Fort Cobb, Camp Supply, and Fort Dodge to Ellis and Fort Hays. This route would have allowed Harris to make use of military roads where they existed and allowed the possibility of military escorts between the forts along the way to Ellis County, Kansas. The mapped route was mostly east of what became known as the Western Trail until it neared Fort Dodge. The route between Fort Dodge and Ellis County was short-lived as the quarantine deadlines changed.[26] This is a rare instance of the application of a drover's name to a mapped cattle route while the trail was in use.

In April 1878 Jonathan Doan established a trading post in Wilbarger County, Texas, near the popular crossing on the Prairie Dog Town Fork of the Red River just upstream of the confluence of the North Fork and the Prairie Dog Town Fork that became known as Doan's Store or Doan's Crossing (fig. 28). Doan's nephew, C. F. Doan, arrived with his family a few months later and managed the operation for the duration of the long cattle drives. Supplies were hauled from the closest towns where they could be obtained—Sherman, Denison, and Gainesville, more than 150 miles to the east—to Doan's to furnish the needs of the drovers on the trail. After a few years, supplies could be obtained and hauled from Wichita Falls.[27] Doan's was located at the present junction of FM 2916 and FM 924 in Wilbarger County. The adobe cabin that was erected in 1881 still stands at that location, along with several trail markers and monuments.

This trail was known by several different names, including simply "the Trail." It has been called Fort Griffin Trail, Fort Dodge Trail, Dodge City Trail, Western Trail, and Texas Cattle Trail. Great Western Trail is currently popular but does not appear to be grounded in fact, as no reference that includes "Great" as part of the name during the trail's period of use is found. The cited maps from 1881 and 1885 designated the trail as Western Trail, Fort Griffin Trail, and Fort Griffin and Dodge City Trail (figs. 2, 17).[28]

After the Western Trail was in use, cattlemen referred to the trail that crossed the Red River at Cooke and Montague Counties as the Eastern and the trail that crossed the Red in Wilbarger County as the Western. It was a simple matter; one was the easternmost northbound cattle trail still in use, and the other was the westernmost northbound cattle trail still in use. The earliest newspaper reference to "eastern trail" and "western trail" appeared in the May 10, 1881, edition of the *Cheyenne Transporter*. Capitalization of the names varied and was likely at the discretion of an editor. In February 1882 the Texas Stockmen's Association passed a resolution regarding the two main northbound trails at their annual convention in Austin; the Eastern crossed the Red River at Red River Station, and the Western crossed the Red River at Doan's Store. The adoption of this resolution regarding the Eastern and Western trails was also reported subsequently in the *Weekly Democratic Statesman* in Austin. The resolution read in part, "We, the committee on trail, beg leave to offer our report, recommending the two trails known as the eastern and western. The eastern trail crossing Red river at Red River station: the western trail crossing Red river at Doan's store."[29]

The Western Trail to Dodge City and beyond was still in use at the time this resolution was passed. This is likely the basis for later claims that the trail from south Texas that crossed the Red River at Montague County was known by drovers as the Eastern Trail; however, no record is found of the name Eastern Trail until after the Western Trail was in use. Despite later claims to the contrary, the Chisholm name as a designated cattle trail is nowhere to be found on any map of Texas from the trail driving era. Within the next few years, however, conditions changed drastically along the northbound cattle trails.

12

The End
of the Trails

As settlers poured into Kansas and Nebraska, the railroads continued to extend into new areas. The cause of Texas fever was still unknown, and restrictions against the importation of Texas cattle increased until Texas herds were eventually prohibited from entering Kansas unless they were wintered north of the thirty-sixth parallel. Meanwhile, a few Kansas towns on the fringes of the quarantine area competed to attract the Texas cattle business. The Indians of the southern plains had been defeated and removed to reservations while the war continued on the northern plains. Land leases and barbed wire slowly choked access to the remaining cattle trails through Indian Territory. The public clamored for Indian lands in Indian Territory to be opened for Anglo settlement. Few traces of the frontier remained, and the days of the open range and long cattle drives were numbered.

The change to the Kansas quarantine law in 1876 closed access to the last remaining cattle markets closest to the north end of Chisholm's Trail. The railroad had not yet reached Caldwell, located on the trail just north of the border between Indian Territory and Kansas. This left Dodge City as the nearest Kansas railhead for Texas drovers. Then in 1879 the railroad arrived in Caldwell, and by summer of 1880 cattle were being shipped from the new railhead. Perhaps leery of the new challenger, the *Dodge City Times* called the cattle business at Caldwell "pretentious and imaginary." Caldwell was located on the southern edge of the quarantine area, and concerns about Texas fever were apparently of little consequence there. Competition spurred a rate war among Caldwell, Hunnewell, and Dodge City, but by October the prospects for Dodge looked good.[1]

Most of the herd traffic had shifted to the Fort Griffin and Dodge

City Trail, but the old trails toward Caldwell had not yet been abandoned. The arrival of the railroad and capacity to ship cattle from Caldwell provided a brief resurgence of activity. A road led from the Cheyenne Agency along the North Canadian River to Fort Supply. This road could be followed from the old trail, which was later called the Chisholm Trail, past Fort Reno along the north side of the river all the way to the newer trail to Dodge City near Camp Supply (fig. 30). A 1915 reference to this road near Fort Reno, based on an 1892 magazine article, might be the basis for later claims of a "West" or "Western" Chisholm Trail.[2]

The Kansas population continued to increase. Most of the state was off-limits to Texas cattle unless they met certain requirements. The use of barbed wire became more common, and there were complaints that access to cattle trails was blocked. Taxes and grazing leases in Indian Territory impacted the economics of a cattle drive and altered the routes of those that did not want to pay. The handwriting was on the wall, and the end of the cattle trails seemed imminent. In February 1883 the *Barbour County Index* reported that "Mr. Hoover, the member from Ford County," had introduced a resolution in the Kansas legislature to ask Congress to create a national cattle trail. The purpose of the resolution was to guarantee that Texas cattle could continue to trail from Texas to the Kansas railroads. A few days later, the *Eaton Democrat* reported that the Kansas legislature refused to pass the national trails resolution. The idea of a national cattle trail was not dead yet and was proposed again soon as conditions gradually worsened along the trails.[3]

The cattle trails to Caldwell, Hunnewell, and Dodge City all passed through the Cherokee Outlet. The names Cherokee Strip and Cherokee Outlet were often used generically, but they were actually two different areas. The Cherokee Outlet was a rectangular strip of land in the northern part of Indian Territory that extended about sixty miles south from the southern line of Kansas between the ninety-sixth and one-hundredth meridians (from roughly the eastern boundary of present-day Osage County west to the eastern edge of the Oklahoma Panhandle). The Cherokee Strip was a strip of land approximately two and one-half miles wide along the north side of the southern border of Kansas from approximately where the Neosho River crosses the southern line of Kansas west to the one-hundredth meridian. When the Outlet was originally surveyed, the surveyor began at the southeast corner of the Osage Reservation in Kansas and extended his line west to the hundredth meridian. The Kansas-Nebraska Act in 1854 set the southern boundary of Kansas along the thirty-seventh parallel, which was just to the south of the original survey. The Strip was claimed by both the Cherokees and the state of Kansas. The matter was settled in 1866 when, by treaty, the contested land was sold to benefit the Cherokees.[4]

Under the terms of the treaty, the United States could settle friendly Indians in the Cherokee land west of the ninety-sixth meridian. By 1876 the Osage, Pawnee, Ponca, Nez Perce, Otoe, and Missouria tribes had been relocated to their new reservations. Their presence blocked access to the Outlet by the Cherokees from their reserve east of the ninety-sixth meridian. The land allocated to these tribes was purchased by the federal government from the Cherokees for its appraised value of just over $0.47 per acre.

The Outlet contained prime grazing country. By 1879 some stockmen had made arrangements with the Cherokees to graze their herds, while others simply moved in. Kansas ranchers moved cattle south into the Outlet to avoid paying tax in Kansas and moved back north into Kansas to avoid paying grazing fees to the Cherokees. On the open range, herds tended to drift and mingle together, which potentially caused conflict regarding ownership. The stockmen who were legitimately grazing herds in the Outlet preferred to settle their own differences. The Cherokee leaders were beginning to realize the revenue potential of grazing fees, and the stockmen did not want to draw any special attention from the federal government. The Cherokee Strip Live Stock Association was formed in the spring of 1880 at Caldwell, Kansas, in order to arrange roundups, settle disputes, and protect herds in a region with little or no organized law or courts.[5]

In 1882, ranchers who had obtained grazing permits in the Outlet erected wire fences on their respective ranges to contain their cattle and prevent others from drifting into their herd. The Cherokee treasurer who collected the grazing tax believed that it was easier to collect the tax if the fences were allowed. The Pennsylvania Oil Company had fenced range that was used by smaller stockmen in the Outlet south of Arkansas City. When conflict arose between the oil company and the stockmen who had the grazing rights, an appeal was made to the US Department of the Interior. An investigation revealed that tracts of land that had been fenced were under the names of individual Cherokees, who had been paid by stockmen for the use of their names. The attorney general viewed this as a land claim by individual Cherokees and therefore an attempt at settlement by the Cherokees, which was prohibited in the Outlet. The commissioner of Indian affairs notified the agent for the Five Civilized Tribes that fences and improvements must be removed within twenty days, or that would be done by the military. The War Department apparently understood the potential consequences of carrying out these actions and asked for confirmation of a provision of law under which military personnel would be protected in such an action. The military understood that removal of fences during the winter placed an undue burden on the cattlemen to move or contain their stock during winter's cold, when grazing conditions were poorest. This might spark unnecessary resistance, as the situation might be settled peacefully in the spring. The matter was delayed, stockmen protested, and the agent was ordered to investigate further.[6]

On March 1, 1883, Indian Agent John Tufts reported that about 950 miles of barbed-wire fence had been erected in the Cherokee Outlet. Out of an estimated three hundred thousand head of cattle in the Outlet, the Cherokees collected a grazing tax on approximately two hundred thousand head. About one hundred thousand head were grazed without permission by Kansas cattlemen. Tufts also reported that "timber extended only along the water courses," and much had been cut, especially along the Cimarron, and carried into Kansas for fuel and fencing. He stated that the timber would be destroyed within three years, which would harm the water supply and therefore render the land useless. He also stated that if the existing fences were permitted to remain and new fences erected "under proper instruction," the destruction would stop, since cattlemen did not allow large-scale cutting of timber on their range. It was decided that fences and improvements could remain if arrangements were made with the Cherokees.[7]

In March 1883 Cherokee chief Dennis W. Bushyhead met with Secretary of the Interior Henry M. Teller and Commissioner of Indian Affairs Hiram Price in Washington. During the same period, the stock association met at Caldwell and incorporated under Kansas law as the Cherokee Strip Live Stock Association. With no law or courts in the Outlet, the association derived its authority from the consent of its members. Meanwhile, Price directed Indian Agent Tufts to remove trespassers and prohibit construction of new fences until arrangements were made with the Cherokees. Bushyhead arranged for a special session of the Cherokee National Council, at which a number of cattlemen sought leases in the Outlet. Despite disagreement among the council members, the Cherokee Strip Live Stock Association secured a five-year lease of the entire Outlet for the sum of one hundred thousand dollars per year. The association agreed that no permanent improvements would be erected on the land and that temporary improvements would become the property of the Cherokee Nation upon expiration of the lease. This placed approximately six million acres under the control of the Cherokee Strip Live Stock Association (fig. 30). Almost one million acres were allocated for quarantine grounds and access to the trails through the Outlet, which left about five million acres available for grazing. After an initial assessment of two cents per acre, members paid the association one and one-fourth cents per acre every six months for their lease.[8]

Also by 1883, much of the Cheyenne and Arapaho Reservation was leased to cattlemen for grazing (fig. 30). The route along the Fort Griffin and Dodge City Trail through Indian Territory past Fort Supply to Dodge and Ogallala became more restricted as more wire fence was erected on the grass leases. Fences also became more of a problem for drovers south of the Red River in Texas, where they sometimes blocked access to public roads, blocked access to public land, or interfered with mail delivery.[9]

Barbed wire provided an effective barrier, but that barrier could be compromised with a pair of cutters. In January 1884 the *Indian Chieftain* reported that fence cutting was a felony in Texas, "the killing of a fence cutter in the act of applying the nippers" was justifiable homicide, and Governor Ireland "as much as says that he will pardon any man convicted of shooting a fence cutter." According to Indian Agent John Miles of the Cheyenne and Arapaho Reservation, "the western cattle trail, which passes through that reservation, and heretofore [has been] used between Texas and Kansas, has been closed in consequence of having been leased for grazing purposes." He requested Congress to act on the matter and reopen the trail.[10]

Conflicts over fences in Texas became more common, and a dim view was taken of the fence cutter, who was described in one article as a "scoundrelly vandal who should be serving the State in the penitentiary, and he is deserving of no sympathy at the hands of the public at large." The problem was not specific to Texas; fence cutters were also at work north of the Red River. Conflicting reports regarding range conditions in the Cherokee Outlet were published, sometimes on the same page of the same newspaper. One source reported "trouble brewing in the Cherokee strip," with hundreds of miles of fence removed by the sheriff of the Cherokee Nation, while the next article reported that the first article was inaccurate: "There is no trouble brewing in the Cherokee Strip so far as the citizens of this nation are concerned." The second article stated that less than fifty miles of fence had been cut. The discrepancies could possibly be attributed to inaccurate sources or to confusion over the initial order to remove all fencing and improvements, which was rescinded.

It is likely that trouble was actually brewing, as cattlemen at Dodge complained to the secretary of the interior that the Cherokee Stock Association had closed the established trails and offered armed resistance to their herds.[11]

Teller ordered an inspector to the region to open all cattle trails that were found closed. Inspector S. S. Benedict found that the "Chisholm and Western trails" were sufficient and ordered a trail that led from Red Fork Ranch to Clark County, Kansas, which had been blocked by the Live Stock Association, to be opened. He also discovered that Indians had been "plundering beeves from the trailmen" and were "so gorged with the stolen meat that they have been selling to butchers the beeves furnished the thieving Indians by the government." Benedict threatened the culprits with military action if they did not stop and made it clear that the government would protect the trail men.[12]

The Chickasaw Council took several actions in October 1884. They established the Office of Collector of Permits based at Tishomingo, imposed a tax of sixteen cents per head on all stock driven through their territory, required herds to travel no less than eight miles per day with deviation of no more than one mile either way from the direct line of travel, and made the carrying of pistols within the Chickasaw Nation illegal, with no exception for travelers.[13] This law did not provide an exception for certain routes, as had been done in the 1869 livestock law. These regulations imposed additional burdens and obstacles to drovers along the trails through the Chickasaw Nation.

Arguments over fences spilled over from the prairies to the halls of government. Chickasaw governor Jonas Wolf called out the militia to assist the sheriff and his posse in cutting the fences of stockmen who had been declared intruders in the Chickasaw Nation. While the legislature argued over an appropriations bill to pay the militia, the governor sent the militia home and declared a thirty-day truce to provide an opportunity for the stockmen to pay their fines and remove their fences voluntarily. The legislature determined that the militia was not on duty if they were at home and refused to include pay for this period in the bill. The governor vetoed the bill, the legislature was unable to muster enough votes to override the veto, and the militia stayed home.[14]

Troubles over fences continued into 1885 in Texas, where B. T. Warren, a former ranger and a witness in a fence cutting trial in Runnels County, was killed while sitting in a hotel lobby in nearby Sweetwater. The incident happened at night, and the shot was fired from the street by an unknown assailant. More than thirty fence cutting cases were on the Runnels County docket at the time; all were delayed because of Warren's assassination and the absence of other witnesses.[15] While these events were specific to a single county, the problem of fence cutting was widespread, and similar incidents occurred throughout the western portion of the state.

The Kansas legislature on March 7, 1885, passed another quarantine law that effectively closed the entire state to Texas cattle. This law made it illegal to drive Texas cattle into any Kansas county. Two exceptions were allowed: cattle that had been wintered since December 1 of the previous year west of the east line of Indian Territory and north of the thirty-sixth parallel could be driven into the state with the proper health certificate, and cattle that were kept in Kansas that had drifted south over the state line could be rounded up and returned under direction of a livestock association recognized by the state.[16]

Northbound herds along the trail were blocked by Kansas cattlemen who ranched, but did not lease or own the land, in the Cherokee Strip. The Texas cattle could not continue north into Kansas unless they were wintered in that country north of the thirty-sixth parallel. An estimated thirty thousand to forty thousand head of cattle that were destined for Colorado ranches were blocked by the Kansas legislature and the situation in the Outlet. Texas stockmen on the trail were faced with the choice of turning around and returning to Texas, turning west near Fort Supply, or selling their herds at a discounted rate in the Cherokee Outlet. In July 1885 Governor John Ireland and Congressman Joseph D. Sayers, both of Texas, wrote letters of protest to Secretary of the Interior Lucius Q. C. Lamar complaining about the actions of Kansas and Nebraska against Texas commerce. They also reminded him that his predecessor had ordered all cattle trails to be kept open.[17]

With access to the markets at Dodge City, Ogallala, and the ranges of the northwest all but closed by the 1885 Kansas quarantine law, cattlemen looked for another route to an outlet for Texas herds. Indian lands in Indian Territory and Montana Territory had been leased for periods of five to ten years at rates ranging from two to twelve cents per acre per year. Relatively few cattlemen had obtained the grazing rights to large tracts of land. The Senate Committee on Indian Affairs began an investigation in January 1885 to attempt to settle the disputes regarding whether the tribes had the authority to lease their land and to propose any legislation necessary to correct the situation. No progress was accomplished by the summer.[18] Meanwhile, Texas cattlemen needed a route to the railheads in Kansas and Nebraska and to the northwestern ranges.

The idea of a national cattle trail, which had failed in the Kansas legislature in 1883, surfaced again. The idea was to provide a dedicated route to remain free from settlement, using public lands, free of charge, to be used for the sole purpose of a cattle trail. Title to these lands would be retained by the US government, and connecting routes through Texas and Indian Territory would also be established. Another benefit of a dedicated national trail was that grazing areas along the route were included for use only by herds using the trail. This meant that herds on the trail were separated or quarantined from local cattle during their entire journey. The concept of a quarantined trail should, at least in theory, address the concerns regarding the spread of Texas fever. The idea of a dedicated national cattle trail from Texas north to the Dominion of Canada had widespread support among the cattlemen of Texas. A lighthearted event was held in San Antonio to generate publicity and draw attention to the issue. For the cost of twenty-five cents per vote, participants could vote for the ugliest stockman in Texas. A fifty-dollar saddle, donated by the firm of Noyes and Langholz, was to be awarded to the winner. Lively competition was expected, "as Texas can boast of a great many cattlemen who rate higher for their wealth and liberality than their good looks."[19]

Texas was still considered to be a vast breeding ground for cattle at that time. As ranges were stocked with Texas cattle in other western states and in the northern and northwest territories, some stockmen introduced high-grade bulls into their herds to improve the quality of the beef. The availability of a better grade of beef helped satisfy slowly changing consumer demands for better table fare. The dramatic increase in the cattle business since the end of the Civil War not only boosted the Texas economy and that of several other states, but also became a major factor in the economy of the United States. Total US beef exports, including live cattle and beef products (preserved beef, canned beef, and so on), for the year ending on June 30, 1884, totaled $41,080,001.[20]

A precedent for setting aside public lands for the proposed trail had been established when public lands were set aside for the construction of railroads. The estimated number of acres required for a cattle trail from Texas to the northern border of the United States was 1,324,800 acres, which amounted to less than 3 percent of the total land concessions for railroad construction.[21] A dedicated cattle trail that provided a highway from a seemingly endless source in Texas to railheads in Nebraska and to the northern ranges seemed to be in the national interest.

On January 17, 1885, Congressman James F. Miller of Texas introduced "A Bill to Establish a Quarantined Live-Stock Trail, and to Regulate Commerce between the States as to Live Stock." The bill called for the secretary of the interior to appoint three commissioners to lay out and establish "a public highway to be known as a quarantined national live-stock trail." The route of the proposed trail is described in sections 2 and 3 of the bill as follows:

> That said quarantined national live-stock trail shall begin on Red River, as near the one hundredth degree of longitude as may be deemed practicable for the purpose of this act; thence running in a northerly and westerly direction through the Indian Territory, following as far as may be practicable the present trail known as the Fort Griffin and Dodge City trail, to the southwest corner of the State of Kansas; thence over the unappropriated public lands belonging to the United States, in a northerly direction, on the most practicable route, to the north boundary line of the United States. That said quarantined national live-stock trail may be of any practicable width not exceeding six miles, and said quarantined grazing-grounds shall not exceed twelve miles square at any one place.

The proposal also designated that the land was to be used exclusively for a quarantined trail and for no other purpose for ten years after the passage of the bill. The proposed trail began at or near Doan's Crossing in Wilbarger County on the Red River, proceeded along the existing Fort Griffin and Dodge City Trail, and as directly as practical to the northern border of the United States (fig. 31). The lack of water along stretches of the route was to be addressed by sinking artesian wells at appropriate distances.[22]

This route skirted the western edge of settlement in Kansas, as the other trails had done in prior years. However, the people of Kansas, who had suffered heavy financial losses from Texas fever, were opposed to the idea of a national trail through any part of their state. The Kansas law passed in March 1885 amounted to a quarantine of the entire state against Texas cattle for nine months of the year. This law allowed Texas cattle into the state only between December 2 and the end of February, when the weather was the coldest, the grazing the poorest, and conditions for cattle drives of any distance were the harshest. Colorado followed suit on March 21, 1885, passing a similar, but not quite as restrictive bill as that of Kansas. In order to avoid Kansas altogether, the proposed route of the national cattle trail was rerouted to turn west at a point north of the thirty-sixth parallel and before reaching the southern boundary of Kansas, at approximately the location of Fort Supply in Indian Territory. The route proceeded north through Colorado just west of the Colorado-Kansas border; passed to the west of Ogallala, Nebraska, and east of Miles City, Montana; and continued on to the northern border of the United States in the vicinity of the 106th meridian.[23]

Advocates of the national trail believed that laws such as those passed in 1885 in Kansas and Colorado unfairly suppressed inter-state commerce, but there was stiff resistance outside of Texas. The December 25, 1884, edition of the *Dodge City Times* reported: "The proposed national cattle trail fifteen miles in width, from Red river in Texas, through the Indian Territory, Kansas, Colorado, Wyoming and Dakota into British North America, is encountering very determined opposition in every state and territory named. The success of the proposition is very dubious."[24]

An article in the February 11, 1885, edition of the *Fort Worth Daily Gazette* made a strong case for the trail. It stated that while Texas cattle are more prolific, the richer grazing of the northern ranges produces larger and better quality beeves, and every Texas calf that grows larger on the plains of the Wyoming and Montana territories adds to the wealth of the United States. Railroad transportation was available from Texas north to Ogallala by 1885. Transport by rail was quicker, but also more expensive. Most Texas stockmen preferred the drive because the slower pace allowed the cattle to acclimate to the climate changes and remain in better condition. There was also the fact that if there were no outlet provided for Texas cattle, the ranges would soon become overstocked, the quality of the cattle would suffer because of the effects of overgrazing, the surplus would lead to depressed prices, and beef consumers, as well as the economy of the country, would suffer. Advocates also felt that the spread of Texas fever would be limited by using the quarantined trail and graz-ing areas. In spring of 1884 Wyoming stock growers endorsed the idea of the national trail; however, less than a year later the *Daily Yellowstone Journal* reported that the danger to the prairie ranges from Texas fever was so great that a national cattle trail is "not only impracticable but dangerous," and it called upon the president of the United States to ask Congress to intervene.[25]

Anglo settlers, sometimes called Boomers, had attempted to settle the Unassigned Lands in the center of Indian Territory since 1879 but were usually rebuffed by the military or by cattlemen. The movement grew stronger as the cattle trails were pushed to the west by Kansas quarantine laws and more of the Kansas prairie was turned by the farmer's plow. Just across the southern border of Kansas lay several million acres of well-watered land in the Outlet, and beyond that lay the Unassigned Lands. By 1884–85 public sentiment was aroused for the Unassigned Lands to be opened for settlement under the Homestead Laws. It was portrayed as injustice that the federal government allowed cattle grazing in the Outlet on land so rich, yet no homes or farmer's plow was permitted. The stockmen operated under the premise that the Cherokees were within their rights to lease their land for grazing and to allow such fencing and temporary improvements as approved by agreement. Congress was urged to open land in Indian Territory to settlement.[26]

During the summer of 1885, drovers continued to complain that they were denied access to the established trails through the Outlet. The secretary of the interior responded by telegram, stating that "no one had a right to obstruct them." The *Waco Daily Examiner* reported that officers of the federal courts in Kansas ignored orders to keep the trails open, and Secretary Lamar requested the US attorney general to instruct the Kansas courts to "cease their opposition to those using the established trails, and to refrain from interfering with cattle drovers while on such trails in the Indian Territory."[27]

Congress passed a law in February 1885 that declared unlawful any enclosure of public land in any state or territory in which the party controlling the enclosure had no legal claim to the land within the enclosure. On August 7, 1885, President Grover Cleveland issued an executive order that declared that unlawful enclosures as described in the February act "exist upon the public domain and that actual, legal settlement thereon is prevented by such enclosures and by force, threats, and intimidation." Cleveland ordered every unlawful enclosure immediately removed and forbade further interference "by force, threats, or intimidation" against anyone who attempted to enter and settle on any part of the public lands subject to entry and settlement.[28]

The executive order rendered the grazing leases in Indian Territory null and void, and with a stroke of the pen the stockmen who held leases became trespassers. The stockmen were not caught totally unaware, but they were suddenly faced with the prospect of immediately removing several hundred thousand head of cattle from Indian Territory. A contingent was sent to Washington to attempt to obtain a delay in enforcement to provide time to find new grounds and to move their cattle. Winter was approaching soon, and a delay until the following spring was sought. Cleveland's position was that the territory was crowded down to the agencies, and the interests of the public took precedence over the stockmen's private interests. The governor of Kansas requested that the army remain in the border area due to concerns of potential trouble. Cleveland reminded the cattlemen that their request had already been answered in a dispatch to the effect that the order could not be modified, and he chastised them for letting twelve days pass to travel and ask again. Cleveland stated: "If any indulgence is shown it must be an application in specific cases, with an evidence that an effort has been made to comply with the order. . . . No argument will induce me to change what has been done. Some loss and inconvenience will no doubt follow, but there is an interest greater than yours which must receive attention."[29]

The cattlemen vacated Indian Territory during the fall. Some sold their herds in place for whatever they could get; others drove north even though range conditions along the way were such that the cattle were in poor condition and their survival through the winter was questionable. The eviction of the cattlemen, although unfair, was legal, and it cleared the way for the land rush that soon followed.[30]

The proposed national trail was the cattlemen's last hope for an outlet over which to drive their herds to northern ranges and markets. Public sentiment grew increasingly against the proposal, due mostly to fears of the spread of Texas fever, the cause of which had not yet been discovered. More settlement on the plains meant more farmers, which meant more plows and more fences. An unnamed Texas cattleman summed up the feeling of many stockmen regarding the nesters:

> They are the ruin of the country, and have everlastingly, eternally, now and forever, destroyed the best grazing land in the world. The range country, sir, was never intended for raising farm truck. It was intended for cattle and horses, and was the best stock-raising land on earth until they got to turning over the sod—improving the country as they call it. Lord forgive them for such improvements! It makes me sick to think of it. I am sick enough to need two doctors, a druggery, and a mineral spring, when I think of onions and Irish potatoes growing where mustang ponies should be exercising, and where four-year-old steers should be getting ripe for market. Fences, sir, are the curse of the country![31]

Cattle and horses thrived on the same prairie grasses as had the bison, but once the prairie sod was broken by the plow, the grass was lost. On the other hand, cattlemen were sometimes portrayed and perceived as scheming land-grabbers. A headline in the *Omaha Daily Bee* on May 7, 1886, read: "The National Cattle Trail—A Proposed Gigantic Land Grab Which Ought to Be Summarily Squelched." The article stated that the presence of the trail would cause thousands of settlers headed for Nebraska's Dundy, Chase, and other border counties to be driven away; that Nebraska senators should say, "No you can't bring your diseased cattle and murderous cow-boys on our soil." It likened the presence of the national trail to placing a small-pox hospital in every section of land.[32]

Opposition to the national trail continued to grow, especially among the Nebraska farmers. They felt that the stockmen should not be allowed to block the path of the settlers, and a six-mile strip through the state on which no settlement would be allowed for years would certainly hinder settlement. The idea of a cattle trail was rejected in favor of new railroads: "The best national trail for all concerned is one which will run on wheels upon iron rails." The farmers called for the stockmen to defer to the needs of the settler and farmer, and the time had come that "he ought to gracefully retire."[33]

In April 1887 the commissioner of Indian affairs declined to designate a cattle trail through the Chickasaw Nation and the Cheyenne and Arapaho country to connect to the Western Trail in Indian Territory. The Chickasaws objected to herds entering their lands wherever they pleased but did not object to cattle passing through "on the regular, established cattle trail (presumably the Abilene trail entering opposite the mouth of Saline creek on the Red river)." On July 27, 1887, the *Daily Morning Astorian* reported: "The national cattle trail is abandoned. Never again in the history of the United States will great herds of Texas cattle be driven northward through Colorado to Wyoming and Montana." Homesteads and fences obstructed the trail, and seventy thousand head of cattle on the trail were turned back toward Texas. While it might still be possible to get through, there was no market at the north end of the trail. By the next year, regardless of whether a market existed, the trail was closed by fences.[34]

Another article in the December 7, 1887, edition of the *Daily Yellowstone Journal* reported the "closing of the National cattle trail this year" and that railroad construction would soon make it possible to ship cattle from Texas all the way north to the Canadian Pacific Railroad.[35] Communities that had once welcomed and sought to attract the cattle trade to their towns now sought to distance themselves from the stockmen and their herds. Fear of the spread of Texas fever, manifested in the restrictive quarantine laws against Texas cattle, along with the settlement and fencing of the planned route could not be overcome by proponents. Although some herds undoubtedly traversed the route of the proposed trail to the ranges in Colorado, Wyoming, and Montana Territory and the Dominion of Canada, the route was not formalized and designated by Congress. Kansas was closed to Texas herds, and there were no other trail options through Indian Territory. With the failure to designate the national cattle trail officially, the dust began to settle on the northbound trails from Texas.

Improvements in windmill technology allowed farmers to operate in areas with little or no access to surface water. More farms on the plains meant more wire fences, which blocked the cattle trails. The improved windmills also led to establishment of ranches in traditionally dry areas of west Texas. Windmills had been used since the 1870s to supply water for railroads in Texas. The early models were inefficient, and the design was improved by the mid-1880s. By 1887 the Magnolia Land and Cattle Company, C. C. Slaughter, the Francklyn Land and Cattle Company, and the XIT Ranch were all using windmills to water stock in the dry areas of west Texas. By 1890 the use of the windmill had spread east across the state. The windmill, combined with barbed wire, enabled the stockmen to operate in areas where it had previously been impossible to sustain a livestock operation. These west Texas ranches provided a "last hoorah" for the cattle driving era. Despite newspaper reports of the trail's demise, there was a brief resurgence as herds were trailed from west Texas ranches through the Panhandle and across the plains of eastern Colorado to Montana. The XIT, 101, N Bar N, Matador, Mill Iron, Hashknife, and Turkey Track were among the ranches said to have trailed herds north to Montana between 1887 and 1896. The XIT alone trailed over fifty-five thousand head of cattle, with estimates of up to more than one hundred thousand head driven up the trail.[36]

By 1897 it was over. The reach of the railroad continued to expand into what had once been the exclusive domain of the bison. The same combination of technology and the overwhelming numbers of settlers that had swept the bison and the Indian from the plains blocked the cattle trails and ended the need for the long drives. Cattle could be trailed shorter distances and shipped to markets in a fraction of the time that was once required. The cause of Texas fever had finally been discovered, and a remedy was forthcoming. The frontier was gone, and life on the plains soon faded into memories. The Texas cattleman who had just a few years earlier stated that the plow was

the ruin of the finest grazing land in the world proved to be eerily prophetic, as millions of acres of prairie sod were plowed under during
the lifetime of the trail drivers. Without the deep, densely rooted prairie grasses to hold it in place, the topsoil blew away during the Dust
Bowl years of the 1930s in what some have called the worst manmade
ecological disaster in the history of the United States.

13

The Chisholm Trail
from Newsprint
to Hollywood

THE TOPIC OF THE NAME, location, and route of the Chisholm Trail has been a controversial subject for decades. As time passed and the men who rode the trails died, the debate periodically intensified, and it is still a point of contention. The crux of the controversy tends to center around whether the Chisholm Trail was known as such along the entire route from south Texas to the destination in Kansas, or whether it was known as the Chisholm Trail only from a point north of the Red River to the destination in Kansas. The divisions are more frequent in Texas, where the stock was gathered and the trail herds originated. Newspapers, books, dime novels, songs, and silent films influenced the public perception of the Chisholm Trail from the trail driving era until the 1920s. Although some accounts reflected reality, many were embellished or sensationalized for public consumption.

In 1931 the Oklahoma House of Representatives passed House Bill 149, which assigned the task of locating and mapping the Chisholm Trail and the Texas Cattle Trail to the Oklahoma State Highway Department.[1] The state of Texas apparently did not take similar action to document the old cattle trails. With no official action on the subject, that left the Texas portion of the trail wide open for individual interpretation. A number of writers have offered different versions regarding the trail's name and location, with various degrees of documentation provided. Gaps in documentation were sometimes filled with unverifiable statements or opinion. Many of these statements came to be accepted as fact and added to the confusion.

Newspapers are valuable sources of information as long as their data are checked against other contemporary sources, such as maps. I obtained information regarding the trail name and general location from newspaper articles and maps of the period from 1867 to 1890. The earliest use of the name Chisholm Trail in newsprint appeared in the April 10, 1869, edition of the *Georgetown Watchman*. It is contained in an announcement from the superintendent of the Union Pacific Railroad: "The last winter's campaign against the hostile Indians of the Plains has resulted in removing them permanently from the Western route due north of Fort Arbuckle known as the "Chisholm Trail," and Drovers can now take that trail for the great bend of the Smoky Hill River with entire security from molestation by Indians or others."[2] The route mentioned in the article lay many miles to the west of the older route that crossed the Red River in Grayson County and led past Fort Gibson toward Baxter Springs—thus the use of the term *Western route*. This should not be confused with what became called the Western Trail, which came along a few years later as settlements and quarantine laws pushed the cattle markets and trails further to the west. The article indicates that the Chisholm Trail lay north of Fort Arbuckle.

In an announcement to the "Cattle Drovers of Texas" in the March 20, 1871, edition of the *Austin Tri-Weekly State Gazette*, W. N. Fant advised the drovers that the Union Pacific Railroad offered better shipping rates than the Kansas Pacific, and he included the following directions to reach the market at Schuyler, Nebraska: "The route to be pursued by Texas drovers to realize the largest prices, is as follows, to wit: Crossing Red River into the Indian Territory, at Red River Station, proceed by the Chisholm trail in a due north course, traveling some twenty miles west of Wichita, and on to Brookville on the Kansas Pacific Railway, west of Abeline [*sic*] and Salina. From Brookville the route continues north to Schuyler, on the Union Pacific Rail-road, a distance of a little less than two hundred miles."[3] This article placed the Chisholm Trail north of the Red River. In addition to these examples, the name Chisholm Trail appeared numerous times in various newspapers during the period between 1867 and 1890. Its usage was usually in conjunction with reporting the geographic location or area of a news event, and in most occurrences the term was used to describe a specific location in Indian Territory or the southern part of Kansas.

Other examples include a report of the murder of two buffalo hunters "on the sand hills, about thirty miles west of the Chisholm trail, on this side of the Salt Fork," and a report regarding a survey of the new town of Clear Water "on the Nennescah River, and directly on the Chisholm trail and state road." George Wood of Salina, Kansas, reported: "While he was on his way to Texas, last Thursday, the stage-coach was stopped on the Chisholm trail only five miles south of Caldwell, by Cheyennes, headed by white men, and himself [*sic*] and the stage compelled to turn back." The Cherokee Strip Live Stock Association appointed M. H. Bennett and J. W. Hamilton to "have the supervision of and power to employ a surveyor for the eastern division from the 96th meridian on the east to the Chisholm trail on the west, and from the state line on the north to the southern line of the Cherokee Nation on the south" in preparation for the survey of the association's leased land. A report of the plan for a pending roundup in the Cherokee Strip stated: "The place of meeting of the eastern round-up will be at Tom Snow's ranch, on Red Rock, then begin working east and south, covering all the country south of Salt Fork and east of the Arkansas river, then swing north and work west over the country between Salt Fork and the state line, as far west as the Chisholm trail, closing up at the Pond Creek ranch." A soldier accidentally drowned when he "drove into the North Fork at the chisholm [*sic*] trail crossing, 18 miles below this [the Cheyenne and Arapaho] agency, for the purpose of watering his team." Four men were killed in a fight west of Oklahoma City on the Canadian River when Chickasaw police refused a group of cattlemen the use of the Chisholm Trail; the cattlemen detoured through the Cheyenne reservation.[4]

The cited articles represent a sample of the cases in which a detailed geographic reference north of the Red River was given in relation to the Chisholm Trail during 1869–89. A few articles were not quite as geographically specific. For example, a report regarding the trade in Texas cattle stated: "Most of the droves are brought through the Indian Territory, on what is known as the Chisholm trail," and a report on the new cattle trade at Wichita stated: "Mr. McCoy visited eastern states to draw hither buyers, and Mr. Bryden rushed to the Chisholm trail to talk Wichita to drovers." The "Mr. McCoy" was Joseph G. McCoy, and "Mr. Bryden" may have been James Bryden from Corpus Christi, described in the *Wichita City Eagle* as a "well-known and extensive Texas cattle dealer" and "a fast friend of Wichita."[5] It seems logical that Bryden intercepted drovers along the trail in southern Kansas or northern Indian Territory, just as W. W. Sugg had intercepted drovers along the trail in 1867. The first example referenced the trail "through the Indian Territory" with no further details. Articles such as these indicate the trail north of the Red River but lack specific details.

Two newspaper articles included a report of news and a geographic reference to the Chisholm Trail in Texas. One was a report from the Waco and Belton area that stated: "Belton lies directly on the Chisholm cattle trail over which all the cattle south of here intended for the Colorado, Kansas, or Wyoming markets are driven year after [year] amounting to some three hundred thousand head annually." The other article reported the passage of ten thousand head of cattle through Valley Mills in Bosque County on "the Chisholm trail."[6] This same news was reported in several other newspapers.

Beginning about 1890, after the long cattle drives up the Chisholm Trail had ended, the nature of articles that referred to the Chisholm Trail changed from predominantly news-oriented to historical sketches and reminiscences of trail men and the old trails. There was still the occasional geographic reference, such as an 1890 article that reported that the road between Bluff Creek and Pond Creek, "where the old Chisholm trail is struck, is level as a floor and always good." However, many articles began to recount days and events of the past and a disappearing way of life. A historical sketch that appeared in the May 4, 1890, edition of the *Wichita Daily Eagle* recalled Jesse Chisholm's connection with the Wichita area and stated: "The great southwestern cattle trail, reaching from Corpus Christi, on the gulf, and from the Rio Grande, in Texas, to the Union Pacific road, crossing the river at the present site of this city, was named for him." The following month an article appeared in the same publication that urged the formation of a historical society to preserve the old buildings, memories, and traditions of Wichita. The city was barely twenty years old, yet the early landmarks were already being lost in the name of progress, and the generation of her founders was passing from this world.[7]

The most common usage and context in newspapers from 1867 to 1890 placed the Chisholm Trail in Indian Territory and southern Kansas. A much smaller number of articles were ambiguous in this regard; one reminiscent article stated that the entire trail was named after Chisholm, and only two articles contained a geographic reference to the trail by the Chisholm name in Texas. In general, articles that described the Chisholm Trail as located north of the Red River can be corroborated by maps from the same historical period on which either the trail or specific referenced landmarks can be located. The Chisholm Trail name as applied to any portion of the trail in Texas cannot be verified by similar sources from the same historical period, as none are found.

In addition to newspapers, popular literature played a role in shaping the public perception of the frontier and the cattle trails. Joseph G. McCoy's account of the opening of the livestock market at

Abilene, Kansas, was first published by Ramsey, Millett, and Hudson in 1874. In *Historic Sketches of the Cattle Trade of the West and Southwest*, McCoy stated in his preface that his purpose was "to convey in simple, unpretentious language, practical and correct information upon the opening, development, and present status of the live stock trade of the Great New West." This was the first book concerning the subject of the cattle trade authored by a major participant and published during the period of the events.[8]

McCoy mentioned the Chisholm Trail once in the entire volume, and gave the following description of this trail:

> But the principal trail now traveled is more direct and is known as "Chisholm trail," so named from a semicivilized Indian who is said to have traveled it first. It is more direct, has more prairie, less timber, more small streams and less large ones, and altogether better grass and fewer flies (no civilized Indian tax or wild Indian disturbances) than any other route yet driven over, and is also much shorter in distance because direct from Red river to Kansas. Twenty-five to thirty-five days is the usual time required to bring a drove from Red river to the southern line of Kansas, a distance of between two hundred and fifty and three hundred miles, and an excellent country to drive over.[9]

McCoy's description obviously applied to the route north of the Red River and did not indicate that the trail name extended in any manner to the trails south of the Red.

A few years later in 1886, *A Texas Cow-Boy; or, Fifteen Years on the Hurricane Deck of a Spanish Pony* by Charles Siringo was published by Siringo and Dobson. The early editions use the common term "cowboy," while later usage changed to "cowboy." While McCoy was the man responsible for establishment of the railhead, stockyards, and stockyards operation at Abilene, Siringo worked as a ranch hand and drover and later as a merchant, detective for the Pinkerton Agency, rancher, and consultant. By 1886, years of newspaper and magazine accounts of the Indian wars on the plains, accounts of outlaws such as Billy the Kid, and accounts of life and dangers on the frontier had placed the "cow-boy" firmly in the public consciousness. William F. Cody, better known as Buffalo Bill, had assembled his famous Wild West Show and was touring the country, playing to crowds of up to ten thousand people at each stop. These factors all combined to create a ready market for Siringo's book, which was the first book published by someone who had been a working cowboy. The book remains popular as of this writing. Siringo referred to the Chisholm

Trail in the title of his chapter 10, "A Start Up the Chisholm Trail," and chapter 20, "Another Start Up the Chisholm Trail." These references are in the title only, with no further mention or geographic details of the trail contained in these chapters. In chapter 15 Siringo referenced several landmarks along the Chisholm Trail in Indian Territory and stated that he got a job with a passing herd at "Saint Joe [*sic*] on the Chisholm trail." His trips up the trail originated in or near Jackson County, Texas, near the Gulf Coast. Siringo offered no details or geographic references to the Chisholm Trail south of "Saint Joe."[10]

During the same period, the publication of dime novels flourished. These were fanciful publications that often included sensational illustrations and story lines in different genres, including tales of the Wild West. While some were written by authors who had some sort of connection, albeit remote, to the frontier, many popular Wild West stories and tales of the frontier were written by "authors whose nearest acquaintance with the great plains was in White Plains, New York." Perhaps the most famous were Beadle's dime novels. Some authors who contributed to Beadle's New York Dime Library early in their career and went on to greater literary fame include Horatio Alger Jr., Daniel Defoe, Victor Hugo, and A. Conan Doyle. Most of the stories were written under pen names, and some wrote under multiple pen names.[11]

Edward Z. C. Judson, better known as Ned Buntline, met William F. Cody in 1869 and wrote *Buffalo Bill, the King of Border Men*, touted as "The Wildest, Truest Story Ned Buntline Ever Wrote." Of course that little book, as well as the rest of the Buffalo Bill series, the western/frontier genre, and the nickel and dime novels in general, was full of sensational exaggerations that fulfilled the public's expectation of a thrilling story. An article in the *New Orleans Republican* described the typical dime novel cover: "On the yellow cover of this attractive literature is depicted the most ferocious pirates and the wretchedest looking Indians, with trappers, all buckskin and Bowie knife, each in the act of taking or saving a life. There are, of course, panthers just springing upon defenseless young ladies, with a tropical tiger, a boa constrictor, and a brigand belted with weapons." Buntline, who was perhaps the most prolific of the dime novelists, allegedly wrote more than four hundred novels and stories of the sea, pirates, the Wild West, and the Buffalo Bill series. He once stated that his formula was to invent a title, then push forward with a story as fast as possible. That left little time to bother with facts. Later in life Buntline wrote, "I found that to make a living I must write 'trash' for the masses, for he who endeavors to write for the critical few, and do his genius justice, will go hungry if he has no other means of support." The dime novelists gave the public what they wanted, and the historical cowboy began the transformation into a mythical character of the plains.[12]

Sometime in the early to mid 1870s the poem "The Old Chisholm Trail" appeared. The author is unknown. It allegedly was written in a book at the Drover's Cottage in Abilene, Kansas, where various trail men added their own, sometimes raunchy, lyrics over the course of a number of years. The lyrics were transformed into a song of the same name, usually beginning with these or similar opening stanzas:

> Come along boys and listen to my tale,
> I'll tell you of my troubles on the Old Chisholm Trail.
> Coma ti yi youpy youpy ya youpy ya,
> Coma ti yi youpy youpy ya.
>
> Oh a ten dollar hoss and a forty dollar saddle,
> And I'm goin' to punchin' Texas cattle.
> Coma ti yi youpy youpy ya youpy ya,
> Coma ti yi youpy youpy ya.

This ditty was one of 112 songs, none of which had previously been in print, that John Lomax collected for *Cowboy Songs and Other Frontier Ballads*, published in 1910. In order to shed light on the life of the cowboy and life on the frontier, Lomax recorded the songs on paper for the first time from oral recitation by those that knew them, and he included the milder lyrics in his book. No one knows for sure how many verses the song included. Lomax reportedly ran across a man who, "under suitable circumstances," could sing 149 stanzas of "The Old Chisholm Trail." Undoubtedly the "suitable circumstances" did not include an audience in which ladies or children might be present. The milder versions of the poem and subsequent song became immensely popular, and even more so during the earlier 1900s as more people gained access to phonographs and recorded music. The song has been recorded by many singers of the Western genre for years and has remained popular for generations.[13]

Technology continued to advance during the 1890s. The technology that had enabled the mass production of newspapers, magazines, and dime novels was advancing toward a new medium: moving pictures. The combination of the invention of flexible film and the invention of the kinetoscope would, in inventor Thomas Edison's words, "do for the eye what the phonograph does for the ear, and that by a combination of the two, all motion and sound could be recorded and reproduced simultaneously."[14] It took a few more years to perfect the marriage of the two technologies, as motion pictures remained silent until 1927.

Technically, the first Western was a short film of less than a minute in length titled "Cripple Creek Bar Room Scene," filmed by Thomas Edison in 1899. It was Western in the sense that it contained a few characters in cowboy garb drinking and playing cards in a bar. "The Great Train Robbery," which is generally recognized as the first Western film, was released in 1903. It was so successful that it sparked a flurry of other Western films. With titles such as "The Hold-Up of the Leadville Stage" (1904) or "Tracked by Bloodhounds: Lynching at Cripple Creek" (1904), they were basically dime novels in motion.[15]

Actor William S. Hart sought to portray the cowboy in a more realistic manner. He dressed according to the style of the traditional cowboy and hired Wyatt Earp, who provided a living link to the heyday of the American West, as a consultant in his desire for authenticity. Hart dominated the Western film landscape from 1914 until about 1920, when studios shifted to flashier costumes and more action, shoot-outs, horseback chases, and such in order to attract audiences and satisfy the public expectation.[16] With stars like Hart, Hoot Gibson, Tom Mix, Harry Carey, and others the Western film genre thrived. Success bred competition, and story lines accordingly became more sensational. Just as with dime novels, the line between entertainment and reality was not always clear, and entertainment was perceived to an extent by the general public as reality. Motion pictures evolved to satisfy the public's expectation of thrills, chills, and a good story. Hollywood continued to transform the historical cowboy and the historical West into the mythical cowboy and the fictional West. The line between reality and imagination became blurred by various means during the latter days of the trail driving period and afterward. Chisholm's Trail suffered a similar fate as fact was slowly nudged aside by fiction.

14

From Chisholm's Trail to Meridian Highway

LIFE IS OFTEN A SERIES of transitions, and so it was with the cattle trails. When its period of usefulness as a cattle trail was over, some segments were simply abandoned and left to nature to be reclaimed. Other portions continued to be used, perhaps as a stagecoach road. Railroad tracks were sometimes laid along the old cattle trails, as they often took the path of least resistance. After its period of use as a cattle trail was over, Chisholm's Trail changed locations and grew in length. It evolved from Chisholm's Trail to the Chisholm Trail, and its name recognition increased in proportion to changes in the trail's alleged length. The changes occurred primarily after 1901, long after the last herd trudged along the trail. The horseless carriage began to replace the horse and wagon as a primary means of transportation. The American public became more mobile as automobiles became more popular and affordable. Communities began to realize that a combination of road improvements, local attractions, and an interesting story appealed to visitors, which boosted local economies. Advances in technology, construction of an international highway, tourism, and desires to commemorate the accomplishments of the drovers combined to contribute to the mythology of the Chisholm Trail.

While herds of Texas longhorns were being driven along the cattle trails leading north from Texas, a different kind of traffic traveled the roads of the eastern United States. The bicycle had become quite popular for transportation and sport. Bicyclists, or wheelmen, as they were called at the time, were sometimes the target of aggression by pedestrians and men whose primary mode of transportation was the horse. Roads were often laced with ruts, which presented safety problems in addition to the other issues. The League of American Wheelmen had been founded in May 1880 at Newport, Rhode Island, to promote paved roads and safer conditions for bicyclists. There seems to be absolutely no connection between a group of Rhode Island bicyclists and Texas drovers, but the actions of the League of American Wheelmen inadvertently affected the public perception of the Chisholm Trail over the next fifty years.[1]

The Good Roads movement was begun in the United States by the league not only to promote good roads as a matter of bicycling safety, but also as a means to help the American farmer move crops to market. A bicycle that became stuck in the mud was of little impact to anyone other than the hapless bicyclist, but the ability to deliver crops to market more efficiently suggested a real economic impact. The seventy-three-page publication *The Gospel of Good Roads: A Letter to the American Farmer*, published in 1891, pointed out the effects of bad weather and the disadvantages of the existing system of dirt roads across the nation. It provided technical and economic data to make a case for road improvement throughout the country and pointed out considerations ranging from improved rural mail delivery to the fact that harvested crops that were stuck in the mud were economically reduced to not much more than livestock feed. In closing, it implored the farmer to be the catalyst for road reform.[2]

The stated purpose of *Good Roads* magazine, which first appeared in January 1892, was "to stimulate the interest of the public concerning the advantages of good roads and streets, and the best methods of constructing and maintaining them." About that same time, Chisholm's Cattle Trail first appeared on a map as a named route south of the North Canadian River. The 1892 *Map of the Oklahoma Country in the Indian Territory* showed the trail by that name between the Canadian River just north of Wayne and the North Canadian River near Council Grove (fig. 32). The trail led past Norman and a location shown as Negro Settlement. This trail segment had been unnamed on previous maps of Indian Territory, and Chisholm's Cattle Trail had been designated only north of the North Canadian River. Negro Settlement appears to be in the approximate location of present-day Slaughterville. This map extended Chisholm's Cattle Trail as a named route south from the North Canadian River to the Canadian River, though the days of the cattle trails were past.[3]

The 1898 and 1902 editions of *Map of Oklahoma Territory* both showed the Abilene Cattle Trail as a named route, as it had appeared on previous maps (fig. 33). The route between the North Canadian and Cimarron Rivers that had been designated as Chisholm's Trail or Chisholm's Cattle Trail on previous maps was visible, but the Chisholm name no longer appeared.[4]

The 1901 US Geological Survey map *Indian Territory, Chickasaw Nation, Addington Quadrangle* (reprinted in a 1916 edition) showed the route past Ryan, Addington, and Duncan that had been designated since 1872 on maps as the Abilene Cattle Trail suddenly designated as the Chisholm Trail (fig. 34).[5] This is the first mapped application of the Chisholm Trail designation to the route that led north from the Red River near Salt Creek past Monument Hill, generally a few miles east of and parallel to the ninety-eighth meridian. This path soon became the general route of the Meridian Highway, presently designated US Highway 81, which passed through the nearby towns of Ryan, Addington, and Duncan. Also notable is the change from the previous designations of Chisholm's Trail or Chisholm's Cattle Trail to Chisholm Trail. This represents a drastic change from previous mapped locations of Chisholm's Trail. The trail disappeared and then reappeared on the map in a new location, and the Abilene Cattle Trail had a new designation as the Chisholm Trail.

Good Roads associations soon began to form in the more populated areas of the country. The Good Roads movement was beginning to take hold in Texas in 1901, with announcements in newspapers and attendance of a Texas delegation at the International Good Roads Congress in Buffalo, New York. The movement was also taking root in Kansas and Oklahoma Territory, with progress faster in some areas than in others. Production of the original Ford Model A began in 1903, and the American public was on the verge of a new era in travel. As early as 1905 the connection between good roads and the prospects and benefits of tourism was realized. The automobile business grew, and Ford began production of the Model T in 1908.[6]

Three years later, in June 1911, the Meridian Road Association was organized in Salina, Kansas, to promote a north-south road across Kansas near the sixth meridian. The Meridian Road or Highway was planned to connect with a north-south road out of Oklahoma, which connected with a north-south road out of Texas. On August 16, 1911, the Chisholm Trail Good Roads Association was formed at Enid, Oklahoma, in response to a movement to establish the north-south road through the state to generally follow the route of the Rock Island Railroad to Texas. This road would be called the Chisholm Trail Road. A historical committee, for the purpose of "securing accurate data as to the true location of the original trail and the compiling of interesting events and adventures which occurred along the trail in pioneer days," was formed at another meeting held on August 29, 1911, at El Reno.[7]

This road from Caldwell, Kansas, south to the Red River was to be designated as Road No. 5, which was "the famous old Texas cattle trail used in reaching Dodge City and Abilene, Kans., and is locally known as the Chisholm trail." This designation apparently either was reported incorrectly or the road designation was changed, as this route appeared on a 1921 preliminary highway designation map issued by the Oklahoma State Highway Commission as State Highway No. 2, from the state line south of Caldwell to the Red River bridge north of Ringgold, Texas. It also appeared on subsequent maps as State Highway No. 2.[8]

By 1912, Good Roads associations had been organized in Nebraska and the Dakotas. Plans called for the Meridian Highway to be one continuous road from Winnipeg, Canada, to Galveston, Texas, and eventually to be extended south to Mexico City. In June 1913 the Oklahoma counties of Grady, Stephens, and Jefferson, which were members of the Tri-County Good Roads Association, began "initial work in perpetuating the Chisholm Trail, and converting it into a public highway." The route from Chickasha south through Rush Springs, Marlow, Duncan, Addington, Waurika, and Ryan to the Red River was soon surveyed for the new road and included the route of the old trail for approximately half of the distance.[9]

Later that year, the first moving assembly line went into production at the Ford automobile plant. This drastically lowered production time of the Model T and reduced its price accordingly, which made it more affordable to the American public.[10] As more citizens transitioned from horse and wagon to the automobile, the Good Roads movement continued to gather momentum.

Communities in Texas began to realize the potential of the new highway and followed the example of the Chisholm Trail Good Roads Association in Oklahoma. So far, the connection between the Good Roads movement and the Chisholm Trail name had occurred north of the Red River, primarily in Oklahoma. Fort Worth joined in the Chisholm Trail plan and sent a delegate to El Reno to represent the Fort Worth Board of Trade. An article appeared in the *Fort Worth Star Telegram* on August 29, 1911, in which it was claimed: "The Chisholm trail, as it was known in the old cattle days, extended from Fort Worth to Wichita, Kan. It is proposed to extend the road to Fort Sam Houston near San Antonio from the northern boundary of Kansas."[11]

A *Dallas Morning News* article from August 1911 described the trail from Fort Worth to Wichita, Kansas, as "the old Chisholm trail," yet it described the trail from the southern part of Texas to Fort Worth as simply "a trail." Yet another article stated that "Texas people should take up the movement which the people of Oklahoma have started and have the trail improved all the way from Fort Worth to Wichita." This article went on to name the landmarks of Monument Hill, Duncan, Marlow, and Rush Springs—all landmarks along the route that was designated since 1872 on multiple military and Department of the Interior maps of Indian Territory as the Abilene Cattle Trail. Plans included extension of the road south of Fort Worth to San Antonio, yet no mention was made that the cattle trail along that route might already have been known as the Chisholm Trail or that the Chisholm Trail name would be extended south of Fort Worth. Were these statements regarding extension of the Chisholm Trail name based on some unstated historical evidence, or simply a result of the publicity and increasing attention to the Meridian Road project?[12]

The Good Roads movement continued to gain traction in Kansas, Oklahoma, and Texas over the next few years. As the Meridian Highway project moved forward, another organization that would influence recognition of the Texas cattle trails got its start. George W. Saunders, who had been successful in the livestock business as a drover, rancher, and businessman, recognized that the life that he once knew and the historical accomplishments of the old trail men would soon pass into history. Saunders and other stockmen attended annual stock conventions, and it was at one of those conventions that Saunders suggested forming an association of former trail drivers (fig. 35). In February 1915 the Old Time Trail Drivers' Association was formed during a meeting at the San Antonio Chamber of Commerce. In March 1915 the new association held their first annual meeting in conjunction with the annual meeting of the Texas Cattle Raisers Association (fig. 36). The following former trail men were elected as the association's first officers: John R. Blocker, president; George W. Saunders, vice president; Luther A. Lawhon, secretary; and Colonel R. B. Pumphrey, treasurer. Membership increased rapidly, and by the second annual meeting the association numbered about five hundred members.[13]

In May 1915 Saunders began to send letters to members in order to solicit written accounts and reminiscences of their experience on the cattle trails for the benefit of the new association. He intended to publish their stories and memories before they were lost, and thus record their place in Texas history. The project was delayed by a number of circumstances, including slow responses, the outbreak of World War I, and the loss of material when the publishing firm declared bankruptcy. Yet through the continued efforts of Saunders, who brought J. Marvin Hunter into the project in 1920, these written accounts were published in *The Trail Drivers of Texas* in 1920. By the time the first volume was published, membership in the Old Time Trail Drivers' Association had grown to over one thousand members. An additional volume was published in 1923, a revised version of volume one was published in 1924, and the volumes were combined into a single volume in 1925.[14]

At the second annual meeting, the association took up the business of attempting to determine the origin and terminus of the Old Chisholm Trail. The names, spelling, and occupations of John Simpson Chisum, the cattleman, and Jesse Chisholm, the trader and interpreter, were apparently confused among some of the old trail men, just as they had been confused in newspapers and various articles for a number of years. W. P. Anderson mentioned different spellings of the trail name: "Chism, . . . Chissum, . . . but probably the correct one is Chisholm." In brief, they determined that a "half-breed" named John Chisholm ranched in Indian Territory and drove a herd to government forts on the Arkansas River; later herds from Texas intersected and followed his trail in Indian Territory, and it therefore became known as the Chisholm Trail. They also determined that Charles Goodnight trailed "Jingle Bobs," or John "Chissum" cattle, north from New Mexico past Old Tascosa to Dodge along the "Chissum" Trail, and the two trails became confused.[15]

In reality, John Chisum left his ranch in Denton County, Texas, to move his operation to New Mexico Territory. Although he reportedly sold a herd a few years earlier somewhere on the Smoky Hill River, Jesse Chisholm was the man who had established a trail in Indian Territory between his trading posts, and it was this trail that intersected a route from Texas to the railheads in Kansas. Setting aside the confusion between Chisholm and Chisum, the conclusion of the association that the route from Texas to the markets in Kansas intersected and followed for some distance the trail laid out by Chisholm in the Indian Territory is corroborated by military and Department of the Interior maps from the historical period.[16]

A few years later, in 1925, a highway numbering system was proposed by the American Association of State Highway Officials, and it was approved by the secretary of agriculture in 1926. By the close of the construction season in 1930, new highway signs had been installed on most of approximately ninety-seven thousand miles of American highways. Named highways, such as the Lincoln or the Bankhead, were replaced by the highway numbering system, with east-west roads designated by even numbers and north-south roads by odd numbers. As more roads were built, improved, or paved, communities took notice of the rising commercial potential of tourism, and competition increased to attract tourist traffic. Organizations realized the potential commercial value of improving and marking roads to encourage tourist trade.[17]

Independent of the Old Time Trail Drivers' Association, P. P. Ackley, a former drover, began a campaign in 1925 to convert the Old Chisholm Trail into a maintained highway and install markers along the route. The *San Antonio Express* reported: "Ackley said the Chisholm Trail is the longest unbroken trail in the world and that it should not be erased," and he proposed to extend the route from the Gulf of Mexico all the way to Canada. By 1929 he was willing to contribute one thousand dollars toward placement of a monument where the route entered Texas. Aside from the fact that this trail, like all the others, was not a single, continuous, unbroken route, the length of the Chisholm Trail suddenly became extended to the same length as the Meridian Highway.[18]

In April 1930 Ackley offered one thousand dollars toward the expense of marking the Old Chisholm Trail across Texas, Oklahoma, and Kansas and on to the Canadian border. He suggested that five hundred markers should be installed from Brownsville to the Red River, with a similar number of markers installed across Oklahoma. It is not clear whether this was the same contribution he announced in 1929 or an additional thousand-dollar contribution. Later that same month, the Texas State Highway Commission decided, because of financial concerns, against the designation of additional roads until the primary road system was completed. At the same meeting, an appeal was made to the highway commission to designate "a road from near San Antonio through Northern Texas to be known as the Chisholm trail. Action on the proposal was delayed pending the mapping of a comprehensive route for the trail." With this proposal the Chisholm name stood to be extended farther south to San Antonio. A route had not yet been selected, and it appears that the emphasis was on a road name rather than the location of the actual cattle trail.[19]

The Texas State Highway Commission requested that J. Frank Dobie study the matter and recommend a route, since it was known that cattle were driven north over multiple trails. It was also known that these cattle trails were called by different names or by no name at all, and that this would be a controversial topic. At the May 1930 highway commission meeting, Dobie proposed a compromise that called for a route from Brownsville to Red River Station in Montague

County by way of San Antonio, Austin, Waco, and Fort Worth, to be known as Old Chisholm Trail. He also proposed a second route from San Antonio to Quanah through Brady, Coleman, Abilene, Stamford, Rule, and Crowell, to be called the Western Chisholm Trail. Apparently the compromise was to name all northbound post–Civil War trails the Chisholm. The state highway commission meeting minutes from May 19, 1930, do not record any further details of Dobie's presentation or reveal any discussion on the subject. The commission authorized the Chisholm Trail Association to locate the trail and to place markers along the trail as long as they did not interfere with the highway, subject to approval of the marker design and location by the state engineer. Despite later claims, there is no indication in the meeting minutes that the highway commission endorsed a particular trail name or route or made any commitment to install or maintain markers.[20]

The proposed marker was to bear an insignia of a Texas longhorn steer head. Dobie subsequently stated: "The original Chisholm Trail did not come south of the Red River," and he described the trail through Texas as "an annex to its southern extremity—an annex longer than the original trail itself" and noted that "it was natural that this southern annex should in popular speech take on the name of the original trail" but that this was not always the case. He stated that the trail was called by those who drove it the Kansas Trail, the Beef Trail, the Texas Trail, the Chisholm Trail, or just the Trail. He also stated that the roads from Brownsville through San Antonio, Austin, Waco, and Fort Worth to Red River Station in Montague County and from Fort Worth to Doan's Crossing in Wilbarger County, should both be called the Chisholm Trail.[21]

Dobie's reasoning remains a mystery, unless he intended to use Chisholm Trail generically. The crossing at Doan's was the main crossing at the Red River on the route between Fort Griffin and Dodge City on the Fort Griffin and Dodge City, or Western, Trail. This route lay well to the west of and did not pass anywhere near the Chisholm Trail. Quanah is located yet another thirty miles to the west and even farther from the proposed namesake. On one hand, Dobie clearly stated that the original Chisholm Trail did not extend south of the Red River and that the trail was called by many names. On the other hand, he proposed to identify two separate routes through Texas that lay approximately one hundred miles apart at the Red River both by the Chisholm name. The reasons for the contradiction are as yet unknown, and statements such as Dobie's have further muddled the issue.

J. Frank Dobie was the head of a committee to mark the trail. The committee used "a map prepared by the Fourth U.S. Cavalry in 1871 in tracing the trail, supplemented with the accounts of the few remaining trail drivers." No further details are found in other newspaper accounts or in Texas Highway Commission minutes regarding the specific map that was used in the project; however, a map titled *Trails Made and Routes Used by the Fourth U.S. Cavalry under Command of General R. S. Mackenzie in Its Operations against Hostile Indians in Texas, Indian Territory (Now Oklahoma), New Mexico, and Old Mexico during the Period of 1871–2–3–4 and 5* contains data that are strikingly similar to Dobie's route recommendation for the highway marking project.[22]

The *Trails Made* map was compiled from military and other surveys by E. D. Dorchester in 1927 and supervised by Captain R. G. Carter, retired, US Army. Carter is listed on the map as the last surviving officer to serve under General Mackenzie. The map shows the locations of towns, military forts, and outposts; the routes of various military expeditions; and old roads and trails. An unusual feature of the map is that a cattle trail was delineated on a military map almost as prominently as General Mackenzie's campaigns. Given the citation and subject matter of the map, it is odd that a route listed as "Jesse Chisholm (Chissum) Trail" is recorded in the legend alongside military notations, is color-coded, and is prominently marked as "Jesse Chisholm Cattle Trail" seven times along its length from San Antonio to the north, while military expeditions or routes such as that of Major Merrill or the Santa Fe expedition are far less prominent and marked only once. Additionally, it is strange that Chisholm's first name was used. This map shows the Jesse Chisholm Cattle Trail rather than the previous designation of Chisholm's Trail or Chisholm's Cattle Trail, which was used on prior military and Department of the Interior maps of Indian Territory. Outside of the military expedition routes, very few roads are labeled on the map.

The Dorchester map dates from 1927, two years after the volumes of *The Trail Divers of Texas* were combined and released as one revised volume. C. H. Rust's account in *Trail Drivers* described the Chisholm Trail through Texas as follows:

> This old Trail that I attempt to tell you about, begins at San Antonio, and from there leading on to New Braunfels, thence to San Marcos, crossing the San Marcos River four miles below town, thence to Austin, crossing the Colorado River three miles below Austin. Leaving Austin, the Trail winds its way on to the right of

Round Rock, thence to the right of Georgetown, on to right of Salado, to the right of Belton, to Old Fort Graham, crossing the Brazos River to the left of Cleburne, then to Fort Worth, winding its way to the right of Fort Worth, just about where Hell's Half Acre used to be, crossing Trinity River just below town. Fort Worth was just a little burg on the bluff where the panther lay down and died. From Fort Worth the next town was Elizabeth, and from there to Bolivar; here the old Trail forked, but we kept the main trail up Elm to Saint Joe [*sic*] on to Red River Station, here crossing Red River.[23]

Rust went on to describe the right-hand fork from Bolivar north to cross the Red River below Gainesville and another main western trail that led past Coleman, Baird, Albany, Fort Griffin, and Double Mountain Fork and crossed the Red River at Doan's Store.[24] The route of the "Jesse Chisholm Cattle Trail" through Texas on the Dorchester map traces almost exactly this description of the Chisholm Trail from San Antonio to Red River Station as related by C. H. Rust. Wardville, the original Johnson County seat, is shown on the map rather than the newer town of Cleburne, and Red River Station is located incorrectly on the map as north of Henrietta, which is about twenty-five miles west of its actual location. Rust mentioned the crossing on the Red River at Doan's Store on the western route north from Fort Griffin but did not indicate this crossing as being on the Chisholm Trail, as Dobie suggested.

There is little doubt that the cattle trails passed exactly as Rust described; however, the description of any of these Texas trails as the Chisholm Trail cannot be corroborated by other maps or documents from the historical period of the cattle drives. Curiously, the main portion of the actual route of the Western Trail from San Antonio past Fort Griffin to Doan's is omitted from the Dorchester map, yet the portion north of Doan's to Dodge is connected to the route farther to the east and labeled "Jesse Chisholm Cattle Trail." Dorchester's specific source for the cattle trail portion of the map is not known. It is also unknown why this cattle trail received such an unusual level of prominence and attention on an otherwise military-oriented map, unless the purpose was to draw attention to the "Jesse Chisholm Cattle Trail" approximately forty years after the trails had closed.

Dobie's recommended trail marking route to the Texas Highway Commission can also be traced along the Jesse Chisholm Cattle Trail on the Dorchester map, following the route north from San Antonio to Fort Worth, then connecting to Red River Station and Doan's Crossing, which were the two most popular herd crossings on the Red River during the post–Civil War period. Much of that route followed the same path as the Meridian Highway. It would have been a simple matter to extend the proposed trail marking route south from San Antonio to Brownsville and thus include the larger cities from the southern tip of Texas north along much of the route of the Meridian Highway to the Red River as described in Dobie's proposal.

The timing of the publication of the Rust account in 1920 and 1925, interest in marking the trail beginning in 1925, publication of the Dorchester map in 1927, Dobie's proposal to the highway commission in 1930, and the similarities between the Rust account, the map, and Dobie's proposal indicate that the events are likely related. The chronology of these events suggests that the Rust account was likely used as the basis for the cattle trail route shown on the Dorchester map, and that this is the map reportedly used by Dobie in the highway commission project. Newspaper reports that the map was prepared by the Fourth US Cavalry in 1871 were misleading, as it was not prepared by the US Cavalry but was actually produced in 1927. The map could easily leave the viewer with the impressions that the Jesse Chisholm Cattle Trail was the only route for northbound herds from Texas and that all northbound cattle trails were designated by the Chisholm name, both of which are false.

After P. P. Ackley had purchased a home at Donna, Texas, in 1929, his wife died and he declared his intent to have the Old Chisholm Trail made into a national highway. Given the fact that Ackley had been advocating that cause for several years, he was undoubtedly involved at some level in the trail marking recommendation to the Texas Highway Commission in April–May 1930. Proponents of the trail marking project were apparently caught off guard when the highway commission authorized their project without further delay; they asked for permission from a state agency to mark a trail, but the location and route of said trail were not defined. The route of the trail to be marked through the Rio Grande Valley was unknown, and Dobie pointed out that neither of the two paved roads in that part of the state represented the trail route and that the actual route would be difficult to determine. The plan, believing that "the trail drivers should pass on the route and have the final word," was to present the results of their research to the Old Time Trails Drivers' Association for final action during the annual convention in October. The *San Antonio Express* reported that Saunders had been reelected as president of the association at the organization's annual meeting in

October 1930. This article also reported that Saunders, in his closing remarks, "declared himself in favor of the proposal by P. P. Ackley of Elk City, Oklahoma, to mark the Chisholm Trail with miniature longhorns."[25]

Progress by the trail marking group was apparently slow. By December 1930 Ackley had contacted the Brownsville Chamber of Commerce regarding the project, and G. C. Richardson of the chamber wrote a letter to the highway commission that expressed the chamber's support for the project. In a letter to the "President of the State Highway Board of Texas" dated December 9, 1930, Ackley envisioned a "Longhorn Trail Highway" that would connect all the Americas. He stated that he had promoted the "Long-Horn Chisholm Trail through western Oklahoma" and had thus been elected president of the Oklahoma group. He learned from Walter Long of the Austin Chamber of Commerce that "your organization [the Texas Highway Commission] has granted us the Traildrivers and Cowboys of Old the privilege of naming and marking a highway in honor of the Old Timers." He expressed frustration that no apparent progress had been made and asked that the president use his authority to allow markers to be placed on existing highway sign posts.[26]

Both Richardson and Ackley asked in their letters for permission to install trail markers on the existing state highway sign posts. In separate responses, Gibb Gilchrist, state highway engineer, stated that no additional signs would be permitted on the existing posts and referred them to Walter Long of the Austin Chamber of Commerce, who was working on a marker design. The *Brownsville Herald* reported on December 3, 1930, that the United States Good Roads Association endorsed the Chisholm Trail from Brownsville, Texas, to Bismarck, North Dakota. There is no record that the matter was studied by the US Good Roads Association to determine the location of the actual cattle trails, yet the name was endorsed for the length of the new highway. By these efforts to mark the cattle trails, and with the endorsement of the US Good Roads Association, the Chisholm Trail moved yet again. The southern terminus was now over seven hundred miles south of Chisholm's Trail, and the new Chisholm Trail was extended about seven hundred miles north to Bismarck from its original northern terminus at Abilene, Kansas. This latest version of the Chisholm Trail was located generally along the route of the new Meridian Highway.[27]

Marking the
Chisholm Trail

THE FIRST MONUMENT to commemorate a cattle trail in Texas appeared in July 1931 north of Vernon, Texas. The granite marker, placed by P. P. Ackley, included the date of his only known trip up the trail rather than the origin date or dates related to the trail. That marker, along with events that occurred within the next few years, prompted speculation among some former trail men that Ackley was more concerned with memorializing his own experience rather than the cattle trail. Members of the Trail Drivers' Association wanted to commemorate the trails and the accomplishments of the drovers while there were still some survivors left. Drovers used various trail names to describe the same trail; a designation had to be selected. A title or trail name was required before a monument was designed and engraved. Monument or marker locations had to be selected and approved by the appropriate entity. The controversy over the name and route of the Chisholm Trail in Texas intensified accordingly.

By August 1931 no markers had been installed as a result of the Texas Highway Commission authorization. For that matter, a design had not been finalized and approved. The *San Antonio Express* reported that George W. Saunders of San Antonio, Walter Long of Austin, and P. P. Ackley of Elk City, Oklahoma, were taking the lead in the project, and several marker designs were being considered that could be cast in iron, mounted on a post, and set in concrete. Saunders submitted a design that consisted simply of two iron longhorn steer heads mounted back-to-back, facing in opposite directions, mounted on a plain iron post with no additional signage.[1] Whether by accident or by design, Saunders's proposal would have served to commemorate the cattle trail without delving into the issues regarding the trail name.

Controversy and uncertainty regarding the names and locations of the old trails continued. Different trail names were proposed in different counties. This controversy, caused by the movement to mark the trail, prompted Saunders to study the matter and review records that he had kept since his days on the trail in the 1870s, along with years of research on the subject. In September 1931 he stated: "The famed Chisholm cattle trail, about which more has been written than any other trail, cannot be traced in Texas for the reason that it never existed in this state." Saunders went on to say that it was understood among those on the trail that the Chisholm was struck north of the Red River, that this was the general understanding until recently, and that some had recently been claiming that all trails were designated as the Chisholm.[2]

Since members of the Old Time Trail Drivers' Association were directly involved in this historic period, the subject was taken up at their annual convention in October 1931. The matter was presented to "insure [sic] uniformity as well as to keep history straight." The following motion was approved:

> Whereas; Since there are conflicting ideas about the location of the Chisholm Trail, and Whereas, there is now a movement to mark cattle trails through Texas, therefore be it Resolved; that it is the understanding of this association at its 17th annual reunion, arrived at the research of its president, George W. Saunders, and many of the oldest members who drove the trail, that the Chisholm Trail proper started at Red River Station and extended north to Abilene, Kan, and be it further Resolved; That the herds originating at all points in Texas drove north over the western or eastern Texas-Kansas Cattle Trails, the eastern branch of which met the Chisholm Trail at Red River Station, and be it further Resolved; That this association and their president do not wish to impose their will on any individual or county in marking of trails but offer this resolution obtained by knowledge of men who first drove cattle north, merely in the interest that Texas history be properly preserved to posterity.[3]

The motion was passed by a unanimous vote. The business meeting records of the Old Time Trail Drivers' Association were not available as of this writing; however, it was reported that "approximately 300 veterans of the cattle trails" were in attendance. Saunders stated

later that "over 500 trailers were present."[4] The purpose of this resolution was to address the question of the trail south of the Red River
and arrive at a consensus as an organization to address the controversy with the trail marking project in Texas.

Later in October a monument was dedicated at the site of Doan's
store in Wilbarger County near the crossing on the Red River. The
granite monument stands 10 feet 6 inches tall and is 5 feet 4 inches
wide and 18 inches thick. A bronze plaque featuring a herd at the
crossing and an inscription is on one side of the monument, and
the other side displays various brands that were used by cattlemen
who used the crossing (fig. 37). The inscription read: "IN HONOR OF
THE TRAIL DRIVERS WHO FREED TEXAS FROM THE YOKE OF DEBT
AND DESPAIR BY THEIR TRAIL TO THE CATTLE MARKETS OF THE FAR
NORTH; WE DEDICATE THIS STONE, SYMBOL OF THEIR COURAGE AND
FORTITUDE, AT THE SITE OF THE OLD DOAN'S STORE, OCTOBER 21–22,
1931. THE LONGHORN CHISHOLM TRAIL AND THE WESTERN TRAIL
1876–1895."[5]

About thirty members of the Trail Drivers Association made
the trip from San Antonio to Vernon on a bus chartered for the
event. J. Frank Dobie was the principal speaker at the dedication
ceremony. The monument was built with funds collected by Bertha Doan Ross, daughter of C. F. Doan, proprietor and namesake of
Doan's Store and Doan's Crossing. Saunders had advised P. P. Ackley
of this monument project and suggested that he should visit Ross.
Ackley followed through and made the largest single contribution
of one thousand dollars, and he apparently was in charge of having
the monument inscribed. He wanted to inscribe Chisholm Trail on
the monument but was told by both Ross and Saunders that it was
incorrect. Ackley persisted and threatened to take back his donation.
Some of the money had already been spent on the project, so Saunders told him to go ahead, but that including Chisholm Trail would
ignore history and ignore the recent unanimous resolution of the
Trail Drivers' Association. Bertha Ross was reportedly furious when
the monument was unveiled at the dedication ceremony. Saunders
stated that he "accepted the monument for the trail drivers Ass'n in
the best chuck wagon language at my command, but felt an aching
void in my heart." The celebrations continued, and afterward the trail
drivers returned to San Antonio.[6]

Up to that point Ackley and Saunders had apparently been working together on the trail marking project that had been authorized
by the Texas Highway Commission. Ackley had submitted a sketch
of a proposed marker design to the commission in December 1930;

it included a longhorn steer head design mounted on top of a post above another sign that designated the highway number. On the front of the steer head was inscribed "LONGHORN CHISHOLM TRAIL HIGHWAY." Ackley's design was not approved by the highway commission or the state engineer; instead, he was referred to W. R. Long of the Austin Chamber of Commerce, who was working on a design for the project. There is no record that they produced a marker proposal for this project. A sketch of a design submitted by Saunders was published in the *San Antonio Express*, and it appeared that it might be the most likely design for the project.[7]

The argument over the inscription on the monument at Doan's intensified. The Trail Drivers' Association had settled the question of whether the Chisholm Trail entered Texas to their satisfaction with their resolution on the subject, yet Ackley seemed determined to spread the name of the Chisholm Trail throughout the state. He had even used himself as the model for the bronze relief on the Doan's monument. He had the inclination and the resources, and he undertook his own trail marking projects. In addition to ignoring the advice of the Doans and the Trail Drivers' Association regarding the monument at Doan's Crossing, Ackley had a granite marker installed just a few miles away from Doan's in July 1931, a short time before the October unveiling. This monument read, "GOING UP THE CHISHOLM TRAIL, P. P. ACKLEY, 1878," and was reported to be the first marker placed on the cattle trail. In January 1932 Ackley announced in a letter to the Brownsville Chamber of Commerce that a marker would be installed at the international bridge at Brownsville to commemorate the Old Chisholm Trail.[8]

Letters between Saunders and Dobie in February 1932 indicate that the matter of the trail name was still a point of contention with Ackley, who campaigned for the "Longhorn Chisholm Trail." Saunders complained that "Ackley sold his story to new comers in Oklahoma and they believed him" and asked Dobie for his opinion on the muddle. Dobie responded a few days later. Ackley had apparently used Dobie's name to justify his choice of trail names, as Dobie stated to Saunders:

Old Ackley is all wrong when he says that I approve of the name "Longhorn Chisholm Trail." As a matter of fact, I disapprove of this name. It is a name that was never used denoting any trail whatsoever. Ackley seems more interested in commemorating his own trail experiences, which were so limited that he seems to know nothing about trail driving, than he is in commemorating the trail itself. On the marker he has made he has the date 1878. That was the date that he himself, he says, went up the trail. I protested to him against putting such a personal allusion on the marker.[9]

Meanwhile, Ackley, frustrated at the lack of progress with the marker project that had been approved by the highway commission, visited Walter Long in Austin to enlist his help in designing a marker for his latest project. The result was a design that consisted of a round, cast-metal marker approximately 24 inches in diameter, with six stars across the top, a longhorn head, a saddle and prickly pear at the bottom, and the inscription "GOING UP THE TEXAS CHISHOLM TRAIL." The proposed marker, to be installed at Brownsville, included the date 1878. According to a 1937 interview with Ackley, 1878 was the year of his first trip up the trail, starting out from near the present location of Wichita Falls, Texas. It is possible that he made more than one trip up the trail; however, he only mentioned the single trip in 1878, with no reference to any additional trips in the interview. In the previously cited letter from J. Frank Dobie to George W. Saunders, Dobie also cited only a single trip up the trail for Ackley in 1878.[10]

In July 1932 Saunders wrote a scathing letter to Ackley, stating, "We [the Trail Drivers' Association] want to keep Texas history straight. . . . We are tired of new comers who are notoriety hunting." Ackley's insistence on marking the trail with the Chisholm name went against the old trail drivers who "drove the trail in the late 60s and early 70s, . . . ignored a resolution passed at our last reunion by over 500 trailers unanimously," and was wrong from a historical perspective. He pointed out that Ackley went to newcomers for information instead of men who had made the trails, and that Ackley's claim to be "the daddy of the trails" looked fine to newcomers, but "you entered the trails eleven years after they opened." Saunders went on to say that "no cattle that crossed the Red River at Doan's ever touched the Chisholm Trail," that "you have ignored all our pleadings and proof that you were wrong, which proves that you are not sincere," that the old trail men had no patience for "imitators and windjammers" who were hunting notoriety, and that trails should be "marked proper or not at all." He suggested that Ackley should put his Chisholm inscription on his sheep trail through Mexico and South America, referencing Ackley's previous experience driving sheep and his desire to link the Americas with his trail.[11]

As Saunders pointed out, Ackley had become known as "Daddy" Ackley, the "daddy" of the Longhorn Chisholm Trail. Whether Ackley or one of his followers was responsible for the moniker is unknown. The *Canadian Record* reported in 1934: "Daddy Ackley, as he is known to thousands of good roads men from Mexico to Canada, is honorary president of the Longhorn Chisholm Trail Association." The following notation appears at the end of the transcript of the 1937 Yates interview: "Editor's Note; This interview is signed 'This is the story of Mr. P. P. Ackley, known as the father of the Chisholm Trail.'" There is no indication whether Ackley mentioned the "father of the Chisholm Trail" title or the interviewer obtained the title from another source. Although Ackley was apparently known affectionately among the Good Roads associations, he evidently did not enjoy the same reputation among the old drovers after the Doan's monument incident, as there are no similar statements of support among the old trail drivers.[12]

Prior to July 1931 it appears that Ackley, Saunders, and the Trail Drivers' Association were working together, at least to some degree, to mark the cattle trails through Texas. Ackley was apparently unwilling to listen to those with much more experience on the trails— the Doans, Saunders, and the unanimous vote of the Trail Drivers Association—and whatever spirit of cooperation existed vanished with his insistence on the Chisholm Trail name for the monuments installed in Wilbarger County during the summer and fall of 1931.

The trail marking project approved by the Texas Highway Commission was apparently never completed. While the commission authorized the Chisholm Trail Association in 1930 to mark a route along the trail, they declined to approve a marker design that included the name Longhorn Chisholm Trail or that was affixed to the same post as a state highway designation. In a 1932 letter to J. Frank Dobie, George W. Saunders stated that he would soon go to Austin to meet with W. R. Long regarding the trail marking project, but due to the worsening depression nothing could be done except to keep the matter alive until the economic situation improved.[13] Pressure from Dobie and Saunders may have had a minimal effect on Ackley, as the name Longhorn Chisholm Trail was replaced, when his markers were cast, by Texas Chisholm Trail, and 1878, the year of his only known trip up the trail, was replaced by 1867, which was the year that the cattle market at Abilene, Kansas, opened and the first herds took that route through Indian Territory toward Abilene (fig. 38).

Ackley continued with his own trail marking project, placing his markers in Texas with permission of each local county commissioners court and with no other apparent historical oversight. County commissioners during the Depression might have been more concerned with the possibility that the markers might help attract travelers and boost the local economy rather than question historical accuracy. The total number of markers purchased and placed is unknown. By 1938 Ackley had placed his markers from Brownsville, Texas, to the Canadian border. Some of his Chisholm Trail markers still exist and can be found in Texas generally along the route of US 81, which is basically the route of the old Meridian Highway, and along the route of the Western Trail that led past Fort Griffin to Doan's Store in Wilbarger County and on to Dodge City. Ackley's markers have been found off of the main route in places such as Ellis County, Texas, and as far away as Bowman, North Dakota. Regarding the Ellis County marker, by 1958 it was known locally that there was a cattle trail in Hill County and a trail from Waxahachie to Fort Worth, but the reason for the Chisholm Trail marker was a mystery. A description of the metal marker fits the description of Ackley's markers. It was found after the sale of a local farm and eventually put on display at a local bank. A notice of the curiosity appeared in a local publication: "Something new has been added at the Waxahachie Bank and Trust Company. Along with a money tree, a lollipop tree, and a few other items, there is now a Chisholm Trail marker on display in the lobby."[14]

Peter Preston Ackley died on April 7, 1940. Although his persistence and determination to mark the trails are admirable, his attachment to the Chisholm name and the location of his markers have confused many and fueled the trail controversy over the decades. Regardless of his intentions and motivation, the fact is that many of his Chisholm Trail markers were placed along the route of the Western Trail, a long way from the Chisholm. Some have disappeared, perhaps removed once it was discovered they were in the wrong place. Regarding his Chisholm Trail markers generally along the US 81 corridor in Texas, many were placed at county courthouses, which might be miles from the old trail but are a more easily accessible and visible location. Although a cattle trail may have passed nearby and the marker is accurate in respect to general proximity to a cattle trail, the inscription "Going Up the Texas Chisholm Trail" represents Ackley's own notion. There is no documentation from the period of the cattle drives to support Ackley's Chisholm Trail markers south of the Red River; between Abilene, Kansas, and Canada; or along the route of the Western Trail.[15]

The inscription on the monument at Doan's was subsequently changed. The original inscription "THE LONGHORN CHISHOLM TRAIL AND THE WESTERN TRAIL 1876–1895," which caused the consternation of Bertha Doan Ross and the Trail Drivers' Association, was removed and replaced by the present inscription on the monument (fig. 39): "THE WESTERN TEXAS–KANSAS TRAIL 1876–1895 / THIS MONUMENT ERECTED BY TEXANS." It is unknown exactly who ordered the change or when the change was made, although, according to a Doan descendant, the inscription was changed within two or three years of the 1931 dedication ceremony. The original engraving was done by G. W. Backus of Backus Monument Company in Vernon, Texas. The later inscription includes the trail designation for this trail from the October 1931 resolution of the Trail Drivers' Association.[16]

George W. Saunders died on July 3, 1933. Honorary pallbearers included Will Rogers, John Nance Garner, and J. Frank Dobie. Another monument to Doan's Crossing was erected by the state of Texas a short distance away from the large monument in 1936. This monument includes the following quote from Will Rogers: "YOU DON'T NEED MUCH MONUMENT IF THE CAUSE IS GOOD. IT'S ONLY THESE MONUMENTS THAT ARE FOR NO REASON AT ALL THAT HAS TO BE BIG. GOOD LUCK TO YOU ALL ANYHOW. YOURS, WILL ROGERS." This quote was taken from a letter that accompanied Rogers's contribution of fifty dollars toward the 1931 monument: "Taint much, but you don't need much monument if the cause is good, its [*sic*] these monuments that are for no reason at all that have to be big. Good luck to you all anyhow." This was likely included on the 1936 monument as a reference to the erroneous original inscription and personal allusions on the large monument. Additionally, it is inscribed, "DEDICATED TO GEORGE W. SAUNDERS, PRESIDENT OF THE OLD TRAIL DRIVERS ASS'N., WHO KEPT THE TRAIL RECORDS STRAIGHT." The wording on this monument suggests that the original inscription on the large monument was still visible in 1936 and might have been changed after that date rather than within two or three years of installation. This monument has since been moved from its original location and is presently located next to the large monument at the site of Doan's Store.[17]

While the project to mark the trail in Texas was proposed by private citizens, and the Texas State Highway Commission left it up to the same private citizens to perform the research and make recommendations, commemorators took a more formal approach north of the Red River. The Oklahoma legislature's House Bill 149, passed in March 1931 and approved by the governor on March 31, required the Oklahoma Highway Department to locate, as near as possible, the location where the Chisholm Trail crossed each section of land in the state from Jefferson County north through Grant County, and to locate the trail that crossed the Red River at Doan's Store. The bill also required the mapping of the trails in relation to the main line of the Rock Island Railway and the Meridian Highway. Whether the decision by Oklahoma officials to take a more formal and organized approach to the issue was influenced by the disagreements and controversy across the Red River in Texas is a matter of speculation.[18]

The final report was prepared in 1933 by H. S. Tennant of the Oklahoma State Highway Commission and published in a 1936 edition of *Chronicles of Oklahoma*. The general route through the Oklahoma counties of Jefferson and Grant, as specified in HB 149, was also the route of the Chisholm Trail Road as designated in 1911 by the Chisholm Trail Good Roads Association as the name of their stretch of the Meridian Highway. This road designation might explain why the entire route through the state was referred to as the Chisholm Trail in HB 149 and why there was no separate mention of the original mapped Chisholm's Trail. Tennant concluded that there was a demarcation at the Red River between the trail that led from south Texas to Red River Station and the continuation of the trail through Indian Territory. He referred to the Texas portion of that trail as the Eastern Trail and the portion of the trail through Indian Territory as the Chisholm Trail. Tennant referred to the trail that crossed the Red River at Doan's Store as the Texas Cattle Trail, or Western Trail. Tennant's conclusion regarding the Eastern Trail and Western Trail through Texas is supported by the Department of the Interior's 1881 *Map of Texas Showing Routes of Transportation of Cattle* (fig. 17).[19]

Based on numerous interviews with surviving trail men, physical evidence of the trails, and relevant surveys, Tennant gave detailed descriptions of the locations of the trails in relation to the township, section, and range positions through the state. The Engineering Department of the Oklahoma State Highway Commission produced two maps in 1933 as a result of this project that showed the trail routes and adjacent section numbers: one map of the route from Red River Station north through Jefferson County and on through Grant County, labeled as the Chisholm Trail, and one map of the route from Doan's Store through Jackson County and on through Harper County, labeled as the Texas Cattle Trail (figs. 40, 41). According to these maps the old trails were still visible at that time in many locations along both routes.[20]

Tennant's assignment was an engineering project to document the location of the specified trails rather than to document the history of the trails. He stated that the history of these trails could be found in practically any library in the state, but to determine the location of the trail was "a wonderful engineering project; it followed the course of least resistance." A certain amount of information that could not be corroborated, such as statements that Jesse Chisholm was employed by Joseph McCoy and that Charles Goodnight first traveled the Chisholm Trail, found its way into Tennant's report. Statements like these, which are now known to be incorrect but were common during the 1930s, do not affect the engineering data. The route described in Tennant's report and marked on the associated 1933 map as the Chisholm Trail closely matches the route of the Abilene Cattle Trail as designated on multiple military and Department of the Interior maps of Indian Territory that date back to 1872 (fig. 40). Since Tennant did not cite any of those maps in his report, it is assumed that their existence was unknown to him at that time.[21]

Between 1892 and 1933, the southern end of Chisholm's Trail as mapped in Indian Territory and Oklahoma, moved more than one hundred miles south and slightly west. The mapped route of the Abilene Cattle Trail remained the same, but the trail name was replaced by the Chisholm name. The Chisholm Trail name was also extended north to Canada and south to the Rio Grande in conjunction with construction of the Meridian Highway. Between 1932 and 1938, P. P. Ackley marked the Meridian Highway as the Chisholm Trail with the blessing of the US Good Roads Association, whose mission was road improvement and development of national highways (fig. 38). Ackley's markers were endorsed by an organization that had nothing to do with cattle drives, and his choice of location and terminology were contradicted unanimously by the Trail Drivers' Association. Ackley's markers, and many others that were subsequently erected, were apparently based upon these changes that occurred a number of years after the trail's period of use. Even when cast in metal or etched in stone, the Chisholm Trail name is often based on a dash of truth, a bucket of folklore, and a wagonload of opinion, especially south of the Red River and north of Abilene, Kansas.

16

Old Chestnuts
and White Lies

THE CHISHOLM TRAIL led from near San Angelo, Texas, to New Mexico. A fork of the Chisholm Trail led from Horsehead Crossing on the Pecos River in Texas through Indian Territory. The cattle trail through Texas was the McCoy Trail. Joseph McCoy hired Jesse Chisholm to blaze the Chisholm Trail from Kansas to the Red River in 1867. Jesse Chisholm blazed a trail from Kansas to Mexico in 1867. Jesse Chisholm drove cattle herds from south Texas to Kansas in 1867. The Texas portion of the cattle trail to Kansas is called the Chisholm Trail because of common usage of the term by drovers. The Texas portion of the cattle trail to Kansas is called the Chisholm Trail because the trail name is documented on maps. These are a few of the claims that have been repeated since the 1930s that are used to promote various versions of Chisholm Trail history. Is there any substance in these old chestnuts or are they mostly empty shells?

Many statements have been made over the years regarding the Chisholm and other trails, and several versions of events have evolved. Some of these can be corroborated by the historical record. Other statements are contradicted by or otherwise not supported by the documentation, yet have come to be accepted as historical fact and woven into the fabric of the cattle trails narrative. It is not uncommon to encounter inconsistent or contradictory information, sometimes from the same source. Some of these statements that fall into this category were published with no footnote or source information. Once a statement appeared in print, it apparently was accepted as factual and subsequently repeated. This is evident by the multiple similar versions of trails history that deviate from the historical record but that have been repeated over the years. Some may have been based on the best information available at the time, based on nothing more than an opinion, or perhaps a combination of fact and opinion. The common denominator among folklore, hearsay, and legend is the lack of proof to substantiate the story. If the information in a narrative cannot be verified, by definition it falls into the category of folklore, hearsay, or legend.

Howard W. Peak was a member of a pioneer family and resident of Fort Worth, Texas. In the fall of 1923, during preparations for the Diamond Jubilee celebrations in Fort Worth, Peak wrote to Charles Goodnight requesting information regarding the cattle trail that passed through the city. Goodnight, who was involved in a business relationship with John Chisum for several years, responded that the trail that passed through Fort Worth should be called the McCoy Trail, since Joseph McCoy established the market at Abilene, Kansas, sent a scout into Indian Territory to intercept and direct herds to Abilene, and was therefore responsible for the presence of the trail. Goodnight also mentioned that the Chisholm Trail "existed in name only" and that John Chisum had never laid a trail anywhere, but followed the Loving and Goodnight Trail to Fort Sumner, New Mexico. A series of concrete McCoy Trail markers was subsequently installed along the route of the old cattle trail through Fort Worth, and the route was included among points of interest marked for the Diamond Jubilee celebration in November 1923.[1]

Peak later wrote "The Old Cattle Trail," part of which was included in *The Story of Old Fort Worth* to commemorate the Texas Centennial and contained information that Goodnight had furnished regarding the cattle trail. However, Peak's version, which he stated was "on the authority of the late Charles Goodnight, a cattle man whose authority is unquestioned," stated that the Chisholm Trail "was the McCoy Trail, properly speaking" and was "named for one of the earlier cattle drivers who drove his stock on the hoof from the coast country to the Kansas markets." Peak also stated: "The Chisholm Trail proper started near San Angelo, crossed the Pecos river at Horse Head Crossing, and branched, one prong going to New Mexico, the other through the Indian Territory, now Oklahoma."[2]

Although Peak mentioned Goodnight as a source, and his statement regarding the McCoy Trail is accurate according to Goodnight's letter, his statements regarding the Chisholm Trail's being named for an earlier cattle driver, the origin of the Chisholm Trail near San Angelo or New Mexico, and a prong of the Chisholm Trail from Horsehead Crossing through Indian Territory were not mentioned in Goodnight's letter. The actual source for that information is unknown, and this version is not supported by any documentation.

Peak also fell victim to the Chisholm/Chisum/Chism confusion; he wrote, "There were two cattlemen of similar names, John Chisholm (heretofore mentioned) and a Chism or Chisum, an Indian of the Indian Territory, so it appears that the matter is somewhat confused."[3] Whether by intentional fabrication or accidental assumptions, Peak perpetuated the muddle between John Chisum and Jesse Chisholm and further confused the trail's history.

For his part, Goodnight did not mention that Chisum had driven a herd along much of the route to New Mexico before Goodnight's and Loving's first trip.[4] His motive for omitting that information is unknown and has been the subject of occasional speculation. Goodnight was likely correct when he said the trail should have been called the McCoy Trail. Given the contributions of Joseph McCoy, the entire trail route from origins in Texas to destination at Abilene, Kansas, could have been named the McCoy Trail if someone had taken the initiative at the time, and it would have been difficult to argue a case to the contrary.

Even the president of the Trail Drivers' Association was not infallible. George W. Saunders stated in September 1931 that Joseph McCoy hired Jesse Chisholm to blaze a trail from Abilene, Kansas, south to a crossing on the Red River during spring of 1867 in time for the 1867 cattle drives. According to J. R. Mead, Chisholm's business associate, Chisholm first made the trip from the Little Arkansas River to the North Canadian River in the fall of 1864. According to Vincente George Chisholm, Jesse's adopted son, that first trip was made in the spring of 1865. At any rate, Chisholm had already traveled most of the route multiple times before the railroad reached Abilene. The route followed the natural lay of the land along a buffalo migration route. Chisholm used the route to travel between his trading posts on the Little Arkansas and the North Canadian Rivers.[5]

After the railhead and stock facilities were established at Abilene during the summer of 1867, McCoy hired T. F. Hersey, a civil engineer, to survey and mark a direct route from Abilene south across the plains to the mouth of the Little Arkansas River (the present site of Wichita, Kansas), which was the end of Chisholm's Trail. There were no landmarks on the plains, and Hersey constructed dirt mounds to mark the shortest route from the Little Arkansas to Abilene, enabling drovers to reach Abilene instead of potentially wandering to a competing town.[6] While it is true that Joseph McCoy hired someone to survey and mark, or "blaze," the portion of the trail between the Little Arkansas River and Abilene, Kansas, that person was T. F. Hersey. McCoy made no mention of an arrangement of any kind with Jesse

Chisholm, and no evidence indicates that McCoy and Chisholm ever met.

Variations on the claim that McCoy hired Chisholm to blaze a trail include versions that Jesse Chisholm blazed a trail from some point in Kansas or Indian Territory south past the Red River, or that Chisholm blazed a trail from various points in Texas all the way to somewhere in Kansas. For example, a proclamation was issued by the Commissioners Court of McLennan County, Texas, on October 19, 2010, for a local Chisholm Trail festival. The proclamation states in the opening line: "Whereas, In 1867, Jesse Chisholm a trading post owner, blazed a trade route and trail that ran from Wichita Kansas— South to Mexico—through Indian Territory known as Chisholm's Trail, which opened the way for railheads in Kansas."[7] Although Jesse Chisholm traveled through various parts of Texas and into Mexico, the primary purpose for these trips was to assist Sam Houston in efforts to negotiate peace on the frontier and to attempt to locate Sequoyah, the inventor of the Cherokee alphabet, in Mexico. All of that travel occurred during the 1840s; railheads at Abilene or Wichita, Kansas, did not exist at that time.

Those activities also occurred well before Chisholm's first trip between the Little Arkansas River and the North Canadian River in 1865. Chisholm was known to be in Kansas and Indian Territory during 1867, where he was involved in trading and negotiations at the National Creek Council, at Fort Gibson, and at the Medicine Lodge Creek Council.[8] These events kept Chisholm occupied during the summer and fall of 1867. The railheads in Kansas were the result of westward movement of the population and associated construction of railroads rather than the result of a single trail as claimed. There is no documentation to indicate that Jesse Chisholm blazed a trail between any point in Texas and any point in Kansas during 1867 or in the years immediately preceding the expansion of the railroads into central Kansas.

Occasional claims are made to the effect that Jesse Chisholm drove cattle from various points in Texas up the trail, and the trail through Texas is therefore named the Chisholm Trail. J. R. Mead wrote in *History of Wichita and Sedgwick County, Kansas*, published in 1910, that Jesse Chisholm drove a herd of four hundred head of cattle from the Canadian River to the Little Arkansas. Mead died the same year the book was published, and no dates or further details were given. Vincente George Chisholm claimed that the herd was driven by a Delaware named Red Blanket and not by Jesse Chisholm.[9]

A modern example of such a claim can be seen on a monument

in Round Rock, Texas, dedicated in 2003, which contains the following inscription: "In the pioneer days of yesterday, a settlement was springing up along a Brushy Creek by a round rock, where pioneers had heard there was a low water crossing. This crossing would become one of the most famous markers along the Chisholm Trail. Jesse Chisholm led his herds along this trail from deep in the south of Texas towards Hays, Kansas, which was fast becoming the hub of a burgeoning cattle industry, each time passing through the growing settlement of Round Rock."[10] This inscription leaves the impression that Jesse Chisholm drove multiple herds of Texas cattle past the crossing at Brushy Creek to Hays, Kansas. According to the Kansas Historical Society, the Union Pacific Railroad first arrived at Ellis County, Kansas, near Fort Hays, in October 1867. The town of Hays was established with the arrival of the railroad. The trail driving season was almost over, as winter was near. During the summer of 1867, Jesse Chisholm attended a National Creek Council on July 4 held in the Creek lands near the present site of Okmulgee; traveled to the mouth of the Little Arkansas for a meeting on July 20 with Indian Agent Jesse Leavenworth, James Mead, George Bent, William Greiffenstein, and representatives of the Comanche, Apache, Kiowa, Arapaho, and Wichita tribes; conducted his trading business; and was present but sick during the Medicine Lodge Creek Council in October.[11]

It is possible that Chisholm acquired some cattle through trade or came into possession of cattle running loose in Indian Territory and moved them in small numbers between his trading posts. It is just as possible that he kept busy with other activities and delegated the moving of any livestock to someone else. At any rate, there is no documentation to indicate that Chisholm drove cattle anywhere in any significant quantity. The cattle business did not reach Hays for a few years after the town was established, and it did not become a major market on the order of Abilene, Wichita, Dodge, or some of the other cow towns.[12] The trip with a herd from "deep in the south of Texas" to Hays, Kansas, would have taken approximately two months, maybe longer. Chisholm was known to be in Indian Territory and southern Kansas during the spring, summer, and fall of 1867.

Before the arrival of the railroad, the establishment of the town, and the capacity to ship cattle, there was no reason to drive a herd to the future site of Hays unless one had a contract to supply beef to Fort Hays. Since Jesse Chisholm was not a cattleman, it is highly unlikely that he possessed such a contract. Chisholm died on March 4, 1868, only a few months after the railroad first arrived at Ellis County,

Kansas, and several years before a cattle market existed at Hays. Chisholm's documented presence in Kansas and Indian Territory, the lack of evidence that he ever drove a large cattle herd anywhere, and the timing of these events contradict the Round Rock narrative. There is no evidence to support the claim that Jesse Chisholm drove herds past the round rock at Brushy Creek to Hays, Kansas.

The book *A Texas Cow-boy; or, Fifteen Years on the Hurricane Deck of a Spanish Pony* (1886), by Charles Siringo, is sometimes mentioned in support of the Chisholm name for the Texas portion of the trail, yet it contains only one reference in the entire book in which a landmark in Texas is linked to the famous trail. Siringo wrote: "The following May I landed in Gainesville, Texas, right side up with care, and from there went to Saint Joe [*sic*] on the Chisholm trail," where he was hired by a passing herd. The Chisholm Trail is mentioned in the title of two chapters; however, the term is used in the titles only, as no further details or information about the trail or landmarks is contained in those chapters. A chapter that described Siringo's return trip from Kansas to Texas contained references to Eagle Chief Creek, the Cimarron River, Turkey Creek, the Chisholm Trail, the Washita River, and Pauls Valley, which were all located along the trail in Indian Territory, and to Gainesville and Saint Jo in Texas.[13]

Siringo traveled from Jackson County, Texas, to Kansas and back. All of his specific references to landmarks along the Chisholm Trail were located in Indian Territory except for Gainesville and Saint Jo, which were both located just south of the Red River in close proximity to the river crossings. The claim that Siringo's mention of Saint Jo and Gainesville or his use of the name Chisholm Trail in the chapter titles somehow indicates a belief on his part that the Chisholm Trail stretched throughout Texas assumes something that is not stated. This assumption is contradicted by the fact that Siringo described landmarks in conjunction with the Chisholm Trail through Indian Territory, yet did not mention a single landmark in relation to the Chisholm Trail between the prairies of the Texas Gulf Coast and the vicinity of the Red River.

One of the more prevalent claims is that the Chisholm name was applied to the Texas portion of the trail because of "common usage" by the drovers. As one gets closer to the historical period of the cattle drives, fewer references to the Chisholm Trail are found, and they tell a contradictory story. The books *Historic Sketches of the Cattle Trade of the West and Southwest* (1874), *Report in Regard to the Range and Ranch Cattle Business of the United States* (1885), *Historical and Biographical Record of the Cattle Industry and the Cattlemen of Texas and Adjacent*

Territory (1895), and *Prose and Poetry of the Live Stock Industry of the United States* (1905) are considered by collectors as the "big four" books on the subject of the early cattle business. *Historic Sketches* and *Report in Regard* were both published during the cattle driving period. *Historical and Biographical Record* and *Prose and Poetry* were published immediately afterward but contain relevant information and biographical sketches of cattlemen who drove the trails. These were the first volumes published after the trails closed, and the information would have been gathered while it was still relatively fresh.

These books contain information from multiple sources: the founder of the cattle market at Abilene, Kansas; the US Bureau of Statistics; the National Live Stock Association; and more than four hundred biographical sketches based on first-person accounts. Among these biographical sketches, only one mention of Chisholm Trail and three mentions of Chisum Trail are found.[14] In all of these volumes there are two references to the Chisholm Trail in Indian Territory, two generic references to the Chisholm Trail with no geographic indication, two references to the Chisum Trail in Texas, one reference to the Chisum Trail to Colorado, two references to the Texas Trail or Texas Cattle Trail, several references to the Fort Griffin or Fort Dodge Trail, and many references using the destination of Abilene, Dodge, Ogallala, and so on.

If a fifth book were considered in the "big five," it might be Siringo's *A Texas Cow-boy*, which was the first book authored by a former drover. This book provided a string of geographic points referenced along the Chisholm Trail in Indian Territory that can be confirmed using the cited maps of Indian Territory from 1875 to 1887. It gives one geographic reference to the Chisholm Trail south of the Red River, at Saint Jo in Montague County. The biographical sketches were written immediately after the trail driving period and therefore tend to reflect the actual terms used by the cattlemen at that time.[15]

A number of newspaper stories published between 1869 and 1890 include a reference to the Chisholm Trail with a geographic reference to a location. The range of dates is relevant, because the first news article to mention the Chisholm Trail appeared in 1869. Trail traffic had been reduced to a mere trickle, and articles changed from reporting news to more of a reminiscent or sentimental tone after 1890. Twenty-five articles refer to the Chisholm Trail. Fourteen of those articles refer to a point in the vicinity of or north of the Cimarron River. Four articles refer to a point in the vicinity of or between the Canadian River and the Cimarron. Five articles include a general reference to a point north of the Red River. Two articles include a reference to a point south of the Red River in Texas. Twenty-seven articles refer to the Texas Cattle Trail and include a geographic reference to a point north of the Red River. Two articles reference the Texas Cattle Trail geographically in Texas. Three articles reference the Eastern Trail in Indian Territory. Two articles reference the Eastern Trail in Texas. Seven articles reference the Abilene Trail. It was not uncommon for articles to be reprinted in subsequent editions of other newspapers; generally, only the first occurrence was counted as a reference.[16]

Mention is often made of an article that appeared in the *Kansas Daily Commonwealth* (Topeka) on May 27, 1870, which was thought to be the first newspaper reference to the Chisholm Trail. Historian and author Wayne Gard stated that the article reported that Osage Indians on a hunt had camped on the Chisholm Trail. At that time the Osages were still located in southern Kansas, and preparations were still being made by the Office of Indian Affairs to relocate them to Indian Territory. It is most likely that their camp described in this article was located in the vicinity of the cattle trail near Caldwell or in the northern part of Indian Territory.[17]

Another article to which reference is often made appeared in the April 28, 1874, edition of the *Denison (Texas) Daily News*. According to Gard, this article referred to cattle going "up the famous Chisholm Trail." Many have seized upon this partial, vague reference as "proof" of the Chisholm name for the trail in Texas. But the writer's intent is clear when the entire sentence from the original newspaper article is considered. The statement is taken from an article about stock raisers and cattle. The original sentence reads: "In 1872 there were four hundred and fifty thousand driven overland from Western Texas to Kansas, through the Indian Territory by Bluff Creek and Caldwell, up the famous Chisholm trail." Gard used the partial quote "up the famous Chisholm Trail" in an explanation of how the Chisholm name came to be applied to the Texas portion of the trail. His reasons for omitting the landmarks are unknown. He also pointed out that the Chisholm name was not used universally. Rather than this being an indication of the trail name in Texas, the specific landmarks described in the original article are along the trail in the northern part of Indian Territory and southern Kansas.[18]

The preponderance of the relevant newspaper articles from the historical period of the cattle drives included geographic or landmark references to the Chisholm Trail at points north of the Red River, while there is an apparent lack of similar newspaper articles from the same period that included geographic or landmark references to the Chisholm south of the Red—only two articles over a twenty-one-year period. The name Texas Cattle Trail appears to have been at least as popular, if not more so, in newsprint than the name Chisholm Trail during the years 1869–90.

The Kansas Pacific Railway published a series of booklets and associated maps from 1871 to 1875 as a marketing tool to provide Texas drovers with a general route to the KP railheads. These booklets, intended to attract Texas cattlemen and drovers, included specific directions from the Red River near Red River Station across Indian Territory to the KP railheads in the general vicinity of Abilene, Ellsworth, Brookville, and Ellis. The written directions include approximate distances and notes regarding the availability of grass, water, and firewood. The maps that accompanied the booklets typically show a network of routes that begin at various points in south Texas and along the Gulf Coast, converge at Red River Station into a direct route north, and then diverge to the various destinations in Kansas like the roots, trunk, and branches of a mighty tree.

The maps were not intended to trace the exact route of a trail, but as a general guide to Red River Station and then to the KP railheads. To serve their purpose as promotional items, the booklets and maps would have used common nomenclature and landmarks that reflected the terminology and usage of the target audience of the historical period; otherwise they would not have been effective. Surviving copies of the booklet and map are rare. The 1874 and 1875 editions of the booklet use the names Great Texas Cattle Trail, Cattle Trail, or Texas Stock Route to describe the overall route from Texas to the destinations in Kansas. The 1872 edition of the map shows the route north of the Red River marked simply as Cattle Trail. The 1873 and 1875 editions of the map show the route north of the Red as the Ellsworth Cattle Trail.[19]

Each of the Kansas Pacific maps shows the route indicated by a double line north of the Red River and single lines south of the Red, which indicates a clear delineation between the trails north and south of the river. The trail north of the Red River was designated with a trail name, while the trails through Texas that converged at Red River Station were unnamed. The name Chisholm Trail or Chisholm Cattle Trail did not appear in any of the cited Kansas Pacific Railway maps or booklets. A summary description of the 1871–75 series by a rare book dealer did not indicate that Chisholm Trail or Chisholm Cattle Trail appeared in any of the other editions. An 1872 article in the *Houston Telegraph* stated that the Kansas Pacific Railway had "prepared and printed a small guide-map of the Texas cattle trail from several points in Texas to Abilene and neighboring points on the railroad." Several different designations of the cattle trail from Texas were used in the Kansas Pacific literature and related articles, but Chisholm Trail or Chisholm Cattle Trail did not appear in this series of advertising.[20]

The claim that the Chisholm Trail name was applied to the Texas portion of the trail by common usage has been repeated often and is typically not supported by any footnote or specific reference. This claim does not appear to be supported by contemporary news-papers, by the Kansas Pacific Railway advertising aimed at attracting the drovers, or by the numerous biographical sketches of the cattle-men themselves that were published in the years immediately after the trails closed. If the name was actually applied to the Texas trail through common usage, one would expect to find more examples of that usage among news reports and advertising from the historical period of 1869–90 or in statements of cattlemen published prior to 1906. Much of this "common usage" appears to have originated later during the period when the Chisholm Trail name was prominent in the news because of its link to the Meridian Highway project.

Cattle trails literature is full of contradictions, and the book *The Trail Drivers of Texas* is no exception. A collection of first-person accounts of experiences on the trails, it is often cited to support opin-ions regarding the Chisholm Trail. These accounts were solicited by George W. Saunders beginning in 1915, approximately thirty years after the long cattle drives were drawing to a close, and they provide valuable insight as long as the reader can recognize that nostalgia, old age, public perception, and selective memory could have been a factor in some of the accounts given so many years after the fact. It is not necessarily that one trail driver was more or less credible than another, but that each one observed events from a different perspec-tive, potentially subject to the aforementioned later influences. This holds true not only for *The Trail Drivers of Texas*, but also for other interviews conducted and books and articles written during the later part of the lifetime of the trail drivers.

A review of *The Trail Drivers of Texas* reveals that out of approx-imately 180 trail drivers who described their trail experience, seven stated or indicated that the Chisholm Trail was struck somewhere south of the Red River in Texas. Ten men stated or indicated that the Chisholm Trail was struck north of the Red River in Indian Territory. Two men described the trail past Red River Station as the Eastern Trail. Two trail drivers referred to the trail by a name other than Chisholm or Eastern, such as Texas Trail or Kansas Trail. Twenty-seven references were geographically ambiguous, and more than eighty trail drivers did not use a trail name, but instead used the generic phrase "up the trail" when they described their experiences on the cattle trail. Many others simply spoke of the destination at the end of the trail, which seemed to be the common custom at the time.[21]

The "common usage" claim is easy to make but difficult to prove, given the fact that for each account that stated that the Chisholm Trail was located in Texas, an equal or greater number of other accounts can be found that stated that the trail was located only north of the Red River. Because of the many contradictions and regardless of the source, statements that were made years or decades after the fact should be compared against other historical data from the period of the cattle drives to arrive at a conclusion. To compare one drover's statement against another's without additional data to corroborate one version or another is futile. It seems obvious that the cattle trail south of Red River Station and Gainesville was much more commonly known by drovers during the historic period of the cattle drives by names other than Chisholm or by no name other than "the trail."

Another common claim is that the Chisholm Trail through Texas is documented on authoritative maps. Maps that have provenance to the particular historical period under study are typically more valuable for research purposes than maps drawn later. Maps from the actual historical period typically reflect a region as it was known at the time, while maps drawn later can potentially be subject to opinion, nostalgia, hindsight, or any number of other influences, especially regarding the subject of the cattle trails. Maps prepared by surveyors and cartographers for an official entity typically have a greater degree of accuracy, and therefore greater research value. Maps that were prepared later can be compared against maps or other documents from the historical period and can then be evaluated accordingly.

Caution is needed because things are not always as they appear. For example, the map *The Old Chisholm Cattle Trail with Subsidiary Trails in Texas, 1873* was thought to date from 1873. But the author of the map, A. W. Ziegelasch, was born in 1893; therefore, the map is not authentic to 1873. Ziegelasch worked as a draftsman for the state of Kansas during the 1920s. The Ziegelasch map closely resembles *The Best and Shortest Cattle Trail from Texas* map published in 1873 by the Kansas Pacific Railway Company. The trail was designated as Ellsworth Cattle Trail and led to Ellsworth, Kansas, on the original map. The designation was changed to Chisholm Trail and rerouted from Ellsworth to Abilene on the Ziegelasch map. Specific reasons for the changes are unknown; however, the Meridian Highway project, publicity regarding naming it the Chisholm Trail Road in certain areas, P. P. Ackley's campaign to name the entire Meridian Highway route the Chisholm Trail, and the suspected appearance of the Ziegelasch map coincidentally occurred within a few years of each other and would account for the changes made from the original to the Ziegelasch map (fig. 42).[22]

The Abilene Cattle Trail first appeared as a designated mapped route on the 1872 *Map of the Chickasaw Country and Contiguous Portions of the Indian Territory* (fig. 23). Chisholm's Trail first appeared as a designated mapped route on the 1875 *Military Map of the Indian Territory*. The designation of Chisholm's Trail changed to Chisholm's Cattle Trail on the 1879 map *Indian Territory*, but the routes remained unchanged (fig. 22). Both routes appeared on the maps *Indian Territory* in 1883 and 1887, and again the routes and designations remained unchanged (fig. 25). These maps were prepared from surveys by military and Department of the Interior authorities. The Abilene Cattle Trail was designated from a point slightly northwest of the vicinity of the confluence of the Red River and Salt Creek at Montague County and led north generally along and east of the ninety-eighth meridian (fig. 23). Chisholm's Trail was designated from a point at or near Council Grove on the North Canadian River and led northwest to merge with the Abilene Cattle Trail near the confluence of the Cimarron River and Uncle John's Creek (fig. 22).[23]

A map of Texas with provenance to the period 1867–87 that indicates any route in the state marked as the Chisholm Trail does not seem to exist. The Chisholm Trail is not indicated on Texas General Land Office maps from the same historical period of twenty-nine Texas counties along the route of the cattle trails from the Rio Grande to the Red River crossings in Cooke and Montague Counties. Notations such as La Bahia Road, Gonzales Road, Old Nacogdoches Road, San Antonio Road, Belton Road, Goliad Road, Road to Fort Graham, Road to Dallas, Road to Meridian, or Caddo Trail can be found, but the Chisholm Trail name does not appear on any of the county maps.[24]

Although many maps can be found that purport to show the Chisholm Trail in Texas, all of them were produced decades after the actual events, were typically associated with a book or article on the topic, and typically do not include a reference to a verifiable source from the cattle driving period. These later maps might be based on a particular drover's recollections; however, the problem is that for every drover who stated that the trail in Texas was the

Chisholm Trail, several contradictory accounts by other drovers can be found. The credentials of a map's author might be impeccable, but the fact remains that a map with provenance to the historical period of the cattle drives that shows any trail in Texas designated as the Chisholm Trail does not seem to exist. Such a map or document has not been cited in support of later maps that show the Chisholm Trail in Texas. Maps of later date might provide a general idea of the overall route of a trail, but cartographic references to the Chisholm Trail name in Texas do not appear to be grounded in fact. The only known map that shows the cattle trail through Texas that crossed the Red River at Montague County and has provenance to the cattle trailing period shows this trail designated as the Eastern Trail or Fort Worth Trail (fig. 17).[25]

Most of these and other similar arguments for the Chisholm Trail in Texas might sound good on the surface, might make a good story or provide interesting speculation, but they simply do not withstand scrutiny. There are usually details such as towns or railheads that did not yet exist, dates or events that do not match, names that were mixed, reasoning that cannot be explained or proven, or claims that were made decades later that are contradicted by documentation. Whether by intention or accident, the cumulative effect of these and other unproven claims has provided plenty of fodder for conversation over the years, but the trail's history has become distorted as a result.

17

National Historic
Trails and
Santa Claus

LIKE THE COALS OF A CAMPFIRE, the Chisholm Trail controversy appears to die but blazes to life with a small puff of wind in the right place. Many articles and maps published after the cattle trailing period ended regarding the trail name and route are inconsistent and contradictory, perhaps because they tend to rely heavily on post-1920 sources. Information contained therein is generally contradicted by data from the cattle trailing period, yet much of it has come to be accepted by many as fact anyway. Between 1911 and 2002 various versions of the story placed the origin point of the Chisholm Trail in Texas at Fort Worth, Ringgold, Denton County, Austin, San Antonio, or Brownsville, somewhere slightly south of Austin, somewhere around Kleberg County, Cuero, or several other places.[1]

Prior to the Meridian Highway project there was not much public concern about the actual origin and route of the Chisholm Trail. Claims of links to the trail increased as the Meridian Highway evolved and community leaders began to realize the benefits of good roads and tourism. Surviving drovers wished to commemorate the old cattle trails before they all died out, but several decades had passed since the actual events and the remains of the old cattle trails in Texas had not been formally surveyed. Information was sketchy, and old memories were tainted by years of outside influences. There was a desire to do something good and worthwhile, and there were potential economic impacts to local communities, all of which set the stage for controversy regarding trail names and routes. The controversy eventually subsided but has been renewed by a more recent proposal to designate the Chisholm Trail as a National Historic Trail. The economic potential of tourism has been a driving factor in the current proposal, and the controversy continues.

Claims regarding the origin of the Chisholm Trail are almost as numerous as the authors who have written about the subject. The mere fact that a statement appeared in print does not necessarily mean that it is true, yet the same or similar stories have circulated for years, and they are often accepted for no reason other than because the author lived near a trail, had a relative who was a drover, lived during the cattle trailing era, or "was a cow-puncher and punchers don't lie." A 1911 article published in the *Topeka State Journal* stated that Jesse Chisholm, who "first blazed the trail in 1867," and John Chisholm, "a cattleman of considerable means," were brothers and Jesse was from Ringgold, Texas. Upon investigation, none of this is true. This is another case of mistaken identity and confusion with John Chisum, who formerly ranched in Denton County and was not Jesse Chisholm's brother. Ringgold was the first town south of the Red River down the proposed extension of the Chisholm Trail Road along the Rock Island Railroad south into Texas.[2] Articles such as this typically offered no supporting documentation and might simply have been an attempt to link Texas towns or regions to the new Chisholm Trail Road. Countless articles claim that John Chisholm or John Chisum blazed the Chisholm or Chisum Trail north to Kansas, but supporting documentation is nowhere to be found.

There was apparently some discussion of how far the Chisholm name should be extended south out of Oklahoma along the Meridian Highway. The question was whether the southern terminus should be at Austin or San Antonio: "The old trail from Fort Worth united with the Texas trail from Austin here . . . and I think Austin would be the proper termination in South Texas instead of San Antonio." By 1930 the story had become so muddled that J. Frank Dobie suggested that there were two Chisholm Trails in Texas, miles apart and leading to different destinations. The different versions are inconsistent, and narratives based on these statements are inconsistent as well.[3]

Maps drawn years after the fact are just as unreliable. Maps can be found that indicate the origin point of the Chisholm Trail variously at some point on the Rio Grande River, San Antonio, Austin, or somewhere between Austin and Brownsville, apparently depending on the opinion of the author. Maps that show the Texas portion of the trail designated as the Chisholm Trail were drawn years later, mostly beginning during the 1920s. Despite the contradictions and inconsistencies, maps that fall into this category seem to be prominent in the public perception, with some proponents pointing to such modern maps as evidence that the Old Chisholm Trail passed through their particular area.[4]

There are a number of cases in which conflicting or inconsistent statements were made by various authors and even by some of the trail men. Many accounts of the trails were written between 1900 and the mid-1930s, while there were still some surviving veterans of the trail with firsthand knowledge of these events. By the time most of these accounts were documented or published during the 1920s and 1930s, up to forty or more years had passed since the long drives had ended. The normal toll of time on human memory, the tendency to reflect on a nostalgic sense of the past, and the possibility of embellishment in the interest of telling a good story were undoubtedly factors in some of these accounts. Sentimental memories of past events decades after the fact and the actual events are often two different things.

By then, Hollywood was well on its way to completing the transition of the historical cowboy to the mythical cowboy that had begun in literature during the latter days of the trails. The poem and song *The Old Chisholm Trail* had been recited and sung countless times since its appearance sometime during the 1870s, often at events such as settler's reunions, stock association meetings, and Trail Drivers' Association conventions. The popularity of the song, with the opening lyric of "Come along boys and listen to my tale, / I'll tell you of my troubles on the Old Chisholm Trail" might have had more influence on the public perception over the decades than any other single item. The name Old Chisholm Trail first appeared in newsprint in 1875. In some instances the name was used in the context of age; at other times it was used as the trail name, as in the 1875 article. When this name first appeared in newsprint, the Chisholm Trail had been in use for less than eight years. This might be an indication of the almost immediate popularity of the poem, as the trail was not that old yet, and the term was not typically applied to other trails as it was to the Chisholm. For example, the name Old Abilene Trail was not found in newsprint until 1889 in a reference to the "Old Abilene Cattle Trail and Stage Road." It had been eighteen or nineteen years since herd traffic shifted to this trail, so it actually was an old trail by 1889. References to the Old Chisholm Trail began shortly after the time the poem is thought to have appeared and continue to this day.[5]

As more time passes between an event and the time a person is asked to recall the event, it becomes less likely that the details can be recalled accurately from memory. Personal experiences, observations, and biases can influence recollections, whether the episode occurred minutes or years before. A dozen different people might witness the same incident at the same time and later give a dozen different accounts of what occurred. This is why eyewitness testimony is now known to be less reliable than once thought. In the case of the postbellum cattle trails history, when one considers that many events were witnessed over approximately a twenty-five-year period by a number of various people of different ages from diverse backgrounds under widely different conditions and circumstances, and recalled after thirty to fifty years of countless outside influences, the contradictions and conflicting versions are no surprise.

In cases in which an individual contradicted themselves or made other questionable statements, it is not an automatic excuse to disregard every other statement from that source.[6] Very few accounts given years after the fact are 100 percent accurate, even from primary sources. For each account that stated that the trail in Texas was the Chisholm, several others can be found that stated that the Chisholm was struck north of the Red River and did not enter Texas. This particular point is usually omitted when someone claims that all drovers called it the Chisholm Trail. This is where debates often focus on credibility of one source over another or center on the source that favors one's own opinion, and at that point the conversation degenerates. For example, proponents of the Chisholm Trail name for the Texas portion of the trail tend to quote the C. H. Rust account from *The Trail Drivers of Texas* to support their position, and those who hold that the Chisholm Trail did not enter Texas tend to quote George W. Saunders from the same volume, and the conversation turns to one trail driver versus another trail driver. Both Rust and Saunders are primary sources who drove herds up the trails during the same historical period. They agree on the general route of the trail but offered contradicting versions regarding the trail name. Both appeared sincere, and there is nothing to indicate that either party intended to hoodwink anyone on the subject. The question of why Rust should be considered more credible than Saunders on this subject has been asked, but no answer has been forthcoming. The conversation usually ends there, which leaves one to wonder if there is a legitimate explanation or if it is simply that Rust's account confirms a closely held belief or opinion of the trail name and therefore contradictory information is rejected.

Rather than the endless argument pitting the credibility of one source over another or simply rejecting information contradictory to one's opinion that has been typical of this old debate, the focus should be on the content of the statement. There is generally a thread of truth running through most of the old accounts. The purpose is to find that thread of truth and determine which statements or pieces of information can be corroborated by documentation from the appropriate historical period and therefore determine and follow the trail of historical evidence. For example, a statement made during the 1930s regarding a cattle trail might agree with another statement made during the same period, but can it be verified by evidence from the cattle driving period?[7] It would be an almost endless chore to research and dissect every statement or version of events ever written on this subject; however, once a historical benchmark is established, any statement or version of events can be compared against that standard. The matter can then be investigated further or conclusions formulated. If additional information is discovered, the benchmark can be adjusted accordingly.

Newspapers, maps, and other documents from the historical period that are consistent in content and can be verified against other sources can be used to establish a benchmark. Documentation that dates to the historical period of the cattle drives, generally 1830–87, presents a snapshot of events in the vernacular of the era and therefore is of greater research value than reminiscences or articles written decades later. The trail appeared consistently both in route and in name on maps of Indian Territory during the post–Civil War trail driving period that ended about 1887.[8] Geographic references in newspaper articles from the same period are consistent with the maps. When written accounts and reminiscences are compared against these documents for verification, some match up with the data from the trailing era while others match data from the post-1905 period.

Fifty-six percent of the cited newspaper articles refer to the Chisholm Trail in the vicinity of or north of the Cimarron River, and ninety-two percent refer to the Chisholm Trail as geographically north of the Red River. These descriptions can be verified using the cited 1875–87 maps of Indian Territory and many drover accounts. Only eight percent of the newspaper articles refer to the Chisholm Trail geographically south of the Red River in Texas. These descriptions cannot be corroborated by a contemporary map, as none are found that show a route in Texas designated with the Chisholm name. Lacking any maps or other documentation with provenance to the years 1867–87, drover accounts that placed the Chisholm Trail name in Texas cannot be verified. There is no documentation from the trail's period of use to indicate that the Texas portion of the trail was generally known to drovers by a trail name other than the origin or destination. The use of trail names came along later as more news articles and stories were written.

Due to the lack of references to the Chisholm Trail in writings and biographical sketches published from 1874 to 1905, it is obvious that the cattlemen who rode the trails did not commonly refer to the trail by the Chisholm name, but more frequently spoke of the destination or simply were not concerned with trail names. The same pattern regarding the lack of use of trail names was apparent from the earliest drives until the end; drovers were simply more concerned with the destination. Of the letters from drovers that were reviewed, none that dated to the trails' historical period of use made reference to a trail by name. A few mentions of Chisholm Trail are found in letters that date after 1910, and these are mostly in the context of "I went up the Chisholm Trail four [or however many] times" with no further details provided by the writer. The Lytle Collection, a collection estimated at over one thousand items that date from the early 1870s to about 1905 regarding the early days of the cattle business in Texas, was also reviewed. The firm of Lytle, McDaniel, Schreiner, and Light was one of the largest organizations that moved cattle up the trails. Many interesting details can be discovered; however, no written reference to a cattle trail by a trail name is found.[9]

The changes in the physical location of the Chisholm Trail can be traced on maps with provenance to 1892–1901, which was after the historic period of use as a cattle trail (figs. 32 and 34).[10] The reason for the change in the Chisholm Trail's mapped location is unknown; however, it coincides with the beginnings of the Good Roads movement. The Abilene Trail from the Red River north to Kansas along the ninety-eighth meridian near the route of what became the Meridian Highway, and later, US 81, was designated on a map as the Chisholm Trail for the first time in 1901 (figs. 23, 24, 25, 34, and 40). This stretch has been referred to as the Old Chisholm Trail since around 1911.

The link between tourism, the Good Roads movement, the Meridian Highway, and the Chisholm Trail name can be traced by numerous newspaper articles published from 1905 to 1930. As plans for the Meridian Highway progressed from north to south through Oklahoma, local Good Roads associations adopted the Chisholm Trail name for their stretch of the road. P. P. Ackley sold the Good Roads associations on his idea regarding the Chisholm Trail from the Rio Grande to Canada, but there were still too many surviving trail men who knew better. Although Ackley found supporters within the Good Roads organizations, he was unable to gather similar support from the trail veterans. The trail name was extended south into Texas along with the new highway, and by 1930 the US Good Roads

Association had endorsed Ackley's idea of the Chisholm Trail from Brownsville, Texas, to North Dakota along the route of the Meridian Highway. Thus, the Meridian Highway became the Chisholm Trail.[11]

Ackley's trail marking project is documented in articles published from 1931 to 1938. He placed his Chisholm Trail markers from the Rio Grande to Canada, generally along the route of the new road and the route of the Western or Fort Griffin and Dodge City Trail. The Chisholm Trail name was applied to the route along the ninety-eighth meridian and south into Texas along the route of the Meridian Highway, later US 81, by "common usage" resulting from a combination of publicity surrounding these events and reminiscent articles written during that period, rather than by the drovers who actually used the trail.[12]

Some may wonder why the Trail Drivers' Association and others were not more vocal on the subject during the 1930s. J. Frank Dobie once said of his uncle, Jim Dobie: "Like the great majority of real cowmen, he disliked the popular exaggeration of so many factors pertaining to range life and was more given to under- than over-statement." The Trail Drivers' Association stated in their 1931 resolution that they "do not wish to impose their will on any individual or county in marking of the trails." It may well be that, rather than extended agitation to promote and convince others of a trail name, the "real cowmen" simply said what they had to say on the matter, avoided the "popular exaggeration," and with the exception of occasional interviews, went back to their lives. Meanwhile, Ackley went on promotional tours in a medicine-show-style rig to promote the Chisholm Trail and the Meridian Highway as an international route from Mexico to Canada.[13]

While some have held that the Texas portion of the trail is called the Chisholm Trail on the authority of the Texas Highway Commission in 1930, the fact is that the highway commission did not approve a marker design that included the name Chisholm Trail.[14] Ackley undertook his own trail marking venture when the project approved by the highway commission stalled. No indication of an endorsement by the highway commission of a route, marker design, marker locations, or other authorization is indicated in the 1930 Texas Highway Commission minutes or subsequent related correspondence.

The Trail Drivers' Association resolution of 1931 is often ignored or dismissed by those who advocate the Chisholm name for the Texas portion of the trail. Although the resolution appears to describe the route of the Abilene Cattle Trail, by that time the Chisholm Trail name had been applied to the route of the Abilene Trail by the Oklahoma Good Roads associations as the name of the Meridian Highway. As it turned out, the Trail Drivers' Association was correct in their contention that the Chisholm Trail was located geographically north of the Red River and did not enter Texas. Although their resolution was not entirely accurate, their purpose was to address how the trail, which was known by multiple names, should be marked by signage or trail markers south of the Red River. The immediate purpose for the resolution was to address whether the Chisholm Trail extended into Texas and how the cattle trail should be recognized.

By the time H. S. Tennant of the Oklahoma State Highway Commission began his project in 1931 to locate the cattle trails pursuant to Oklahoma HB 149, the Chisholm Trail had been in its new location along the route of the Abilene Cattle Trail for thirty years. The Meridian Highway along that route had been designated as the Chisholm Trail Road for twenty years. Based on information gathered during his project, Tennant referred in his final report to the trail south of Red River Station in Texas as the Eastern and the trail north of the Red River in Oklahoma as the Chisholm. The map produced as a result of Tennant's report showed the Chisholm Trail leading north from the Red River along and just east of US 81, along what had been designated as the Abilene Cattle Trail up until 1901 (fig. 40).[15]

Tennant did not cite any of the 1872–87 maps of Indian Territory and may have been unaware of their existence. A few months after Tennant's report was published, cow puncher and pioneer O. E. Brewster mentioned an 1883 survey map and stated at the annual meeting of the Oklahoma Historical Society that his research showed that Texas cattle were driven principally over the Eastern or Abilene Trail. Brewster concluded that Texas drovers named the Chisholm Trail because they intersected the trail at Red Fork (the present site of Dover, Oklahoma) and followed the trail north to Abilene. Dover is located just north of the Cimarron River, in the vicinity of the intersection of Chisholm's Trail with the Abilene Cattle Trail. He also stated that Tennant's report should be considered the final chapter and "leaves no further need of discussion."[16] Both Tennant's and Brewster's findings regarding the Chisholm, Eastern, and Western trails are consistent with the findings of the Texas Stockmen's Association in 1882 and the Trail Drivers' Association in 1931. While the question of whether the Chisholm Trail extended into Texas was argued by what appears to be a vocal minority south of the Red River in Texas, the matter appeared to be settled and uncontested among Texas cattlemen and north of the Red River in Oklahoma.

Since the 1940s, occasional articles have appeared that claimed either the Eastern or the Chisholm name for the Texas portion of the trail, depending on the point of view of the author. This kept the matter alive and spurred occasional debates among interested parties. Then it escalated slightly in 1968, when several cattle trails were considered for inclusion in the national trails system. The Shawnee Trail, the Chisholm Trail, and the Western Trail were studied for possible inclusion in the national trails system under the 1968 National Trails System Act. A study completed in 1975 determined that these cattle trails did not meet the criteria for inclusion as a national scenic trail, noting that "The historical integrity and appearance of the study corridors have been almost completely altered by man's activities."[17]

Congress created a new category with new criteria for a trail to be included in the national trails system as a National Historic Trail under the National Trails System Act of 1978. In 1991 a bill was introduced to establish the Chisholm Cattle Drive Trail, the Ellsworth Cattle Drive Trail, the Dodge City or Western Cattle Drive Trail, and the Smoky Hill/David Butterfield Overland Dispatch Stage Trail. The bill did not pass. The Shawnee Trail was not included in this second attempt. In 2005 another bill was introduced to designate the Chisholm Trail from Brownsville, Texas, to Abilene, Kansas, and alternative Kansas destinations and the Great Western Trail from the vicinity of San Antonio, Texas, to Dodge City, Kansas. This bill did not pass but was reintroduced in 2007, and another bill was introduced a few months later which called for studies of the Chisholm Trail and Great Western Trail for possible inclusion in the national trails system. Neither of those two bills passed, but provisions for study of the cattle trails were included in the Omnibus Public Lands Management Act of 2009. Under provisions of that act, the secretary of the interior was to conduct a study of the two trails, with responsibility for conducting the study delegated to the National Park Service. A series of public meetings was held, and periodic reports were released along with public comments on the subject.[18]

This proposal has fired up the old debate once again. After the 1991 bill failed, and prior to the passage of the Omnibus Public Lands Management Act, a 1999 article in the *Fort Worth Star Telegram* discussed marketing the Chisholm Trail for tourism purposes. The article discussed including the Chisholm Trail as a Texas Travel Trail and the importance of signs, markers, and marketing. Chisholm Trail marker posts began to appear in Fort Worth in 2000. Historical markers may be placed by private organizations or individuals without the permission or oversight of the Texas Historical Commission, and these marker posts were placed by a private organization. Requirements for

markers placed by individuals or private entities are left to the discretion of the individual or group. For example, the group that erects
the Chisholm Trail marker posts has minimal requirements to obtain
a marker. The requesting party is asked to make a commitment to
locate the Chisholm Trail in their location, do their own research, get
necessary approval from landowner and appropriate authorities for
the marker, coordinate for the installation and dedication ceremony,
and make a donation to cover or help with the cost of the marker
(fig. 38). Although local historical commissions are contacted, this
process includes no documented requirement for due diligence or
historical oversight by another party that has no vested interest in
the matter. This can therefore result in questions regarding the historical accuracy of the markers.[19]

There is an old saying that history repeats itself. The current sce-
nario regarding marking the Chisholm Trail in Texas is strikingly
similar to the trail marking efforts during the 1930s, except that the
proponents of the Chisholm Trail name in Texas were better prepared this time and there are no surviving trail drivers left who knew
the trails firsthand to offer opposition from a primary source. Like
P. P. Ackley, who undertook his own private trail marking projects
during the 1930s, a private group has done the same in recent years
in Texas. On one side of the fence are those who desire, driven by
marketing and tourism interests, to have the Chisholm Trail designated by a government entity, and on the other side of the fence are
many descendants of trail drivers and those who believe that historical accuracy should be the priority, and the true history will speak
for itself.[20]

The Texas Department of Transportation (TXDOT) has also apparently been enlisted in the modern trail marking venture. Although
according to the original 1930 Texas Highway Commission meeting
minutes the commission did not commit to providing or installing
markers, identifying a route, endorsing a trail name, or granting
P. P. Ackley the authority to designate and mark a trail, TXDOT was
recently involved in the casting of new markers and installation or
replacement of thirty-seven of the Ackley markers. Reasons for the
missing markers are unknown; perhaps they were lost during construction projects, stolen, or possibly removed over the years if it was
discovered that they were not accurate. Seven of the original markers
remain, and the rest are being installed along the route of US 81.[21] At
least one county historical commission, the Atascosa County Historical Commission, has rejected the new markers placed by TXDOT
because of the trail name on the marker.[22] Ackley's markers repre-

sented his own idea of the trail and his promotion of the Meridian Highway as the Old Chisholm Trail, rather than the trail itself. The proliferation of Chisholm Trail markers since the 1999 *Star Telegram* article and the Omnibus Public Lands Management Act of 2009 is undoubtedly linked to the National Historic Trails proposal and the sesquicentennial anniversary of the Chisholm Trail.

Despite the fact that members of the Trail Drivers' Association were the ones who did the work and took the risks on the trails, they were ultimately ignored by P. P. Ackley during the 1930s. They are usually dismissed by proponents of the Chisholm name for the Texas portion of the trail and have been largely disregarded during the recent project. The term *historical purist* seems to have entered this conversation about 2001, about the same time that Chisholm Trail marker posts began to appear in Texas as efforts to obtain a national trail designation increased. The term is usually used by promoters or advocates of the Chisholm Trail name in Texas and applied to those who hold that the Chisholm Trail was located north of the Red River and did not enter Texas. Debate and public comments, especially in Texas, have tended to center on the route and name of the Chisholm Trail and, to a lesser degree, of the Western Trail. The trail that became known as the Shawnee Trail, the first northbound trail, is usually overshadowed, and the earliest eastbound trails are rarely mentioned. Since the initial attempt to obtain national trail designations in 1968, the focus has narrowed to only two trails: the Chisholm and the Western. The final recommendation to Congress by the National Park Service is over a year overdue as of this writing, and no details have been made public.[23]

So, where was the Chisholm Trail located? Chisholm's Trail was a segment of a longer route—part of a network of trails that led through Indian Territory north of the Red River, with the southernmost end of the trail located near Council Grove on the North Canadian River (figs. 22, 25). The trail that led north from the vicinity of Red River Station is designated as the Abilene Cattle Trail; it intersected Chisholm's Trail near the present site of Kingfisher, Oklahoma, near the Cimarron River (figs. 23, 24, 25). The trail north of the Cimarron is designated on maps of Indian Territory as the Abilene Cattle Trail (fig. 24). The trail past the present site of Wichita to Abilene is designated on an 1871 map of Kansas as the Texas Cattle Trail (fig. 26). The Chisholm Trail, or Chisholm's Trail, does not appear on any of the cited maps north of the Cimarron River. A map from that period showing the Chisholm Trail designated anywhere north of the Cimarron River was not found. The Red River was a clear demarcation between the trail in Texas and the trail in Indian Territory, probably because of the river's size, potential for danger, and status as a border. The trail was at least as commonly known by the public and by drovers by names other than Chisholm Trail; drovers rarely referred to the trail, especially the Texas portion of the trail, by a formal trail name other than customary use of the destination.

The only contemporary maps that show cattle trails designated in Texas indicate the trail that crossed the Red River in Montague County as the Eastern or Fort Worth Trail and the trail that crossed the Red River at Doan's in Wilbarger County as the Western, Fort Griffin, or Fort Griffin and Dodge City Trail (figs. 2, 17). This fits the custom of the period, incorporating landmarks, geography, or origin/destination into a road name, as evidenced by other maps from the same historical period. The Chisholm name was transferred to the mapped location of the Abilene Cattle Trail for reasons unknown, and the route that led north from the vicinity of Red River Station first appeared on a map as the Chisholm Trail in 1901 (fig. 34). The general application of the Chisholm name to the trail from Red River Station past Monument Hill, Addington, Duncan, and Kingfisher occurred after 1901. The general application of the Chisholm name to the Texas portion of the trail occurred after 1911, mainly during the 1930s. This establishes benchmarks based on verifiable data against which various statements or versions of the story can be measured. The modern narrative in which the Chisholm Trail name extends to various origins in Texas is supported by later reminiscence, literature, and public perception rather than documentation from the cattle driving days.

It is difficult to construct a logical argument in which folklore trumps documentation, yet the folklore seems to have trumped the documentation regarding the public perception over the years where the Chisholm Trail is concerned. It is apparent that there are two Chisholm Trails; one is established by documentation with provenance to the historical period of 1867–87, while the other was founded after the fact in the folklore and fiction that has skewed public perception since the dust had barely settled on the trails. One is based on documentation from the appropriate historical period, and the other is based on statements and claims that were made years after the fact, that upon further investigation are inconsistent, cannot be proven, and therefore fall into the category of folklore, legend, or hearsay. While the documentation cited herein may not settle all of the trails issues, it provides relevant data against which information can be evaluated objectively.

The Chisholm Trail name can be verified north of the Red River; however, since a trail name cannot be corroborated south of the Red prior to 1881, the question of what the Texas portion of the trail or the trail as a whole should be called remains. During the period of 1867–87 the trail was called by a variety of names, by no name, or more commonly by the destination. Had the trail been named early on for Black Beaver, who traveled the route prior to Jesse Chisholm, or Joseph McCoy, who established the cattle market at Abilene, or had the anonymous author of the famous poem written "let me tell you of my troubles on the Abilene Trail," the matter of the trail name might have been immediately settled long ago. Perhaps the Department of the Interior, the Stockmen's Association, and the Trail Drivers' Association provided the answer in 1881, 1882, and 1931. In the absence of a trail name that is supported by anything other than folklore, legend, or hearsay, the name Eastern Texas-Kansas Trail for the Texas portion of the trail, as recommended in 1931 for trail marking purposes by the same trail veterans who actually rode the trail, incorporates geographic references that reflect the genuine custom of the period. The combination of "Chisholm and Eastern Texas-Kansas Trail" would provide a single descriptive name that is historically defensible for the entire trail from its origins in Texas to its destinations in Kansas.[24]

To consider any version of events that includes the Chisholm Trail name south of the Red River requires the cited military maps, Department of the Interior maps, and numerous newspaper articles to be either explained away or ignored in favor of folklore that cannot be proven. To explain away the documentation requires one to demonstrate how various correspondents, military engineers, surveyors, draftsmen, agents of the Department of the Interior, and cartographers all independently managed to be so consistent during the years 1869–87, yet somehow were all incorrect regarding the Chisholm Trail. The evidence cannot be simply side-stepped or dismissed as being the opinion of "historical purists." If a Texas map with provenance to the historical period of 1867–87 that shows a route anywhere in Texas designated as the Chisholm Trail ever existed, why has it not been cited in previous works or produced in over one hundred years of research on this topic? If the cattlemen who drove several million head of cattle and horses up the trail through Texas actually called it by the Chisholm name, why is this not reflected in the accounts and biographical sketches published between 1874 and 1905?

Advances in technology have afforded greater access to information now than at any time in the past. It is hoped that this work will shed light into some dark corners of the trails' history and perhaps prompt further research and discussion on the subject. The sad fact is that the more time that has passed since the Trail Drivers "crossed the Great Divide," the more muddled the trails' history has become. The risks and hardships on the trail were real, while much of the modern trail's narrative is based on partial information and false perceptions. Accounts of the Chisholm Trail name in Texas cannot be verified against other data from 1867 to 1887 because such data do not seem to exist. The reason that they do not exist could be because they have not been discovered, or more likely because the claim that the name was applied to the trail in Texas simply was not so. But conclusions must be formulated based on known information, where it exists, rather than opinion, folklore, or theory. Many details of this period of history may never be known. The Trail Drivers, the old-time cow men, lived in the saddle, slept on the ground, took the risks, and did the work. They rescued the state of Texas from the brink of bankruptcy and built the foundation of the modern livestock industry in the western United States. They deserve to have their history recorded as truthfully as possible.

Colonel Jack M. Potter stated in his 1939 book *Cattle Trails of the Old West*, "If I should tell you that the Chisholm Trail never did enter Texas, what would you think? It would be like telling you there was no Santa Claus."[25] The arguments raised back then were much the same as the current arguments over what to call the trail in Texas. In the typical fashion of the old trail men, Potter was direct and to the point with his analogy. Although Chisholm's Trail was an important segment of the trail to central Kansas, there is much more to the history of the cattle trails than a single trail name. The accomplishments of the men (and a few women) who faced the dangers and did the work should not be overshadowed by publicity and hype over a trail name for the sake of tourism. The same people faced the same risks and hardships and drove the same cattle and horses up the same trails to the same destinations. The only part of that history that has been consistently inconsistent since the early 1900s is the trail name. The same stories that history aficionados and tourists thrive on can still be told; the only difference is the trail name. The history is more interesting than the folklore, which tends to change with each retelling.

The Chisholm Trail of fact or the Chisholm Trail of folklore—the trail that is found depends upon the trail that is sought. The sun has set on the days of the long trail drives, but the sun may never set on the old debate over the Chisholm Trail. George Rainey, author of *The*

Cherokee Strip, stated in 1936: "The true historian seeks to be exact, unbiased, and faithful to the truth; for history is but the preservation of the records of truth, the enemy of oblivion, the witness of the past and director of the future. . . . Nothing save error need fear the historian." This work is offered, as the Trail Drivers' Association stated in 1931, "merely in the interest that Texas history may be properly preserved to posterity." The Chisholm Trail of folklore is so well marked that a greenhorn could find it, but it leads to nowhere. Just as the drover's grave was obscured by the prairie grass, the actual, historical Chisholm Trail is obscured by the legend and commercial promotions, but it is there for those who wish to find it.[26]

Appendix

It is difficult to construct a timeline of the cattle trails using the various post-1900 narratives because of the many contradictions and inconsistencies. The following timeline provides an overview of major events related to the history of the cattle trails and the subsequent Chisholm Trail controversy through the 1930s. Key dates in the trails' history and related events that influenced the cattle drives are included.

1493   Christopher Columbus brings Iberian cattle to Santo Domingo. The Texas longhorn evolves from these Iberian cattle over the next three hundred–plus years (fig. 1).[1]

1521   Gregorio de Villalobos brings cattle to New Spain (Mexico) from Santo Domingo.[2]

1690   San Francisco de los Tejas, the first Spanish mission in Texas, is established. The mission's cattle herd is the first herd intentionally driven from Mexico into Texas.[3]

1779   The first organized cattle drive from Texas is ordered by Governor Domingo Cabello in response to a request by Bernardo de Gálvez. A herd is driven from the present site of Goliad County east to Opelousas.[4] This trail is used later to drive Texas cattle to New Orleans.

1824   "The Old Three Hundred" arrive in Texas to settle Stephen F. Austin's first colony.[5]

1820s   Cattle are driven east to New Orleans from Austin's Colony on the Brazos.[6] The trails east eventually become known as the Opelousas Trail, Beef Trail, or Beef Road.

1830   The Indian Removal Act of 1830 is passed by the US Congress, paving the way for forced relocations of eastern tribes to west of the Mississippi River and eventually into Indian Territory.[7]

1836   The Republic of Texas is formed.[8]

1836   Samuel Colt is awarded a patent for his revolving-cylinder pistol design, and the Colt Paterson model goes into production.[9] The Colt Paterson allows multiple shots to be fired before reloading. Prior to this, most pistols had to be reloaded after each shot.

1840s–50s   Small herds that average less than two hundred head are driven east to the cattle market at New Orleans.[10]

1845   Texas is admitted to the United States.[11]

1846   Edward Piper drives what is believed to be the first large cattle herd northward from Texas to Ohio.[12] Piper's route from Texas to Ohio is unknown.

1847   The Colt Walker revolver goes into production.[13]

Early to mid-1850s   Herds are driven west to California during the California Gold Rush.[14]

Mid-1850s   Outbreaks of Spanish fever, also known as Texas fever, in Missouri result in quarantine laws and armed resistance to Texas herds.[15]

1854–55   John Simpson Chisum establishes his ranch at Bolivar in Denton County, Texas. He manages cattle on shares, gathers herds, and drives a herd of about five hundred head to Shreveport.[16]

1855   A small herd of Texas cattle arrives in New York, driven by way of Illinois, and sells for eleven to thirteen cents per pound.[17]

1855   Major Merrill's expedition travels north from Fort Belknap past the mouth of the Little Arkansas River.[18]

1858   Oliver Loving and John Durkee drive a herd from Palo Pinto County, Texas, to Illinois.[19]

Late 1850s   Jesse Chisholm establishes a trading post on the North Canadian River at Council Grove in Indian Territory.[20]

1860   Oliver Loving and John Dawson drive a herd from Palo Pinto County, Texas, to Pueblo, Colorado.[21]

1860   Benjamin T. Henry is granted a patent for the Henry rifle, the first practical lever-action repeating rifle.[22]

1861   The Missouri Pacific Railroad arrives at Sedalia, Missouri.[23]

1861–65   The War of the Rebellion or War for Southern Independence, more commonly known as the Civil War, occurs.[24] Railroad construction ceases west of the Mississippi River during the war.

1861   Colonel William Emory is ordered to consolidate and evacuate all Union forces from forts in Indian Territory to Fort Leavenworth.

Guided by Black Beaver, he follows the same route Merrill had taken to the Little Arkansas.[25]

1863   John Chisum begins to relocate cattle from Denton County to a new ranch in Coleman County.[26] His exact trail route is unknown, but it is likely that he followed the Butterfield stage route as much as possible.

1864   John Chisum drives a small herd from his ranch at Coleman County into New Mexico Territory.[27] The best route from Chisum's Coleman County ranch is along the Middle Concho River, across eighty to ninety miles of waterless plains to Horsehead Crossing, and up the Pecos River into New Mexico Territory. Chisum's route from Denton County and this route are later called Chisum's Trail, Chisum's Western Trail, or the Chisum trail.

1864   Jesse Chisholm establishes a trading post at the mouth of the Little Arkansas River in Kansas.[28]

1864–66   Jesse Chisholm makes the first trip with supply wagons from his trading post at the Little Arkansas River to his post at Council Grove over the route that becomes known locally as Chisholm's Trail. This is part of the same route that Merrill, Emory, and Black Beaver used previously. Various dates given for this event range between 1864 and 1866. The exact date is unknown; however, Vincente George Chisholm, Jesse's adopted son, stated that the journey occurred in 1865.[29]

1865   The Civil War ends. Railroad construction resumes. Cattle drives from Texas, which were slowed but not stopped during the war, resume. The Union Stock Yard and Transit Company of Chicago is organized; the four existing stockyards in Chicago can no longer meet the demand.[30]

1866   Thornton Chisholm drives a herd from DeWitt County, Texas, to Saint Joseph, Missouri.[31] Thornton Chisholm's trail is sometimes claimed to be the famous Chisholm Trail; however, the Chisholm Trail led to Abilene, Kansas; there was no cattle market at Abilene until the summer of 1867; and Thornton Chisholm's trail took a different route to Saint Joseph.

1866   Charles Goodnight and Oliver Loving drive their first herd together. Their trail begins near Fort Belknap in Young County, Texas, and leads past Horsehead Crossing and up the Pecos River into New Mexico Territory.[32] Although John Chisum had likely covered much of the same route along the Butterfield trail past Fort Griffin and Buffalo Gap when he relocated from Denton County in 1863 and when he drove a herd along the route from the Middle

Concho River to Horsehead Crossing and up the Pecos into New Mexico Territory in 1864, the overall trail from near Fort Belknap eventually takes on the name of Goodnight and Loving.

1866   The Winchester Model 1866 lever-action repeating rifle is introduced.[33]

1867   John Chisum arrives with a herd at Bosque Redondo, near the current site of Fort Sumner, New Mexico.[34] He continues to move cattle from his Coleman County ranch into New Mexico Territory.

1867   The Kansas legislature sets the cattle quarantine deadline basically at the sixth principal meridian (just west of Abilene); the restrictions apply to all portions of the state east of the sixth principal meridian and north of the line of township 19 (just west of the present site of Hillsboro).[35]

1867   Joseph G. McCoy negotiates with officials of the Eastern Division of the Union Pacific Railroad to establish a railhead at Abilene, Kansas, for the purpose of hauling Texas cattle. McCoy hires T. F. Hersey to survey and mark a trail south from Abilene to the end of Chisholm's Trail at the mouth of the Little Arkansas.[36]

1867   The first herd reaches the new railhead at Abilene during the late summer.[37]

1867   The Union Pacific Railroad completes a rail line west along the Platte River through Nebraska.[38]

1869   The name Chisholm Trail appears in the April 10 edition of the *Georgetown (Texas) Watchman*.[39] This is the first use of the name in newsprint.

1870   The name Shawnee Trail appears in the January 28 edition of the *Emporia (Kansas) News*.[40] This is the first use of the name in newsprint.

1870s   The dime novel begins to transform the American West and its characters into sensationalized fictional characters and places.

Early to mid-1870s   "I woke up one morning on the old Chisholm trail, / Rope in my hand and a cow by the tail"; the poem "The Old Chisholm Trail," author unknown, appears.[41]

1870   A cattle market opens at Schuyler, Nebraska.[42]

1871   Cattle are shipped from Newton, Kansas, on the Atchison, Topeka & Santa Fe Railway. The Union Stock Yards Corporation and the Missouri Pacific Stock Yards are consolidated into the Kansas Stock Yard Company, located on the state line at Kansas City, Kansas.[43]

1871   The Creek Nation authorizes a tax for the use of wood, water, and grazing livestock within Creek territory.[44]

1872   The Kansas legislature moves the quarantine deadline along a zig-zag line approximately fifty miles west of the sixth principal meridian.[45]

1872   The Atchison, Topeka & Santa Fe Railway reaches Wichita, Kansas. The Wichita Stockyards are completed.[46]

1872   The Drovers Cottage is moved from Abilene to Ellsworth.[47]

1872   The first herds of 1872 arrive in Ellsworth.[48]

1872   The Atchison, Topeka & Santa Fe Railway reaches Fort Dodge.[49]

1872   The Abilene Cattle Trail first appears as a mapped route generally along and east of the ninety-eighth meridian in Indian Territory (see fig. 23).[50]

1873   The Colt Single Action Army revolver, also known as the Peacemaker, and the Winchester Model 1873 repeating rifle are introduced.[51]

1874   John T. Lytle drives a herd from Medina County, Texas, past Fort Griffin, Camp Supply, and Fort Dodge to the Red Cloud Agency in Nebraska.[52] Much of this route becomes known as the Fort Griffin, Fort Dodge, or Western Trail.

1874   A patent for a practical design for two-strand barbed wire is awarded to Joseph Glidden. Glidden's design is still in use.[53]

1874   The Union Pacific Railroad builds holding pens and loading chutes for cattle at Ogallala, Nebraska.[54]

1875   The cattle trade is forced out of Wichita.[55]

1875   The Quahadi Comanches, led by Quanah Parker, surrender at Fort Sill. This represents the last holdouts of the southern plains and removes the last barrier to settlement of the area known as the Comancheria.[56]

1875   Chisholm's Trail first appears as a mapped route in Indian Territory.[57]

1875   The name Old Chisholm Trail appears in the May 13 edition of the *Milan (Tennessee) Exchange*. This is the first use of the name in newsprint.[58]

1876   The Kansas legislature moves the quarantine deadline west to a point about twenty-four miles east of Fort Dodge.[59]

1876   The first herds of the season arrive at Dodge City.[60]

1876   The Atchison, Topeka & Santa Fe Railway builds stockyards at Dodge City.[61]

1876   Charles Goodnight establishes the first ranch in Palo Duro Canyon in the Texas Panhandle.[62] This was the former domain of the Comanches. Quanah Parker and Goodnight become friends, and Parker later visits Goodnight at his ranch.

1877   Crazy Horse, Oglala Lakota war chief, and his followers surrender; Sitting Bull, Hunkpapa Lakota holy man, and his followers flee into Canada. This ends the Indian war on the northern plains.[63]

1878   Jonathan Doan establishes Doan's Store, also known as Doan's Crossing, on the Prairie Dog Town Fork of the Red River in Wilbarger County, Texas.[64]

1880   The Atchison, Topeka & Santa Fe Railway reaches Caldwell, Kansas.[65]

1881   Cattle trails in Indian Territory are described as the "Eastern" and "Western" in the May 10 edition of the *Cheyenne Transporter*. This is the first appearance of these terms in newsprint used to describe the cattle trails.[66]

1882   A resolution recommended by the Texas Stockmen's Association Committee on Trails and passed by the stockmen's convention in Austin, Texas, identifies the trail that crossed the Red River at Red River Station as the "eastern" and the trail that crossed the Red River at Doan's Store as the "western."[67]

1884   Grass leases in the Cheyenne and Arapaho Reservation in Indian Territory block access to the Western cattle trail through the reservation. The Eastern Trail was already closed due to fears of Texas fever.[68]

1884   The trail through the Cherokee Strip to Dodge City is blocked with wire fences and armed resistance on land leased by the Cherokee Stock Association in Indian Territory.[69]

1885   The Kansas legislature passes a quarantine law that prohibits driving Texas cattle into any Kansas county unless the cattle were wintered north of the thirty-sixth parallel and the owner possesses the proper certificate.[70] This act in effect closes Kansas to Texas drovers.

1885   A bill is introduced to designate a quarantined national livestock trail from the Red River to the northern border of the United States to provide an outlet for Texas cattle.[71]

1885   President Grover Cleveland issues an executive order that declares grazing leases in Indian Territory null and void. Cattlemen who

hold herds in Indian Territory must get out or be evicted as trespassers.[72]

1887   No official action is taken to designate a national livestock trail;
farms and fences obstruct the route, and herds are stopped on
the trail or turned back.[73] Between 1887 and 1896 a few West Texas
ranches continue to trail a few herds up what is left of the trail to
Montana. By 1897 the trail is closed by fences and farmland. Any
future cattle drives from Texas to Montana require permission
from landowners to pass.

1890   About 1890, newspaper articles that mention the Chisholm Trail
shift predominantly to reminiscence of days past rather than
deliver news.

1892   *Good Roads* magazine is published. This magazine promotes the
advantages of road improvements at a time when most roads in
the United States are unpaved dirt roads.[74]

1892   Chisholm's Cattle Trail first appears on a map south of the North
Canadian River (fig. 32).[75]

1893   After about twenty-five years of research, the common cattle tick
is discovered to transmit Texas fever, also known as splenic fever,
and findings are published in *BAI Bulletin No. 1* (1893).[76]

1901   Delegates travel from Texas to the International Good Roads Congress in New York.[77]

1901   The Abilene Cattle Trail designation for the trail past Monument
Hill east of Addington, Oklahoma, is replaced by the designation
of Chisholm Trail.[78] This is the first mapped application of the
Chisholm name to the trail leading from Red River Station past
Monument Hill, Duncan, Chickasha, El Reno, Kingfisher, and
Enid (figs. 23, 24, 25, and 34).

1903   *The Great Train Robbery* is the first in a long line of popular silent
Western films. As competition increases, plots become more
sensational, costumes flashier, and characters more exaggerated
in order to attract more customers and satisfy the public perception.[79]

1905   The connection between good roads and the economic potential
of tourism is recognized.[80]

1911   The Meridian Road Association is formed at Salina, Kansas, to
promote a new highway along the sixth meridian across Kansas,
which will eventually link to a north-south road from Oklahoma
and Texas.[81]

1911   The Chisholm Trail Good Roads Association is formed at Enid, Oklahoma. A subsequent meeting is held at El Reno, and the road from Caldwell, Kansas, along the Rock Island Line to Texas is endorsed as the Chisholm Trail Road.[82]

1911   A claim that the Chisholm Trail started at Fort Worth is published in a local newspaper; Texans are urged to take up the movement and improve the trail from Wichita, Kansas, into Fort Worth.[83]

1911   In an article titled "Fort Worth Joins in Chisholm Trail Plan," it is stated that the Chisholm Trail extended from Fort Worth, Texas, to Wichita, Kansas.[84]

1912   The Meridian Highway is envisioned to stretch from Canada into Mexico. Good Roads associations have been formed along the route from the Dakotas to Texas. [85]

1913   The Oklahoma Tri-County Good Roads Association begins to survey a route through Chickasha, Rush Springs, Marlow, Duncan, Addington, Waurika, and Ryan for the Chisholm Trail Road. This association includes Grady, Stephens, and Jefferson Counties.[86]

1915   The Old Time Trail Drivers' Association is organized and established in San Antonio, Texas, by George W. Saunders.[87]

1925   Saunders solicited written accounts of members' experiences and published *The Trail Drivers of Texas*, vol. 1 in 1920 and vol. 2 in 1923; the combined volumes are published under one cover in 1925.[88] The last version is still in print.

1925   P. P. Ackley, a former drover who went up the trail in 1878, campaigns to convert the old trail into a maintained highway and mark it as "The Old Chisholm Trail" from the Gulf of Mexico to Canada. He states that the route will pass Fort Sam Houston, Fort Worth, Fort Griffin, Fort Supply, Fort Dodge, and Fort Laramie.[89] However, most of these landmarks are along the route of the Western Trail, a long way from the Chisholm Trail.

1929   Ackley moves to Donna, Texas, and states his intention to have the Old Chisholm Trail made into a national highway.[90]

1930   The Texas State Highway Commission authorizes the Chisholm Trail Association to place markers or monuments that are approved by the commission or the state highway engineer along the trail as long as they do not interfere with the highway.[91]

1930   J. Frank Dobie is the head of the committee to mark the trails. The *Berkeley (California) Daily Gazette* reports that Dobie will use a map prepared in 1871 by the Fourth US Cavalry, along with statements by surviving drovers, to trace the route of the trail. A map compiled by E. D. Dorchester closely matches the description in the article and Dobie's subsequent recommendation; however, the map dates to 1927.[92] The map was not prepared by the Fourth Cavalry in 1871, but represents General R. S. Mackenzie's expeditions during that period.

1930   Dobie proposes a compromise that includes a route from Brownsville through San Antonio, Austin, Waco, Fort Worth, and Red River Station as Old Chisholm Trail; and a route from San Antonio through Brady, Coleman, Abilene, Stamford, Rule, Crowell, and Quanah as Western Chisholm Trail. Dobie also states: "The original Chisholm Trail did not come south of the Red River."[93]

1930   The US Good Roads Association endorses Ackley's idea of the Chisholm Trail from Brownsville, Texas, to Bismarck, North Dakota.[94] The organization had nothing to do with cattle drives; their mission is road improvement.

1931   P. P. Ackley places the first trail marker in Texas along the highway nine miles north of Vernon.[95] The marker is currently located at a roadside park along US 283 north of Vernon and is a granite marker with the inscription "Going Up the Chisholm Trail, P. P. Ackley, 1878." Although this is the first trail marker in the state, it includes the date of Ackley's only known trip up the trail, leaving the impression that he may have commemorated his experience instead of the trail. This Chisholm Trail marker is along the route of the Western Trail near Doan's Store and is approximately ninety-six miles west of the Red River crossing that led to Chisholm's Trail.

1931   The controversy and disagreement over the trail marking project approved by the Texas Highway Commission leads the Trail Drivers' Association to research the topic. At their October 1931 annual convention the matter is presented and discussed, and a resolution that states that Texas cattle were driven over the Western and Eastern Texas-Kansas Trails, and that the Chisholm Trail was struck north of the Red River and did not enter Texas, is passed unanimously.[96]

1931   A large monument is dedicated on October 21–22 at Doan's Store. About thirty members of the Trail Drivers' Association are present for the dedication ceremony. P. P. Ackley, who contributed the largest single amount towards the cost of the monument and is in charge of the inscription, ignores the advice of Bertha Doan Ross, George W. Saunders, and the Trail Drivers' Association and has Longhorn Chisholm Trail inscribed on the monument. Ackley also uses himself as the model for the bronze relief on the monument.[97]

1932   The trail marking project that was approved by the Texas Highway Commission stalls due to disagreement, controversy, and the Depression. Ackley proceeds with his own trail marking project and erects round, cast metal markers that include the words "GOING UP THE TEXAS CHISHOLM TRAIL."[98] Ackley has the endorsement of the US Good Roads Association but ignores the Trail Drivers' Association. Some of the original markers can still be found (fig. 38).

1936   A smaller monument including a quote from Will Rogers is placed near Doan's Store by the state of Texas. This monument is later moved and is presently located next to the large 1931 monument at Doan's. At some point, likely after 1936, the original inscription "THE LONGHORN CHISHOLM TRAIL AND THE WESTERN TRAIL 1876–1895" is removed from the large monument and replaced by "THE WESTERN TEXAS–KANSAS TRAIL 1876–1895."[99]

1938   P. P. Ackley completes his trail marking project, placing Chisholm Trail markers from Brownsville, Texas, to the Canadian border. No indication that the Texas Highway Commission approved his marker design or placements is included in the 1930 meeting minutes or subsequent correspondence. The project approved by the Texas Highway Commission was never completed.[100] The Ackley markers remain controversial among historians and trails enthusiasts to this day.

Notes

Chapter 1

1. J. Marvin Hunter, ed., *The Trail Drivers of Texas*, 2nd ed., rev., 690.

2. Robert H. Thonhoff, *The Texas Connection with the American Revolution*, 48–51, referencing Croix to Cabello, August 16, 1779, Bexar Archives, Austin, Texas, Bexar Archives Translation (BAT) 2C342, vol. 85, 112–14.

3. Thonhoff, *Texas Connection*, 63–64; Robert Torrez, "Pueblo Revolt of 1680," Office of the State Historian, Santa Fe, New Mexico, New Mexico History, http://newmexicohistory.org/people/pueblo-revolt-of-1680, accessed October 2, 2016; W. W. Newcomb Jr., *The Indians of Texas*, 86–90, 156–57.
   The Comanches first appeared in New Mexico shortly after 1700, when they migrated down the Arkansas River to the plains of what is now eastern Colorado and western Kansas and then south into New Mexico, where the Pueblos had been conquered by the Spanish. They likely came into possession of horses subsequent to the Pueblo Revolt of 1680. They mimicked some Spanish customs, such as mounting from the right side; made some innovations, such as substituting bridles made of lightweight horsehair or rawhide in place of the heavier Spanish bits and bridles; and became perhaps the finest riders on the plains. Horses were previously unknown upon the plains, but by the mid-1700s they were common across the plains and into Canada.

4. US Census, *Compendium of the Tenth Census (June 1, 1880), Compiled Pursuant to an Act of Congress Approved August 7, 1882*, rev. ed., Part I, Table II, "Aggregate Population at Each Census," 4.

5. US Census, *Population of the United States in 1860 . . . Eighth Census, Compiled from the Original Returns of the Eighth Census, under the Direction of the Secretary of the Interior, Superintendent of Census, Bureau of the Census Library*; "State & County Quickfacts," US Department of Commerce, US Census Bureau, www.census.gov/quickfacts/fact/table /US/PST045216, accessed March 10, 2013.
   Total population of the United States in 1860 was 31,443,321, population west of the Mississippi River was 4,536,475, and Texas population was 604,215. Estimated population in 2010 as of April 1: New York,

19,378,104; New Jersey, 8,791,898; Connecticut, 3,574,097; Dallas County, Texas, 2,368,139; Tarrant County, Texas, 1,809,039; Parker County, Texas, 116,927; and Denton County, Texas, 662,614.

6. US Census, *Population of the United States in 1860*, iv, and "Area and Density of Population," xvi. By comparison, according to the US Census Bureau there was an average of more than ninety-six persons per square mile in Texas in 2010.

7. S. E. Forman, "Railroad Lines in Actual Operation, 1860," Map 02889, in *Advanced American History*; J. H. Colton, *Colton's New Railroad & County Map of the United States and the Canadas &c.*

8. Joseph Nimmo, *Report in Regard to the Range and Ranch Cattle Business of the United States*, 28; Jerome C. Smiley and National Live Stock Association of the United States, *Prose and Poetry of the Live Stock Industry of the United States*, 1:707; B. Byron Price, introduction to J. Marvin Hunter, ed., *The Trail Drivers of Texas*, v. This edition is taken from the second edition, revised, published in 1925 by Cokesbury Press. Estimates of six million to ten million head of cattle driven north from Texas can also be found in other works and on various monuments and historical markers.

9. Nimmo, *Report*, 28.

10. Ibid., 58–59.

11. Ibid., 67–69.

12. Hunter, *Trail Drivers*, 453; T. C. Richardson, "Cattle Trails of Texas," *Texas Geographic Magazine* 1, no. 2 (November 1937): 29; J. Evetts Haley, *Charles Goodnight, Cowman and Plainsman*, 245–46. The organization was originally founded as the Old Time Trail Drivers' Association. By about 1940 it was also called the Old Trail Drivers' Association. Later, presumably after the original trail drivers had died, it was called the Trail Drivers' Association.

    Goodnight stated that his outfits consisted of sixteen to eighteen men plus a cook and a wrangler for an average herd of three thousand head of cattle. The number of drovers on a given drive depended on variables such as the herd size, the trail boss, the experience level of the drovers, and so on.

13. Deborah M. Liles, "Southern Roots, Western Foundations: The Peculiar Institution and the Livestock Industry on the Northwestern Frontier of Texas, 1846–1864," PhD diss., University of North Texas, 2013, 18, 70, 100, 121, 142, 172, 185, 203, 243, and 250, referencing Clay County Tax Records, 1861–63; Denton County Tax Records, 1855–64; Jack County Tax Records, 1857–64; Montague County Tax Records, 1858–64; Palo Pinto County Tax Records, 1857–64; Parker County Tax Records, 1856–64; Stephens County Tax Records, 1861–1910; and Wise County Tax Records, 1857–64. Clay, Palo Pinto, Stephens, and Wise county records are all on microfilm, Willis Library, University of North Texas, Denton; Denton, Jack, Montague, and Parker County records are from each respective county courthouse.

    The northwestern frontier in this context was generally the area south of the Red River and west of the present Texas counties of Cooke, Denton, and Tarrant.

14.   Hunter, *Trail Drivers*, 295–305; Johnye C. Sturcken, "Amanda and William Franklin Burks: A Nueces County Partnership," *East Texas Historical Journal* 30, no. 2 (October 1992).

15.   Richardson, "Cattle Trails," 17.

Chapter 2

1.   James Cox, *Historical and Biographical Record of the Cattle Industry and the Cattlemen of Texas and Adjacent Territory*, 600–601.

2.   J. Frank Dobie, *The Longhorns*, 72–73. A cypress knee is a structure that grows upward from the root of a cypress tree.

3.   Ibid., 41–42.

4.   Dan Kilgore, "The Spanish Missions and the Origins of the Cattle Industry in Texas," *The Cattleman*, January, 1983; "History of the Texas Longhorns," US Fish and Wildlife Service, Wichita Mountains Wildlife Refuge, Oklahoma, www.fws.gov/refuge/Wichita_Mountains/wildlife /longhorns/history.html, accessed June 19, 2012.

5.   K. K. Kidd et al., "Immunogenetic and Population Genetic Analyses of Iberian Cattle," Paper no. 2341, Laboratory of Genetics, University of Wisconsin–Madison, December 5, 1979, www.texaslonghorn conservancy.org.

6.   "Breeds of Livestock, Department of Animal Science," Oklahoma State University, Department of Animal Science, www.ansi.okstate.edu /breeds/cattle/, referencing Marleen Felius, *Genus Bos: Cattle Breeds of the World*, and I. L. Mason, *A World Dictionary of Livestock Breeds, Types, and Varieties*, 4th ed.

7.   William E. Doolittle, "Las Marismas to Panuco to Texas: The Transfer of Open Range Cattle Ranching from Iberia through Northeastern Mexico," *Yearbook of the Conference of Latin Americanist Geographers*, January 1987, 13, ResearchGate, www.researchgate.net/publication /242201609, accessed August 6, 2015, referencing D. E. Chipman, *Nuño de Guzmán and the Province of Pánuco in New Spain, 1518–1533*, 157, 198, 199, 203, 211, 217.

8.   Doolittle, "Las Marismas."

9.   Dobie, *Longhorns*, 4.

10.   Kilgore, "Spanish Missions," referencing José Antonio Pichardo, *Pichardo's Treatise on the Limits of Louisiana and Texas*, ed. and annot. Charles Wilson Hackett, 4:308.

11.   Dobie, *Longhorns*, 30.

12.   "The Fight against the Cattle-Tick," *Scientific American* 87, supp. 2260 (April 26, 1919): 266–67.

13.   J. Evetts Haley, *Charles Goodnight, Cowman and Plainsman*, 256.

14.   Tom B. Saunders IV, interview with the author, Weatherford, Texas, November 19, 2012; "Legacy of the Texas Longhorns," International Texas Longhorn Association, Glen Rose, Texas, www.itla.com /Longhorn-Legacy, accessed June 15, 2013.

15.   Dobie, *Longhorns*, 161–62.

16.   Ibid., 168.

17.   Ibid., 33–34.

18.   Ibid., 222; Robin Dutton, "Olive, Isom Prentice," Handbook of Texas Online, Texas State Historical Association, https://tshaonline.org/handbook/online/articles/fol12.

19.   Dobie, *Longhorns*, 206, 207, referencing *Chicago Tribune*, February 6, 1900.

20.   Ibid., 207–8; Alan Rogers, "The Truth about Champion's Horns," National Texas Longhorn Museum, Kansas City, Missouri, www.longhornmuseum.com/Champion.htm, accessed August 2, 2012.

21.   Dobie, *Longhorns*, 209, 213. The term *mossy-horned* refers to wrinkles that form on a steer's horns with age.

22.   "Yates Horn Collection" (formerly Howdy Fowler, "Historic Yates Texas Longhorn Collection"), Cattlemen's Texas Longhorn Registry, Hondo, Texas, www.ctlr.org/ewExternalFiles/Yates%20Horn%20Collection.pdf, accessed November 27, 2017.

23.   "Dogie Almost as Scarce as Dodo," *Miami (Oklahoma) Daily News-Record*, May 22, 1927; "Longhorn Cattle Almost Extinct," *Perry (Oklahoma) Journal*, September 5, 1927; Lawrence Clayton, *Longhorn Legacy: Graves Peeler and the Texas Cattle Trade*; Will C. Cradduck, Herd Manager, Official State of Texas Longhorn Herd, Fort Griffin State Historic Site, Texas Historical Commission, Albany, Texas, to the author, e-mail, March 21, 2017.

24.   "Butler Foundation Cattle: One of the Original Seven Families with an Interesting History," http://longhornroundup.com/butler-foundation-cattle/, accessed June 26, 2017; "The Seven Families (Plus One) Revisited," reprinted from *Texas Longhorn Journal*, July–August 1993, Butler Texas Longhorns, Info Center, www.butlertexaslonghorns.com/history/sevenfamilies.html, accessed June 26, 2017; "The Seven Families of Texas Longhorns," reprinted from *Texas Longhorn Trails*, in Double Helix Ranch, www.doublehelixranch.com/SevenFamilies.html, accessed June 26, 2017. Butler apparently bred longhorns to achieve specific characteristics without introducing genes from other breeds. Some of these characteristics became hallmarks of the Butler line.

25.   D. Phillip Sponenberg, Professor, Pathology and Genetics, Virginia-Maryland College of Veterinary Medicine, Blacksburg, Virginia, to the author, e-mail, March 2, 2017; Debbie Davis, president, Cattlemen's Texas Longhorn Conservancy, Tarpley, Texas, interview with the author, March 2, 2017; Cora Oltersdorf, "A Dying Breed?," *Alcalde*, Volume 91, Number 2, November/December 2002, Cattlemen's Texas Longhorn Registry, www.ctlr.org/ewExternalFiles/Alcalde.pdf, accessed December 6, 2017; "Unacceptable Traits," Debbie Davis to the author, e-mail, March 2, 2017.
       The pure Texas longhorn possesses certain observable characteristics (its phenotype). A typical longhorn should exhibit a long, narrow head with a straight profile from the poll to the muzzle, with the poll the same approximate width as the muzzle, and the head should show masculinity or femininity according to the animal's sex. A bull's horns typically grow laterally from the poll with a forward and upward sweep, evolved as a dominance trait from fighting. The "Texas Twist" is usually present in the horns of cows and steers. The long, lateral horn growth is a trait that evolved to allow the animal to protect its

flank or its calf. Ears should be short to medium, set horizontally directly under the horns, with long hairs to help protect against parasites. The body should be of good length, angular (for heat adaptation), with a slender head and shoulders (for ease of calving). Bulls will be thicker and more muscular through the neck and shoulders.

The Texas longhorn is a medium-bodied breed. Size and weight will vary according to the quality of its range. The tail should be long (evolved to swish and swat to repel flies). The legs should be long in comparison to those of other breeds; long legs meant the ability to travel long distances. Coloration can be varied; the most common colors among the wild Texas cattle were red, black, brown, dun (tan), or roan (reddish brown). Lines should be clean with little or no loose skin. These are a few of the general characteristics. Traits such as large ears; long, flattened horns; U-shaped horns; poll bump; dished nose bridge; round rump; short face; loose skin; and greater body depth indicate crossbreeding with Watusi, Brahman, or English breeds.

Genetic testing (genotyping) involves comparison of the percentage of the indicine genome in a particular animal with that of other animals of known ancestry. The actual percentage can vary but must fall within a certain range. A high percentage of the indicine genome indicates more Indian or African ancestry, such as Brahman or Watusi. A lower percentage of the indicine genome might indicate more European or English ancestry, rather than Iberian.

26.   Cradduck to the author, e-mail.

Chapter 3

1.   S. E. Forman, "Railroad Lines in Actual Operation, 1860," Map 02889 in *Advanced American History*; J. H. Colton, *Colton's New Railroad & County Map of the United States and the Canadas &c.*; "Railroad Ties," Sedalia, MO, Come Grow with Us, http://ci.sedalia.mo.us/about, accessed September 12, 2012.

2.   Horace Capron, *Report of the Commissioner of Agriculture on the Diseases of Cattle in the United States*, 82.

3.   Ibid.

4.   J. Marvin Hunter, ed., *The Trail Drivers of Texas*, 2nd ed., rev., 696–99. Some accounts of this incident state that Daugherty was tied to a tree with his own picket rope and whipped severely with switches; however, Daugherty did not mention this in his account of the incident recorded in *The Trail Drivers of Texas*.

5.   Capron, *Report of the Commissioner*, 82–132.

6.   Ibid., 1, 183.

7.   Ibid., 1, 184.

8.   Ibid., 85–86.

9.   Ibid., 122–23.

10.   Ibid., 118–19.

11.   Ibid., 200–202.

12.   Ibid., 179.

13.   Ibid., 124.

14.   Dixon Ryan Fox, "Map Showing Trunk Line Railway Systems Disregarding Minor Branches, 1875," Map 3350, in *Harper's Atlas of American History*; Gaylord Watson, *Centennial American Republic and Railroad Map of the United States and of the Dominion of Canada*, 1875. A trunk line is a main line that carries through traffic; a branch line is a secondary line that branches off of a main route, also sometimes called a spur.

15.   "The Pan Handle Trails," *Dodge City Times*, August 7, 1880.

16.   Ida Ellen Rath, *The Rath Trail*, 143–44; "Pan Handle Trails." The requirement regarding cattle wintered "west of the Wichitas and north of the Brazos" referred to the Big Wichita and Little Wichita Rivers in the area north or northwest of Baylor County. The Texas Panhandle stockmen also passed a resolution that approved efforts to improve the bloodlines of their herds by importing "bulls of good blood." "Bulls of good blood" referred to domestic English breeds such as Hereford, Durham, Angus, or other heavier, stockier breeds. This marked perhaps the first organized effort to improve beef production in Texas by cross-breeding the longhorn.

17.   H. Allen Anderson, "Winchester Quarantine," Handbook of Texas Online, Texas State Historical Association, www.tshaonline.org /handbook, accessed October 5, 2012.

18.   J. Evetts Haley, *Charles Goodnight, Cowman and Plainsman*, 361–62.

19.   Joseph Nimmo, *Report in Regard to the Range and Ranch Cattle Business of the United States*, 90.

20.   Ibid., 25–26.

21.   Ibid., 138, 164.

22.   *Railroad Company v. Husen*, 95 U.S. 465 (1877), Legal Information Institute, Cornell University Law School, www.law.cornell.edu, accessed October 9, 2012.

23.   Nimmo, *Report*, 137.

24.   Ibid., 141–42.

25.   Ibid., 134–35. The thirty-seventh parallel represents the southern border of Kansas; therefore, all cattle that entered the state across its southern border were assumed to be a threat, and owners or persons in charge of those cattle were assumed to know that their cattle were capable of spreading the fever. The area of the twenty-first meridian of longitude west from Washington and north of the thirty-fourth parallel of north latitude is the same general area that was specified in the Winchester Quarantine: generally north or northwest of the Brazos and west of Clay County, Texas. This 1885 law effectively closed Kansas to herd traffic.

26.   Ibid., 136.

27.   Julius Bien, *The Range and Ranch Cattle Area of the United States, 1884*, Map 1, in Nimmo, *Report*.

28.   "The Fight against the Cattle Tick," *Scientific American* 87, supp. 2260 (April 26, 1919): 266–67; Myron Schultz, "Theobald Smith," *Emerging Infectious Diseases* 14, no. 12 (December 2008); Theobald Smith and Fred Lucius Kilborne, *Investigations into the Nature, Causations, and*

Prevention of Texas or Southern Cattle Fever, Bureau of Animal Industry Bulletin No. 1 (1893).

29. "Fight against the Cattle Tick."

30. "King Ranch's Legacy" (formerly "The End of the War and Building a Business"), King Ranch, 2017, www.king-ranch.com, accessed December 5, 2017; "Fight against the Cattle Tick."

31. Randolph Garner, "A New Piece of History Discovered and a Note of Thanks," *Cleburne (Texas) Times-Review*, January 8, 2012.

Chapter 4

1. J. Marvin Hunter, ed., *The Trail Drivers of Texas*, 2nd ed., rev., 427–28; Philip Durham and Everett L. Jones, *The Negro Cowboys*, 166. If broken horses fell in with a herd of wild mustangs, they quickly reverted to their feral condition. For that reason the wild mustangs, which were so numerous in some areas that they were considered pests, were sometimes simply shot.

2. James H. Cook, *Fifty Years on the Old Frontier as Cowboy, Hunter, Guide, Scout, and Ranchman*, 64–69.

3. Frederick Law Olmsted, *A Journey through Texas; or, A Saddle Trip on the Southwestern Frontier: With a Statistical Appendix*, 372.

4. John C. Ewers, *The Horse in Blackfoot Indian Culture with Comparative Material from Other Western Tribes*, Bureau of American Ethnology Bulletin no. 159, 59–64.

5. Hunter, *Trail Drivers*, 427; David Dary, *Cowboy Culture: A Saga of Five Centuries*, 137, referencing Lee Moore et al., *Letters from Old Friends and Members*, 33–34.

6. Hunter, *Trail Drivers*, 338–45.

7. Cook, *Fifty Years on the Old Frontier*, 10, 16.

8. Ibid., 19–20.

9. David Dary, "Cattle Brands," Handbook of Texas Online, Texas State Historical Association, https://tshaonline.org/handbook/online/articles/auc01, accessed August 31, 2015.

10. Hunter, *Trail Drivers*, 338–47; Dary, *Cowboy Culture*, 138–39.

11. Dary, *Cowboy Culture*, 190–91, 352, referencing Hans Peter Nielsen Gammel, comp., *Laws of Texas, 1822–1897*, sess. 12 (1871), 119. While the use of road brands may have been a common practice prior to this law, only a few references to their use in the years immediately preceding 1871 were found. All other references to the use of road brands were after 1871.

12. "Herd Delivered to John Lytle, Medina County, Texas, April 12, 1877," leather-bound pocket notebook, John T. Lytle Collection, Box 2, Cattle Raisers Museum, Texas and Southwestern Cattle Raisers Foundation, Fort Worth.

13. J. Evetts Haley, *Charles Goodnight, Cowman and Plainsman*, 245; Philip Ashton Rollins, *The Cowboy: His Characteristics, His Equipment, and His Part in the Development of the West*, 252.

14. Jerome C. Smiley and National Live Stock Association of the United States, *Prose and Poetry of the Live Stock Industry of the United States*,

vol. 1, 596–97; Haley, *Charles Goodnight*, 244–49, 254, 431–36; Dary, *Cowboy Culture*, 191–92; Rollins, *Cowboy*, 252–54. Charles Goodnight's lead steer, Old Blue, wore a bell fastened around his neck. The herd soon learned to follow the sound of the bell up the trail. A leather strap was placed around the clapper at night to silence the bell and removed the next morning when the herd was ready to move.

15.   Haley, *Charles Goodnight*, 246–48, 253.

16.   Ibid., 244–49.

17.   Ibid., 248; Durham and Jones, *Negro Cowboys*, 40.

18.   Cook, *Fifty Years on the Old Frontier*, 40.

19.   "Receipt from Frank E. Conrad & Co., Fort Griffin, Texas, to Messrs. Lytle & Schreiner, May 14, 1881," John T. Lytle Collection, Box 1, Folder E, Cattle Raisers Museum, Texas and Southwestern Cattle Raisers Foundation, Fort Worth.

20.   "Receipt from York, Parker, Draper Mercantile Co., Dodge City, Kansas, to Messrs. Lytle & Shriner [*sic*], June 19, 1881," Folder O, and "Receipt from L. Aufdengarten to Shriner [*sic*] & Lytle, Ogallala, Nebraska, July 20, 1881," Folder X, both in John T. Lytle Collection, Box 1, Cattle Raisers Museum, Texas and Southwestern Cattle Raisers Foundation, Fort Worth.

21.   J. C. Davis to Dicy Clark, May 28, 1882, collection of R. W. Hewett, Henrietta, Texas; Jack Bailey, *A Texas Cowboy's Journal Up the Trail to Kansas in 1868*, ed. David Dary, 54.

22.   Hunter, *Trail Drivers*, 236.

23.   Ibid., 236–37.

24.   Ibid., 239–40.

25.   Ibid., 378.

26.   Tom B. Saunders IV, interview with the author, Weatherford, Texas, February 16, 2011.

27.   Ibid.

28.   Hunter, *Trail Drivers*, 105–8. Sometimes the drovers stripped their clothes, wrapped them in oilcloth or stowed them in the wagon to keep them dry, and swam the herd while naked.

29.   Haley, *Charles Goodnight*, 145–46.

30.   Cook, *Fifty Years on the Old Frontier*, 102.

31.   Haley, *Charles Goodnight*, 250–51.

32.   Cook, *Fifty Years on the Old Frontier*, 106–7.

33.   Rollins, *Cowboy*, 260.

34.   Smiley and National Live Stock Association, *Prose and Poetry*, 400; Hunter, *Trail Drivers*, 23, 44, 81, 97, 122, 149–50, 186, 234, 432, 448, 502, 559–60, 757–58, 819, 927, 965.

35.   Smiley and National Live Stock Association, *Prose and Poetry*, 700–702.

36.   Dary, *Cowboy Culture*, 190–91.

37.   Rollins, *Cowboy*, 187–88; Haley, *Charles Goodnight*, 257.

38.   Hunter, *Trail Drivers*, 120.

39.   Joseph C. McConnell, *The West Texas Frontier*, 2:104; Hunter, *Trail Drivers*, 1025.

Chapter 5

1. Dan Kilgore, "The Spanish Missions and the Origins of the Cattle Industry in Texas," *The Cattleman*, January 1983; "New Orleans and Mobile Mail Line," *True American* (New Orleans), April 8, 1837; "House of Representatives," *True American* (New Orleans), February 22, 1839.

2. Andres Tijerina, "Tejano Origins in Mexican Texas," May 4, 1998, Alamo de Parras Hispanic Studies, Sons of DeWitt Colony Texas, www.tamu.edu, accessed April 8, 2013; Robert H. Thonhoff, *The Texas Connection with the American Revolution*, 48.

3. Date in History, "The Revolution Day by Day" (formerly "Revolutionary War"), National Park Service, www.nps.gov, accessed November 27, 2017; Thonhoff, *Texas Connection*, 48–51, referencing Croix to Cabello, August 16, 1779, Bexar Archives, Bexar Archives Translation (BAT) 2C342, 85:112–14.

4. "La Bahia Road," Handbook of Texas Online, Texas State Historical Association, https://tshaonline.org/handbook/online/articles/exl01, accessed May 5, 2013; Robert H. Thonhoff, "Galvez, Bernardo de," Handbook of Texas Online, Texas State Historical Association, https://tshaonline.org/handbook/online/articles/fga10, accessed May 15, 2013.

5. Jim Bob Jackson, *They Pointed Them East First*, 5th ed., xi; Mickie Baldwin, "White, James Taylor," Handbook of Texas Online, Texas State Historical Association, https://tshaonline.org/handbook/online/articles/fwh21, accessed May 15, 2013; "New Orleans Cattle Market," *New Orleans Daily Crescent*, September 14, 1848; January 13, 1849. The September 14, 1848, advertisement is the earliest found for beef cattle prices at the New Orleans cattle market.

6. *Regulations of the Army of the United States and General Orders in Force on the 17th of February, 1881*, 170; Joseph Nimmo, *Report in Regard to the Range and Ranch Cattle Business of the United States*, 74.
   Net weight, or carcass weight, was calculated based on a percentage of live weight; 55 percent if the animal weighed thirteen hundred pounds or more, 50 percent when it weighed eight hundred to thirteen hundred pounds, and 40 percent for animals that weighed less than eight hundred pounds. Another method to determine net weight was to slaughter several animals that represented the average size in the herd and weigh the carcasses. The weight estimate of 950–1,050 pounds was for well-fed steers on the prairie grass of the northern ranges, which was more nutritious than that found in southern climates. A longhorn steer fresh off the trail to New Orleans likely weighed slightly less.

7. "Texas," *Houston Telegraph and Texas Register*, May 25, 1842; Carl A. Brasseaux and Keith P. Fontenot, *Steamboats on Louisiana's Bayous: A History and Directory*, 25; "The Atchafalaya," *Houston Telegraph and Texas Register*, June 1, 1842.

8. Jackson, *They Pointed Them East First*, 40–41.

9. "Diary of William B. Duncan, Liberty County, Texas," October 23–December 14, 1853, and October 2–4, 1854, transcribed by Mrs. Julia Duncan Welder, Liberty, Texas, formatted by Tom Patin, Leander, Texas, San Jacinto Museum of History, Houston, 19–21.

10. "Cow Boat Establishment, Bayou la Rose," *Southern Sentinel* (Plaquemine, Louisiana), July 4, 1857; Jackson, *They Pointed Them East First*, 1–4.

11. "Diary of William B. Duncan," 19–21; Jackson, *They Pointed Them East First*, 43–44.

12. "Diary of William B. Duncan," 23, 30–31.

13. In "New Orleans Cattle Market," *New Orleans Daily Crescent*, May 9, 1851, prices were advertised as $0.035 to $0.05 per pound for Texas cattle, while "Beef Cattle" were advertised as $0.07–$0.075 per pound. In "Cattle Market," *Thibodaux Minerva*, March 3, 1855, prices were advertised as $0.06 to $0.12 per pound. "Cattle Market," *Harrisonburg (Louisiana) Independent*, November 24, 1858, advertised prices of $22 to $40 per head for good to fine grades and $6 per head for inferior grades. "Cattle Market," *New Orleans Daily Crescent*, September 10, 1860, advertised prices of $16 to $40 per head, ordinary to choice grades.

14. Bobby D. Weaver, "Texas Road," Encyclopedia of Oklahoma History and Culture, Oklahoma Historical Society, Oklahoma City, www .okhistory.org, accessed October 28, 2013; Grant Foreman, "The Centennial of Fort Gibson," *Chronicles of Oklahoma* 2, no. 2 (June 1924): 119–20. Fort Smith was established in 1817 and Fort Gibson in 1824.

15. Christopher D. Long, "Old Three Hundred," Handbook of Texas Online, Texas State Historical Association, https://tshaonline.org /handbook/online/articles/um001, accessed October 11, 2016; Ray Allen Billington and Martin Ridge, "The Southern Mississippi Valley Frontier, 1815–1830," map, in *Westward Expansion: A History of the American Frontier*, 109; US Census, "Guide to 2010 State and Local Census Geography," Missouri, US Census Bureau, Census Blogs, www .census.gov/newsroom/blogs/random-samplings/2011/10/us-census -bureau-releases-2010-guide-to-state-and-local-census-geography.html, accessed September 9, 2013; *State of Missouri Formed, but Name of Missouri Territory Retained for the Undivided Portion of Louisiana Purchase*, map, Serial Set 4312, 57th Cong., 1st sess., H. Doc. 15, Part 3, map 15, 987, 1821.

16. US Census, "Guide to 2010 Census Geography," Arkansas and Missouri. The original spelling of Arkansas' name, "Arkansaw," was changed to Arkansas in 1881. The eastern border of the Texas Panhandle lies along the one-hundredth meridian, and its northern border lies along thirty-six degrees, thirty minutes north latitude.

17. Billington and Ridge, *Westward Expansion*, 111–13; Earl A. Shoemaker, *The Permanent Indian Frontier: The Reason for the Construction and Abandonment of Fort Scott, Kansas during the Dragoon Era*, 9–10, referencing Francis Paul Prucha, *American Indian Policy in the Formative Years: The Indian Trade and Intercourse Acts, 1790–1834*, 140–43.

18. Billington and Ridge, *Westward Expansion*, 40–41.

19. Ibid., 107–14; George Catlin, *United States Indian Frontier in 1840, Showing the Position of the Tribes That Have Been Removed West of the Mississippi*, map, Serial Set 3016, 52nd Cong., 1st sess., H. Misc. Doc. 340, Part 15, 44, map 2.

20. *The History of Pettis County, Missouri*, 355.

21.   Billington and Ridge, *Westward Expansion*, 113; Shoemaker, *Permanent Indian Frontier*, 19–20; Catlin, *United States Indian Frontier*, map.

22.   Wayne Gard, *The Chisholm Trail*, 23; J. H. Colton and Company, *Texas*, map, 1855.
        In 1855 the only counties between San Antonio and the Rio Grande were Bexar, Uvalde, Kinney (shown as McKinney on the Colton 1855 map), San Patricio, Webb, Nueces, Starr, Hidalgo, and Cameron. Over the course of time these counties were divided into the current counties of Bexar (1829), Wilson (1860), Medina (1848), Val Verde (1885), Kinney (1850), Uvalde (1850), Atascosa (1856), Frio (1858), Zavala (1858), Maverick (1856), Dimmit (1858), La Salle (1858), McMullen (1858), Live Oak (1856), Bee (1857), San Patricio (1829), Nueces (1846), Jim Wells (1911), Duval (1858), Webb (1848), Zapata (1858), Jim Hogg (1913), Brooks (1911), Starr (1848), Hidalgo (1852), Willacy (1911), Cameron (1848), and Kenedy (1921). "Texas County Creation Dates and Parent Counties," Family Search, Church of Jesus Christ of Latter Day Saints, www.familysearch.org/wiki/en/Texas_County_Creation_Dates_and_Parent_Counties, accessed May 16, 2013.

23.   Colton and Company, *Texas*, map; Charles W. Pressler, *Grayson*, map.

24.   Wayne Gard, "The Shawnee Trail," *Southwestern Historical Quarterly* 56 (July 1952–April 1953): 361, 362; C. Roeser, *Indian Territory*, map, 1879, Serial Set 1885, 46th Cong., 2d sess., S. Exec. Doc. 124, 12.

25.   Roeser, *Indian Territory*, map, Serial Set 1885.

26.   J. Marvin Hunter, ed., *The Trail Drivers of Texas*, 2nd ed., rev., 963; Colton and Company, *Texas*. George W. Saunders listed these counties as part of the main route from the Rio Grande to the post–Civil War railheads of central Kansas that opened beginning in 1867. It is logical that the same route was the best route to move cattle herds from the Rio Grande to the Brazos crossings prior to the war as well. Depending upon the origin point, herds could also reach the Travis County area from San Patricio County through the counties of Bee, Goliad, DeWitt, Gonzales, Caldwell, and Bastrop.

27.   Colton, *Texas*.

28.   Roeser, *Indian Territory*, map, Serial Set 1885. The trail route was also compared with *Oklahoma 1997–98 Official State Map* to determine the Oklahoma counties.

29.   *History of Pettis County, Missouri*, 404–10.

30.   Ibid., 461.

31.   Nathaniel Thompson Allison, ed., *History of Cherokee County, Kansas, and Representative Citizens*, 135, 151–53; *The Opening of the Great Southwest, 1870–1970: A Brief History of the Origin and Development of the Missouri-Kansas-Texas Railroad, Better Known as the KATY*, 3–7.

32.   Roeser, *Indian Territory*, map, Serial Set 1885.

33.   US War Department, *Reports of the Secretary of War, with Reconnaissances of Routes from San Antonio to El Paso, by Brevet Lt. Col. J. E. Johnston; Lieutenant W. F. Smith; Lieutenant F. T. Bryan; Lieutenant N. H. Michler; and Captain S. G. French, of Q'rmaster's Dep't.; Also, the Report of Capt. R. B. Marcy's Route from Fort Smith to Santa Fe; and the Report of Lieut. J. H. Simpson of an Expedition into the Navajo Country;*

and the Report of Lieutenant W. H. C. Whiting's Reconnaissances of the
Western Frontier of Texas, 31st Cong., 1st sess., S. Exec. Doc. 64 (July 24,
1850), 173.

34.   "Texan Cattle," *Emporia (Kansas) News*, January 28, 1870. This is an
        obvious reference to the trail branch previously cited on the 1879
        Roeser map of Indian Territory (Serial Set 1885).

35.   Jean T. Hannaford, "Old Preston Road," Handbook of Texas Online,
        Texas State Historical Association, https://tshaonline.org/handbook
        /online/articles/exo03, accessed November 2, 2013; Pressler, *Grayson*;
        Morris L. Britton, "Colbert's Ferry," Handbook of Texas Online, Texas
        State Historical Association, https://tshaonline.org/handbook/online
        /articles/rtc01, accessed November 2, 2013; Sandra L. Myres, "Fort
        Graham," Handbook of Texas Online, Texas State Historical Associa-
        tion, https://tshaonline.org/handbook/online/articles/qbf21, accessed
        November 2, 2013; Brian Hart, "Towash, TX," Handbook of Texas
        Online, Texas State Historical Association, https://tshaonline.org
        /handbook/online/articles/hvt53, accessed November 2, 2013.

36.   Roeser, *Indian Territory*, map, Serial Set 1885; *Opening of the Great
        Southwest*, 12, 14. The trail route was also compared with *Oklahoma
        1997–98 Official State Map* to determine the Oklahoma river crossings.

Chapter 6

1.   Fannie G. Chisholm, *The Four State Chisholm Trail*, 9; Louise Artrip and
        Fullen Artrip, *Memoirs of (the Late) Daniel Fore (Jim) Chisholm and the
        Chisholm Trail*, 18–19.

2.   Artrip, *Memoirs*, 18–19; Chisholm, *Four State Chisholm Trail*, 82.

3.   Chisholm, *Four State Chisholm Trail*, 26–27. Regarding speculation
        that Thornton and Jesse were related, according to DeWitt Historical
        Commission, *The History of DeWitt County, Texas*; "DeWitt Colony
        Biographies," Surnames A–G, Sons of DeWitt Colony, Texas, www
        .sonsofdewittcolony.org/dewittbiosa-g2.htm; and Stan Hoig, "The
        Genealogy of Jesse Chisholm," *Chronicles of Oklahoma* 67, no. 2
        (Summer 1989): 194–205, there is no mention of a family relationship
        between Thornton Chisholm and Jesse Chisholm.

4.   Charles Moreau Harger, "Cattle-Trails of the Prairies," *Scribner's
        Magazine* 11, no. 6 (January–June 1892): 734. The relevant text reads as
        follows: "The most famous of these was the 'Chisholm Trail.' It was
        named after John Chisholm, an eccentric frontier stockman, who was
        the first to drive over it. Chisholm lived at Paris, Texas, was a bachelor,
        and had many thousand head of cattle on the ranges in the southern
        part of the State. Later he removed to New Mexico, and died a few
        years ago, leaving almost uncounted droves upon his ranches. There
        was through Texas, reaching down from the Red River, the irregular
        "Southern Texas Trail," ending at the north near Cooke County. From
        the Red River, Chisholm broke the way to Kansas, riding ahead of his
        herd and selecting what seemed the most favorable route."

5.   "The Chisholm Trail," *Wichita Daily Eagle*, March 14, 1893; "County
        News," *Golden Era* (Lincoln, New Mexico), January 1, 1885; "Notes for
        the Stock Man," *Indian Chieftain* (Vinita, Indian Territory), January 8,
        1885; *National Live-Stock Journal* 16 (January–December 1885).

6. Clara M. Love, "History of the Cattle Industry in the Southwest," *Southwestern Historical Quarterly* 19 (July 1915–April 1916): 393–94; Edmond Franklin Bates, *History and Reminiscences of Denton County*, 167–68; Mary Jo Cowling, *Geography of Denton County*, 25.

    Later in Bates, *History and Reminiscences*, another contributor, I. D. Ferguson, mentioned Chisum, the Chisum trail, and Chisum's movement of cattle from Denton County eventually to New Mexico. Ferguson did not make the same claim regarding the connection to the northern markets (305–306). On page 406, Bates states in closing: "In the perusal of these reminiscences the reader may have observed an occasional tendency to embellish narrative with a few gems of fiction, despite the fact that truth is supposed to be stranger than fiction. But this tendency to allow free rein to one's fancy is pardonable. Do we not live in a world of romance, a world of make-believe? . . . We wish to make things more attractive than they are, hence the sugar coating on the pill. . . . These embellishments that approach the realm of fiction give zest to facts that might otherwise be lost to future citizens of Denton County." This all but states that not everything in the book is true.

7. Hoig, "Genealogy of Jesse Chisholm," 198, 201–2, referencing "Heirs of Jesse and William E. Chisholm," Shawnee War Claims File, 24, Archives and Manuscripts Division, Oklahoma Historical Society. See also "Valuable Data for History of Chisholm Trail Offered," *Enid (Oklahoma) Daily Eagle*, September 7, 1911.

8. "Old Skeleton Found," *Oklahoma City Evening Free Press*, December 13, 1910, "old skeleton found near the 'old Chism Trail.'" *Peoples Press* (El Reno, Oklahoma), December 22, 1911, "The Chism trail north of town is like the lost chord in music. Hard to find and difficult to follow when it is found." "Bad Spelling of the Pioneers," *Muskogee Daily Phoenix*, October 13, 1911. "Chism it is, not Chisholm." *Enid (Oklahoma) Events*, October 19, 1911, "Let's call it Chism Trail instead of Chis-holm Trail." "Markers for Chisholm Trail Being Put in Place," *Medford (Oklahoma) Patriot*, April 17, 1913. The last article used two spellings. The headline read "Markers for Chisholm Trail Being Put in Place," but the article read "the signal code adopted to designate the Chism Trail or official route."

9. *Arizona Silver Belt* (Globe City, Arizona), January 17, 1885.

10. J. G. Clift, "Notes on the Early History of Stephens County," *Chronicles of Oklahoma* 20, no. 1 (March 1942): 53. By their own statement the Cowpunchers Association offered no evidence, only an assumption or opinion that the trail was named for a cattleman rather than a trader. "Dr. Thoburn" is likely a reference to historian and author Joseph B. Thoburn, who served on the staff of the Oklahoma Historical Society and edited *Chronicles of Oklahoma*. Thoburn retired in 1931.

11. Clifford R. Caldwell, *John Simpson Chisum: The Cattle King of the Pecos Revisited*, 52–53, referencing William A. Keleher, *The Fabulous Frontier, 1846–1912*, 58.

12. Stan Hoig, *Jesse Chisholm, Ambassador of the Plains*, 91, 94–95, 115, 118; John Rossel, "The Chisholm Trail," Kansas Historical Quarterly 5 (1936): 6. Fort Holmes, originally designated Camp Holmes, was located near the confluence of Little River and the Canadian River.

Chisholm's cabin was located east of the present site of Asher, Oklahoma.

13.   Rossel, "Chisholm Trail," 3–5, referencing Captain R. B. Marcy, *Map of Western Trails*, and Joseph Stroud, *Memories of Old Western Trails in Texas Longhorn Days*, 9. See also US War Department, *Reports of the Secretary of War, with Reconnaissances of Routes from San Antonio to El Paso, by Brevet Lt. Col. J. E. Johnston; Lieutenant W. F. Smith; Lieutenant F. T. Bryan; Lieutenant N. H. Michler; and Captain S. G. French, of Q'rmaster's Dep't.; Also, the Report of Capt. R. B. Marcy's Route from Fort Smith to Santa Fe; and the Report of Lieut. J. H. Simpson of an Expedition into the Navajo Country; and the Report of Lieutenant W. H. C. Whiting's Reconnaissances of the Western Frontier of Texas*, 31st Cong., 1st sess., S. Exec. Doc. 64 (July 24, 1850), 173–74; Julius Bien, *Map of the Territory of the United States from the Mississippi River to the Pacific Ocean; Ordered by Jeff'n Davis, Secretary of War to Accompany the Reports of the Explorations for a Railroad Route*. References to military officers typically include their full name or initials. It is assumed that "Major Merrill" named on the map is Major Hamilton Wilcox Merrill, who was at Fort Worth and Fort Belknap at that time.

14.   *The War of the Rebellion: A Compilation of the Official Records of the Union and Confederate Armies* (hereafter cited as *Official Records*), series I, 1:656, 667; Rossel, "Chisholm Trail," 6, 7, referencing James R. Mead, "The Chisholm Trail," *Wichita Eagle*, March 1, 1890; Letter to the author (Rossel) from George Rainey; and Joseph B. Thoburn, "The Chisholm Trail," *Rock Island Magazine* 5, no. 19 (December 1924), 4. See also letter from George Rainey, in "Letters and Documents," *Southwestern Historical Quarterly* 44: 249; and Muriel H. Wright, "A History of Fort Cobb," *Chronicles of Oklahoma* 34 (Spring 1956): 57–59, referencing *Official Records*, series I, 1:648, 649.

15.   Rossel, "Chisholm Trail," 6; Hoig, *Jesse Chisholm*, 141, 161, referencing Mead, "Little Arkansas," Collections of the Kansas State Historical Society 10 (1908); *Wichita Eagle*, March 7, 1890; *Daily Oklahoman* (Oklahoma City), November 17, 1907; Philip McCusker to Thomas Murphy, November 15, 1867, Letters Received, Wichita Indian Agency, 1867–75, RG 75, NA; and Jesse Leavenworth to Wichita Agency, Letters Received, April 23, 1868, Kiowa Indian Agency, 1864–68, RG 75, NA. See also Ado Hunnius, *Military Map of the Indian Territory*.

Chapter 7

1.   Stan Hoig, *Jesse Chisholm, Ambassador of the Plains*, 7–11, referencing John Chisholm to Governor Shelby, January 24, 1795, Draper Collection, II, 53, Western History Collections, University of Oklahoma, 5, 11, referencing affidavit by John Chisholm (Jesse's brother), January 25, 1842, Records of the First Board of Cherokee Commissioners, Folder 1106, RG 75, NA; and 11–12, 20, and 115, referencing US Congress, Senate, *Correspondence on the Subject of the Emigration of Indians*, 23d Cong., 1st sess., S. Exec. Doc. 512. On the affidavit, see also Stan Hoig, "The Genealogy of Jesse Chisholm," *Chronicles of Oklahoma* 67, no. 2 (Summer 1989): 198–99. This affidavit establishes the identity of Jesse's mother as Corn Tassel's sister.

The questionable circumstances of Ignatius Chisholm's departure from Tennessee involve Ignatius's allegedly entering another man's slave quarters and "abusing a Negro man." Hoig, *Jesse Chisholm*, 11, referencing Knox County Court Minutes I, entry for February 4, 1797, and II, entry for April 13, 1802, Knox County Archives, Knoxville, Tennessee; John Rossel, "The Chisholm Trail," *Kansas Historical Quarterly* 5 (1936): 6.

2. Marie Giles, "Tehuacana Creek Councils," Handbook of Texas Online, Texas State Historical Association, https://tshaonline.org/handbook /online/articles/mgt01, accessed March 21, 2014; "By the President of the Republic of Texas, Proclamation," *Northern Standard* (Clarksville, Texas), March 20, 1844; Hoig, *Jesse Chisholm*, 21, 52, referencing Grant Foreman, *Advancing the Frontier*, 38; Hoig, "Genealogy," 199–200. The Tehuacana Creek Councils were a series of meetings between various Indian tribes and representatives of the Republic of Texas held at various locations from Tehuacana Creek in McLennan County to Bird's Fort on the Trinity River in present-day Tarrant County.

    It has not been established whether Ignatius Chisholm's second wife, Martha Rogers, and Sam Houston's second wife, Diana Rogers, were sisters. It is possible that Diana (not Tiana or Talihina) was Martha's aunt or cousin.

3. Hoig, *Jesse Chisholm*, 91, 94–95, 118, referencing T. U. Taylor, *Jesse Chisholm*, 47, 132–33.

4. US Census, *1860 Federal Census—Slave Schedules*, Creek Nation, Indian Territory, File 1 of 5, State: Arkansas, County: Indian Lands, Sheet 406A, 2, Reel No. M653–54, Division: Creek Nation West of the State of Arkansas, Enumerated on September 8th, 1860; Hoig, *Jesse Chisholm*, 120, 131, referencing Joseph B. Thoburn and Muriel H. Wright, *Oklahoma: A History of the State and Its People*. In the census Sahkahkee Chisholm is shown as Sar Kar Ke.

5. Hoig, *Jesse Chisholm*, 93–94.

6. Ibid., 48, 49–50, referencing Statement of George Brinton, September 19, 1845; Lames Logan to commissioner of Indian Affairs, September 28, 1845; and Bill of Sale by Jesse Chisholm to Lucinda Edwards, January 24, 1841, all in Office of Indian Affairs, Special Files, 5, 35–47, RG 75, NA; Joseph W. Robertson to James S. Mayfield, April 7, 1841, in 32d Cong., 1st sess., S. Exec. Doc. 14, 3:57–58; and Grant A. Foreman, *A Traveler in Indian Territory: The Journal of Ethan Allen Hitchcock, Late Major-General in the United States Army*, 156. See also Joseph W. Robertson to James S. Mayfield, April 7, 1841, in Dorman H. Winfrey and James M. Day, eds., *Indian Papers of Texas and the Southwest 1825–1916*, 1:122–23; and Grant Foreman, "Early Trails through Oklahoma," *Chronicles of Oklahoma* 3, no. 2 (June 1925): 103–4, referencing *Annual Report of the American Historical Association for 1908* 2, no. 1 (1911): 107ff. The issue that drew the attention of Presidents Harrison and Tyler was whether the Republic of Texas (a foreign power) had a right to demand the return of the slaves. No documentation was found to indicate that the US government was investigating the specific slave dealings of Jesse Chisholm, as some have suggested.

7. Joseph B. Thoburn and Muriel H. Wright, "The Story of a Mexican Captive," *Oklahoma: A History of the State and Its People*, 2:823–24.

According to Thoburn, Vincente could not spell, and his last name (de Huersus) is spelled phonetically. Vincente was kept as a slave by the Comanche warrior who captured him. The warrior was later killed while on another raid. During a ceremony for the dead warrior, Vincente was instructed to don some of his former master's best apparel and mount his finest horse. As he sat waiting for the ceremony to begin, another Comanche from another band approached, looked at him for a long moment, and left. The strange warrior returned and instructed Vincente to dismount and remove the garments. This warrior had traded a horse for Vincente and was his new master. He later told Vincente that, had he not intervened, the boy would have been killed along with his master's horse according to Comanche custom so that both horse and slave could be with their master in the afterlife.

8. Hoig, Jesse Chisholm, 106–19.

9. *Official Records*, series I, 1:656, 659, 665.

10. Ibid., 667.

11. Julius Bien, *Map of the Territory of the United States from the Mississippi River to the Pacific Ocean; Ordered by Jeff'n Davis, Secretary of War to Accompany the Reports of the Explorations for a Railroad Route*; US War Department, *Reports of the Secretary of War, with Reconnaissances of Routes from San Antonio to El Paso, by Brevet Lt. Col. J. E. Johnston; Lieutenant W. F. Smith; Lieutenant F. T. Bryan; Lieutenant N. H. Michler; and Captain S. G. French, of Q'rmaster's Dep't.; Also, the Report of Capt. R. B. Marcy's Route from Fort Smith to Santa Fe; and the Report of Lieut. J. H. Simpson of an Expedition into the Navajo Country; and the Report of Lieutenant W. H. C. Whiting's Reconnaissances of the Western Frontier of Texas*, July 24, 1850, 31st Cong., 1st sess., S. Exec. Doc. 64 (July 24, 1850), 173–74; Rossel, "Chisholm Trail," 6, 7, referencing James R. Mead, "The Chisholm Trail," *Wichita Eagle*, March 1, 1890; letter to the author (Rossel) from George Rainey; and Joseph G. Thoburn, "The Chisholm Trail," *Rock Island Magazine* 5, no. 19 (December 1924): 4. See also letter from George Rainey in "Letters and Documents," *Southwestern Historical Quarterly* 44 (July 1940–April 1941): 249, and Muriel H. Wright, "A History of Fort Cobb," *Chronicles of Oklahoma* 34 (Spring 1956): 57–59, referencing *Official Records*, Series I, 1:648, 649.

12. Hoig, *Jesse Chisholm*, 131–32.

13. *Official Records*, Series I, 1:652; Hoig, *Jesse Chisholm*, 135, referencing *Galveston Weekly News*, September 3, 1861, in Barker Texas History Center, University of Texas at Austin; and Albert Pike, *Report of Albert Pike on Mission to the Indian Nations*, 8–19.

14. *Official Records*, Series IV, 1:542–54; Hoig, *Jesse Chisholm*, 136; Wright, "History of Fort Cobb," 59–60.

15. Hoig, *Jesse Chisholm*, 138, 139–41, referencing Elias Rector to Jesse Chisholm, December 1861, and bill of goods purchased from J. Shirley by J. Chisholm, January 25, 1862, both in Letters Sent, Records of the Southern Superintendency of Indian Affairs, Confederate Records, RG 75, NA; S. S. Scott to Gen. Holmes, November 2, 1862, *Official Records*, Series I, 13:919–21; F. Johnson to William P. Dole, January 20, 1863, cited in Annie Heloise Abel, *The American Indian as Slaveholder and Secessionist*, 329–30n590; Angie Debo, *The Road to Disappearance*, 151–52;

Charles B. Johnson Papers, Special Collections Department, University of Arkansas; and C. B. Johnson to Gen. William Steele, *Official Records*, Series I, vol. 22, pt. 2, 1020–21.

16. Hoig, *Jesse Chisholm*, 141, 142–43, 150, referencing Chisholm to Leavenworth, February 16, 1865, Letters Received, Kiowa Indian Agency, 1864–68, RG 75, NA; and James R. Mead, "The Little Arkansas," *Collections of the Kansas State Historical Society, 1907–8*, 10 (1908): 11; Rossel, "Chisholm Trail," 6; *Wichita Eagle*, March 7, 1890; *Daily Oklahoman* (Oklahoma City), November 17, 1907. See also Rossel, "Chisholm Trail," 6; and Edward E. Dale, "Additional Letters of General Stand Watie," *Chronicles of Oklahoma* 1, no. 2 (October 1921): 140–43.

    Chisholm worked on behalf of Confederate Commissioner Albert Pike early in the war, and his work for Union Comanche-Kiowa Agent Jesse Leavenworth late in the war has been viewed by some as traitorous toward the Confederacy. Chisholm was not known to have taken sides; Pike and Leavenworth were among his friends on both sides, and he acted on their behalf. All indications are that Chisholm's interests were neither Confederate nor Union, but with the Indians. While acting on behalf of Agent Leavenworth he advised the Indians to ignore the proposal of the Union officers; this is not the action of someone who had switched sides.

17. *Official Records*, Series I, vol. 48, part 1, 1096–97; Hoig, *Jesse Chisholm*, 152, referencing *Official Records*, Series I, vol. 48, part 2, 687–88, and 155, referencing J. H. Leavenworth to D. N. Colley, December 1, 1865, Letters Received, Kiowa Indian Agency, 1864–68, RG 75, NA. Chisholm's trading with the tribes hostile to the Union is another indication that his loyalty was to the Indians rather than to the Confederacy or the Union.

18. Hoig, *Jesse Chisholm*, 164–67, referencing Record Book of Chief Sam Checote, Archives-Manuscript Division, Oklahoma Historical Society; Creek File, Foreign Relations File, Archives and Manuscripts Division, Oklahoma Historical Society; *Daily Missouri Democrat* (Saint Louis), July 13, 1867; Henry Shanklin to James Wortham, September 1, 1867, in US Office of Indian Affairs, *Report on Indian Affairs by the Acting Commissioner for the Year 1867*, 321–23; and *Leavenworth Daily Conservative*, September 27, 1867.

19. Hoig, *Jesse Chisholm*, 167–70, referencing *Wichita Eagle*, May 9 and May 23, 1890; Aloise Hopkins to Joseph Thoburn, October 20, 1913, Edwards Trading Post File, Grant Foreman Collection, Archives and Manuscripts Division, Oklahoma Historical Society; James Wortham to N. G. Taylor, June 27, 1868, Letters Received, Creek Indian Agency, 1864–68, RG 75, NA; and Geo. T. Robinson to George Reynolds, March 31, 1868, and Captain George T. Robinson to George A. Reynolds, March 31, 1868, both in Letters Received, Kiowa Indian Agency, 1864–68, RG 75, NA.

20. Hoig, *Jesse Chisholm*, 170–72, referencing *Wichita Eagle*, March 7, 1890, and Jesse Chisholm Papers, Barker Texas History Center, University of Texas at Austin. Some accounts state that Chisholm died of cholera and some, cholera morbus. To address potential confusion, cholera and cholera morbus are essentially the same ailment. Webster's defines cholera morbus as a "gastrointestinal illness characterized by

cramps, diarrhea, and sometimes vomiting—not used technically." Cholera is defined by Webster's as "a serious disease that causes severe vomiting and diarrhea and that often results in death." According to James Byars Carter, MD, "Disease and Death in the Nineteenth Century: A Genealogical Perspective," *National Genealogical Society Quarterly* 76 (December 1988), cholera is defined as an acute infectious disease, caused by feces-contaminated food and water, with the same symptoms described above, that often results in death within three to five days. The word *morbus* is Latin for "disease." In the nineteenth century the term was associated with a qualifying noun to describe a disease; for example, *morbus cordis* for heart disease or *cholera morbus* for cholera. The term *morbus* is no longer typically used.

Witnesses reported that Chisholm died of cholera morbus caused by eating bear grease cooked in a brass kettle (Wayne Gard, *The Chisholm Trail*, 74). Chisholm was known to have been sick in the days prior to his death and had been in areas of exposure; he could already have had the disease, or the bear grease could have been contaminated. Either way, the result was the same.

Chapter 8

1. US Census, *Compendium of the Tenth Census (June 1, 1880), Compiled Pursuant to an Act of Congress Approved August 7, 1882*, rev. ed., Part I, Population, Table II, Aggregate Population at Each Census, 4; US Census, *Ninth Census of the United States,* vol. 1, *The Statistics of the Population of the United States (June 1, 1870)*, Table XX, "The United States," 595. The number of dwellings increased from an average of 1.48 dwellings per square mile in 1850 to 2.77 dwellings per square mile in 1860.

2. Richard Peters, ed., *The Public Statutes at Large of the United States of America from the Organization of the Government in 1789 to March 3, 1845*, vol. 4; "United States Statutes at Large," 23rd Cong., 1st sess., 729–30, "A Century of Lawmaking for a New Nation: US Congressional Documents and Debates," Library of Congress, https://memory.loc.gov /ammem/amlaw/lwsl.html, accessed January 2, 2014. The Permanent Indian Frontier lay west of the ninety-fifth meridian. A "foreigner" was defined as anyone who was not Indian.

3. Kansas-Nebraska Act (1854), National Archives and Records Administration, www.ourdocuments.gov, accessed January 2, 2014.

4. "The Result" and "Incidents of Yesterday," *Kansas Herald of Freedom* (Wakarusa, Kansas Territory), March 31, 1855.

5. "The Excitement of the Last Week," *Kansas Herald of Freedom*, February 19, 1859. The amnesty law applied to criminal acts caused by political differences of opinion committed in the counties of Lykins, Linn, Bourbon, McGee, Allen, and Anderson.

6. US Census, *Compendium of the Tenth Census*, 4; Ray Allen Billington and Martin Ridge, *Westward Expansion: A History of the American Frontier*, 245; S. E. Forman, "Railroad Lines in Actual Operation, 1860," Map 02889 in *Advanced American History*; J. H Colton, *Colton's New Railroad & County Map of the United States and the Canadas &c.*

7.   Joseph G. McCoy, *Historic Sketches of the Cattle Trade of the West and Southwest*, ed. Ralph Bieber, 47–49, 108.

8.   Ibid., 49–50, referencing *New York Daily Tribune*, November 6, 1867, and *Kansas Daily Commonwealth* (Topeka), August 15, 1871. See also Joseph Nimmo, *Report in Regard to the Range and Ranch Cattle Business of the United States*, 28; and Horace Capron, *Report of the Commissioner of Agriculture on the Diseases of Cattle in the United States*, 179. Joseph G. McCoy was considered an expert on the matter, and his estimate may have been used for this report.

9.   McCoy, *Historic Sketches*, 19, 94, referencing *Daily Illinois State Journal*, May 12; June 9, 13, 20; July 4, 11, 23, 28; August 13, 15, 29; December 29, 1866; February 9; April 20; May 1, 4, 8, 11, 15, 22, 23; June 5, 15, 19, 26, 29; October 29, 1867; and Charles F. Martin, comp., *Proceedings of the Second Annual Convention of the National Live Stock Association, Denver, Colorado, January 24, 25, 26, and 27, 1899*, 323.

10.   McCoy, *Historic Sketches*, 51–52, referencing *Laws of the State of Missouri Passed at the Regular Session of the Twenty-Third General Assembly, 1867*; *Laws of the State of Kansas, Passed at the Seventh Session of the Legislature, Commenced at the State Capital on Tuesday, Jan. 8, 1867*, 263–67; E. Estabrook, *The Statutes of Nebraska, 1867*; *General Laws, Joint Resolutions, Memorials, and Private Acts of the Territory of Colorado*, Sixth Session, 1866–67; *Acts of the Commonwealth of Kentucky Passed by the General Assembly at the Adjourned Session, January 3, 1867*; and *Public Laws of the State of Illinois Passed by the Twenty-Fifth General Assembly, Convened January 7, 1867*, 169.
      Applicable text from *Laws of the State of Kansas*, 263–67, chapter 152, "An Act for the Protection of Stock from Disease," Sec. 12, states:

> The provisions of this Act shall apply to all that portion of the State east of the sixth principal meridian; also, to all that portion of the State north of township nineteen (19), but shall not apply to that portion of southwest Kansas west of the sixth principal meridian and south of township eighteen (18), as above provided; And provided further, That all persons herding or driving the description of stock mentioned in the First Section of this Act in that portion of Kansas west of the sixth principal meridian and south of township eighteen (18), within five miles of any highway or any ranche [*sic*], or other settlement, without the consent of the settler or owner of such ranche [*sic*], shall be liable as provided for in the First and Fifth Sections of this Act; And provided further, That any person, association or company, may, upon execution of a bond in the penal sum of ten thousand dollars, payable to the State of Kansas, approved by the Governor and filed with the Secretary of State, conditioned to pay all damages that may be incurred by any citizen of the State of Kansas, select a route from some point in southwest Kansas, west of the sixth principal meridian, and south of township eighteen, to some point on the U.P.R., E.D., west of the first guide meridian west of the sixth principal meridian, where such cattle may be shipped out of the State, but in no case unloaded within the State; And provided further, That said person, association or company shall not locate said route or drive said stock or allow them to range on any persons premises

or within five [miles] of any settler, without his or her consent in writing, and shall not drive said cattle along or allow them to feed on or near any public road or highway, and any person violating any provision of this section shall be liable to all the penalties provided in the First and Fifth Sections of this Act.

The U.P.R., E.D. was the Union Pacific Railway, Eastern Division.

11.   McCoy, *Historic Sketches*, 51–52 and 55–56, referencing Davis County, Kansas, District Court, *Joseph G. McCoy vs. the Kansas Pacific Railway Company*, copy of the record of the judgment and proceedings, 1871, 59, manuscript, Supreme Court of Kansas, Topeka (hereafter cited as *McCoy vs. Kansas Pacific*), and Kansas Supreme Court, *Brief of the Defendant in Error, Kansas Pacific Railway Company vs. Joseph G. McCoy*. Ellsworth was founded in spring 1867 shortly after passage of the new law in February. The Union Pacific Railroad opened for business in Ellsworth in July 1867.

12.   McCoy, *Historic Sketches*, 51–52, 56, 116, referencing Dickinson County, Kansas, Deed Record A, 496, manuscript, Recorder of Deeds Office, Abilene; and *Laws of the State of Kansas*, 263–67.

13.   Bieber's footnotes in McCoy, *Historic Sketches*, 119–20. See also *Laws of the State of Kansas*, 263–67.

14.   McCoy, *Historic Sketches*, 120–21, referencing *Junction City (Kansas) Weekly Union*, August 31, 1867. See also "Cheap Beef from Texas: The Story of a Cattle Speculator," *Alexandria (Virginia) Gazette*, November 22, 1867.

Chapter 9

1.   Stan Hoig, *Jesse Chisholm, Ambassador of the Plains*, 148–50, referencing Evans to Barde, Barde Collection, Archives-Manuscript Division, Oklahoma Historical Society; *Wichita Eagle*, March 7, 1890; and *Daily Oklahoman*, November 17, 1907.

2.   "As 'Wichita Town,'" *Wichita Daily Eagle*, March 27, 1900.

3.   Hoig, *Jesse Chisholm*, 94–95, 148, and 161, referencing T. U. Taylor, *Jesse Chisholm*, 132–34, 147–48, 151; Joseph B. Thoburn, *A Standard History of Oklahoma*, 364–66; and Philip McCusker to Thomas Murphy, November 15, 1867, Letters Received, Wichita Indian Agency, 1867–75, and Jesse Leavenworth to Wichita Agency, Letters Received, April 23, 1868, Kiowa Indian Agency, 1864–68, both in RG 75, NA. See also Stan Hoig, "The Genealogy of Jesse Chisholm," *Chronicles of Oklahoma* 57, no. 2 (Summer 1989): 198–202; Julius Bien, *Map of the Territory of the United States from the Mississippi River to the Pacific Ocean; Ordered by Jeff'n Davis, Secretary of War, to Accompany the Reports of the Explorations for a Railroad Route*.

Merrill's route shown on Bien's map is slightly west of the ninety-eighth meridian through Indian Territory and well to the west of Council Grove, where Chisholm maintained a trading post on the North Canadian. The cattle trail exited Indian Territory and entered Kansas east of the ninety-eighth meridian. The routes are in the same general vicinity from about the Cimarron River north to the Little Arkansas. See Muriel H. Wright, "A History of Fort Cobb," *Chronicles of*

Oklahoma, 34 (Spring 1956): 57–59, referencing *Official Records*, Series I, 1:648–49.
   The Wichita Agency was established in 1859. Fort Cobb was established in 1859 near the Wichita Agency to protect the Wichitas and other Texas tribes removed from the Brazos reservations from raids by the Comanches and Kiowas.

4.   Hoig, *Jesse Chisholm*, 146–48, 161, referencing O. H. Bentley, *History of Wichita and Sedgwick County Kansas*, 1:119; and George W. Conover, *Sixty Years in Southwest Oklahoma*, 103–4. See also "Cattle," *Emporia (Kansas) News*, August 6, 1864. The quote from J. R. Mead is from *History of Wichita and Sedgwick County*.

5.   Hoig, *Jesse Chisholm*, 148, referencing "Old Settlers," *Wichita Eagle*, March 7, 1890. See also *Atchison Daily Champion*, September 10, 1865; Records of the Central Superintendency of Indian Affairs, 1813–78, Kansas Historical Society microfilm rolls MF6903–MF7010, National Archives Microfilm Publication M856, Kansas Historical Society, Topeka, www.kshs.org, accessed April 30, 2014. The article "Old Settlers" is a reminiscent story of the early settlers around Wichita, Kansas. Mead offered no details regarding the cattle herd other than to state that some "were driven out of the territory over the route which afterwards became the great Chisholm trail." It is not known whether Jesse Chisholm was actually involved in moving the cattle. Chisholm may have acted temporarily as an agent for Enoch Stevens, who did business with the Sac and Fox Agency. Stevens drowned crossing a creek near the agency in September 1865, and that was likely the end of the arrangement.

6.   J. Marvin Hunter, ed., *The Trail Drivers of Texas*, 2nd ed., rev., 963.

7.   Julius Bien, *Map of Texas Showing Routes of Transportation of Cattle, 1881*. The trail that crossed the Red River in Montague County is designated as the Eastern Trail or Fort Worth Trail. According to a 1946 article, this rare map was likely intended for inclusion in a report contained in the Tenth Census of the United States. See Ralph H. Brown, "Texas Cattle Trails," *Texas Geographic Magazine* 10, no. 1 (Spring 1946): 1–2.

8.   Hunter, *Trail Drivers*, 115, 119, 139, 210, 412, 482, 646, 703, 781, 865; E. H. Ruffner, *Map of the Chickasaw Country and Contiguous Portions of the Indian Territory*; "Cheap Beef from Texas: The Story of a Cattle Speculator," *Alexandria (Virginia) Gazette*, November 22, 1867. It is likely that the bulk of the herd traffic passed through Red River Station, also known as Salt Creek, and the other locations near Gainesville tend to be overlooked despite their use in 1867–71. Trail drivers who stated that they crossed the Red River near Gainesville included J. N. Byler, B. A. Borroum, G. N. Steen, C. H. Rust, W. A. Peril, P. B. Butler, T. J. Garner, Leo Tucker, E. P. Byler, and W. B. Slaughter.

9.   Ado Hunnius, *Indian Territory with Parts of Neighboring States and Territories*, map; Ado Hunnius, *Military Map of the Indian Territory*; C. Roeser, *Indian Territory*, map, 1879, Serial Set 1885, 46th Cong., 2d sess., S. Exec. Doc. 124, 12.

10.   Ruffner, *Map of the Chickasaw Country*; Jon D. May, "Leon," Susan L. Webb and Sandra L. Thomas, "Love County," and Michael Tower,

"Pauls Valley," all in Encyclopedia of Oklahoma History and Culture, Oklahoma Historical Society, www.okhistory.org/, accessed May 15, 2014; Roeser, *Indian Territory*, map, Serial Set 1885. Love's may have been a ranch owned by a prominent Chickasaw, Overton Love. Smith Paul was an intermarried citizen of the Chickasaw Nation.

11.   Ruffner, *Map of the Chickasaw Country*; Roeser, *Indian Territory*, map, Serial Set 1885. This trail is sometimes referred to as the Middle or Western Shawnee Trail; however, it led in a different direction to different destinations than did the earlier Shawnee Trail. It likely developed as a cattle trail after Abilene opened in 1867 and led north past Arkansas City into central Kansas. The earlier Shawnee Trail led past Preston and Shawneetown on the Red River and past Boggy Depot, the Shawnee Hills, and Fort Gibson toward the northeast. These are separate trails to different destinations with different periods of use and are most likely related in name only.

12.   Chickasaw Nation, *General Laws of the Legislature of the Chickasaw Nation*, 1867, 1868, 1869, and 1870.

13.   Tom Weger, "North to Kansas, Identifying the Primary and Secondary Cattle Trails in Montague County, Texas, 1866–1885," paper, Saint Jo, Texas, 2016, 16, 19, 29, 33, referencing Commissioners Court Meeting Minutes, Montague County, Texas, July 10, 1873, May 10, 1877, and May 10, 1880; Tom Weger, interview with the author, November 6, 2016, Saint Jo, Texas.

Cattle trails were often located along or parallel to military or other roads and skirted around communities and towns. In some cases where there were no previous public roads, parts of the cattle trail became public roads. The Commissioner's Court records provide rare details regarding road locations, descriptions, and references to the cattle trail. Many similar Texas historic records have been lost to courthouse fires and other disasters. The 1873 record establishes roads from Head of Elm to Red River Station and from Head of Elm to Spanish Fort Bend as "first class" roads. The town of Spanish Fort did not yet officially exist under that name, but was known as Burlington. Spanish Fort Bend was an apparent reference to the nearby bend in the Red River.

The 1877 record stated "that a road be opened leading from Red River Station Montague Co Tex [*sic*] via Eagle Point, Thence on the nearest and most practicable route to intercept the old beef trail between the crossing on Farmers Creek and the Burlington and St Joe [*sic*] road." This establishes that the cattle trail crossed Farmer's Creek near Eagle Point, and that the cattle trail location was so well defined that county commissioners used it as a geographical reference. The 1880 record described a road "beginning at the end of Montague street [*sic*] in the town of Red River Station, Thence SE along the present Road to the line of Cardwell's farm, thence east with cattle trail to Farmers Creek, crossing said creek at the cattle trail ford." This is another instance in which the cattle trail was so well defined that county commissioners used it as a geographical reference. These records confirm that the cattle trail crossed Farmer's Creek near Eagle Point and approached Red River Station from the east.

14. "Restoration of the Monument at the Initial Point of the Public Land Surveys of Oklahoma," *Chronicles of Oklahoma* 3, no. 1 (April 1925): 81–85; Ruffner, *Map of the Chickasaw Country.*

15. Hunnius, *Military Map*; Roeser, *Indian Territory*, map, Serial Set 1885.

16. Roeser, *Indian Territory*, map, Serial Set 1885; G. P. Strum, *Indian Territory*, map, 1883, Serial Set 2261, 48th Cong., 2d sess., S. Exec. Doc. 17, 220; G. P. Strum, *Indian Territory*, map, 1887, Serial Set 2432, 49th Cong., 1st sess., H. Misc. Doc. 15, pt., 2, 852.

17. *Oklahoma 1997–98 Official State Map*, Oklahoma Department of Transportation, Oklahoma City.

18. *Guide Map of the Great Texas Cattle Trail from Red River Crossing to the Old Reliable Kansas Pacific Railway*, 1874.

19. Ibid., 13–16.

20. Joseph G. McCoy, *Historic Sketches of the Cattle Trade of the West and Southwest*, ed. Ralph Bieber, 188–89.

21. "Important to Drovers," *Austin Republican*, April 28, 1868.

22. "Letter from Kansas—Interesting to Cattle Drivers," *Dallas Herald*, May 16, 1868; McCoy, *Historic Sketches*, 116; *Ninth Census of the United States*, vol. 1, *The Statistics of the Population of the United States (June 1, 1870)*, Population of Each State and Territory by Counties, Table II, State of Kansas, 29.

23. "State Items," *Emporia (Kansas) News*, July 26, 1867; McCoy, *Historic Sketches*, 291, referencing *Kansas Daily Commonwealth* (Topeka), March 28 and May 30, 1871; Robert W. P. Muse, "History of Harvey County, Kansas," in *Edwards' Historical Atlas of Harvey County, Kansas*, reprinted in *Harvey County Clippings, 1878–1999*, 1:88–124; and William G. Cutler, *History of the State of Kansas*, 771–81. See also "State News," *Emporia (Kansas) News*, June 2, 1871.

24. "Town and Country," *Emporia (Kansas) News*, July 21, 1871; McCoy, *Historic Sketches*, 299; "City and County News," *Wichita City Eagle*, June 7, 14, 21, 1872; "Correspondence of the Topeka Commonwealth, Wichita," *Wichita City Eagle*, October 24, 1872.

25. "City and County News," *Wichita City Eagle*, November 14, 1872; April 16, 1874; McCoy, *Historic Sketches*, 186–87. "Mr. Bryden" may have been James Bryden from Corpus Christi, described as a "well-known and extensive Texas cattle dealer" and "a fast friend of Wichita."

26. "State News," *White Cloud Kansas Chief*, September 14, 1871; "Texan Cattle," *Leavenworth Weekly Times*, May 23, 1872; "Texas Cattle—Objective Points," *Wichita City Eagle*, March 20, 1873.

27. William G. Cutler, "Sumner County," in *History of the State of Kansas*, Kansas Collection, www.kancoll.org, accessed June 26, 2014; "The Cattle Trail," *Wichita City Eagle*, February 25, 1875; E. H. Ross, *Railroad and Sectional Map of Kansas*. There are only two known copies of the Ross map.

Chapter 10

1. Clifford R. Caldwell, *John Simpson Chisum: The Cattle King of the Pecos Revisited*, 28–33; Harwood P. Hinton, "Chisum, John Simpson," Handbook of Texas Online, Texas State Historical Association, https://

tshaonline.org/handbook/online/articles/fch33, accessed November 1, 2016; Skipper Steely, *Forty-Seven Years: A New Look at Early Texas History, 1830–77.*

2.   Caldwell, *John Simpson Chisum*, 38–40; Hinton, "Chisum, John Simpson"; Steely, *Forty-Seven Years.* Most accounts claim that Chisum's partner was Stephen K. Fowler; some accounts claim it was Oliver Keep. Chisum allegedly purchased twelve hundred head of cattle in Colorado County, Texas, and drove them to his new ranch in Denton County. While this is likely, no documentation is cited in support of the claim. Some have claimed that the trail north from south Texas should be the Chisum Trail because Chisum drove a herd of cattle from Colorado County to Denton County. This was a one-time drive to stock a ranch. Chisum may have driven that herd in 1854 over part of the route that appeared on an 1881 map as the Eastern Trail, but trails and roads at that time were typically named for an origin/destination or geographic landmark. No examples of the use of the name Chisum Trail to describe the route from Colorado County to Denton County were found until after 1900, when various stories began to surface that claimed a connection to the trail.

3.   Steely, *Forty Seven Years*; Hinton, "Chisum"; J. Evetts Haley, *Charles Goodnight, Cowman and Plainsman*, 13–20, referencing C. Goodnight to J. Evetts Haley, July 10, 1928; D. W. Moore to J. Evetts Haley, February 2, 1932; and G. W. Lockhart, *Sixty Years on the Brazos*, 328. Black Springs was located at the present site of Oran, Texas, in Palo Pinto County.

4.   Julia Cauble Smith, "Loving, Oliver," Handbook of Texas Online, Texas State Historical Association, https://tshaonline.org/handbook/online/articles/flo38, accessed October 11, 2016; Haley, *Charles Goodnight*, 20–21.

5.   E. H. Ruffner, *Map of the Chickasaw Country and Contiguous Portions of the Indian Territory.* It is possible, though unknown, that Loving and Dawson followed a part of the route shown as Abilene Cattle Trail toward the Arkansas River.

6.   Caldwell, *John Simpson Chisum*, 50–53, referencing William A. Keleher, *The Fabulous Frontier*, 58.

7.   Caldwell, *John Simpson Chisum*, 52–53; Haley, *Charles Goodnight*, 121–22.

8.   Haley, *Charles Goodnight*, 126–39; Charles Kenner, "The Origins of the 'Goodnight' Trail Reconsidered," *Southwestern Historical Quarterly* 77 (July 1973–April 1974): 390–94.

9.   Caldwell, *John Simpson Chisum*, 54, 57; Haley, *Charles Goodnight*, 162–84; J. Marvin Hunter, ed., *The Trail Drivers of Texas*, 2nd ed., rev., 904.
     According to a map marked by J. Evetts Haley at the direction of Charles Goodnight on July 24, 1925, Goodnight and Loving joined herds twelve miles south of Fort Belknap and generally followed the route described previously. The map shows that they continued south along the South Concho River, then turned west and traveled generally along the southern border of the present counties of Tom Green, Irion, Reagan, and Upton through Castle Gap to Horsehead Crossing. From there they followed the Pecos River, crossed at Pope's Crossing,

and continued up the Pecos to Fort Sumner. A notation on the map indicates that Loving had his fight with the Indians seven miles below Carlsbad. *Map of Goodnight-Loving Trail*, marked by J. Evetts Haley under direction of Charles Goodnight, Goodnight Ranch, Texas, July 24, 1925, N. S. Haley Memorial Library, Midland, Texas.

10. Haley, *Charles Goodnight*, 162–65. Hoop iron was the metal that formed the iron hoops that held a barrel together. Indians stripped the hoops from captured barrels and fashioned tools or arrow points from the iron. A shoe pincher is a tool used to remove a horseshoe, also called a puller or pull-off.

11. Ibid., 166–84. Loving thought that he would die before daybreak, and he talked Wilson into leaving during the night for help. They calculated that if Wilson could swim past the Comanches and backtrack their trail, he should meet the herd in a day and a half. Loving said that he would hold out as long as he could but would shoot himself rather than be taken alive and tortured to death. Wilson took Loving's Henry repeating rifle, which fired metallic cartridges and would therefore function when wet, left five revolvers and a rifle for Loving's defense, and started out after the moon set. He stripped down to his drawers, undershirt, and hat, hid his clothes and pocketknife underwater where they would not be found by the Indians, and swam downstream. Swimming with the rifle was difficult, so he jammed the rifle muzzle-down in the river bottom and braced the stock against an overhanging bank. With his good arm free, he swam past a Comanche sentry and escaped.

Unknown to Wilson, Goodnight had decided to stop and rest the herd before entering New Mexico Territory, so help was twice as far away as Wilson and Loving had calculated. For three days Wilson walked barefoot across the hot, rock-strewn, cactus-covered ground with no food or water. Goodnight thought he saw a man at the mouth of a cave on a hill, and thinking it was an Indian, suspected an attack. When Wilson came out again and waved, Goodnight recognized him. After he recovered enough to talk, Wilson told his story. Goodnight rode off to find his partner. He found the site of the attack and found Wilson's clothes, pocketknife, and rifle exactly where Wilson had told him they were hidden. There was no sign of Loving, and he assumed that Loving had shot himself, fallen into the river, and floated off downstream to deny the Indians the opportunity to mutilate his body.

Loving, however, had held out for two days, but when help did not come he determined that either Wilson did not make it or the crew had been killed by Indians. On the third night after Wilson left, Loving slipped into the water and managed to swim upstream. He correctly figured that his attackers would expect him to go downstream. He managed to get to a trail crossing about six miles upstream, where he was found by some passers-by and taken by wagon to Fort Sumner. A man named Burleson, who, like Loving, had ridden ahead to arrange the sale of his cattle, was waiting at Fort Sumner for the arrival of his herd, which was following behind the Goodnight-Loving herd. When Burleson headed back for his herd, he encountered the wounded wagon passenger along the road, and when he later found Goodnight further back up the trail, he informed him that Loving was alive and in Fort Sumner.

12. *Map of Goodnight-Loving Trail*; Haley, *Charles Goodnight*, 135–37, referencing Goodnight to J. Evetts Haley, September 29, 1929, and Jack Potter to J. Evetts Haley, August 26, 1932; Caldwell, *John Simpson Chisum*, 56. Where the route in the Goodnight-Loving map is indicated along a county line, both counties are listed. Bear in mind that most Texas counties west of the one-hundredth meridian were not organized at the time of Goodnight's 1866–67 drives to New Mexico Territory.

13. Caldwell, *John Simpson Chisum*, 50–51.

14. Haley, *Charles Goodnight*, 140.

15. Kenner, "Goodnight Trail Reconsidered," 393–94, referencing Carleton to Shoemaker, September 2, 1865, Department of New Mexico, Letters Sent, 16:402, Records of United States Army Continental Commands, 1821–1920, RG 393, NA; Haley, *Charles Goodnight*, 138. General James H. Carleton was commander of the Department of New Mexico. Captain William R. Shoemaker was the quartermaster at Fort Union, New Mexico. Captain Thomas S. Roberts, James (Jim) Patterson, and Tom Patterson (James's brother) were stock contractors at Forts Sumner and Stanton.

16. Caldwell, *John Simpson Chisum*, 56; Haley, *Charles Goodnight*, 140; "The Goodnight Trail," *Austin Weekly Statesman*, March 25, 1886. I found no newspaper reference to a trail name applied to the trail through Texas along the Pecos River into New Mexico Territory from 1864 to 1887.

Chapter 11

1. The markers were installed by P. P. Ackley at his expense and with no additional historical oversight. Chisholm's Trail merged with the Abilene Cattle Trail and led to the railheads of central Kansas, beginning with Abilene in 1867. The two trails were just over 100 miles apart where they left Indian Territory and entered Kansas. They were approximately 100 miles apart at the fords on the Red River between Texas and Indian Territory. The original destinations for each trail were Abilene, Kansas, in 1867 and Dodge City, Kansas, over 150 miles to the west, in 1876.

    The Kansas City Board of Trade estimated that 5,201,132 head of cattle were driven north from Texas for the years 1866–84. Approximately 2,400,000 head went up the trails prior to the opening of the Fort Griffin and Dodge City Trail in 1876. Approximately 2,800,000 head were driven north from 1876 to 1884. The Fort Griffin Trail was in use for several additional years for which official estimates were not available, and portions of the trail continued to be used until the mid-1890s. Volume estimates are referenced in Joseph Nimmo, *Report in Regard to the Range and Ranch Cattle Business of the United States*, 28.

2. *Statistics of the Population of the United States at the Tenth Census, June 1, 1880*, Department of the Interior, Census Office, The Progress of the Nation: 1790–1880, General Discussion of the Movements of Population, 1790 to 1880, vols. 18 and 19; *Compendium of the Tenth Census (June 1, 1880)*, rev. ed., Part I, 1885, Table III, Percentage of Increase of Population, 6, and Table XVIII, Aggregate Population by Counties, Kansas, 29; Ray Allen Billington and Martin Ridge, *Westward Expansion: A History of the American Frontier*, 111, 113. The western edge of the

frontier line of the country in 1860 was determined to be a line along 99 degrees, 30 minutes west. The frontier line was defined as the area having an average population density of two inhabitants per square mile as calculated by the most recent census; this was considered the limit of settlement. By 1870 the frontier line had moved farther west to 99 degrees, 45 minutes west. The distance of a minute of longitude at 38 degrees north latitude is 0.91 miles.

3. "Report on the Indian War," *Emporia (Kansas) News*, July 19, 1867; *Report on Indian Affairs by the Acting Commissioner for the Year 1867*, 260, 297, 312; Progress of Their Road, West from Omaha, Nebraska, across the Continent; E. H. Ross, *Railroad and Sectional Map of Kansas*. There are only two known copies of this map.

4. General U. S. Grant to Edwin M. Stanton, Secretary of War, January 15, 1867, in Ulysses S. Grant, *The Papers of Ulysses S. Grant*, vol. 17 (January 1–September 30, 1867), 21; *Personal Memoirs of P. H. Sheridan*, 2:297.

5. "Indian Civilization," *White Cloud Kansas Chief*, April 14, 1870.

6. Ibid.

7. David D. Smits, "The Frontier Army and the Destruction of the Buffalo, 1865–1883," *Western Historical Quarterly* 25, no. 3 (Autumn 1994): 317, referencing *Army-Navy Journal* 6 (June 26, 1869): 705.

8. Smits, "Frontier Army," 315, referencing William F. Cody, "Famous Hunting Parties of the Plains," *Cosmopolitan* 17 (June 1894): 138–39; Paul Andrew Hutton, *Phil Sheridan and His Army*, 213–14; Cody, "Famous Hunting Parties," 141.

9. Smits, "Frontier Army," 326; Allen Lee Hamilton, "Warren Wagontrain Raid," Handbook of Texas Online, Texas State Historical Association, https://tshaonline.org/handbook/online/articles/btw03, accessed July 2, 2014.

10. Smits, "Frontier Army," 326, 327–28. The buffalo rifles of the hide hunters were much more efficient than the standard-issue army rifles and ammunition. The hide hunters were numerous, and the army could save its manpower and ammunition, as there were millions of bison on the plains.

11. Ibid., 328, referencing US Congress, House, *Report of Bvt. Maj. Gen. John Pope*, 43rd Cong., 2d sess. (1874–75), H. Exec. Doc. 1, part 2, 30; Frederick Barde, *Life and Adventures of Billy Dixon of Adobe Walls, Texas Panhandle*, 233.

12. "Proposals for Fresh Beef and Beef Cattle," *Nebraska Advertiser* (Brownville, Nebraska), May 19, 1870; *Nebraska Advertiser* (Brownville, Nebraska), July 21, 1870; "Texas Cattle," *Dallas Herald*, December 10, 1870.

13. *Wichita City Eagle*, July 15, 1875; Kansas, *The Laws of the State of Kansas, Passed at the Twelfth Session of the Legislature, Commenced at the State Capital on Tuesday, Jan. 8, 1872*, 387–91.

14. "Echoes from the Frontier," *Leavenworth Weekly Times*, May 18, 1876; *Wichita City Eagle*, July 15, 1875.

15. Kansas, *Laws of the State of Kansas*, 388; Kansas, *Session Laws of 1876, and Memorials, Passed at the Sixteenth Annual Session of the Legislature, Commenced at the State Capitol on Tuesday, January 11, 1876*, 316–17.

16. "New Military and Cattle Road," *Dallas Daily Herald*, February 18, 1874. Presumably "Mr. Ingalls" was Senator John J. Ingalls of Kansas, whose state stood to benefit by the presence of a dedicated road from Texas to Kansas.

17. Frank Collinson, *Life in the Saddle*, 31–40. This account by Frank Collinson described the first known cattle drive over the route that became known as the Western Trail. It also illustrates how military roads or trails were used by cattlemen when it made sense to do so. The material for this book was gathered between 1926 and Collinson's death in 1943 and edited and published by Mary Whatley Clarke in 1963. John Lytle has been credited with blazing this trail, but partial credit should go to the unnamed military scout who guided him between Fort Griffin and Camp Supply. This does not diminish Lytle's accomplishment, and many herds would follow his route into the next decade.

18. Frances T. McCallum and James Mulkey Owens, "Barbed Wire," Handbook of Texas Online, Texas State Historical Association, https://tshaonline.org/handbook/online/articles/aob01, accessed August 5, 2015; Advertisement, *Los Angeles Daily Herald*, May 7, 1875.

19. "Echoes from the Frontier," *Leavenworth Weekly Times*, June, 1, 1876; "Southwest," *Emporia (Kansas) News*, June 16, 1876.

20. J. Marvin Hunter, ed., *The Trail Drivers of Texas*, 2nd ed., rev., 409, 963; A. R. Roessler, *New Map of Texas Prepared and Published for the Bureau of Immigration of the State of Texas*.
    When discussing trail routes, it should be remembered that a herd was not necessarily restricted to a single route in the manner that a vehicle is restricted to pavement. It was reported in 1875 that "the main cattle trail now passes through Henrietta" (Clay County, Texas) and in 1877 that "a movement is being made to open a new cattle trail from Fort Worth, crossing Red river at the mouth of the Little Wichita [*sic*]." "State Items," *Denison (Texas) Daily Cresset*, April 10, 1875, and "A Raid on Our Exchanges," *Frontier Echo* (Jacksboro, Texas), June 8, 1877.

21. Julius Bien, *Map of Texas Showing Routes of Transportation of Cattle, 1881*; Julius Bien, *The Range and Ranch Cattle Area of the United States, 1884*, Map 1 in Nimmo, *Report*.

22. Emma Estill-Harbour, "Greer County," *Chronicles of Oklahoma* 12, no. 2 (June 1934): 145–60; "Adams-Onis Treaty of 1819," New Spain Index, Sons of DeWitt Colony Texas, www.sonsofdewittcolony.org//adamonis.htm, accessed April 28, 2017; Roessler, *New Map of Texas*.

23. H. S. Tennant, "The Two Cattle Trails," *Chronicles of Oklahoma* 14, no. 1 (March 1936): 87–99. Tennant had the task of locating the trails from an engineering perspective as a result of Oklahoma House Bill 149, passed in 1931. At that time remnants of the cattle trails were still visible in many places in Oklahoma, and surviving veterans of the trails were interviewed.

24. Gary Kraisinger and Margaret Kraisinger, *The Western: The Greatest Texas Cattle Trail*, Map 7-4, 130; Map 7-5, 133; John Kay et al., "Nebraska Historic Buildings Survey: Reconnaissance Survey Final Report of Keith County, Nebraska," Nebraska State Historical Society, State His-

toric Preservation Office, March 1, 1990, 11–12, www.nebraskahistory
.org, accessed August 12, 2015.

25.   Kraisinger and Kraisinger, *The Western*, Map 9-1, 170; Map 10-1, 220;
       Map 11-1, 240; and Map 11-13, 262.

26.   *The Best and Shortest Cattle Trail from Texas*, map; Joseph G. McCoy,
       Historic Sketches of the Cattle Trade of the West and Southwest, ed. Ralph
       Bieber, 88–89; John C. Henderson, "Tom Green County," Handbook
       of Texas Online, Texas State Historical Association, https://tshaonline
       .org/handbook/online/articles/hct07, accessed August 5, 2015;
       Kraisinger and Kraisinger, *The Western*, 28–30, referencing A. W. Ziege-
       lasch, *The Old Chisholm Cattle Trail, with Subsidiary Trails in Texas,
       1873*, map.
              It was recently discovered that A. W. Ziegelasch was born in or
       about 1893, worked as a draftsman for the State of Kansas in Topeka
       during the 1920s, and therefore could not have drawn this map in 1873.
       The Ziegelasch map likely dates from the 1920s and is likely based on
       the *Best and Shortest Cattle Trail* route map published by the Kansas
       Pacific Railway in 1873; many details match the original, but the label
       "Ellsworth Cattle Trail" that appeared on the original was changed to
       "Chisholm Trail" on the later Ziegelasch map.

27.   Hunter, *Trail Drivers*, 777–79.

28.   Bien, *Map of Texas*, 1881; Bien, *Range and Ranch Cattle Area*, map.

29.   "The New Trail," *Cheyenne Transporter* (Darlington, Indian Territory),
       May 10, 1881; "From Austin," *Waco Daily Examiner*, February 17, 1882;
       "Stockmen's Convention," *Austin Weekly Democratic Statesman*, Febru-
       ary 23, 1882. The *Cheyenne Transporter* article described a new trail in
       Indian Territory connecting the "eastern, or Caldwell Trail" with the
       western trail.

Chapter 12

1.   Kansas, *Session Laws of 1876, and Memorials, Passed at the Sixteenth
       Annual Session of the Legislature, Commenced at the State Capitol on
       Tuesday, January 11, 1876*, 316–17; "Caldwell," *Leavenworth Weekly Times*,
       November 13, 1879; William G. Cutler, "Sumner County," *History of
       the State of Kansas*, transcribed by Kat Thompson, Kansas Collection,
       www.kancoll.org, accessed June 26, 2014; "The Cattle Trade," *Dodge
       City Times*, June 26, 1880; "Over the State," *Emporia (Kansas) News*,
       August 20, 1880; "Among Our Neighbors," *Emporia (Kansas) News*,
       October 1, 1880.

2.   G. P. Strum, *Indian Territory*, map, 1883, Serial Set 2261, 48th Cong. 2d
       sess., S. Exec. Doc. 17, 220; Anna Lewis, "History of the Cattle Industry
       in Oklahoma," MA thesis, University of California, 1915, 31. Lewis refer-
       enced Charles Moreau Harger, "Cattle-Trails of the Prairies," *Scribner's
       Magazine* 11:736; however, that article claimed that Dodge City was
       "on the Chisholm trail's western offshoot to Ellsworth." Dodge City is
       located almost 130 miles southwest of Ellsworth, a long way from the
       "Chisholm trail's western offshoot to Ellsworth."
              The road to Fort Supply, shown as "Road from Cheyenne Agy. to
       Camp Supply" on the Strum 1883 map, intersected the Abilene Cattle
       Trail where it crossed the North Canadian River about fifteen miles

east of the ninety-eighth meridian. This was about twenty-eight miles south of the intersection of the Abilene Cattle Trail and Chisholm's Cattle Trail. The Abilene Cattle Trail was later called the Chisholm Trail.

3. *Barbour County Index* (Medicine Lodge, Kansas), February 2, 1883; "At Home," *Eaton (Ohio) Democrat*, February 8, 1883. "Mr. Hoover" was likely G. M. Hoover, who served as a county commissioner and as representative in the state legislature. See William G. Cutler, "Ford County," *History of the State of Kansas*.

4. C. W. McCampbell, "W. E. Campbell, Pioneer Kansas Livestockman," *Kansas Historical Quarterly* 16, no. 3 (August 1948), referencing J. Stanley Clark, "The Northern Boundary of Oklahoma," *Chronicles of Oklahoma* 15:271–90; George W. Martin, "The Boundary Lines of Kansas," *Kansas Historical Collections* 11:55–56; Charles J. Kappler, comp. and ed., *Indian Affairs: Laws and Treaties* 2:947; and George Rainey, *The Cherokee Strip*, 30–42. See also Strum, *Indian Territory*, map, 1883.

5. Joe B. Milam, "The Opening of the Cherokee Outlet," *Chronicles of Oklahoma* 9, no. 3 (September 1931): 268–69; Edward Everitt Dale, "The Cherokee Strip Live Stock Association," *Chronicles of Oklahoma* 5, no. 1 (March 1927): 61–63.

6. Dale, "Cherokee Strip," 64–66, referencing Price to Secretary of Interior, December 28, 1882; and Price to Tufts, December 30, 1882, both in 48th Cong., 1st sess., S. Exec. Doc. 54, 4:129–31.

7. Dale, "Cherokee Strip," 66–67, referencing John Q. Tufts, Report to the Commissioner, March 1, 1883, in *Annual Report of the Commissioner of Indian Affairs to the Secretary of the Interior*, 1883, 48th Cong., 1st sess., S. Exec. Doc. 54, 4:148–49. See also "Agent Tufts Report," *Indian Chieftain* (Vinita, Indian Territory), March 30, 1883; *Cheyenne Transporter* (Darlington, Indian Territory), March 12, 1883.

In a report dated March 1, 1883, by Indian Agent John Tufts, described in the March 30 *Indian Chieftain* article, the Pennsylvania Oil Company is named, while in the March 12 *Cheyenne Transporter* article the Standard Oil Company is named in what appears to be the same incident. The company bought out the stockmen, dealt directly with the Cherokee government, and continued to erect fences and move cattle into the fenced range. Some suspected the cattle were a cover for oil prospecting in the area.

8. Dale, "Cherokee Strip," 67–71.

9. Strum, *Indian Territory*, 1883; Wayne Gard, "Fence Cutting," Handbook of Texas Online, Texas State Historical Association, https://tshaonline.org/handbook/online/articles/auf01, accessed March 18, 2016, referencing Hans Peter Nielsen Gammel, comp., *Laws of Texas, 1822–1897*. The Cherokee Strip Live Stock Association lease is denoted on the Strum 1883 map, as well as leases in the Cheyenne and Arapaho Reserve.

10. *Indian Chieftain* (Vinita, Indian Territory), January 24, 1884; "Legislature," *Fort Worth Daily Gazette*, January 13, 1884.

11. "Views of an Old Timer," *San Antonio Light*, January 3, 1884; "Are We Communists," *Austin Weekly Statesman*, February 7, 1884; "Over the

State," *Galveston Daily News*, February 22, 1884; *San Antonio Light*, July 3, 1884; *Indian Chieftain* (Vinita, Indian Territory), July 17, 1884.

12. "Telegraphic News," *San Antonio Light*, July 2, 1884; "Notes for the Stock Raiser," *Indian Chieftain* (Vinita, Indian Territory), July 17, 1884; "U.S. Indian Inspector After Them," *Indian Journal* (Muskogee, Indian Territory), July 31, 1884. Red Fork Ranch was located near the present site of Dover, Oklahoma.

13. "The Chickasaw Council," *Indian Chieftain* (Vinita, Indian Territory), October 23, 1884.

14. Ibid.; John Bartlett Meserve, "Governor Jonas Wolf and Governor Palmer Simeon Mosely," *Chronicles of Oklahoma* 18, no. 3 (September 1840): 244. Jonas Wolf was elected governor of the Chickasaw Nation in August 1884.

15. *Norton's Union Intelligencer* (Dallas, Texas), February 14, 1885; "The Festive Fence Cotters [*sic*] Much Elate," *Austin Weekly Statesman*, March 26, 1885.

16. Joseph Nimmo, *Report in Regard to the Range and Ranch Cattle Business of the United States*, 134–35.

17. "Cattlemen's Appeal," *Fort Worth Daily Gazette*, July 4, 1885.

18. "Indian Leased Lands," *Emporia (Kansas) Weekly News*, January 1, 1885.

19. Nimmo, *Report*, 27; "For the Ugliest Stockman," *San Antonio Light*, December 12, 1884.

20. Nimmo, *Report*, 22, 69. "High-grade" bulls were generally considered to be the heavier, stockier breeds such as Hereford, Angus, or short-horn. These were crossbred with the native Texas cattle to improve the grade of cattle on the range. The longhorn was almost improved out of existence.

21. Ibid., 30. As of June 30, 1884, the total amount of land granted to states and corporations in aid of railroad construction was 47,620,046 acres. The estimated number of acres required for a cattle trail from Texas to the northern border of the United States was 1,324,800 acres. That amounted to only 2.78 percent of the total land concessions by Congress for railroad construction and was far less than the 2,935,163 acres conceded just for the Atchison, Topeka and Santa Fe Railroad.

22. Ibid., 27, 160.

23. Ibid., 134–36; Julius Bien, *The Range and Ranch Cattle Area of the United States, 1884*, Map no. 1 in Nimmo, *Report*.

24. "Prospective," *Dodge City Times*, December 25, 1884. The legislation specified a width of no more than six miles; the reported trail width was more than doubled in the article. This could have been an honest mistake, or it could have been an effort to undermine the legislation.

25. "Advantages of a National Cattle Trail," *Fort Worth Daily Gazette*, February 11, 1885; "Wyoming Stockmen," *Sun River (Montana) Sun*, April 17, 1884; "The Legislature," *Daily Yellowstone Journal* (Miles City, Montana), January 18, 1885.

26. Jerome C. Smiley and National Live Stock Association of the United States, *Prose and Poetry of the Live Stock Industry of the United States*, 1:686–88; Dan W. Peery, "Colonel Crocker and the Boomer Movement," *Chronicles of Oklahoma* 13, no. 3 (September 1935): 274, 279–80.

27.   "The Cattle Trail Question," *Waco Daily Examiner*, Waco, Texas, July 9, 1885.

28.   "A Fence Cutter," *Waco Daily Examiner*, August 11, 1885; Smiley and National Live Stock Association, *Prose and Poetry*, 689.

29.   "The President and the Cattlemen," *Denison (Texas) Sunday Gazetteer*, August 23, 1885; Smiley and National Live Stock Association, *Prose and Poetry*, 689.

30.   Smiley and National Live Stock Association, *Prose and Poetry*, 689–90.

31.   Ibid., 686.

32.   "The National Cattle Trail—A Proposed Gigantic Land Grab Which Ought to be Summarily Squelched," *Omaha Daily Bee*, May 7, 1886.

33.   "The National Trail," *Omaha Daily Bee*, May 10, 1886.

34.   "Through the Territory," *Galveston Daily News*, April 20, 1887; "Abandoning the Trail," *Daily Morning Astorian* (Astoria, Oregon), July 27, 1887. The Abilene Cattle Trail led from near Salt Creek, also known as Red River Station, north through the Chickasaw Nation toward Caldwell, Kansas.

35.   "General Brisbin's Views," *Daily Yellowstone Journal* (Miles City, Montana), December 7, 1887.

36.   Daniel B. Welborn, "Windmills," Handbook of Texas Online, Texas State Historical Association, https://tshaonline.org/handbook/online/articles/aowo1, accessed July 8, 2014; Gary Kraisinger and Margaret Kraisinger, *The Western Cattle Trail, 1874–1897: Its Rise, Collapse, and Revival*, 474–75, referencing J. Evetts Haley, *The XIT Ranch of Texas, and the Early Days of the Llano Estacado*, 127, 136, 143, 233.

Chapter 13

1.   H. S. Tennant, "The Two Cattle Trails," *Chronicles of Oklahoma* 14, no. 1 (March 1936): 84–85.

2.   *Georgetown (Texas) Watchman*, April 10, 1869. Previously, the earliest known newspaper reference to the Chisholm Trail was dated May 18, 1870, as cited in Wayne Gard, *The Chisholm Trail*, 75.

3.   "To the Cattle Drovers of Texas," *Austin Tri-Weekly State Gazette*, March 20, 1871.

4.   "Buffalo Hunters Murdered," *Emporia (Kansas) News*, November 24, 1871; "Clear Water," *Wichita City Eagle*, April 26, 1872; "Indian Alarm," *Leavenworth Weekly Times*, May 15, 1873; "From Caldwell," *Barbour County Index* (Medicine Lodge, Kansas), June 1, 1883; "Cherokee Strip Round-up May 26th," *Barbour County Index* (Medicine Lodge, Kansas), May 14, 1886; "Accidental Drowning," *Cheyenne Transporter* (Darlington, Indian Territory), August 12, 1886; "On the March," *Austin Weekly Statesman*, April 25, 1889.

5.   "The Texas Cattle Trade," *Emporia (Kansas) News*, September 30, 1870; "The Texas Cattle Trade," *Wichita City Eagle*, October 24, 1872; *Wichita City Eagle*, April 16, 1874.

6.   "From Texas," *Pulaski (Tennessee) Citizen*, June 12, 1879; "State News," *Galveston Daily News*, April 21, 1876.

7.   "Bluff City Items," *Wichita Daily Eagle*, March 23, 1890; "A Historical Character," *Wichita Daily Eagle*, May 4, 1890; "A Historical Society," *Wichita Daily Eagle*, June 12, 1890.

8.   Joseph G. McCoy, *Historic Sketches of the Cattle Trade of the West and Southwest*, ed. Ralph Bieber, 73.

9.   Ibid., 159–60. Ralph Bieber's extensive footnotes included a statement that the Chisholm Trail was between Wichita, Kansas, and a point on or near the North Canadian River, that the trail was later extended north into central Kansas and south into northern Texas, and that the entire trail was popularly called the Chisholm Trail. No references were offered in support of the statement that the entire trail was popularly called the Chisholm Trail. Bieber also mentioned in his notes on page 163 that maps published by the US government during the 1870s and 1880s called it the Abilene Cattle Trail.

10. "The Wild West," *Omaha Daily Bee*, July 11, 1883; Charles A. Siringo, *A Texas Cow-boy; or, Fifteen Years on the Hurricane Deck of a Spanish Pony*, 95–102, 141–49, 186–95.

11. Edmund Pearson, *Dime Novels; or, Following an Old Trail in Popular Literature*, 105; W. C. Miller, *Dime Novel Authors, 1860–1900*.

12. "Ned Buntline's Great Story!" *Stark County Democrat* (Canton, Ohio), December 15, 1869; "The Buntline Business," *New Orleans Republican*, May 15, 1874; Jay Monaghan, *The Great Rascal: The Life and Adventures of Ned Buntline*, 250, 283.

13. John A. Lomax, *Cowboy Songs and Other Frontier Ballads*, xvii–xxvi, 58; "Collecting Cowboy Ballads," *Topeka State Journal*, March 6, 1913.

14. Frank Lewis Dyer and Thomas Commerford Martin, *Edison: His Life and Inventions*, 2:537.

15. Jeremy Agnew, *The Old West in Fact and Film: History Versus Hollywood*, 46–51.

16. Ibid.

Chapter 14

1.   "Wheelmen in Consultation," *New York Sun*, September 19, 1880; "Mission and History," The League of American Bicyclists, Washington, DC, www.bikeleague.org/content/mission-and-history.

2.   Isaac B. Potter, *The Gospel of Good Roads: A Letter to the American Farmer*, University of Michigan Library, Internet Archive, Open Library, www.archive.org, accessed May 10, 2015.

3.   *Good Roads* 1, no. 1 (January 1892); *Map of the Oklahoma Country in the Indian Territory*, 1892. A page number appears at the bottom of this map, indicating that it may have been published in an atlas or other publication. Another copy of the map was subsequently located at the same source with the notation "Watson—Chicago—1891" written at the bottom. Another reference to this map was found in a George Cram 1889 atlas.

4.   M. Hedges, *Map of Oklahoma Territory*, Serial Set 3918, H. Doc. 8 (1898), map 3, 743; *Map of Oklahoma Territory*, Serial Set 4461, 57th Cong., 2d sess. (1902), H. Doc. 5, map 3, 495.

5. *Indian Territory, Chickasaw Nation, Addington Quadrangle*, map, 1901; *Indian Territory, Chickasaw Nation, Addington Quadrangle*, map, 1916.

6. "County Commissioners Have Decided to Send Good Roads Bonds to Austin for Approval," *Shiner (Texas) Gazette*, November 20, 1901; "Business League Delegates," *Houston Daily Post*, September 4, 1901; "Bryan Business League," *Bryan (Texas) Morning Eagle*, September 12, 1901; "Attracting the Tourist," *San Angelo Press*, June 1, 1905; "Model T Facts," Ford Motor Company, Media Center, https://media.ford.com, accessed December 7, 2016.

7. "Mexico City as the Ultimate Southern Terminus of Big Road," *Grand Forks Evening Times*, February 17, 1912; "Chisholm Trail Road," *Kansas City Star*, August 31, 1911.

8. "A Criss-Cross of 8 Highways," *Tulsa Daily World*, November 29, 1911; *Preliminary Designation of the State Highway System*, map; *Oklahoma State Highway System*, map.

9. "Mexico City," *Grand Forks Evening Times*, February 17, 1912; "To Perpetuate the Old Trail," *Dallas Morning News*, June 16, 1913.

10. "Celebrating the Moving Assembly Line in Pictures," Ford Motor Company, Media Center, https://media.ford.com, accessed December 7, 2016.

11. "Fort Worth Joins in Chisholm Trail Plan," *Fort Worth Star Telegram*, August 29, 1911.

12. "Favors National Road," *Dallas Morning News*, August 26, 1911; "Postmaster Drove Last Herd over Chisholm Trail," *Fort Worth Star Telegram*, August 25, 1911.

13. J. Marvin Hunter, ed., *The Trail Drivers of Texas*, 2nd ed., rev., 4–12.

14. B. Byron Price, introduction to Hunter, *Trail Drivers*, vi–ix, from the second edition, revised, published in 1925 by Cokesbury Press.

15. Hunter, *Trail Drivers*, 12–15. The name had apparently been spelled differently in letters from various men. The confusion of cattleman John Chisum with Jesse Chisholm, the Indian trader and interpreter, has contributed to the trails' historical muddle.

16. Ado Hunnius, *Military Map of the Indian Territory*; C. Roeser, *Indian Territory*, map, Serial Set 1885, 46th Cong., 2d sess., S. Exec. Doc. 124 (1879), 12.

17. "Highway Numbering System Will Be Complete by End This Year," *Sandusky (Ohio) Register*, June 22, 1930; *Milwaukee Journal*, June 22, 1930; "Numbered Highways," *Dallas Morning News*, June 28, 1930, Collection of Pete Charlton, Fort Worth, Texas.

18. "Oklahoma Urges Chisholm Trail Be Preserved," *San Antonio Express*, December 11, 1925; "Old Chisholm Trail Again Is Traveled," *San Antonio Express*, December 18, 1929.

19. "Chisholm Trail Marks Proposed," *San Antonio Express*, April 13, 1930; "$2,099,413 Road Contracts Awarded by Commission," *San Antonio Express*, April 24, 1930.

20. "Marking the Chisholm Trail," *San Antonio Express*, May 21, 1930; Texas, Department of Transportation, Office of Commission Support, "Minutes of the One Hundred and Forty-Fifth Meeting of the State Highway Commission," Minute No. 2861, May 19, 1930. Minute No. 2861

reads as follows: "Moved by Mr. Johnson, seconded by Judge Ely, that the Chisholm Trail Association is authorized by the State Highway Commission to place appropriate markers and monuments along said trail as the same has been laid out and located by said Association, provided that such markers and monuments are so located as to not interfere with the highway, and with the understanding that the location and markers will first be submitted to the Commission or the State Highway Engineer for approval."

21. "Marking the Chisholm Trail"; "Designation of Chisholm Trail Nears," *Dallas Morning News*, June 1, 1930, Collection of Pete Charlton, Fort Worth, Texas.

22. "Old Chisholm Cattle Trail to Be Marked," *Berkeley (California) Daily Gazette*, June 3, 1930, collection of Pete Charlton, Fort Worth; "Cattle Trail To Be Marked," *Oakland (California) Tribune*, June 20, 1930; E. D. Dorchester, *Trails Made and Routes Used by the Fourth U.S. Cavalry under the Command of General R. S. Mackenzie in Its Operations against Hostile Indians in Texas, Indian Territory (Now Oklahoma), New Mexico, and Old Mexico during the Period of 1871-2-3-4 and 5*, map (1927).

23. Hunter, *Trail Drivers*, 1925 ed., 37–39.

24. Ibid., 40.

25. "Oklahoma Urges Chisholm Trail Be Preserved," *San Antonio Express*, December 11, 1925; "Cowboy Plans Making Trail a National Highway," *Vernon (Texas) Daily Record*, April 29, 1929; "Marking of Chisholm Trail Is Delayed," *Brownsville (Texas) Herald*, June 1, 1930; "Saunders Again Heads Drivers," *San Antonio Express*, October 5, 1930. Saunders agreed with Ackley about the type of marker, but not necessarily on the trail route or name, which had not yet been determined.

26. G. C. Richardson to the State Highway Board, December 3, 1930, and P. P. Ackley to the State Highway Board, December 9, 1930, both in G-C-3 Chisholm Trail (1930), Texas Department of Transportation, Texas Highway Department Historical Records, Archives, and Information Services Division, Texas State Library and Archives Commission.

27. Gibb Gilchrist to G. C. Richardson, letter transcript, December 5, 1930, and Gibb Gilchrist to P. P. Ackley, letter transcript, December 12, 1930, both in G-C-3 Chisholm Trail (1930), Texas Department of Transportation, Texas Highway Department Historical Records, Archives, and Information Services Division, Texas State Library and Archives Commission; "City One End of New Trail to Be Marked," *Brownsville (Texas) Herald*, December 3, 1930.

Chapter 15

1. "Movement to Mark Trails Plan Signs in 49 Counties," *San Antonio Express*, August 30, 1931.

2. "Trail Historian Corrects Errors," *San Antonio Express*, September 19, 1931.

3. "Official Trail Names Adopted," *San Antonio Express*, October 16, 1931. According to the government maps cited previously, the resolution was not entirely geographically accurate. The route described in the resolution is the route of the Abilene Cattle Trail. There is no indication that any of these maps were known to or used by the association

in their research. It is true that the routes described were the two main cattle trails to Kansas. The implication that the Chisholm Trail was located north of the Red River is also correct according to these maps.

4. Ibid.; "Old Trail Drivers Laughed At Knocks and Depression," *Lubbock Morning Avalanche*, October 10, 1931; George W. Saunders to P. P. Ackley, July 14, 1932, Collection of Tom B. Saunders IV, Weatherford, Texas. The Chisholm Trail name first appeared on a map along the route of the Abilene Cattle Trail and what became the route of the Meridian Highway in Oklahoma in 1901. The effect of this name change from the Abilene Cattle Trail to the Chisholm Trail, plus publicity surrounding the Good Roads Associations' promotion of the road as the Chisholm Trail Highway, is not known. The resolution indicated a delineation between the trail north and south of the Red River, which was also indicated in the Kansas Pacific Railway advertising literature from 1871 to 1875.

5. "Monument Erected to Trail Drivers," *The Cattleman* 18, no. 7 (December 1931), Texas and Southwestern Cattle Raisers Association, Coliseum Building, Stock Yards, Fort Worth.

6. Saunders to Ackley, July 14, 1932. "Trail Drivers Return to S.A. Following Ceremony," *San Antonio Light*, October 23, 1931.

7. P. P. Ackley to the State Highway Board, December 9, 1930, and Gibb Gilchrist to P. P. Ackley, letter transcript, December 12, 1930, both in G-C-3 Chisholm Trail (1930), Texas Department of Transportation, Texas Highway Department Historical Records, Archives and Information Services Division, Texas State Library and Archives Commission; "Movement to Mark Trails," *San Antonio Express*, August 30, 1931.

8. "Going Up the Chisholm Trail, P. P. Ackley, 1878" monument with the silhouette of a longhorn head and an arrow pointing north, Wilbarger County, Texas. As of this writing the monument is located in a roadside park along US Highway 283 approximately nine miles north of Vernon, Texas. See also "First Marker Placed on Old Cattle Trail," *Bryan (Texas) Eagle*, July 29, 1931; "Chisholm Marker to Go on Bridge," *Brownsville (Texas) Herald*, January 13, 1932.

    In February 1932 J. Frank Dobie wrote that Ackley, because of his personal allusions of including his name and the date of his trip up the trail in 1878, was more interested in commemorating his own experience than in commemorating the trail. J. Frank Dobie to George W. Saunders, letter transcript, February 8, 1932, Harry Ransom Center, University of Texas, Austin, Collection of Tom B. Saunders IV, Weatherford, Texas.

9. George W. Saunders to J. Frank Dobie, February 3, 1932, Harry Ransom Center, University of Texas, Austin, Collection of Tom B. Saunders IV, Weatherford, Texas; Dobie to Saunders, February 8, 1932. The "new comers" that Saunders spoke of likely included the Good Roads Associations.

10. Walter E. Long, "Notes on the Longhorn-Chisholm Trail," *Southwestern Historical Quarterly* 60 (July 1956–April 1957): 73–74; "Marking the Old Chisholm Trail," *Canyon (Texas) News*, May 12, 1932; P. P. Ackley interview with Ethel Mae Yates, Interview 4544, June 24, 1937, Oklahoma Federation of Labor Collection, M452, Box 5, Folder 2, Western History

Collections, University of Oklahoma, Norman, https://digital.libraries
.ou.edu, accessed June 21, 2012; Dobie to Saunders, February 8, 1932.
According to Long, his and Tip's Engine works in Austin assisted in
the marker design, and the original markers cost about twelve dollars
each, which was paid by P. P. Ackley. His plan was to place two markers
in each county along a route between Brownsville and Oklahoma. It is
not clear whether the original markers were cast by Tip's or by another
company.

   According to Scott Southwell, the Southwell Company of San
Antonio possesses the original master mold for the Ackley markers,
but his records do not date as far back as the 1930s, so he was unable
to provide further information regarding the original markers. Billy
Southwell stated in an interview with Bob and Kelli Phillips of the
television show *Texas Country Reporter* that the Southwell Company
has been making Texas Historical Commission markers since 1960.
The Ackley markers appear to originate from a manufacturing process
similar to that of markers made by Southwell. Modern reproductions
of the Ackley marker installed at a roadside park in Hill County, Texas,
in 2016 and at the Hill County courthouse bear the Southwell name
stamped on the back. A similar manufacturer's mark is not visible
on original markers at the Wise County courthouse. It is therefore
unknown whether the Southwell Company cast the original markers or acquired the original master mold from another company at
some point. Scott Southwell to the author, e-mail, November 29, 2016.
See also "Texas State Historical Markers," Show 1527, *Texas Country Reporter*, December 3–4, 2016, www.texascountryreporter.com,
accessed February 27, 2017.

11.   Saunders to Ackley, July 14, 1932; Ackley interview with Yates.

12.   "To Honor P. P. Ackley at Elk City Celebration," *Canadian (Texas)
Record*, August 9, 1934; Ackley interview with Yates. Nothing was found
to explain how someone who made their first trip up a trail that had
already been in use for eleven years could be considered the father of
the trail. No record from the cattle trailing era was found of a cattle
trail designated as the Longhorn Chisholm Trail.

13.   George W. Saunders to J. Frank Dobie, April 7, 1932, Harry Ransom
Center, University of Texas, Austin, Collection of Tom B. Saunders IV,
Weatherford, Texas.

14.   Long, "Notes on the Longhorn-Chisholm Trail," 73–74; "Oklahoman
Inspecting Chisholm Trail Marks," *Pampa Daily News*, April 3, 1938;
Emma Wright Feltenberger, comp., *Texas Genealogical Records: Ellis
County*, vol. 16, 1800–1962, Book 1962, 61–62, University of North Texas
Libraries, Portal to Texas History, crediting Nicholas P. Sims Library
and Lyceum, Waxahachie, Texas, www.texashistory.unt.edu, accessed
October 14, 2012.

   Some of the trail landmarks where Ackley placed his markers
given in the *Pampa Daily News* article are along the route of the Western or Fort Griffin and Dodge City Trail, not the route of the Chisholm
Trail.

15.   "Chisholm Trailer Dies at Elk City," *Pampa Daily News*, April 7, 1940.

16.   Tip Igou, interview with the author, Vernon, Texas, April 30, 2015.

17. "Texas Patriarch Borne to Grave," *Lubbock Morning Avalanche*, July 5, 1933; "Doan's Crossing on the Red River," monument erected by the State of Texas, 1936, located at the site of Doan's Store, Wilbarger County, Texas; Will Rogers to Bertha Doan Ross, letter postmarked August 4, 1931, Red River Valley Museum, Vernon, Texas.

18. H. S. Tennant, "The Two Cattle Trails," *Chronicles of Oklahoma* 14, no. 1 (March 1936): 84–85.

19. Ibid., 84–85, 86–87, 109; "Chisholm Trail Road," *Kansas City Star*, August 31, 1911; Julius Bien, *Map of Texas Showing Routes of Transportation of Cattle, 1881*.

20. *Map of a Portion of Oklahoma Showing the Location of the Chisholm Trail*, and *Map of a Portion of Oklahoma Showing the Location of the Old Texas Cattle Trail*.

21. Tennant, "Two Cattle Trails," 121; E. H. Ruffner, *Map of the Chickasaw Country and Contiguous Portions of the Indian Territory*, map; Ado Hunnius, *Military Map of the Indian Territory*; C. Roeser, *Indian Territory*, map, Serial Set 1885, 46th Cong. 2d sess., S. Exec. Doc. 124, 12; G. P. Strum, *Indian Territory*, map, 1883, Serial Set 2261, 48th Cong., 2d sess., S. Exec. Doc. 17, 220; G. P. Strum, *Indian Territory*, map, 1887, Serial Set 2432, 49th Cong. 1st sess., H. Misc. Doc. 15, part 2, 852.

Chapter 16

1. Charles Goodnight to Howard Peak, letter transcript, October 26, 1923, Tarrant County Historical Commission, Tarrant County Archives, Fort Worth, Texas, collection of Tom B. Saunders IV, Weatherford, Texas; "Location for Markers, McCoy Cattle Trail," Tarrant County Historical Commission, Tarrant County Archives, Fort Worth, Texas, collection of Roland Jary, Fort Worth. The inscription was "McCoy Cattle Trail, 1867." The concrete markers were located as follows:

> No. 1 at Ryan Place and College Avenue, No. 2 at Hemphill and Elizabeth Blvd., No. 3 at Grainger and Laurel, No. 4 at Laurel and St. Louis Ave, No. 5 at So. Main and Broadway, No. 6 at Broadway across from Presbyterian Church, No. 7 at NE Corner of Haynes Fountain opposite T&P Depot, No. 8 at Front east of T&P Freight Depot, No. 9 at 14th and Commerce, No. 10 at 13th and Jones, No. 11 at No. West Corner near Fort Worth and D.C. Freight Depot, No. 12 at East Third and Grove, No. 13 at 1107 Belknap St., No. 14 at Cold Springs Road between Rock Island and M K & T RR. Tracks, No. 15 at So. West corner of bridge (county) as it crosses Trinity River, No. 16 at No. East corner of same bridge on North Side.

The McCoy markers have disappeared over the years. See *From Frontier to Metropolis: Fort Worth, Texas, Diamond Jubilee*.

2. Howard W. Peak, *The Story of Old Fort Worth*, 7.

3. Howard W. Peak, "The Old Cattle Trail," undated transcript, Tarrant County Historical Commission, Tarrant County Archives, Fort Worth, Texas, collection of Tom B. Saunders IV, Weatherford, Texas. The date is not visible; however, the document contains information from Goodnight's letter of October 26, 1923, and information that was included in *The Story of Old Fort Worth*, which was published to celebrate the 1836

Texas Centennial. Peak also confused the last names of Chisholm, Chisum, and Chism.

4. Goodnight to Peak, October 26, 1923.

5. "Trail Historian Corrects Errors," *San Antonio Express*, September 19, 1931; "As Wichita Town," *Wichita Daily Eagle*, March 27, 1900; Stan Hoig, *Jesse Chisholm, Ambassador of the Plains*, 148, referencing Joseph B. Thoburn, *A Standard History of Oklahoma*, 364–66.

6. Joseph G. McCoy, *Historic Sketches of the Cattle Trade of the West and Southwest*, ed. Ralph Bieber, 188–89.

7. McLennan County, Texas, "A Proclamation of the Commissioners Court of McLennan County, Texas, Recognizing & Commemorating the Chisholm Trail Festival 'Across the Brazos at Waco,'" October 19, 2010.

8. Hoig, *Jesse Chisholm*, 53–65, 66, 76–83, 148, 164–69.

9. Ibid., 161, referencing George W. Conover, *Sixty Years in Southwest Oklahoma*, 103–4, and O. H. Bentley, *History of Wichita and Sedgwick County Kansas*, 1:119.

10. "The Crossing," marker at Brushy Creek Crossing, Round Rock, Texas.

11. William G. Cutler, "Ellis County," *History of the State of Kansas*, Kansas Collection, transcribed by Sally M. Snell and John Matthews, www.kancoll.org, accessed June 26, 2014; Hoig, *Jesse Chisholm*, 164–67, referencing Record Book of Chief Sam Checote, Archives Manuscript Division, Oklahoma Historical Society, and Leavenworth to Mix, August 18, 1867, Letters Received, Kiowa Indian Agency, 1864–68, RG 75, National Archives.

12. Gary Kraisinger and Margaret Kraisinger, *The Western: The Greatest Texas Cattle Trail*, 58, 122.

13. Charles A. Siringo, *A Texas Cow-boy; or, Fifteen Years on the Hurricane Deck of a Spanish Pony*, 95–102, 141–49, 186–95.

14. James Cox, *Historical and Biographical Record of the Cattle Industry and the Cattlemen of Texas and Adjacent Territory*, 434, 531, 613, 662.

15. Siringo, *Texas Cow-boy*, 148.

16. Articles referring to a point north of the Cimarron River: "Buffalo Hunters Murdered," *Emporia (Kansas) News*, November 24, 1871; "Clear Water," *Wichita City Eagle*, April 26, 1872; "City of Wichita," *Wichita City Eagle*, December 12, 1872; "Indian Alarm," *Leavenworth Weekly Times*, May 15, 1873; "Cattle Raising," *Milan (Tennessee) Exchange*, May 13, 1875; "The Cattle Conclave at Caldwell," *Emporia (Kansas) News*, March 25, 1881; "Live Stock," *Galveston Daily News*, June 23, 1882; "From Caldwell," *Barbour County Index* (Medicine Lodge, Kansas), June 1, 1883; *Cheyenne Transporter* (Darlington, Indian Territory), June 10, 1883; "To the Drovers of Southern Cattle," *Barbour County Index* (Medicine Lodge, Kansas), June 6, 1884; "Notes for the Stock Raiser," *Indian Chieftain* (Vinita, Indian Territory), July 17, 1884; "Prairie Fires," *Barbour County Index* (Medicine Lodge, Kansas), November 27, 1885; "Cherokee Strip Round-up May 26th," *Barbour County Index* (Medicine Lodge, Kansas), May 14, 1886; "Stock Raisers and Cattle," *Denison (Texas) Daily News*, April 28, 1874.

Articles referring to a point between the Canadian and the Cimar-ron Rivers: "Live Stock Notes," *Saint Johns (Arizona Territory) Herald*, June 17, 1886; "Accidental Drowning," *Cheyenne Transporter* (Darling-ton, Indian Territory), August 12, 1886; "On the March," *Austin Weekly Statesman*, Austin, Texas, April 25, 1889; "Bluff City Items," *Wichita Daily Eagle*, March 23, 1890.

Articles generally referring to a point north of the Red River: *Georgetown (Texas) Watchman*, April 10, 1869; "The Texas Cattle Trade," *Emporia (Kansas) News*, September 30, 1870; "Circular," *Austin Tri-Weekly State Gazette*, March 20, 1871; "Texas Cattle and Indian Ferries," *Austin Tri-Weekly State Gazette*, May 19, 1871; "Southwestern Kansas," *Leavenworth Times*, June 8, 1871.

Articles referring to a point south of the Red River: "State News," *Galveston Daily News*, April 21, 1876; "From Texas," *Pulaski (Tennes-see) Citizen*, June 12, 1879. Due to the lack of articles that refer to the Chisholm Trail south of the Red River, additional searches did not yield any other examples.

Articles referring to the Texas Cattle Trail, including a point north of the Red River: "From Butler County," *Emporia (Kansas) News*, June 11, 1869; "Letter from Friend Stanley," *Emporia (Kansas) News*, September 10, 1869; "New Town," *Emporia (Kansas) News*, September 2, 1870; "Texas Long Horns," *Shreveport (Louisiana) South-Western*, August 10, 1870; "Sumner County," *Emporia (Kansas) News*, December 2, 1870; *Fayette County (Ohio) Herald*, March 2, 1871; "Great Excitement at Park City," *Emporia (Kansas) News*, March 24, 1871; "A.T. and S.F. Railroad Items," *Emporia (Kansas) News*, March 31, 1871; "Park City," advertisement, *Emporia (Kansas) News*, March 31, 1871; *Saline County Journal* (Salina, Kansas), May 25, 1871; "Southern Kansas Items," *Leavenworth Weekly Times*, July 20, 1871; "Letter from the West," *Western Reserve Chronicle* (Warren, Ohio), August 2, 1871; "From Caldwell," *Leavenworth Weekly Times*, November 16, 1871; "The Texas Cattle Trade," *Houston Telegraph*, February 15, 1872; "Letter from Our Traveling Correspondent," *Highland Weekly News* (Hillsborough [Hillsboro], Ohio), October 24, 1872; "Sumner County," *Emporia (Kansas) News*, April 25, 1873; "Sumner County," *Wichita City Eagle*, July 17, 1873; "The Cattle Trail," *Wichita City Eagle*, February 25, 1875; "Quarantine Ground," *Wichita City Eagle*, April 29, 1875; "The Kansas Legislature," *Emporia (Kansas) News*, February 25, 1876; "Locations for Stock Ranches," *Dodge City Times*, June 23, 1877; "Railroad Business at Wichita," *Wichita City Eagle*, January 10, 1878; "On the Nebraska Ranges," *Saint Landry Democrat* (Opelousas, Louisiana), June 12, 1880; "Our Washington Letter," *New North-west* (Deer Lodge, Montana), January 28, 1881; "On to Dodge," *Dodge City Times*, February 16, 1882; "Round-Up at Erin Springs," *Cheyenne Transporter* (Darlington, Indian Territory), April 12, 1883; *Phillipsburg (Kansas) Herald*, March 27, 1884.

Articles referring to the Texas Cattle Trail in Texas: "Commercial Matters," *New Orleans Bulletin*, May 1, 1875; "Southern Items," *New Orleans Democrat*, June 5, 1876.

Articles referring to the Eastern Trail in Indian Territory: "The New Trail," *Cheyenne Transporter* (Darlington, Indian Territory), May 10, 1881; "Notice to Texas Cattle Drovers and Others," *Barbour County*

Index (Medicine Lodge, Kansas), November 30, 1883; "Legislature," *Fort Worth Daily Gazette*, January 13, 1884.

    Articles referring to the Eastern Trail in Texas: "Live Stock Notes," *Galveston Daily News*, April 4, 1880; "From Austin," *Waco Daily Examiner*, February 17, 1882.

    Articles referring to the Abilene Trail: "Letter from Kansas," *Highland Weekly News* (Hillsborough, Ohio), July 28, 1870; "A Hunt for the South Line of the State," *Emporia (Kansas) News*, July 29, 1870; "Through the Territory," *Galveston Daily News*, April 20, 1887; "To Oklahoma," *Rock Island (Illinois) Daily Argus*, April 9, 1889; "Matthewson City, the Future Great," *Wichita Eagle*, July 9, 1889; "From the Panhandle," *Fort Worth Daily Gazette*, May 4, 1890; "Another Victory," *Wichita Daily Eagle*, June 1, 1890.

17.   Wayne Gard, *The Chisholm Trail*, 75, referencing *Kansas Daily Commonwealth* (Topeka), May 27, 1870; *Annual Report of the Commissioner of Indian Affairs to the Secretary of the Interior for the Year 1870*, 6.

18.   Gard, *Chisholm Trail*, 76, referencing *Denison (Texas) Daily News*, April 28, 1874; "Stock Raisers and Cattle," *Denison (Texas) Daily News*, April 28, 1874.

19.   *Guide Map of the Great Texas Cattle Trail from Red River Crossing to the Old Reliable Kansas Pacific Railway*, 1874; *Guide Map of the Great Texas Cattle Trail from Red River Crossing to the Old Reliable Kansas Pacific Railway*, 1875, reprint 1958; *The Best and Shortest Cattle Route from Texas*, map, 1872; *The Best and Shortest Cattle Trail from Texas*, map, 1873; *The Best and Shortest Cattle Trail from Texas*, map, 1875, reprint 1958.

20.   *Best and Shortest Cattle Trail*, 1873; "Texas Cattle Trade," *Houston Telegraph*, February 15, 1872.

21.   J. Marvin Hunter, ed., *The Trail Drivers of Texas*, 2nd ed., rev., 37–39, 115, 118, 122, 169, 215, 231, 254, 294, 296, 306, 482, 499, 598, 607, 772, 781, 840, 963, 1026.

22.   A. W. Ziegelasch, *The Old Chisholm Cattle Trail, with Subsidiary Trails in Texas, 1873*, map; Kansas State Census Collection, www.ancestry.com, accessed August 19, 2014; Topeka, Kansas, City Directory, 1924, 556; 1926, 475; 1927, 543; 1929, 49, in US City Directories, 1822–1995, National Archives at Fort Worth, Kansas Historical Society, www.ancestry.com, accessed August 19, 2014; *Best and Shortest Cattle Trail* (1873). Kansas Memory, Kansas State Historical Society, has since changed their citation to include Ziegelasch's year of birth and year of death, 1893–1930, to clarify the map's provenance.

23.   E. H. Ruffner, *Map of the Chickasaw Country and Contiguous Portions of the Indian Territory*; Ado Hunnius, *Military Map of the Indian Territory*; C. Roeser, *Indian Territory*, map, 1879, Serial Set 1885, 46th Cong. 2d sess., S. Exec. Doc. 124, 12; G. P. Strum, *Indian Territory*, map, 1883, Serial Set 2261, 48th Cong., 2d sess., S. Exec. Doc. 17, 220, and G. P. Strum, *Indian Territory*, map, 1887, Serial Set 2432, 49th Cong., 1st sess., H. Misc. Doc. 15, part 2, 852.

24.   The following Texas General Land Office county maps that I consulted are listed here in order from south to north following the cattle drives: A. B. Langermann, *Map of Hidalgo County*, April 1880; A. B. Langer-

mann, *Map of Starr County*, March 1880; Texas General Land Office,
Nueces County, map, 1879; Texas General Land Office, *Map of San Patri-
cio County*, 1879; Otto Groos, *Live Oak County*, map, December 1878;
Texas General Land Office, *McMullen County*, map, 1877; F. H. Arlitt,
Map of La Salle County, 1877; A. B. Langermann, *Frio County*, map, May
1879; A. B. Langermann, *Atascosa County*, map, September 1879; Louis
Klappenbach, *Wilson County*, map, February 1872; Louis Klappenbach,
Bexar County, map, July 1871; Otto Groos, *Map of Comal County*, March
3, 1874; F. G. Blau, *Guadalupe County*, map, 1877; Herman Lungkwitz,
Map of Caldwell County, 1871; A. B. Langermann, *Map of Hays County*,
September 1877; Texas General Land Office, *Travis County*, map,
May 14, 1870; A. B. Langermann, *Map of Williamson County*, December
1876; George J. Thielepape, *Bell County*, map, December 1877; George J.
Thielepape, *Coryell County*, map, June 1883; F. Schenck, *Map of Falls
County*, December 1874; F. G. Blau, *McLennan County*, map, May 1878;
George J. Thielepape, *Bosque County*, map, December 1876; Louis
Klappenbach, *Hill County*, map, November 1871; George J. Thielepape,
Johnson County, map, June 1874; A. L. Lucas, *Tarrant County*, map, April
1873; F. G. Blau, *Map of Denton County*, April 1877; George J. Thielepape,
Wise County, map, October 1878; Max Stakemann, *Cooke County*, map,
March 1876; and Max Stakemann, *Montague County*, map, October
1875.

25.   Julius Bien, *Map of Texas Showing Routes of Transportation of Cattle,
1881*. This map indicates that this trail was known as the Eastern
during the period when the map was made. No indication was found
that the trail was known as the Eastern prior to 1876.

Chapter 17

1.   "Postmaster Drove Last Herd over Chisholm Trail," *Fort Worth Star
Telegram*, August 25, 1911; "Is Historic Route," *Topeka State Journal*,
October 14, 1911; Edmond Franklin Bates, *History and Reminiscences
of Denton County*, 167–68; "Auto Tour along Chisholm Trail Barkley's
Plan," *Fort Worth Star Telegram*, November 10, 1911; J. Marvin Hunter,
ed., *The Trail Drivers of Texas*, 2nd ed., rev., 37; "Marking the Chisholm
Trail," *San Antonio Express*, May 21, 1930; T. C. Richardson, "Cattle
Trails from Texas," *Texas Almanac and Industrial Guide, 1933*, 178–79,
University of North Texas Libraries, Portal to Texas History, crediting
Texas State Historical Association, Austin, www.texashistory.unt.edu,
accessed June 21, 2012; T. C. Richardson, "Cattle Trails and Trail Driv-
ing," *Texas Almanac and State Industrial Guide,1936*, 260–61; "Texans
Driven by Chisholm Trail Debate," *Houston Chronicle*, November 25,
2001.

2.   "Is Historic Route," *Topeka State Journal*, October 14, 1911; "Chisholm
Trail Road," *Kansas City Star*, August 31, 1911. The location of the
Chisholm Trail Road from Caldwell south along the Rock Island
Railroad to Texas was endorsed by Good Roads boosters at a meeting
held on August 29, 1911, at El Reno, Oklahoma. Continuing into Texas,
Ringgold was the first town along the Rock Island south of the Red
River.

3.   "Cowmen Asked to Aid Highway Move," *Fort Worth Star Telegram*,
August 30, 1911; "Marking the Chisholm Trail," *San Antonio Express*,

May 21, 1930. Apparently, because of the controversy and multiple trail names, J. Frank Dobie suggested marking two separate trails as the Chisholm in an apparent compromise to get past the trail name issue, but this is speculation.

4. Wayne Gard, *The Chisholm Trail*, 77, 229; E. D. Dorchester, *Trails Made and Routes Used by the Fourth U.S. Cavalry under the Command of General R. S. Mackenzie in Its Operations against Hostile Indians in Texas, Indian Territory (Now Oklahoma), New Mexico, and Old Mexico during the Period of 1871-2-3-4 and 5*, map; Richardson, "Cattle Trails and Trail Driving," 1936, 260–61. Text in Richardson's 1936 article that accompanied the map stated, "This was the route that has come to be known as the Chisholm Trail," and "the name of Chisholm's Trail was eventually applied to the southern extension." See also *Hoffman & Walker's Pictorial & Historical Map of Texas*. The Hoffman and Walker map is undated but is believed to date to the 1960s. See also Lewis Atherton, "Frontier Federal Forts and Cattle Trails, 1867–1886," map, in *Atlas of Texas*; and *The Chisholm Trail: Exploring the Folklore and Legacy*, map, Texas Historical Commission brochure, 2002.

5. "Cattle Raising," *Milan (Tennessee) Exchange*, May 13, 1875; "To Oklahoma," *Rock Island (Illinois) Daily Argus*, April 9, 1889. The *Milan Exchange* article placed the Old Chisholm Trail at Caldwell, Kansas: "On the Old Chisholm Trail, from May 1 to November 11, 1872, 292 drovers passed Caldwell, Kan., with 349,275 cattle, making the average per drove very nearly 1,200."

6. For example, J. Frank Dobie seemingly contradicted himself in 1930 when he proposed to name the Old Chisholm Trail and Western Chisholm Trail through Texas and stated that the original Chisholm Trail did not extend into Texas. Perhaps he intended to apply the names generically for trail marking purposes, but this is speculation. In another case, George W. Saunders stated in 1931 that Joseph McCoy hired Jesse Chisholm to blaze a trail from Abilene, Kansas, to the Red River. The statement is partially true: McCoy hired T. F. Hersey to mark a trail from Abilene south to the mouth of the Little Arkansas River, which was the north end of Jesse Chisholm's trail. These are only two examples. Many sources contain similar miscues, but that does not necessarily disqualify the source in all matters.

7. Multiple sources over the years have claimed that the Chisholm Trail was blazed by and is named for cattleman John S. Chisum, but none have offered documentation to place Chisum in Abilene, Kansas, when the first herds arrived during the summer of 1867 or explained how he managed to blaze a trail across Indian Territory to Abilene at the same time he was establishing his operation in New Mexico Territory. Other sources have claimed that the trail north from Texas to Kansas is so named because Chisum cattle were the first to be driven over it, or because of the volume of Chisum cattle driven over it, yet no documentation to this effect has surfaced or been cited. In cases like this there might be multiple sources that repeat the same or similar stories, but the events cannot be verified.

A different kind of example is C. H. Rust's detailed description of the Chisholm Trail in *The Trail Drivers of Texas* (37–41). Although the described route of the trail is accurate, the trail name was disputed by others who drove the same trail, and there is no documentation from the trail's period of use to support the Chisholm name for this trail. Less emphasis should be placed on the source and more emphasis should be placed on the statement content and whether any of the information can be verified by documentation, such as newspapers, maps, etc., from the appropriate historical period.

8.   E. H. Ruffner, *Map of the Chickasaw Country and Contiguous Portions of the Indian Territory*; Ado Hunnius, *Military Map of the Indian Territory*; C. Roeser, *Indian Territory*, map, 1879, Serial Set 1885, 46th Cong., 2d sess., S. Exec. Doc. 124; G. P. Strum, *Indian Territory*, 1883, Serial Set 2261, 48th Cong, 2d sess., S. Exec. Doc. 17; G. P. Strum, *Indian Territory*, 1887, Serial Set 2432, 49th Cong., 1st sess., H. Misc. Doc. 15, pt. 2.

9.   John T. Lytle Collection, Cattle Raisers Museum, Texas and Southwestern Cattle Raisers Foundation, Fort Worth.

     A collection of letters from former drovers was also reviewed at the Tales 'N' Trails Museum in Nocona, Texas. These letters were in response to an ad placed in the *Denison Daily Herald* in August 1910 which read: "Wanted—To correspond with persons familiar with the early history of Cooke, Montague, and Clay Counties, Texas. Also with persons who have driven cattle over the Chisholm Trail. Address Box No. 11, Nocona, Texas." Most of the letters were little more than acknowledgement of the ad and willingness to correspond, as in this example: "I saw your notice in the News and wish to say that I lived in Cook [*sic*] Co from 1866 to 1870, and drove cattle over the Chisholm trail to Kansans [*sic*] from '70 to '75. Would like to correspond with you." Some letters provided a few details of life on the trail but no specific details of the trail name or route other than general references to the Chisholm Trail and the ad. Price Quote for Advertisement, *Denison Daily Herald*, August 10, 1910; and E. A. Jordan, letter response to advertisement, undated, both in Tales 'N' Trails Museum, Nocona, Texas.

10.   *Map of the Oklahoma Country in the Indian Territory*, 1892; M. Hedges, *Map of Oklahoma Territory*, 1898, Serial Set 3918., H. Doc. 8, map 3, 743; *Map of Oklahoma Territory*, 1902, Serial Set 4461, 57th Cong., 2d sess., H. Doc. 5, map 3, 495; *Indian Territory, Chickasaw Nation, Addington Quadrangle*, map, 1901. The 1892 map is believed to be the first time the Chisholm Trail appeared on a map south of the North Canadian River. Chisholm's Trail or Chisholm's Cattle Trail did not appear on the 1898 and 1902 maps; the route from near Council Grove to the Abilene Cattle Trail near the Cimarron River was indicated, but it was not named. The Chisholm Trail appeared in a distinctly different location on the 1901 map.

11.   "Attracting the Tourist," *San Angelo Press*, June 1, 1905; "Mexico City as the Ultimate Southern Terminus of Big Road," *Grand Forks Evening Times*, February 17, 1912; "Chisholm Trail Road," *Kansas City Star*, August 31, 1911; "A Criss-Cross of 8 Highways," *Tulsa Daily World*, November 29, 1911; "To Perpetuate the Old Trail," *Dallas Morning News*, June 16, 1913; "Fort Worth Joins in Chisholm Trail Plan," *Fort Worth Star Telegram*, August 29, 1911; "Favors National Road," *Dallas Morning News*, August 26, 1911; "Postmaster Drove Last Herd over Chisholm Trail," *Fort Worth Star Telegram*, August 25, 1911; "Numbered High-

ways," *Dallas Morning News*, June 28, 1930, Collection of Pete Charlton, Fort Worth, Texas; "Oklahoma Urges Chisholm Trail Be Preserved," *San Antonio Express*, December 11, 1925; "Old Chisholm Trail Again Is Traveled," *San Antonio Express*, December 18, 1929; "City One End of New Trail to Be Marked," *Brownsville (Texas) Herald*, December 3, 1930.

12. "Going Up the Chisholm Trail, P. P. Ackley, 1878" monument, Wilbarger County, Texas. As of this writing the monument is located in a roadside park along US Highway 283 approximately nine miles north of Vernon, Texas. "First Marker Placed on Old Cattle Trail," *Bryan (Texas) Eagle*, July 29, 1931; "Chisholm Marker to Go on Bridge," *Brownsville (Texas) Herald*, January 13, 1932; Walter E. Long, "Notes on the Longhorn-Chisholm Trail," *Southwestern Historical Quarterly* 60 (July 1956–April 1957): 73–74; "To Honor P. P. Ackley at Elk City Celebration," *Canadian (Texas) Record*, August 9, 1934; "Oklahoman Inspecting Chisholm Trail Marks," *Pampa Daily News*, April 3, 1938.

13. J. Frank Dobie, *The Longhorns*, 207; "Official Trail Names Adopted," *San Antonio Express*, October 16, 1931; Gordon Wilkison, "Progress Report Austin: Legends of Austin 2," newsreel, 1962, Texas Archive of the Moving Image, Austin, showing newsreel footage of P. P. Ackley on a promotional tour in 1934.

14. "Marking the Chisholm Trail," *San Antonio Express*, May 21, 1930; Texas, Department of Transportation, Office of Commission Support, "Minutes of the One Hundred and Forty-Fifth Meeting of the State Highway Commission," Minute No. 2861, May 19, 1930; Gibb Gilchrist to G. C. Richardson, December 5, 1930, and Gibb Gilchrist to P. P. Ackley, December 12, 1930, both in G-C-3 Chisholm Trail (1930), Texas Highway Department Records, Texas State Library and Archives.

15. H. S. Tennant, "The Two Cattle Trails," *Chronicles of Oklahoma* 14, no. 1 (March 1936): 84–86, 109; *Map of a Portion of Oklahoma Showing the Location of the Chisholm Trail*, 1933.

16. "Addresses Delivered at the Annual Meeting of the Oklahoma Historical Society," *Chronicles of Oklahoma* 14, no. 2 (June 1936): 231–33.

17. Frank Norris, "Cattle Trails—Statement of Significance," March 20, 2012, 1, U.S. Department of the Interior, National Park Service, National Trails Intermountain Region, Santa Fe, New Mexico..

18. Ibid., 1–2.

19. "Blazing a Trail," *Fort Worth Star Telegram*, November 5, 1999; Billy Cate and Steve Myers, "The Chisholm Trail Marker Project: Marking the Chisholm Trail in Texas," 2012, paper in author's collection. Requirements to obtain a marker are from a 2012 document. As of this writing, e-mail requests for updated information or a copy of a narrative in support of any of the markers that have been installed have gone unanswered.

20. Frank Norris and Brooke Safford, "Scoping Report, Chisholm and Great Western National Historic Trail Feasibility Study and Environmental Assessment," September 2010, 22–91, US Department of the Interior, National Park Service, National Trails Intermountain Region, Santa Fe, New Mexico. A review of the public comments, pp. 22–91, shows an emphasis on tourism and economic opportunity. See also "Texas Cattle Route Drives Controversy," *Daily Oklahoman* (Oklahoma

City), December 10, 2001, Collection of Tom B. Saunders IV, Weatherford, Texas. This article states, "Eastern doesn't have the same ring to
it as Chisholm does and it doesn't attract tourism dollars—especially
in the Lone Star State." That argument is sometimes used as justification for the Chisholm name applied to the Texas portion of the trail.

21.   Texas, Department of Transportation, "2014 Chisholm Trail Marker
Restoration Project," PowerPoint presentation, Austin, November
2014. The marker restoration project is based on the narrative in
Hidalgo County Historical Commission, "Texas Cattle Trails," paper,
Mission, Texas, 2009, 4–8. This narrative may have been based on the
best information that was available at the time, but it omits important, relevant parts of the story. The television series *History Detectives*
is referenced as a source, but their conclusions that P. P. Ackley was
"frequently off course when marking the trail," and that the trail
north from south Texas led "to" the Chisholm Trail but was not the
Chisholm Trail, were not included in the Hidalgo County paper.

Regarding the claim on p. 7 of the paper that Ackley "secured
permission from the Texas Highway Commission to put markers
on a route Ackley designated," according to the meeting minutes
from May 19, 1930, the highway commission granted permission to
the Chisholm Trail Association to lay out a route and erect markers,
pending approval of the location and marker design by the commission or the state engineer. Nothing in the minutes indicates that the
commission granted permission to Ackley to personally designate
a route and select a trail name. No indication was found that the
highway commission approved Ackley's marker design or proposed
locations. Searches for subsequent meeting minutes regarding Ackley
or the Chisholm Trail have failed to reveal any changes to the original
minutes. J. Frank Dobie was asked to research and recommend a
route. Ackley's marker design was not approved, and he was referred
to Walter Long of Austin, who was working on a design.

The Hidalgo County Historical Commission narrative also states
that Ackley moved to southwest Texas as a boy, but according to Ackley
in a 1937 interview he came to Texas in 1877 at about age nineteen,
when he drove sheep from Dodge City south past Fort Supply to the
Pease River. He referred to that trail past Fort Supply as the Chisholm
Trail, but it was over one hundred miles west of Chisholm's trail.
Ackley mistakenly referred to the trail to Dodge City as the Chisholm
Trail and placed his "Chisholm Trail" markers along the trail by
which he came to Texas. This Hidalgo County Historical Commission
narrative is also apparently used as justification for Texas Historical
Commission Marker 15868, "P. P. Ackley and the Texas Chisholm Trail,"
installed in Donna, Texas, in 2009.

When all of the information regarding P. P. Ackley is considered
in its entirety, the narrative changes considerably. Much of the
information in the 2009 narrative supporting the Texas Department
of Transportation Ackley Chisholm Trail marker project and Texas Historical Commission Marker 15868 is contradicted, and the markers are
therefore questionable. See also Chris Chambers, Texas Department
of Transportation, to the author, e-mail, September 21, 2016; "Minutes
of the One Hundred and Forty-Fifth," May 19, 1930; "Investigations:
Chisholm Trail," *History Detectives: Special Investigations*, transcript,

Episode 1, Season 4, 2006; Gilchrist to Ackley, December 12, 1930; "Marking the Chisholm Trail," *San Antonio Express*, May 21, 1930; and Ethel Mae Yates, interview 4544, P. P. Ackley, June 24, 1937, Oklahoma Federation of Labor Collection, M452, Box 5, Folder 2, Western History Collections, University of Oklahoma, Norman, https://digital.libraries .ou.edu, accessed June 21, 2012.

22.   Chris Chambers, Texas Department of Transportation, San Antonio, to Barbara Westbrook, Atascosa County Historical Commission, Leming, Texas, June 3, 2016, and Barbara Westbrook to Chris Chambers, June 9, 2016, both in Atascosa County Historical Commission. In the first letter Chris Chambers described the marker replacement project for the approaching 150th anniversary of the Chisholm Trail and asked permission to install markers at the Atascosa County courthouse. In the return letter Westbrook denied permission because the cattle trail through that county was not the Chisholm Trail, and installation of Chisholm Trail markers would be "a distortion of our history," although markers commemorating the Western Trail were welcomed.

23.   "Chisholm Trail Designated, but Purists Object," *New York Times*, November 29, 2001, and "Texas Cattle Route Drives Controversy," *Daily Oklahoman* (Oklahoma City), December 10, 2001, both in collection of Tom B. Saunders IV, Weatherford, Texas; Frank Norris to the author, e-mail, March 4, 2016.

24.   "Official Trail Names Adopted," *San Antonio Express*, October 16, 1931; "From Austin," *Waco Daily Examiner*, February 17, 1882; Julius Bien, *Map of Texas Showing Routes of Transportation of Cattle, 1881*; Julius Bien, *The Range and Ranch Cattle Area of the United States, 1884*, Map 1 in Joseph Nimmo, *Report in Regard to the Range and Ranch Cattle Business of the United States*.

25.   Jack M. Potter, *Cattle Trails of the Old West*, ed. and comp. Laura R. Krehbiel, 15. Potter started working with herds on the trail at age twelve; by age seventeen he was a trail boss.

26.   "Addresses Delivered," *Chronicles of Oklahoma* 14, no. 2 (June 1936): 229; "Official Trail Names Adopted," *San Antonio Express*, October 16, 1931.

Appendix

1.   Dan Kilgore, "The Spanish Missions and the Origins of the Cattle Industry in Texas," *The Cattleman*, January 1983.

2.   "History of the Texas Longhorns," United States Fish and Wildlife Service, Wichita Mountains Wildlife Refuge.

3.   Kilgore, "Spanish Missions."

4.   Robert H. Thonhoff, *The Texas Connection with the American Revolution*, 48–51.

5.   Christopher D. Long, "Old Three Hundred," Handbook of Texas Online, Texas State Historical Association, https://tshaonline.org /handbook/online/articles/umoo1.

6.   Jim Bob Jackson, *They Pointed Them East First*, 38–39.

7.   "Indian Removal Act," Primary Documents in American History, Web Guides, Library of Congress, www.loc.gov/rr/program/bib/ourdocs /Indian.html, accessed January 4, 2017.

8. "The Republic of Texas," Texas State Library and Archives Commission, Austin, www.tsl.texas.gov/treasures/republic/index.html, accessed January 4, 2017.

9. "History," Colt's Manufacturing Company, LLC, www.colt.com /Company/History, accessed January 4, 2017.

10. Jackson, *They Pointed Them East First*, 41.

11. C. T. Neu, "Annexation," Handbook of Texas Online, Texas State Historical Association, www.tshaonline.org/handbook/online/articles /mga02, accessed January 4, 2017.

12. Wayne Gard, *The Chisholm Trail*, 23; "United States Meat Production, Texas," *Johnson's (Revised) Universal Cyclopaedia: A Scientific and Popular Treasury of Useful Knowledge*, 8:751. This issue of *Johnson's* contains the earliest reference to the Piper drive in 1846 that I found.

13. "History," Colt's Manufacturing Company.

14. Jerome C. Smiley and National Live Stock Association of the United States, *Prose and Poetry of the Live Stock Industry of the United States*, 1:392.

15. Gard, *Chisholm Trail*, 29–33.

16. Clifford R. Caldwell, *John Simpson Chisum: The Cattle King of the Pecos Revisited*, 38, 40–41.

17. "Markets," *Austin State Gazette*, September 16, 1855.

18. Julius Bien, *Map of the Territory of the United States from the Mississippi River to the Pacific Ocean; Ordered by Jeff'n Davis, Secretary of War to Accompany the Reports of the Explorations for a Railroad Route.*

19. J. Evetts Haley, *Charles Goodnight, Cowman and Plainsman*, 20–21; Gard, *Chisholm Trail*, 34–35.
     It has also been reported that Loving sent his son, William, up the trail to Illinois with a herd in 1857. See Julia Cauble Smith, "Loving, Oliver," Handbook of Texas Online, Texas State Historical Association, https://tshaonline.org/handbook/online/articles/flo38, accessed October 11, 2016.

20. Stan Hoig, *Jesse Chisholm, Ambassador of the Plains*, 94–95, 118.

21. Haley, *Charles Goodnight*, 20–21.

22. Thomas Henshaw, ed., *The History of Winchester Firearms, 1866–1992*, 6th ed., 7–8.

23. *The History of Pettis County, Missouri*, 404.

24. Ralph A. Wooster, "Civil War," Handbook of Texas Online, Texas State Historical Association, https://tshaonline.org/handbook/online /articles/qdc02, accessed October 11, 2013.

25. *Official Records*, series I, 1:667; John Rossel, "The Chisholm Trail," *Kansas Historical Quarterly* 5 (1936): 6.

26. Caldwell, *John Simpson Chisum*, 51.

27. Ibid., 52.

28. Hoig, *Jesse Chisholm*, 141.

29. Ibid., 148.

30. Smiley and National Live Stock Association, *Prose and Poetry*, 394–96; *Evansville (Indiana) Daily Journal*, January 20, 1865.

31. Fannie G. Chisholm, *The Four State Chisholm Trail*, 7–9.

32. Caldwell, *John Simpson Chisum*, 53–62.

33. Henshaw, *History of Winchester Firearms*, 10–12.

34. Caldwell, *John Simpson Chisum*, 55.

35. *Laws of the State of Kansas*, 263–67.

36. Joseph G. McCoy, *Historic Sketches of the Cattle Trade of the West and Southwest*, ed. Ralph Bieber, 55–56, 188–89.

37. Ibid., 120–21.

38. *Progress of Their Road, West from Omaha, Nebraska, across the Continent*, The Union Pacific Railroad Company.

39. *Georgetown (Texas) Watchman*, April 10, 1869.

40. "Texan Cattle," *Emporia (Kansas) News*, January 28, 1870.

41. David J. Wishart, ed., "Folk Songs," *Encyclopedia of the Great Plains*, Lincoln: University of Nebraska-Lincoln, http://plainshumanities.unl .edu/encyclopedia/, accessed January 4, 2017.

42. *Nebraska Advertiser* (Brownville, Nebraska), July 21, 1870.

43. "State News," *Emporia (Kansas) News*, June 2, 1871; "The Kansas Stock Yard Company," *Emporia (Kansas) Weekly News*, October 13, 1871.

44. "Important to Cattle Drovers," *Austin Tri-Weekly State Gazette*, April 21, 1871.

45. *The Laws of the State of Kansas, Passed at the Twelfth Session of the Legislature, Commenced at the State Capital on Tuesday, January 9, 1872*, 387–91.

46. *Wichita City Eagle*, June 7, 1872.

47. McCoy, *Historic Sketches*, 187.

48. "Texan Cattle," *Leavenworth Weekly Times*, May 23, 1872.

49. Joseph W. Snell and Don W. Wilson, "The Birth of the Atchison, Topeka, and Santa Fe Railroad," *Kansas Historical Quarterly* 34, no. 3 (Autumn 1968): 325–56, transcribed by Barbara J. Scott.

50. E. H. Ruffner, *Map of the Chickasaw Country and Contiguous Portions of the Indian Territory*.

51. "History," Colt's Manufacturing Company; Henshaw, *History of Winchester Firearms*, 10–12.

52. Frank Collinson, *Life in the Saddle*, 31–40.

53. Frances T. McCallum and James Mulkey Owens, "Barbed Wire," Handbook of Texas Online, Texas State Historical Association, https:// tshaonline.org/handbook/online/articles/aob01, accessed August 5, 2015.

54. John Kay et al., "Nebraska Historic Buildings Survey, Reconnaissance Survey Final Report of Keith County, Nebraska," 11–12.

55. *Wichita City Eagle*, July 15, 1875.

56. James L. Haley, "Red River War," Handbook of Texas Online, Texas State Historical Association, https://tshaonline.org/handbook/online /articles/qdr02, accessed August 12, 2015.

57. Ado Hunnius, *Military Map of the Indian Territory*.

58. "Cattle Raising," *Milan (Tennessee) Exchange*, May 13, 1875.

59.   Kansas, *Session Laws of 1876, and Memorials, Passed at the Sixteenth Annual Session of the Legislature, Commenced at the State Capitol on Tuesday, January 11, 1876*, 316–17.

60.   "Echoes from the Frontier," *Leavenworth Weekly Times*, May 18, 1876.

61.   "Southwest," *Emporia (Kansas) News*, June 16, 1876.

62.   Haley, *Charles Goodnight*, 280–94; H. Allen Anderson, "JA Ranch," Handbook of Texas Online, Texas State Historical Association, https://tshaonline.org/handbook/online/articles/apj01, accessed March 2, 2013.

63.   US Office of Indian Affairs, *Annual Report of the Commissioner of Indian Affairs to the Secretary of the Interior for the Year 1877*, 16–17.

64.   J. Marvin Hunter, ed., *The Trail Drivers of Texas*, 2nd ed., rev., 777–79.

65.   William G. Cutler, "Sumner County," in *History of the State of Kansas*.

66.   "The New Trail," *Cheyenne Transporter* (Darlington, Indian Territory), May 10, 1881.

67.   "Stockmen's Convention," *Austin Weekly Democratic Statesman*, February 23, 1882.

68.   "Legislature," *Fort Worth Daily Gazette*, January 13, 1884.

69.   "Telegraphic News," *San Antonio Light*, July 2, 1884.

70.   Joseph Nimmo, *Report in Regard to the Range and Ranch Cattle Business of the United States*, 134–35.

71.   Ibid., 160.

72.   "A Fence Cutter," *Waco Daily Examiner*, August 11, 1885.

73.   "Abandoning the Trail," *Daily Morning Astorian* (Astoria, Oregon), July 27, 1887.

74.   *Good Roads* 1, no. 1 (January–June 1892).

75.   *Map of the Oklahoma Country in the Indian Territory.*

76.   Myron Schultz, "Theobald Smith," *Emerging Infectious Diseases* 14, no. 12 (December 2008).

77.   "Business League Delegates," *Houston Daily Post*, September 4, 1901.

78.   *Indian Territory, Chickasaw Nation, Addington Quadrangle*, map, 1901.

79.   Jeremy Agnew, *The Old West in Fact and Film: History versus Hollywood*, 46–51.

80.   "Attracting the Tourist," *San Angelo Press*, June 1, 1905.

81.   "Mexico City as the Ultimate Southern Terminus of Big Road," *Grand Forks Evening Times*, February 17, 1912.

82.   "Chisholm Trail's Road," *Kansas City Star*, August 31, 1911.

83.   "Postmaster Drove Last Herd over Chisholm Trail," *Fort Worth Star Telegram*, August 25, 1911.

84.   "Fort Worth Joins in Chisholm Trail Plan," *Fort Worth Star Telegram*, August 29, 1911.

85.   "Mexico City," *Grand Forks Evening Times*, February 17, 1912.

86.   "To Perpetuate the Old Trail," *Dallas Morning News*, June 16, 1913.

87.   Hunter, *Trail Drivers* (1925), 4–12.

88.   B. Byron Price, introduction to Hunter, *Trail Drivers*, 2nd ed., rev., 6th printing (2008): vi–ix.

89. "Oklahoma Urges Chisholm Trail Be Preserved," *San Antonio Express*, December 11, 1925.

90. "Cowboy Plans Making Trail a National Highway," *Vernon (Texas) Daily Record*, April 29, 1929.

91. Texas Department of Transportation, Office of Commission Support, "Minutes of the One Hundred and Forty-Fifth Meeting of the State Highway Commission," Minute No. 2861, May 19, 1930.

92. "Old Chisholm Cattle Trail to Be Marked," *Berkeley (California) Daily Gazette*, June 3, 1930, Collection of Pete Charlton, Fort Worth, Texas; E. D. Dorchester, *Trails Made and Routes Used by the Fourth U.S. Cavalry under the Command of General R. S. Mackenzie in Its Operations against Hostile Indians in Texas, Indian Territory (Now Oklahoma), New Mexico, and Old Mexico during the Period of 1871-2-3-4 and 5*, map.

93. "Marking the Chisholm Trail," *San Antonio Express*, Texas, May 21, 1930; "Designation of Chisholm Trail Nears," *Dallas Morning News*, June 1, 1930, Collection of Pete Charlton, Fort Worth, Texas.

94. "City One End of New Trail to Be Marked," *Brownsville (Texas) Herald*, December 3, 1930.

95. "First Marker Placed On Old Cattle Trail," *Bryan (Texas) Eagle*, July 29, 1931.

96. "Official Trail Names Adopted," *San Antonio Express*, October 16, 1931.

97. "Monument Erected to Trail Drivers," *The Cattleman* 18, no. 7 (December 1931); George W. Saunders to P. P. Ackley, July 14, 1932, Collection of Tom B. Saunders IV, Weatherford, Texas; Monument, October 21–22, 1931, inscribed with cattle brands on one side and bronze relief on the other side, located at the site of Doan's Store, Wilbarger County, Texas. The bronze relief includes a likeness of P. P. Ackley with his name inscribed.

98. Walter E. Long, "Notes on the Longhorn-Chisholm Trail," *Southwestern Historical Quarterly* 60 (July 1956–April 1957): 73–74.

99. "Doan's Crossing on the Red River," monument erected by the State of Texas, 1936, located at the site of Doan's Store, Wilbarger County, Texas; Will Rogers to Bertha Doan Ross, postmarked August 4, 1931, Red River Valley Museum, Vernon, Texas. The inscription on the 1936 monument was taken from the letter from Will Rogers to Bertha Doan Ross. See also the October 21–22, 1931, monument located at the site of Doan's Store.

100. "Oklahoman Inspecting Chisholm Trail Marks," *Pampa Daily News*, April 3, 1938; Texas, Department of Transportation, "Minutes," Minute No. 2861, May 19, 1930; Gibb Gilchrist to P. P. Ackley, December 12, 1930, in G-C-3 Chisholm Trail (1930), Texas Department of Transportation, Texas Highway Department Historical Records, Archives and Information Services Division, Texas State Library and Archives Commission. I have found no records for the duration of Ackley's trail marking project, which ended in 1938, to indicate that there were any changes to the original 1930 Highway Commission minutes. No record has been found to indicate that the Highway Commission approved any of the Ackley markers.

Bibliography

Collections and Archives

Ancestry.com.

    Kansas State Census Collection, 1865–1925.

    US City Directories, 1822–1995.

Cattle Raisers Museum, Texas and Southwestern Cattle Raisers Foundation, Fort Worth.

    John T. Lytle Collection.

County Courthouses

    Denton County Tax Records, 1846–64.

    Jack County Tax Records, 1857–64.

    Montague County Tax Records, 1858–64.

    Parker County Tax Records, 1856–64.

Kansas Historical Society, Topeka

    Kansas State Censuses.

Knox County Archives, Knoxville, Tennessee.

    Knox County Court Minutes I and II.

Oklahoma Historical Society, Archives and Manuscripts Division.

    Barde Collection.

    Creek File, Foreign Relations File.

    Grant Foreman Collection, Edwards Trading Post File.

    Record Book of Chief Sam Checote.

    Shawnee War Claims File.

Oklahoma State University, Edmon Low Library.

    Oklahoma Digital Maps Collection

        McCasland Collection.

        Russal Brawley Collection.

Private Collections

    Pete Charlton, Fort Worth, Texas.

    R. W. Hewett, Henrietta, Texas.

Roland Jary, Fort Worth, Texas.
Tom B. Saunders IV, Weatherford, Texas
San Jacinto Museum of History, Houston.
Tarrant County (Texas) Historical Commission, Fort Worth.
Tarrant County Archives.
Texas State Library and Archives
Texas Highway Department Records
University of Arkansas Libraries, Special Collections.
Charles B. Johnson Papers.
University of Oklahoma Libraries, Western History Collections.
Draper Collection.
Oklahoma Federation of Labor Collection.
University of Texas at Austin, Eugene C. Barker Texas History Collection.
Jesse Chisholm Papers.
Harry Ransom Center, J. Frank Dobie Collection.
US National Archives.
Records of the Bureau of Indian Affairs, RG 75.
Creek Indian Agency, 1864–68, Letters Received.
Kiowa Indian Agency, 1864–68, Letters Received.
Office of Indian Affairs, Special Files, 5, 35–47.
Records of the Central Superintendency of Indian Affairs, 1813–78.
Records of the First Board of Cherokee Commissioners, Folder
1106.
Southern Superintendency of Indian Affairs, Confederate Records,
Letters Sent.
Wichita Indian Agency, 1867–75, Letters Received.
Records of United States Army Continental Commands, 1821–1920,
RG 393.
Department of New Mexico, Letters Sent, vol. 16, 402, RG 393.4.
Willis Library.
Clay County Tax Records, 1861–63.
Palo Pinto County Tax Records, 1857–64.
Stephens County Tax Records, 1861–1910.
Wise County Tax Records, 1857–64.

Public Documents

"An Act to Organize the Territories of Nebraska and Kansas," 1854. General
Records of the United States Government, RG 11, National Archives.
Capron, Horace. *Report of the Commissioner of Agriculture on the Diseases
of Cattle in the United States*. Washington: Government Printing Office,
1871. University of California Libraries, Internet Archive, Open Library.
www.archive.org, accessed September 12, 2012.
Chickasaw Nation. *General Laws of the Legislature of the Chickasaw Nation*,
1867, 1868, 1869, and 1870. N.p.: Chickasaw Nation, Oklahoma, [1871?].

Library of Congress, American Indian Constitutions and Legal Materials. https://lccn.loc.gov/06020309, accessed November 16, 2016.

Colorado. *General Laws, Joint Resolutions, Memorials, and Private Acts of the Territory of Colorado*, Sixth Session, 1866–67. Central City: David C. Collier, 1867.

Estabrook, E. *The Statutes of Nebraska, Embracing All of the General Laws of the State in Force August 1, 1867*. Chicago: Culver, Page, and Hoyne, 1867.

Ewers, John C. *The Horse in Blackfoot Indian Culture with Comparative Material from Other Western Tribes*. Smithsonian Institution, Bureau of American Ethnology, Bulletin 159. Washington: Government Printing Office, 1955. Internet Archive, Open Library. www. archive.org, accessed October 6, 2016.

Gammel, Hans Peter Nielsen, comp. *Laws of Texas, 1822–1897*. 10 vols. Austin: Gammel, 1898.

Garrison, George P., ed. "Diplomatic Archives of the Republic of Texas." In *Annual Report of the American Historical Association for the Year 1908*, vol. 2. Washington: Government Printing Office, 1909.

Illinois. *Public Laws of the State of Illinois Passed by the Twenty-Fifth General Assembly, Convened January 7, 1867*. Springfield: Baker, Bailhache and Co., 1867.

Kansas. *The Laws of the State of Kansas, Passed at the Seventh Session of the Legislature, Commenced at the State Capital on Tuesday, Jan. 8, 1867*. Leavenworth: Bulletin Book and Job Office, 1867. Stanford University Library, Internet Archive, Open Library. www.archive.org, accessed August 15, 2015.

———. *The Laws of the State of Kansas, Passed at the Twelfth Session of the Legislature, Commenced at the State Capital on Tuesday, January 9, 1872*. Topeka: Commonwealth State Printing House, 1872. Collection unknown, Internet Archive, Open Library. www.archive.org, accessed August 15, 2015.

———. *Session Laws of 1876, and Memorials, Passed at the Sixteenth Annual Session of the Legislature, Commenced at the State Capitol on Tuesday, January 11, 1876*. Topeka: Geo. W. Martin, Kansas Publishing House, 1876. Stanford Library, Internet Archive, Open Library. www.archive .org, accessed June 3, 2015.

———, Davis County. *McCoy, Joseph G., vs. the Kansas Pacific Railway Company*. Copy of the Record of the Judgment and Proceedings of the District Court for Davis County, Kansas, 1871. Manuscript. Supreme Court of Kansas, Topeka.

———, Supreme Court. *Brief of the Defendant in Error, Kansas Pacific Railway Company vs. Joseph G. McCoy*. July 1871.

Kappler, Charles J., comp. and ed. *Indian Affairs: Laws and Treaties*, vol. 2. Washington: Government Printing Office, 1904.

Kentucky. *Acts of the Commonwealth of Kentucky Passed by the General*

Assembly at the Adjourned Session, January 3, 1867, vol. 1. Frankfort: Kentucky Yeoman Office, John H. Harney, 1867.

Missouri. *Laws of the State of Missouri Passed at the Regular Session of the Twenty-Third General Assembly, 1867*. Jefferson City: 1867.

Nimmo, Joseph. *Report in Regard to the Range and Ranch Cattle Business of the United States*. Washington: US Department of the Treasury, Bureau of Statistics, 1885.

Norris, Frank. "Cattle Trails—Statement of Significance," March 20, 2012. US Department of the Interior, National Park Service, National Trails Intermountain Region, Santa Fe, New Mexico. https://parkplanning .nps.gov, accessed on April 3, 2014.

———, and Brooke Safford. "Scoping Report, Chisholm and Great Western National Historic Trail Feasibility Study and Environmental Assessment," September 2010. US Department of the Interior, National Park Service, National Trails Intermountain Region, Santa Fe, New Mexico. https://parkplanning.nps.gov, accessed April 3, 2014.

Peters, Richard, ed. *The Public Statutes at Large of the United States of America from the Organization of the Government in 1789 to March 3, 1845*, vol. 4 (Boston: Charles C. Little and James Brown, 1846).

Shoemaker, Earl A. *The Permanent Indian Frontier: The Reason for the Construction and Abandonment of Fort Scott, Kansas, during the Dragoon Era*. Washington: National Park Service, 1986. Clemson University Libraries, Internet Archive, Open Library. www.archive.org, accessed March 7, 2016.

Smith, Theobald, and Fred Lucius Kilborne. *Investigations into the Nature, Causations, and Prevention of Texas or Southern Cattle Fever*. Bureau of Animal Industry Bulletin No. 1. Washington: Government Printing Office, 1893. University of North Texas Libraries, Portal to Texas History, crediting University of Texas Health Sciences Libraries. www .texashistory.unt.edu, accessed November 26, 2017.

Texas, Department of Transportation, "2014 Chisholm Trail Marker Restoration Project." PowerPoint presentation, Austin, November, 2014.

———, Office of Commission Support. "Minutes of the One Hundred and Forty-Fifth Meeting of the State Highway Commission." Minute No. 2861, May 19, 1930. State Office Building, Austin, Texas.

Texas, McLennan County. "A Proclamation of the Commissioners Court of McLennan County, Texas, Recognizing & Commemorating the Chisholm Trail Festival 'Across the Brazos at Waco.'" Proclamation. State of Texas, County of McLennan, October 19, 2010.

Texas, Montague County. Commissioner's Court Meeting Minutes, July 10, 1873; May 10, 1877; May 10, 1880.

Tufts, John Q. Report to the Commissioner, March 1, 1883, in *Annual Report of the Commissioner of Indian Affairs to the Secretary of the Interior*, 1883. S. Doc. 54, 48th Cong., 1st sess., vol. 4.

US Census. *Compendium of the Tenth Census (June 1, 1880), Compiled Pursuant to an Act of Congress Approved August 7, 1882*, rev. ed., Part I. Washington: Government Printing Office, 1885.

———. *1860 Federal Census—Slave Schedules*, Creek Nation, Indian Territory. File 1 of 5, State: Arkansas, County: Indian Lands, Sheet 406A, 2, Reel M653–54, Division: Creek Nation West of the State of Arkansas. Enumerated on September 8, 1860, by Israel G. Vore, Ass't. Marshal. Transcribed by Teri Padgett and proofread by Maggie Stewart for USGenweb. http://files.usgwarchives.net, accessed March 20, 2014.

———. "Guide to 2010 State and Local Census Geography." United States Census Bureau, Census Blogs. www.census.gov/newsroom/blogs /random-samplings/2011/10/us-census-bureau-releases-2010-guide-to -state-and-local-census-geography.html.

———. *Ninth Census of the United States*, vol. 1, *The Statistics of the Population of the United States (June 1, 1870)*. Washington: Government Printing Office, 1872.

———. *Population of the United States in 1860 . . . Eighth Census, Compiled from the Original Returns of the Eighth Census, under the Direction of the Secretary of the Interior, Superintendent of Census, Bureau of the Census Library*. Washington: Government Printing Office, 1864. University of California Libraries, Internet Archive, Open Library. www.archive.org, accessed February 18, 2015.

———. "State & County Quickfacts." US Department of Commerce, United States Census Bureau. www.census.gov/quickfacts/fact/table/US /PST045216, accessed March 10, 2013.

———. *Statistics of the Population of the United States at the Tenth Census, June 1, 1880*. Washington: Government Printing Office.

US Congress, House. *Report of Bvt. Maj. Gen. John Pope*. H. Exec. Doc. 1, pt. 2, 43rd Cong., 2d sess., 1874–75.

———, Senate. *Correspondence on the Subject of the Emigration of Indians*. S. Exec. Doc. 512, 23d Cong., 1st sess, 1834.

US Office of Indian Affairs. *Annual Report of the Commissioner of Indian Affairs to the Secretary of the Interior for the Year 1870*. Washington: Government Printing Office, 1870. Internet Archive, Open Library. www.archive.org, accessed December 12, 2015.

———. *Annual Report of the Commissioner of Indian Affairs to the Secretary of the Interior for the Year 1877*. Washington: Government Printing Office, 1877. Prelinger Library, Internet Archive, Open Library www .archive.org, accessed August 12, 2015.

———. *Report on Indian Affairs by the Acting Commissioner for the Year 1867*. Washington: Government Printing Office, 1868. Prelinger Library, Internet Archive, Open Library. www.archive.org, accessed June 28, 2014.

US War Department. *Regulations of the Army of the United States and*

General Orders in Force on the 17th of February, 1881. Washington: Government Printing Office, 1881. Stanford University Libraries, Google Books. https://books.google.com, accessed October 11, 2016.

———. *Reports of the Secretary of War, with Reconnaissances of Routes from San Antonio to El Paso, by Brevet Lt. Col. J. E. Johnston; Lieutenant W. F. Smith; Lieutenant F. T. Bryan; Lieutenant N. H. Michler; and Captain S. G. French, of Q'rmaster's Dep't.; Also, the Report of Capt. R. B. Marcy's Route from Fort Smith to Santa Fe; and the Report of Lieut. J. H. Simpson of an Expedition into the Navajo Country; and the Report of Lieutenant W. H. C. Whiting's Reconnaissances of the Western Frontier of Texas*. 31st Cong., 1st sess., S. Exec. Doc. 64, July 24, 1850. Washington: Printed at the Union Office, 1850. Ghent University, Google Books. books.google .com, accessed October 25, 2013.

———. *War of the Rebellion: A Compilation of the Official Records of the Union and Confederate Armies*, series I, vols. 1, 13, 22, and 48. Washington: Government Printing Office, 1880–98. Department of History, Ohio State University. http://ehistory.osu.edu/books/official-records, accessed March 13, 2014.

———. *The War of the Rebellion: A Compilation of the Official Records of the Union and Confederate Armies*, series IV, vol. 1. Washington: Government Printing Office, 1900. Making of America, Cornell University Library Digital Collections. https://newcatalog.library.cornell.edu /digitalcollections, accessed July 6, 2015.

Published Works

Abel, Annie Heloise. *The American Indian as Slaveholder and Secessionist*. Lincoln: University of Nebraska Press, 1992.

"Addresses Delivered at the Annual Meeting of the Oklahoma Historical Society." *Chronicles of Oklahoma* 14, no. 2 (June 1936). Oklahoma Historical Society, Oklahoma City. Oklahoma State University Library Electronic Publishing Center, Stillwater. http://digital.library.okstate .edu, accessed October 29, 2015.

Agnew, Jeremy. *The Old West in Fact and Film: History versus Hollywood*. Jefferson, NC, and London: McFarland and Company, 2012.

Allison, Nathaniel Thompson, ed. *History of Cherokee County, Kansas, and Representative Citizens*. Chicago: Biographical Publishing Company, 1904. Internet Archive, Open Library. www.archive.org, accessed November 2, 2013.

Artrip, Louise, and Fullen Artrip. *Memoirs of (the Late) Daniel Fore (Jim) Chisholm and the Chisholm Trail*. N.p.: Artrip Publications, 1959.

Bailey, Jack. *A Texas Cowboy's Journal Up the Trail to Kansas in 1868*. Edited by David Dary. Norman: University of Oklahoma Press, 2006.

Barde, Frederick. *Life and Adventures of Billy Dixon of Adobe Walls, Texas*

Panhandle. Guthrie, OK: Co-Operative Publishing Company, 1914. Internet Archive, Open Library. www.archive.org, accessed June 29, 2014.

Bates, Edmond Franklin. *History and Reminiscences of Denton County*. Denton, TX: McNitzky Printing Company, 1918.

Bentley, O. H. *History of Wichita and Sedgwick County Kansas*, vol. 1. Chicago: C. F. Cooper and Co., 1910.

Billington, Ray Allen, and Martin Ridge. *Westward Expansion: A History of the American Frontier*, 6th ed. Albuquerque: University of New Mexico Press, 2001.

Brasseaux, Carl A., and Keith P. Fontenot. *Steamboats on Louisiana's Bayous: A History and Directory*. Baton Rouge: Louisiana State University Press, 2004.

Brown, Ralph H. "Texas Cattle Trails." *Texas Geographic Magazine* 10, no. 1 (Spring 1946).

Caldwell, Clifford R. *John Simpson Chisum: The Cattle King of the Pecos Revisited*. Santa Fe: Sunstone Press, 2010.

Carter, James Byars, MD. "Disease and Death in the Nineteenth Century: A Genealogical Perspective." *National Genealogical Society Quarterly* 76 (December 1988). www.chartiers.com/, accessed June 30, 2016.

Chipman, D. E. *Nuño de Guzmán and the Province of Pánuco in New Spain, 1518–1533*. Glendale, CA: Arthur H. Clarke Co., 1967.

Chisholm, Fannie G. *The Four State Chisholm Trail*. N.p.: Munguia Printers, 1966.

Clark, J. Stanley. "The Northern Boundary of Oklahoma." *Chronicles of Oklahoma* 15, no. 3 (September 1937): 271. Oklahoma Historical Society, Oklahoma City. Oklahoma State University Library Electronic Publishing Center, Stillwater, http://digital.library.okstate.edu, accessed June 20, 2014.

Clayton, Lawrence. *Longhorn Legacy: Graves Peeler and the Texas Cattle Trade*. Abilene, TX: Cowboy Press, 1994. Cattlemen's Texas Longhorn Conservancy. www.ctlr.org, accessed March 2, 2017.

Clift, J. G. "Notes on the Early History of Stephens County." *Chronicles of Oklahoma* 20, no. 1 (March 1942). Oklahoma Historical Society, Oklahoma City. Oklahoma State University Library Electronic Publishing Center, Stillwater. http://digital.library.okstate.edu, accessed November 3, 2015.

Cody, William F. "Famous Hunting Parties of the Plains." *Cosmopolitan* 17 (June, 1894).

Collinson, Frank. *Life in the Saddle*. Norman: University of Oklahoma Press, 1963; reprint, 1997. Google Books. https://books.google.com, accessed June 10, 2015.

Conover, George W. *Sixty Years in Southwest Oklahoma*. Anadarko: N. T. Plummer Book & Job Printers, 1927.

Cook, James H. *Fifty Years on the Old Frontier as Cowboy, Hunter, Guide, Scout, and Ranchman*. New Haven: Yale University Press, 1923. Hathi-Trust Digital Library. www.hathitrust.org, accessed April 13, 2013.

Cowling, Mary Jo. *Geography of Denton County*. Dallas: Banks Upshaw and Company, 1936. University of North Texas Libraries, Portal to Texas History, crediting Denton Public Library, Denton, Texas. www.texashistory.unt.edu, accessed October 28, 2015.

Cox, James. *Historical and Biographical Record of the Cattle Industry and the Cattlemen of Texas and Adjacent Territory*. Saint Louis: Woodward & Tiernan Printing Co., 1895.

Cutler, William G. *History of the State of Kansas*. Chicago: A. T. Andreas, 1883. Kansas Collection. www.kancoll.org, accessed June 26, 2014.

Dale, Edward E. "Additional Letters of General Stand Watie." *Chronicles of Oklahoma* 1, no. 2 (October 1921). Oklahoma Historical Society, Oklahoma City. Oklahoma State University Library Electronic Publishing Center, Stillwater. http://digital.library.okstate.edu, accessed March 15, 2014.

———. "The Cherokee Strip Live Stock Association." *Chronicles of Oklahoma* 5, no. 1 (March 1927). Oklahoma Historical Society, Oklahoma City. Oklahoma State University Library Electronic Publishing Center, Stillwater. http://digital.library.okstate.edu, accessed June 20, 2014.

Dary, David. *Cowboy Culture: A Saga of Five Centuries*. Lawrence: University Press of Kansas, 1981.

Debo, Angie. *The Road to Disappearance*. Norman: University of Oklahoma Press, 1941.

Dobie, J. Frank. *The Longhorns*. Austin: University of Texas Press, 2010.

Doolittle, William E. "Las Marismas to Panuco to Texas: The Transfer of Open Range Cattle Ranching from Iberia through Northeastern Mexico." *Yearbook of the Conference of Latin Americanist Geographers*, January 1987. Department of Geography, University of Texas, Austin. ResearchGate. www.researchgate.net/publication/242201609, accessed August 6, 2015.

Durham, Philip, and Everett L. Jones. *The Negro Cowboys*. New York: Dodd, Mead, and Company, Cornwall Press, 1965.

Dyer, Frank Lewis, and Thomas Commerford Martin. *Edison: His Life and Inventions*, vol. 2. New York and London: Harper & Brothers Publishers, 1910. University of Michigan Library, Google Books. https://books.google.com, accessed May 5, 2013.

Ely, Glen Sample. *The Texas Frontier and the Butterfield Overland Mail, 1858–1861*. Norman: University of Oklahoma Press, 2016.

Estill-Harbour, Emma. "Greer County." *Chronicles of Oklahoma* 12, no. 2 (June 1934). Oklahoma Historical Society, Oklahoma City. Oklahoma State University Library Electronic Publishing Center, Stillwater. http://digital.library.okstate.edu, accessed March 3, 2014.

Felius, Marleen. *Genus Bos: Cattle Breeds of the World*. Rahway, NJ: Merck & Co., 1985.

Feltenberger, Emma Wright, comp. *Texas Genealogical Records, Ellis County*, vol. 16, 1800–1962. Waxahachie, TX: Genealogical Records Committee, Rebecca Boyce Chapter, Daughters of the American Revolution, 1962. University of North Texas Libraries, Portal to Texas History, crediting Nicholas P. Sims Library and Lyceum, Waxahachie, Texas. www.texashistory.unt.edu, accessed October 14, 2012.

"The Fight against the Cattle-Tick." *Scientific American* 87, supplement 2260 (April 26, 1919). Google Books. https://books.google.com/books?id=kwQ9AQAAIAAJ&pg=PA266&lpg, accessed August 2, 2012.

Foreman, Grant. *Advancing the Frontier, 1830–1860*. Norman: University of Oklahoma Press, 1933.

———. "The Centennial of Fort Gibson." *Chronicles of Oklahoma* 2, no. 2 (June 1924). Oklahoma Historical Society, Oklahoma City. Oklahoma State University Library Electronic Publishing Center, Stillwater. http://digital.library.okstate.edu, accessed October 28, 2013.

———. "Early Trails through Oklahoma." *Chronicles of Oklahoma* 3, no. 2 (June 1925). Oklahoma Historical Society, Oklahoma City. Oklahoma State University Library Electronic Publishing Center, Stillwater. http://digital.library.okstate.edu, accessed February 20, 2015.

———, ed. *A Traveler in Indian Territory: The Journal of Ethan Allen Hitchcock, Late Major-General in the United States Army*. Cedar Rapids, IA: Torch Press, 1930.

From Frontier to Metropolis: Fort Worth, Texas, Diamond Jubilee. Fort Worth: Bateman-Millican Adv. Agency, 1923. University of North Texas Libraries, Portal to Texas History, crediting Fort Worth Public Library. www.texashistory.unt.edu, accessed February 9, 2012.

Gard, Wayne. *The Chisholm Trail*. Norman: University of Oklahoma Press, 1954.

———. "The Shawnee Trail." *Southwestern Historical Quarterly* 56 (July 1952–April 1953). University of North Texas Libraries, Portal to Texas History, crediting Texas State Historical Association, Austin. www.texashistory.unt.edu, accessed October 29, 2013.

Good Roads 1, no. 1 (January–June 1892). Published by the Roads Improvement Bureau of the League of American Wheelmen, New York. Harvard University Library, Google Books. https://books.google.com, accessed May 10, 2015.

Grant, Ulysses S. *The Papers of Ulysses S. Grant*, vol. 17, January 1–September 30, 1867. Edited by John W. Simon. Carbondale and Edwardsville: Southern Illinois University Press, 1991.

Haley, J. Evetts. *Charles Goodnight, Cowman and Plainsman*. Norman: University of Oklahoma Press, 1949.

———. *The XIT Ranch of Texas, and the Early Days of the Llano Estacado*.

Chicago: Capitol Reservation Lands, 1929; reprint, Norman: University of Oklahoma Press, 1967.

Harger, Charles Moreau. "Cattle-Trails of the Prairies." *Scribner's Magazine* 11, no. 6 (June 1892): 732–42. Google Books. www.google.com, accessed April 19, 2015.

Henshaw, Thomas, ed. *The History of Winchester Firearms, 1866–1992*, 6th ed. Clinton, NJ: Winchester Press, 1993.

The History of Pettis County, Missouri. N.p., 1882. New York Public Library, Internet Archive, Open Library. www.archive.org, accessed October 11, 29, 2013.

Hoig, Stan. "The Genealogy of Jesse Chisholm." *Chronicles of Oklahoma* 67, no. 2 (Summer 1989), Bob L. Blackburn, ed. University of Oklahoma Printing Services.

———. *Jesse Chisholm, Ambassador of the Plains.* Boulder: University Press of Colorado, 1991; reprint, Norman: University of Oklahoma Press, 2005.

Hunter, J. Marvin, ed. *The Trail Drivers of Texas*, 2nd ed., rev. Published under the Direction of George W. Saunders. Nashville: Cokesbury Press, 1925; reprint, with introduction by B. Byron Price, Austin: University of Texas Press, 1985.

Hutchins, Joe H. *The History of DeWitt County, Texas.* Dallas: DeWitt County Historical Commission, 1991.

Hutton, Paul Andrew. *Phil Sheridan and His Army.* Lincoln and London: University of Nebraska Press, 1985.

Jackson, Jim Bob. *They Pointed Them East First*, 5th ed. Houston: Kemp and Company, 2014.

Johnson's (Revised) Universal Cyclopaedia: A Scientific and Popular Treasury of Useful Knowledge, vol. 8. New York: A. J. Johnson & Co., 1886. https://books.google.com, accessed December 1, 2012.

Keleher, William A. *The Fabulous Frontier, 1846–1912.* Albuquerque: University of New Mexico Press, 1962; reprint, Santa Fe: Sunstone Press, 2008.

Kenner, Charles. "The Origins of the 'Goodnight' Trail Reconsidered." *Southwestern Historical Quarterly* 77 (July 1973–April 1974). University of North Texas Libraries, Portal to Texas History, crediting Texas State Historical Association. www.texashistory.unt.edu, accessed June 26, 2017.

Kilgore, Dan. "The Spanish Missions and the Origins of the Cattle Industry in Texas." *The Cattleman*, January 1983.

Kraisinger, Gary, and Margaret Kraisinger. *The Shawnee-Arbuckle Cattle Trail, 1867–1870.* Newton, KS: Mennonite Press, 2016.

———. *The Western: The Greatest Texas Cattle Trail.* Newton, KS: Mennonite Press, 2004.

———. *The Western Cattle Trail, 1874–1897: Its Rise, Collapse, and Revival.* Newton, KS: Mennonite Press, 2014.

"Letters and Documents." *Southwestern Historical Quarterly* 44 (July 1940–April 1941). University of North Texas Libraries, Portal to Texas History, crediting Texas State Historical Association. www.texashistory.unt.edu, accessed March 13, 2014.

Lomax, John A. *Cowboy Songs and Other Frontier Ballads*. New York: Sturgis & Walton Company, 1910. Sloan Foundation, Library of Congress, Internet Archive, Open Library. www.archive.org, accessed May 19, 2011.

Long, Walter E. "Notes on the Longhorn-Chisholm Trail." *Southwestern Historical Quarterly* 60 (July 1956–April 1957). University of North Texas Libraries, Portal to Texas History, crediting Texas State Historical Association, Austin. www.texashistory.unt.edu., accessed June 21, 2012.

Love, Clara M. "History of the Cattle Industry in the Southwest." *Southwestern Historical Quarterly* 19 (July 1915–April 1916). University of North Texas Libraries, Portal to Texas History, crediting Texas State Historical Association, Austin, Texas. www.texashistory.unt.edu, accessed October 28, 2015.

Mahoney, Sylvia Gann. *Finding the Great Western Trail*. Lubbock: Texas Tech University Press, 2015.

Martin, Charles F., comp. *Proceedings of the Second Annual Convention of the National Live Stock Association, Denver, Colorado, January 24, 25, 26, and 27, 1899*. Denver: News Job Printing Co., 1899.

Martin, George W. "The Boundary Lines of Kansas." *Kansas Historical Collections* 11 (1910): 53–74.

Mason, I. L. *A World Dictionary of Livestock Breeds, Types, and Varieties*, 4th ed. Wallingford, Oxon, UK: CAB International, 1996.

McCampbell, C. W. "W. E. Campbell, Pioneer Kansas Livestockman." *Kansas Historical Quarterly* 16, no. 3 (August 1948). Kansas Historical Society, Topeka, Kansas. www.kshs.org, accessed June 20, 2014.

McConnell, Joseph C. *The West Texas Frontier*, vol. 2. Palo Pinto, TX: Texas Legal Bank & Book Co., 1939.

McCoy, Joseph G. *Historic Sketches of the Cattle Trade of the West and Southwest*. Edited by Ralph Bieber. Kansas City, MO: Ramsey, Millett & Hudson, 1874; reprint, Lincoln and London: University of Nebraska Press, 1939.

Mead, James R. "The Chisholm Trail." *Wichita Eagle*, March 1, 1890.

Mead. "Little Arkansas." *Collections of the Kansas State Historical Society* 10 (1908). Allen County Americana, Internet Archive, Open Library. www.archive.org, accessed December 4, 2017.

Meserve, John Bartlett. "Governor Jonas Wolf and Governor Palmer Simeon Mosely." *Chronicles of Oklahoma* 18, no. 3 (September 1940). Oklahoma Historical Society, Oklahoma City. Oklahoma State University Library Electronic Publishing Center, Stillwater. http://digital.library.okstate.edu, accessed November 25, 2016.

Milam, Joe B. "The Opening of the Cherokee Outlet." *Chronicles of Okla-*

homa 9, no. 3 (September 1931). Oklahoma Historical Society, Oklahoma City. Oklahoma State University Library Electronic Publishing Center, Stillwater. http://digital.library.okstate.edu, accessed June 20, 2014.

Miller, W. C. *Dime Novel Authors, 1860–1900*. Grafton, MA: Ralph R. Cummings, 1933. University of California, HathiTrust Digital Library. www.hathitrust.org, accessed April 20, 2013.

Monaghan, Jay. *The Great Rascal: The Life and Adventures of Ned Buntline*. Boston: Little, Brown, & Co., 1952. Universal Digital Library, Internet Archive, Open Library. www.archive.org, accessed April 20, 2013.

"Monument Erected to Trail Drivers." *The Cattleman* 18, no. 7 (December 1931). Texas and Southwestern Cattle Raisers Association, Fort Worth.

Moore, Lee, et al. *Letters from Old Friends and Members*. Cheyenne: Wyoming Stock Growers Association, 1923.

Muse, Robert W. P. "History of Harvey County, Kansas." In *Edwards' Historical Atlas of Harvey County, Kansas*. Reprinted in *Harvey County Clippings, 1878–1999*, vol. 1. Topeka: Kansas State Historical Society, n.d.

National Live-Stock Journal 16 (January–December 1885). University of Wisconsin Library, HathiTrust Digital Library. www.hathitrust.org, accessed November 3, 2015..

Newcomb, W. W., Jr. *The Indians of Texas*. Austin and London: University of Texas Press, 1961.

Olmsted, Frederick Law. *A Journey through Texas; or, A Saddle Trip on the Southwestern Frontier: With a Statistical Appendix*. New York: Dix, Edwards & Co.; London: Sampson Low, Son, & Co.; Edinburg: Thos. Constable & Co., 1857. Portal to Texas History, University of North Texas Libraries, Denton. www.texashistory.unt.edu, accessed April 13, 2013.

The Opening of the Great Southwest, 1870–1970: A Brief History of the Origin and Development of the Missouri-Kansas-Texas Railroad, Better Known as the KATY. Dallas: M-K-T-RR Co., 1970.

Peak, Howard Wallace. *The Story of Old Fort Worth*. Fort Worth: Naylor Company, n.d. Portal to Texas History, crediting Fort Worth Public Library. www.texashistory.unt.edu, accessed February 9, 2012.

Pearson, Edmund. *Dime Novels; or, Following an Old Trail in Popular Literature*. Boston: Little, Brown, and Company, 1929.

Peery, Dan W. "Colonel Crocker and the Boomer Movement." *Chronicles of Oklahoma* 13, no. 3 (September 1935). Oklahoma Historical Society, Oklahoma City. Oklahoma State University Library Electronic Publishing Center, Stillwater. http://digital.library.okstate.edu, accessed June 20, 2014.

Personal Memoirs of P. H. Sheridan, vol. 2. New York: Charles L. Webster and Company, 1888. Lincoln Financial Foundation Collection. Internet Archive, Open Library. www.archive.org, accessed June 28, 2014.

Pichardo, José Antonio. *Pichardo's Treatise on the Limits of Louisiana and Texas*, vol. 4. Edited and annotated by Charles Wilson Hackett. Austin: University of Texas Press, 1931.

Pike, Albert. *Report of Albert Pike on Mission to the Indian Nations*. Richmond, VA: Enquirer Book and Job Press, 1861; reprint, Washington: Supreme Council, 1968.

Potter, Isaac B. *The Gospel of Good Roads: A Letter to the American Farmer*. New York: The Evening Post Printing House, 1891. University of Michigan Library, Internet Archive, Open Library. www.archive.org, accessed May 10, 2015.

Potter, Jack M. *Cattle Trails of the Old West*. Edited and compiled by Laura R. Krehbiel. Clayton, NM: Laura R. Krehbiel, 1939.

Progress of Their Road, West from Omaha, Nebraska, across the Continent. New York: Union Pacific Railroad Company, C. A. Alvord, Printer, 1868. University of Michigan Library, Internet Archive, Open Library. www .archive.org, accessed June 28, 2014.

Prucha, Francis Paul. *American Indian Policy in the Formative Years: The Indian Trade and Intercourse Acts, 1790–1834*. Lincoln: University of Nebraska Press, 1972.

Rainey, George. *The Cherokee Strip*. Guthrie, OK: Co-operative Publishing Co., 1933.

Rath, Ida Ellen. *The Rath Trail*. Wichita, KS: McCormick-Armstrong Co., 1961. Ford County Historical Society, the Kansas Collection. www .kancoll.org/books/rath, accessed October 5, 2012.

"Restoration of the Monument at the Initial Point of the Public Land Surveys of Oklahoma." *Chronicles of Oklahoma* 3, no. 1 (April 1925). Oklahoma Historical Society, Oklahoma City. Oklahoma State University Library Electronic Publishing Center, Stillwater. http://digital .library.okstate.edu, accessed March 22, 2014.

Richardson, T. C. "Cattle Trails of Texas." *Texas Geographic Magazine* 1, no. 2 (November 1937).

———. "Cattle Trails from Texas." *Texas Almanac and State Industrial Guide, 1933*. Dallas: A. H. Belo Corporation, 1933. University of North Texas Libraries, Portal to Texas History, crediting Texas State Historical Association, Austin. www.texashistory.unt.edu, accessed June 21, 2012.

———. "Cattle Trails and Trail Driving." *Texas Almanac and State Industrial Guide, 1936*. Dallas: A. H. Belo Corporation, 1936.

Rollins, Philip Ashton. *The Cowboy: His Characteristics, His Equipment, and His Part in the Development of the West*. New York: Charles Scribner's Sons, 1922. University of California Libraries, Internet Archive, Open Library. www.archive.org, accessed September 25, 2015.

Rossel, John. "The Chisholm Trail." *Kansas Historical Quarterly* 5 (1936). Kansas Historical Collections, vol. 22. Kansas State Historical Society, Topeka. Prelinger Library, Internet Archive, Open Library. www .archive.org, accessed November 6, 2012.

Schultz, Myron. "Theobald Smith." *Emerging Infectious Diseases* 14, no. 12 (December 2008). National Center for Biotechnology Information, US National Library of Medicine, Bethesda, Maryland. www.ncbi.nlm.nih .gov/pmc/articles, accessed October 9, 2012.

Siringo, Charles A. *A Texas Cow-boy; or Fifteen Years on the Hurricane Deck of a Spanish Pony.* Chicago: Siringo & Dobson, Publishers, 1886. Sloan Foundation, Library of Congress, Internet Archive, Open Library. www .archive.org, accessed September 13, 2015.

Smiley, Jerome C., and National Live Stock Association of the United States. *Prose and Poetry of the Live Stock Industry of the United States,* vol. 1. Kansas City: Franklin Hudson Publishing Company, 1905. University of Wisconsin Library. https://books.google.com, accessed August 21, 2015.

Smits, David D. "The Frontier Army and the Destruction of the Buffalo: 1865–1883." *Western Historical Quarterly* 25, no. 3 (Autumn 1994). Utah State University. Western History Association. www.history.msu.edu, accessed July 2, 2014.

Snell, Joseph W., and Don W. Wilson. "The Birth of the Atchison, Topeka, and Santa Fe Railroad." *Kansas Historical Quarterly* 34, no. 3 (Autumn 1968). Transcribed by Barbara J. Scott. Kansas Collection, Kansas State Historical Society. www.kancoll.org, accessed June 28, 2014.

Steely, Skipper. *Forty-Seven Years: A New Look at Early Texas History, 1830–77.* Paris, TX: Wright Press, 2011.

Stroud, Joseph. *Memories of Old Western Trails in Texas Longhorn Days.* Williston, ND: Interstate Press, ca. 1932.

Sturcken, Johnye C. "Amanda and William Franklin Burks: A Nueces County Partnership." *East Texas Historical Journal* 30, no. 2 (October 1992). Stephen F. Austin State University ScholarWorks. http:// scholarworks.sfasu.edu/ethj/vol30/iss2/, accessed November 10, 2017.

Taylor, T. U. *Jesse Chisholm.* Bandera, TX: Frontier Times, 1939.

Tennant, H. S. "The Two Cattle Trails." *Chronicles of Oklahoma* 14, no. 1 (March 1936). Oklahoma Historical Society, Oklahoma City. Oklahoma State University Library Electronic Publishing Center, Stillwater. http://digital.library.okstate.edu, accessed October 15, 2012.

Thoburn, Joseph B. "The Chisholm Trail." *Rock Island Magazine* 19 (December, 1924): 4.

———. *A Standard History of Oklahoma.* Chicago and New York: American Historical Society, 1916.

———, and Muriel H. Wright. *Oklahoma: A History of the State and Its People.* New York: Lewis Historical Publishing, 1929.

Thonhoff, Robert H. *The Texas Connection with the American Revolution.* Austin: Eakin Press, 2000.

Wallis, Jonnie Lockhart, and Laurance L. Hill. *Sixty Years on the Brazos: The Life and Letters of Dr. John Washington Lockhart, 1824–1900*. Los Angeles: privately published, 1930.

Webb, Walter P. "The Chisholm Trail." *Southwestern Historical Quarterly* 44 (July 1940–April 1941). University of North Texas Libraries, Portal to Texas History, crediting Texas State Historical Association. www.texashistory.unt.edu, accessed March 13, 2014.

Winfrey, Dorman H., and James M. Day, eds. *Indian Papers of Texas and the Southwest, 1825–1916*. Austin: Texas State Historical Association, 1995.

Wishart, David J., ed. "Folk Songs." *Encyclopedia of the Great Plains*. Lincoln: University of Nebraska–Lincoln.

Wright, Muriel H. "A History of Fort Cobb." *Chronicles of Oklahoma* 34 (Spring 1956). Oklahoma Historical Society, Oklahoma City. Oklahoma State University Library Electronic Publishing Center, Stillwater. http://digital.library.okstate.edu, accessed March 13, 2014.

Dissertations, Theses, and Papers

Cate, Billy, and Steve Myers. "The Chisholm Trail Marker Project: Marking the Chisholm Trail in Texas." Paper. 2012. In author's collection.

Hidalgo County Historical Commission. "Texas Cattle Trails." Paper. Mission, Texas, 2009. http://agenda.hidalgocounty.us/docs/2016/CC/20160105_2660/52685_09HG05%20narrative%20(1).pdf.

Kay, John, David Anthone, Robert Kay, and Christina Hugly. "Nebraska Historic Buildings Survey: Reconnaissance Survey Final Report of Keith County, Nebraska." Nebraska State Historical Society, State Historic Preservation Office, March 1, 1990. www.nebraskahistory.org, accessed August 12, 2015.

Kidd, K. K., W. H. Stone, C. Crimella, C. Carenzi, M. Casati, and G. Rognoni. "Immunogenetic and Population Genetic Analyses of Iberian Cattle." Paper No. 2341. Laboratory of Genetics, University of Wisconsin–Madison, December 5, 1979. www.texaslonghornconservancy.org, accessed June 19, 2012.

Lewis, Anna. "History of the Cattle Industry in Oklahoma." MA thesis, University of California, 1915. University of California Library, 1918. HathiTrust Digital Library. www.hathitrust.org, accessed July 27, 2016.

Liles, Deborah M. "Southern Roots, Western Foundations: The Peculiar Institution and the Livestock Industry on the Northwestern Frontier of Texas, 1846–1864." PhD diss., University of North Texas, August, 2013.

Weger, Tom. "North to Kansas, Identifying the Primary and Secondary Cattle Trails in Montague County, Texas, 1866–1885." Paper, included in *North to Kansas, The Real Chisholm Trail: Identifying the Primary and Secondary Cattle Trails in Montague County Texas, 1866–1885*. Sweetwater, TX: All Things Printed, 2017.

Maps

Arlitt, F. H. *Map of La Salle County*. Austin: Texas General Land Office, 1877. University of North Texas Libraries, Portal to Texas History. www .texashistory.unt.edu, accessed December 23, 2015.

Atherton, Lewis. "Frontier Federal Forts and Cattle Trails, 1867–1886." Map. In *Atlas of Texas*. Austin: University of Texas at Austin, Bureau of Business Research, 1976. Perry Castaneda Library Map Collection. www.lib.utexas.edu, accessed June 18, 2015.

The Best and Shortest Cattle Trail from Texas. Map. Kansas Pacific Railway. Kansas City, MO: K. C. Lith. Co., 1875. Reprint, Pecos, TX: Bill Leftwich, 1958. Collection of Pete Charlton, Fort Worth, Texas.

The Best and Shortest Cattle Trail from Texas. Map. Kansas Pacific Railway. Saint Louis: Levison and Blythe, 1873. Dorothy Sloan Rare Books, Austin, Texas. www.dsloan.com, accessed May 29, 2014.

The Best and Shortest Cattle Route from Texas. Map. Kansas Pacific Railway. Saint Louis: Levison and Blythe, 1872. Kansas State Historical Society, Topeka. www.kansasmemory.org, accessed December 12, 2015.

Bien, Julius. *Map of the Territory of the United States from the Mississippi River to the Pacific Ocean; Ordered by Jeff'n Davis, Secretary of War, to Accompany the Reports of the Explorations for a Railroad Route*. Washington: War Department, 1858. Library of Congress Catalog Number 76695833. Library of Congress, Geography and Map Division, Washington, DC. www.loc.gov/resource/g4050.np000063/, accessed March 13, 2014.

———. *Map of Texas Showing Routes of Transportation of Cattle, 1881*. US Department of the Interior. New York: Julius Bien Lith., 1881. Geography and Map Division, Library of Congress, Washington, DC.

———. *The Range and Ranch Cattle Area of the United States, 1884*. Map. New York: Julius Bien & Co., 1885. Map 1 in Joseph Nimmo, *Report in Regard to the Range and Ranch Cattle Business of the United States*. Washington: US Department of the Treasury, Bureau of Statistics, 1885. Geography and Map Division, Library of Congress, Washington, DC.

Blau, F. G. *Guadalupe County*. Map. Austin: Texas General Land Office, 1877. University of North Texas Libraries, Portal to Texas History. www .texashistory.unt.edu, accessed December 23, 2015.

———. *Map of Denton County*. Austin: Texas General Land Office, April 1877. University of North Texas Libraries, Portal to Texas History. www .texashistory.unt.edu, accessed December 29, 2015.

———. *McLennan County*. Map. Austin: Texas General Land Office, May 1878. University of North Texas Libraries, Portal to Texas History. www .texashistory.unt.edu, accessed December 29, 2015.

Catlin, George. *United States Indian Frontier in 1840, Showing the Position of the Tribes That Have Been Removed West of the Mississippi*. Map. Serial

Set 3016, 52nd Cong., 1st sess., H. Misc. Doc. 340, Part 15, p. 44, map 2. Washington: Government Printing Office, 1840. Edmon Low Library, Oklahoma State University, Oklahoma Digital Maps Collection, McCasland Collection. www.library.okstate.edu, accessed September 10, 2013.

The Chisholm Trail: Exploring the Folklore and Legacy. Map and brochure. Austin: Texas Historical Commission, 2002.

Colton, J. H. *Colton's New Railroad & County Map of the United States and the Canadas &c*. New York: J. H. Colton, 1860. Geography and Map Division, Library of Congress, Washington, DC. www.loc.gov, accessed November 4, 2016.

———, and Company. *Texas*. Map. New York: J. H. Colton, 1855. University of North Texas Libraries, Portal to Texas History, crediting University of Texas at Arlington Library, Arlington, Texas. www.texashistory.unt .edu, accessed October 29, 2013.

Dorchester, E. D. *Trails Made and Routes Used by the Fourth U.S. Cavalry under the Command of General R. S. Mackenzie in Its Operations against Hostile Indians in Texas, Indian Territory (Now Oklahoma), New Mexico, and Old Mexico during the Period of 1871–2–3–4 and 5*. Map. Compiled from Military and Other Surveys. Supervised by Capt. R. G. Carter, Retired, Last Surviving Officer under Gen'l Mackenzie. Freeport, TX: E. D. Dorchester, 1927. University of North Texas Libraries, Portal to Texas History, crediting Hardin-Simmons University Library, Abilene, Texas. www.texashistory.unt.edu, accessed October 2, 2014.

Forman, S. E. "Railroad Lines in Actual Operation, 1860." Map 02889. In *Advanced American History*. New York: The Century Company, 1919. Florida Center for Instructional Technology, College of Education, University of South Florida. http://etc.usf.edu/maps, accessed September 27, 2012.

Fox, Dixon Ryan. "Map Showing Trunk Line Railway Systems Disregarding Minor Branches, 1875." Map 3350. In *Harper's Atlas of American History*. New York: Harper & Brothers Publisher, 1920. Florida Center for Instructional Technology, College of Education, University of South Florida. http://etc.usf.edu/maps, accessed October 5, 2012.

Groos, Otto. *Live Oak County*. Map. Austin: Texas General Land Office, December 1878. University of North Texas Libraries, Portal to Texas History. www.texashistory.unt.edu, accessed December 23, 2015.

———. *Map of Comal County*. Austin: Texas General Land Office, March 3, 1874. University of North Texas Libraries, Portal to Texas History. www .texashistory.unt.edu, accessed December 23, 2015.

Guide Map of the Great Texas Cattle Trail from Red River Crossing to the Old Reliable Kansas Pacific Railway. Kansas City, MO: Ramsey Millett and Hudson, Steam Printers Book Binders and Engravers, Published by the Kansas Pacific Railway, 1875; reprint, Pecos, TX: Bill Leftwich, 1958. Collection of Pete Charlton, Fort Worth, Texas.

Guide Map of the Great Texas Cattle Trail from Red River Crossing to the Old Reliable Kansas Pacific Railway. Kansas City, MO: Ramsey Millett and Hudson, Steam Printers Book Binders and Engravers, Published by the Kansas Pacific Railway, 1874. Kansas State Historical Society. www .kansasmemory.org, accessed May 29, 2014.

Hedges, M. *Map of Oklahoma Territory*. Serial Set 3918., H. Doc. 8, map 3, 743. Compiled from the official records of the General Land Office and other sources. Washington: Norris-Peters Co., Photo Litho., 1898. Edmon Low Library, Oklahoma State University, Oklahoma Digital Maps Collection, McCasland Collection. www.library.okstate.edu, accessed March 6, 2013.

Hoffman & Walker's Pictorial & Historical Map of Texas. N.p.: n.d. University of North Texas Libraries, Portal to Texas History, crediting Hardin-Simmons University Library, Abilene, Texas. www.texashistory.unt .edu, accessed October 2, 2014.

Hunnius, Ado. *Indian Territory with Parts of Neighboring States and Territories*. Map. Prepared by Order of Maj. Gen. J. M. Schofield. Compiled under Direction of 1st Lieut. Henry Jackson, 7th US Cavalry. Bvt. Maj. Gen. A. A. Humphries, Chief of Engineers. Drawn by Ado Hunnius. J. Bien photolith. Washington: US War Department, September 1869. David Rumsey Historical Map Collection.

———. *Military Map of the Indian Territory*. Drawn and Engraved by Ado Hunnius. Compiled under the Direction of 1st Lieut. E. H. Ruffner, Chief Engineer, Department of the Missouri. Washington: US Army, 1875. American Geographical Society Library. University of Wisconsin–Milwaukee Libraries. http://collections.lib.uwm.edu, accessed December 15, 2015.

Indian Territory, Chickasaw Nation, Addington Quadrangle. Map. US Geological Survey. C. H. Fitch, Topographer in Charge. Van. H. Manning, Topographer, Assistant in Charge. Triangulation by C. F. Urquhart. Topography by J. Ahern, A. D. Morton, and R. A. Farmer. Surveyed in 1897–98. Washington: US Geological Survey, 1901. University of North Texas Libraries, Portal to Texas History, crediting UNT Libraries, Government Documents Department, Denton, Texas. www.texashistory .unt.edu, accessed August 30, 2015.

Indian Territory, Chickasaw Nation, Addington Quadrangle. Map. US Geological Survey. C. H. Fitch, Topographer in Charge. Van. H. Manning, Topographer, Assistant in Charge. Triangulation by C. F. Urquhart. Topography by J. Ahern, A. D. Morton, and R. A. Farmer. Surveyed in 1897–98. Washington: US Geological Survey, 1916. Edmon Low Library, Oklahoma State University, Oklahoma Digital Maps Collection,

McCasland Collection. www.library.okstate.edu, accessed on March 6, 2013.

Klappenbach, Louis. *Bexar County*. Map. Austin: Texas General Land Office, July 1871. University of North Texas Libraries, Portal to Texas History. www.texashistory.unt.edu, accessed December 23, 2015.

———. *Hill County*. Map. Austin: Texas General Land Office, November 1871. University of North Texas Libraries, Portal to Texas History. www .texashistory.unt.edu, accessed December 29, 2015.

———. *Wilson County*. Map. Austin: Texas General Land Office, February 1872. University of North Texas Libraries, Portal to Texas History.

Langermann, A. B. *Atascosa County*. Map. Austin: Texas General Land Office, September 1879. University of North Texas Libraries, Portal to Texas History. www.texashistory.unt.edu, accessed December 23, 2015.

———. *Frio County*. Map. Austin: Texas General Land Office, May 1879. University of North Texas Libraries, Portal to Texas History.

———. *Map of Hays County*. Austin: Texas General Land Office, September 1877. University of North Texas Libraries, Portal to Texas History. www .texashistory.unt.edu, accessed December 29, 2015.

———. *Map of Hidalgo County*. Austin: Texas General Land Office, April 1880. University of North Texas Libraries, Portal to Texas History. www .texashistory.unt.edu, accessed December 23, 2015.

———. *Map of Starr County*. Austin: Texas General Land Office, March 1880. University of North Texas Libraries, Portal to Texas History. www .texashistory.unt.edu, accessed December 23, 2015.

———. *Map of Williamson County*. Austin: Texas General Land Office, December 1876. University of North Texas Libraries, Portal to Texas History. www.texashistory.unt.edu, accessed December 29, 2015.

Lucas, A. L. *Tarrant County*. Map. Austin: Texas General Land Office, April 1873. University of North Texas Libraries, Portal to Texas History. www .texashistory.unt.edu, accessed December 29, 2015.

Lungkwitz, Herman. *Map of Caldwell County*. Austin: Texas General Land Office, 1871. University of North Texas Libraries, Portal to Texas History. www.texashistory.unt.edu, accessed December 29, 2015.

Map of Goodnight-Loving Trail. Marked by J. Evetts Haley under direction of Charles Goodnight. Goodnight Ranch, Texas, July 24, 1925. N. S. Haley Memorial Library, Midland, Texas.

Map of the Oklahoma Country in the Indian Territory. 1892. Edmon Low Library, Oklahoma State University, Oklahoma Digital Maps Collection, Russal Brawley Collection. www.library.okstate.edu, accessed March 6, 2013.

Map of Oklahoma Territory. Serial Set 4461, 57th Cong., 2d sess., H. Doc. 5, map 3, p. 495. Compiled from the Official Records of the General Land Office and from Data on File in the Executive Office of the Territory, to

Accompany the Annual Report of the Governor of the Territory. Washington: Government Printing Office, 1902. Edmon Low Library, Oklahoma State University, Oklahoma Digital Maps Collection, McCasland Collection. www.library.okstate.edu, accessed March 6, 2013.

Map of a Portion of Oklahoma Showing the Location of the Chisholm Trail. Oklahoma City: State Highway Commission, Engineering Department, 1933. Edmon Low Library, Oklahoma State University, Oklahoma Digital Maps Collection, McCasland Collection. www.library .okstate.edu, accessed October 17, 2015.

Map of a Portion of Oklahoma Showing the Location of the Old Texas Cattle Trail. Oklahoma City: State Highway Commission, Engineering Department, 1933. Edmon Low Library, Oklahoma State University, Oklahoma Digital Maps Collection, McCasland Collection. www .library.okstate.edu, accessed October 17, 2015.

Marcy, R. B. *Map of Western Trails.* Division of Maps, Library of Congress.

Oklahoma 1997–98 Official State Map. Oklahoma Graphics. Oklahoma City: Oklahoma Department of Transportation.

Oklahoma State Highway System. Map. Oklahoma City: State Highway Commission, 1925. www.okladot.state.ok.us, accessed May 10, 2015.

Preliminary Designation of the State Highway System. Map. Oklahoma City: State Highway Commission, 1921. www.okladot.state.ok.us, accessed May 10, 2015.

Pressler, Charles W. *Grayson.* Map. Austin: Texas General Land Office, December 29, 1853. University of North Texas Libraries, Portal to Texas History. www.texashistory.unt.edu, accessed May 16, 2013.

Roeser, C. *Indian Territory.* Map. Serial Set 1885, 46th Cong., 2d sess., S. Exec. Doc. 124. Department of the Interior, General Land Office. Julius Bien. 16 & 18 Park Place, New York. Washington: Government Printing Office, 1879. Edmon Low Library, Oklahoma State University, Oklahoma Digital Maps Collection, McCasland Collection. www .library.okstate.edu, accessed March 6, 2013.

———. *Indian Territory.* Map. Serial Set 1989, 47th Cong., 1st sess., S. Exec. Doc. 75, p. 9. Department of the Interior, General Land Office. Washington: Government Printing Office, 1879. Edmon Low Library, Oklahoma State University, Oklahoma Digital Maps Collection, McCasland Collection. www.library.okstate.edu, accessed March 6, 2013.

Roessler, A. R. *New Map of Texas Prepared and Published for the Bureau of Immigration of the State of Texas.* New York: Ed W. Welcke & Bro., 1874. University of North Texas Libraries, Portal to Texas History, crediting University of Texas at Arlington Library. www.texashistory.unt.edu, accessed May 21, 2012.

Ross, E. H. *Railroad and Sectional Map of Kansas.* Entered According to Act of Congress, 1870, by E. H. Ross in the clerk's office of the US for the eastern district of Mo. Saint Louis: A. McLean Lith., 1871. Huntington Library, Huntington Rare Book Maps, San Marino, California. http:// hdl.huntington.org, accessed June 3, 2014.

Ruffner, E. H., 1st Lieut. *Map of the Chickasaw Country and Contiguous Portions of the Indian Territory*. 1st Lieut. E.H. Ruffner, Chief Engineer, Military Division of the Missouri. Fort Leavenworth, Kansas. Published under the Direction of Major J. W. Barlow, Chief Engineer, Military Division of the Missouri. By Order of Lt. Genl. P. H. Sheridan, Commanding. Washington: Library of Congress Geography and Map Division, November 1872. Catalog Number 2007630424. www.loc.gov /item/2007630424/, accessed December 15, 2015.

Schenck, F. *Map of Falls County*. Austin: Texas General Land Office, December 1874. University of North Texas Libraries, Portal to Texas History. www.texashistory.unt.edu, accessed December 30, 2015.

Stakemann, Max. *Cooke County*. Map. Austin: Texas General Land Office, March 1876. University of North Texas Libraries, Portal to Texas History. www.texashistory.unt.edu, accessed December 29, 2015.

———. *Montague County*. Map. Austin: Texas General Land Office, October 1875. University of North Texas Libraries, Portal to Texas History. www .texashistory.unt.edu, accessed December 29, 2015.

State of Missouri Formed, but Name of Missouri Territory Retained for the Undivided Portion of Louisiana Purchase. Map. Serial Set 4312, 57th Cong., 1st sess., H. Doc. 15, Part 3, map 15, 987. Washington: Government Printing Office, 1821. Edmon Low Library, Oklahoma State University, Oklahoma Digital Maps Collection, McCasland Collection. www.library.okstate.edu, accessed August 27, 2013.

Strum, G. P. *Indian Territory*. Map. Serial Set 2432, 49th Cong., 1st sess., H. Misc. Doc. 15, pt. 2. Julius Bien & Co., 139 Duane St., N.Y. Department of the Interior, General Land Office. Washington: Government Printing Office, 1887. Edmon Low Library, Oklahoma State University, Oklahoma Digital Maps Collection, McCasland Collection. www .library.okstate.edu, accessed March 6, 2013.

———. *Indian Territory*. Map. Serial Set 2261, 48th Cong, 2d sess., S. Exec. Doc. 17. Department of the Interior, General Land Office. Julius Bien & Co., 139 Duane St., N.Y. Washington: Government Printing Office, 1883. Edmon Low Library, Oklahoma State University, Oklahoma Digital Maps Collection, McCasland Collection. www.library.okstate.edu, accessed March 6, 2013.

Texas General Land Office. *Map of San Patricio County*. Austin: 1879. University of North Texas Libraries, Portal to Texas History. www .texashistory.unt.edu, accessed December 23, 2015.

———. *McMullen County*. Map. Austin: 1877. University of North Texas

Libraries, Portal to Texas History. www.texashistory.unt.edu, accessed December 23, 2015.

———. *Nueces County*. Map. Austin: 1879. University of North Texas Libraries, Portal to Texas History. www.texashistory.unt.edu, accessed December 23, 2015.

———. *Travis County*. Map. Austin: May 14, 1870. University of North Texas Libraries, Portal to Texas History. www.texashistory.unt.edu, accessed December 29, 2015.

Thielepape, George J. *Bell County*. Map. Austin: Texas General Land Office, December 1877. University of North Texas Libraries, Portal to Texas History. www.texashistory.unt.edu, accessed December 29, 2015.

———. *Bosque County*. Map. Austin: Texas General Land Office, December 1876. University of North Texas Libraries, Portal to Texas History. www.texashistory.unt.edu, accessed December 29, 2015.

———. *Coryell County*. Map. Austin: Texas General Land Office, June 1883. University of North Texas Libraries, Portal to Texas History. www.texashistory.unt.edu, accessed December 30, 2015.

———. *Johnson County*. Map. Austin: Texas General Land Office, June 1874. University of North Texas Libraries, Portal to Texas History. www.texashistory.unt.edu, accessed December 29, 2015.

———. *Wise County*. Map. Austin: Texas General Land Office, October 1878. University of North Texas Libraries, Portal to Texas History. www.texashistory.unt.edu, accessed December 29, 2015.

Watson, Gaylord. *Centennial American Republic and Railroad Map of the United States and of the Dominion of Canada*. Washington: Geography and Map Division, Library of Congress, 1875. www.loc.gov, accessed November 4, 2016.

Ziegelasch, A. W. *The Old Chisholm Cattle Trail, with Subsidiary Trails in Texas, 1873*. Map. Item Number HISMAP.0039, Oklahoma Historical Society, Oklahoma City.

Monuments and Markers

"The Crossing." Marker at Brushy Creek Crossing, Round Rock, Texas.

"Doan's Crossing on the Red River." Monument erected by the State of Texas, 1936. Located at the site of Doan's Store, Wilbarger County, Texas.

"Going Up the Chisholm Trail, P. P. Ackley, 1878." Monument with the silhouette of a longhorn head and an arrow pointing north. Wilbarger County, Texas.

Monument, October 21–22, 1931, inscribed with cattle brands on one side and bronze relief on the other side. Located at the site of Doan's Store, Wilbarger County, Texas.

Web Pages

"Adams-Onis Treaty of 1819." New Spain Index, Sons of DeWitt Colony Texas. www.sonsofdewittcolony.org//adamonis.htm, accessed April 28, 2017.

Anderson, H. Allen. "Winchester Quarantine." Handbook of Texas Online, Texas State Historical Association. https://tshaonline.org/handbook/online/articles/azw01, accessed October 5, 2012.

———. "JA Ranch," Handbook of Texas Online, Texas State Historical Association. https://tshaonline.org/handbook/online/articles/apj01, accessed March 2, 2013.

Baldwin, Mickie. "White, James Taylor." Handbook of Texas Online, Texas State Historical Association. https://tshaonline.org/handbook/online/articles/fwh21, accessed May 15, 2013.

"Breeds of Livestock, Department of Animal Science." Oklahoma State University, Department of Animal Science. www.ansi.okstate.edu/breeds/cattle/, accessed June 20, 2012.

Britton, Morris L. "Colbert's Ferry." Handbook of Texas Online, Texas State Historical Association. https://tshaonline.org/handbook/online/articles/rtc01, accessed November 2, 2013.

"Butler Foundation Cattle." Butler Foundation Cattle: One of the Original Seven Families with an Interesting History. http://longhornroundup.com/butler-foundation-cattle/, accessed June 26, 2017.

"Celebrating the Moving Assembly Line in Pictures." Ford Media Center, Ford Motor Company. https://media.ford.com/content/fordmedia/fna/us/en/features/celebrating-the-moving-assembly-line-in-pictures.html.

"A Century of Lawmaking for a New Nation: US Congressional Documents and Debates." Library of Congress. https://memory.loc.gov/ammem/amlaw/.

Dary, David. "Cattle Brands." Handbook of Texas Online, Texas State Historical Association. https://tshaonline.org/handbook/online/articles/auc01, accessed August 31, 2015.

"DeWitt Colony Biographies." Surnames A–G. Sons of DeWitt Colony, Texas. www.sonsofdewittcolony.org/dewittbiosa-g2.htm.

Dutton, Robin. "Olive, Isom Prentice." Handbook of Texas Online, Texas State Historical Association. https://tshaonline.org/handbook/online/articles/fol12, accessed June 3, 2015.

Fowler, Howdy. "Historic Yates Texas Longhorn Collection." Cattlemen's Texas Longhorn Registry. Hondo, Texas. www.ctlr.org, accessed August 2, 2012.

Gard, Wayne. "Fence Cutting." Handbook of Texas Online, Texas State Historical Association. https://tshaonline.org/handbook/online/articles/auf01, accessed March 18, 2016.

Giles, Marie. "Tehuacana Creek Councils." Handbook of Texas Online, Texas State Historical Association. https://tshaonline.org/handbook /online/articles/mgt01, accessed March 21, 2014.

Haley, James L. "Red River War." Handbook of Texas Online, Texas State Historical Association. https://tshaonline.org/handbook/online /articles/qdr02, accessed August 12, 2015.

Hamilton, Allen Lee. "Warren Wagontrain Raid." Handbook of Texas Online, Texas State Historical Association. https://tshaonline.org /handbook/online/articles/btw03, accessed July 2, 2014.

Hannaford, Jean T. "Old Preston Road." Handbook of Texas Online, Texas State Historical Association. https://tshaonline.org/handbook/online /articles/ex003, accessed November 2, 2013.

Hart, Brian. "Towash, TX." Handbook of Texas Online, Texas State Historical Association. https://tshaonline.org/handbook/online/articles /hvt53, accessed November 2, 2013.

Henderson, John C. "Tom Green County." Handbook of Texas Online. Texas State Historical Association. https://tshaonline.org/handbook /online/articles/hct07, accessed August 5, 2015.

Hinton, Harwood P. "Chisum, John Simpson." Handbook of Texas Online, Texas State Historical Association. https://tshaonline.org/handbook /online/articles/fch33, accessed November 1, 2016.

"History," Colt's Manufacturing Company. www.colt.com/Company /History, accessed January 4, 2017.

"History of the Texas Longhorns." United States Fish and Wildlife Service, Wichita Mountains Wildlife Refuge, Oklahoma. www.fws.gov /refuge/Wichita_Mountains/wildlife/longhorns/history.html, accessed June 19, 2012.

"Indian Removal Act." Primary Documents in American History, Web Guides, Library of Congress. www.loc.gov/rr/program/bib/ourdocs /Indian.html, accessed January 4, 2017.

International Texas Longhorn Association. Glen Rose, Texas. www.itla .com/.

"Investigations: Chisholm Trail." *History Detectives: Special Investigations*. Transcript, Episode 1, Season 4, 2006. www.pbs.org/opb /historydetectives/investigation/chisholm-trail/, accessed December 29, 2014.

"King Ranch's Legacy." King Ranch, 2017. www.king-ranch.com, accessed December 5, 2017.

"La Bahia Road." Handbook of Texas Online, Texas State Historical Association. https://tshaonline.org/handbook/online/articles/exl01.

"Legacy of the Texas Longhorns." International Texas Longhorn Association, Glen Rose, Texas. www.itla.com/Longhorn-Legacy, accessed June 15, 2013.

Long, Christopher D. "Old Three Hundred." Handbook of Texas Online, Texas State Historical Association. https://tshaonline.org/handbook /online/articles/um001, accessed October 11, 2016.

May, Jon D. "Leon." Encyclopedia of Oklahoma History and Culture, Oklahoma Historical Society. www.okhistory.org/publications/enc/entry .php?entry=LE014, accessed May 15, 2014.

McCallum, Frances T., and James Mulkey Owens. "Barbed Wire." Handbook of Texas Online, Texas State Historical Association. https:// tshaonline.org/handbook/online/articles/aob01, accessed August 5, 2015.

"Mission and History." The League of American Bicyclists, Washington, DC. www.bikeleague.org/content/mission-and-history.

"Model T Facts." The Ford Motor Company Media Center, Ford Motor Company. https://media.ford.com, accessed December 7, 2016.

Myres, Sandra L. "Fort Graham." Handbook of Texas Online, Texas State Historical Association. https://tshaonline.org/handbook/online /articles/qbf21, accessed November 2, 2013.

Neu, C. T. "Annexation." Handbook of Texas Online, Texas State Historical Association. https://tshaonline.org/handbook/online/articles/mga02, accessed January 4, 2017.

Oltersdorf, Cora. "A Dying Breed?" *Alcalde* 91, no. 2 (November–December 2002). Cattlemen's Texas Longhorn Registry. www.ctlr.org /ewExternalFiles/Alcalde.pdf, accessed December 6, 2017.

Railroad Company v. Husen. 95 U.S. 465 (1877). Justia, US Supreme Court. Institute, Cornell University Law School. https://supreme.justia.com /cases/federal/us/95/465/case.html, accessed October 9, 2012.

"Railroad Ties." Sedalia, MO, Come Grow with Us. http://ci.sedalia.mo.us /about, accessed September 12, 2012.

"The Republic of Texas." Texas State Library and Archives Commission, Austin. www.tsl.texas.gov/treasures/republic/index.html.

"The Revolution Day by Day." The American Revolution, National Park Service. www.nps.gov/revwar/about_the_revolution/revolution_day _by_day.html.

Rogers, Alan. "The Truth about Champion's Horns." National Texas Longhorn Museum, Kansas City, Missouri. www.longhornmuseum.com /Champion.htm, accessed August 2, 2012.

"The Seven Families (Plus One) Revisited." Butler Texas Longhorns. Reprinted from *Texas Longhorn Journal*, July–August 1993. www .butlertexaslonghorns.com/history/sevenfamilies.html, accessed June 26, 2017.

"The Seven Families of Texas Longhorns." Double Helix Ranch. Reprinted from *Texas Longhorn Trails*. http://doublehelixranch.com /SevenFamilies.html, accessed June 26, 2017.

Smith, Julia Cauble. "Loving, Oliver." Handbook of Texas Online, Texas State Historical Association. https://tshaonline.org/handbook/online/articles/flo38, accessed October 11, 2016.

"Statutes at Large," "A Century of Lawmaking for a New Nation: US Congressional Documents and Debates." Library of Congress. https://memory.loc.gov/ammem/amlaw/lwsl.html.

"Texas County Creation Dates and Parent Counties." Family Search, Church of Jesus Christ of Latter Day Saints. www.familysearch.org/wiki/en/Texas_County_Creation_Dates_and_Parent_Counties, accessed May 16, 2013.

Thonhoff, Robert H. "Galvez, Bernardo de." Handbook of Texas Online, Texas State Historical Association. https://tshaonline.org/handbook/online/articles/fga10, accessed May 15, 2013.

Tijerina, Dr. Andres. "Tejano Origins in Mexican Texas." May 4, 1998. Alamo de Parras Hispanic Studies, Sons of DeWitt Colony. www.tamu.edu, accessed April 8, 2013. www.sonsofdewittcolony.org/adp/archives/feature/tejano/tejano.html.

Torrez, Robert. "Pueblo Revolt of 1680." Office of the State Historian, Santa Fe, New Mexico. New Mexico History. http://newmexicohistory.org/people/pueblo-revolt-of-1680, accessed October 2, 2016.

Tower, Michael. "Pauls Valley." Encyclopedia of Oklahoma History and Culture, Oklahoma Historical Society, Oklahoma City. www.okhistory.org/publications/enc/entry.php?entry=PA019, accessed May 15, 2014.

Weaver, Bobby D. "Texas Road." Encyclopedia of Oklahoma History and Culture. Oklahoma Historical Society, Oklahoma City. www.okhistory.org/publications/enc/entry.php?entryname=TEXAS%20ROAD, accessed October 28, 2013.

Webb, Susan L., and Sandra L. Thomas. "Love County." Encyclopedia of Oklahoma History and Culture, Oklahoma Historical Society. www.okhistory.org/publications/enc/entry.php?entry=LO020, accessed May 15, 2014.

Welborn, Daniel B. "Windmills." Handbook of Texas Online, Texas State Historical Association. https://tshaonline.org/handbook/online/articles/aow01.

Wilkison, Gordon. "Progress Report Austin: Legends of Austin 2." Newsreel. 1962. Texas Archive of the Moving Image, Austin. www.texasarchive.org/library/index.php/Progress_Report_Austin_-_Legends_of_Austin_2, accessed March 29, 2012.

Wooster, Ralph A. "Civil War." Handbook of Texas Online, Texas State Historical Association. https://tshaonline.org/handbook/online/articles/qdc02.

"Yates Horn Collection." Cattlemen's Texas Longhorn Registry, Hondo, Texas. www.ctlr.org/ewExternalFiles/Yates%20Horn%20Collection.pdf, accessed November 27, 2017.

Newspapers

Alexandria (Virginia) Gazette. Chronicling America: Historic American Newspapers, Library of Congress. www.chroniclingamerica.loc.gov, accessed September 15, 2015.

Arizona Silver Belt (Globe City, Arizona). Chronicling America: Historic American Newspapers, Library of Congress. www.chroniclingamerica .loc.gov, accessed November 3, 2015.

Army-Navy Journal.

Atchison Daily Champion. Historical Newspaper Archives. www.newspapers .com, accessed April 25, 2014.

Austin Republican. Fort Worth Public Library, Newsbank, Inc., America's GenealogyBank. www.infoweb.newsbank.com, accessed June 13, 2014.

Austin State Gazette. University of North Texas Libraries, Portal to Texas History, crediting Dolph Briscoe Center for American History, Austin, Texas. www.texashistory.unt.edu, accessed July 30, 2014.

Austin Tri-Weekly State Gazette. University of North Texas Libraries, Portal to Texas History, crediting Dolph Briscoe Center for American History, Austin, Texas. www.texashistory.unt.edu, accessed March 8, June 13, 2014.

Austin Weekly Democratic Statesman. Chronicling America: Historic American Newspapers, Library of Congress. www.chroniclingamerica.loc .gov, accessed June 23, 2014.

Austin Weekly Statesman. Chronicling America: Historic American Newspapers, Library of Congress. www.chroniclingamerica.loc.gov, accessed June 7, 2014; June 16, 2016. University of North Texas Libraries, Portal to Texas History, crediting UNT Libraries, Denton, Texas. www.texashistory.unt.edu, accessed March 18, 2016.

Barbour County Index (Medicine Lodge, Kansas). Chronicling America: Historic American Newspapers, Library of Congress. www .chroniclingamerica.loc.gov, accessed June 7, July 2, 2014; January 7, 2016.

Berkeley (California) Daily Gazette. Collection of Pete Charlton, Fort Worth, Texas.

Brownsville (Texas) Herald. Newspapers.com Historical Newspaper Archive. www.newspapers.com, accessed April 23, 2015; September 2, 2016.

Bryan (Texas) Eagle. Newspapers.com Historical Newspaper Archive. www .newspapers.com, accessed April 23, 2015.

Bryan (Texas) Morning Eagle. Chronicling America: Historic American Newspapers, Library of Congress. www.chroniclingamerica.loc.gov, accessed May 10, 2015.

Canadian (Texas) Record. University of North Texas Libraries, Portal to Texas History, crediting Hemphill County Library, Canadian, Texas. www.texashistory.unt.edu, accessed June 21, 2012.

Canyon (Texas) News. Newspapers.com Historical Newspaper Archive. www.newspapers.com, accessed May 7, 2015.

Cheyenne Transporter (Darlington, Indian Territory). Chronicling America: Historic American Newspapers, Library of Congress. www .chroniclingamerica.loc.gov, accessed June 7, 23, July 2, 2014; January 7, March 18, 2016.

Chicago Tribune.

Cleburne (Texas) Times-Review. www.cleburnetimesreview.com, accessed January 21, 2012.

Corsicana (Texas) Daily Sun. Newspapers.com Historical Newspaper Archive. www.newspapers.com, accessed July 26, 2017.

Daily Crescent (New Orleans).

Daily Illinois State Journal.

Daily Missouri Democrat (Saint Louis).

Daily Morning Astorian (Astoria, Oregon). Chronicling America: Historic American Newspapers, Library of Congress. www.chroniclingamerica .loc.gov, accessed October 17, 2012.

Daily Oklahoman (Oklahoma City).

Daily Yellowstone Journal (Miles City, Montana). Chronicling America: Historic American Newspapers, Library of Congress. www .chroniclingamerica.loc.gov, accessed October 17, 2012.

Dallas Daily Herald. Chronicling America: Historic American Newspapers, Library of Congress. www.chroniclingamerica.loc.gov, accessed June 28, 2014.

Dallas Herald. Chronicling America: Historic American Newspapers, Library of Congress. www.chroniclingamerica.loc.gov, accessed June 13, 28, 2014.

Dallas Morning News. Fort Worth Public Library, Newsbank, Inc., America's GenealogyBank. www.infoweb.newsbank.com, accessed May 12, 2015; Collection of Pete Charleton, Fort Worth, Texas.

Denison (Texas) Daily Cresset. University of North Texas Libraries, Portal to Texas History, crediting Grayson County Frontier Village, Denison, Texas. www.texashistory.unt.edu, accessed February 20, 2015.

Denison (Texas) Daily News. University of North Texas Libraries, Portal to Texas History, crediting Grayson County Frontier Village. www .texashistory.unt.edu, accessed July 15, 2016.

Denison (Texas) Sunday Gazetteer. University of North Texas Libraries, Portal to Texas History, crediting Grayson County Frontier Village, Denison, Texas. www.texashistory.unt.edu, accessed August 21, 2015.

Dodge City Times. Chronicling America: Historic American Newspapers, Library of Congress. www.chroniclingamerica.loc.gov, accessed October 17, 2012; June 12, July 2, 2014; January 7, 2016.

Eaton (Ohio) Democrat. Chronicling America: Historic American Newspapers, Library of Congress. www.chroniclingamerica.loc.gov, accessed July 2, 2014.

Emporia (Kansas) News. Chronicling America: Historic American Newspapers, Library of Congress. www.chroniclingamerica.loc.gov, accessed July 10, 2012; April 24, May 29, June 7, 23, 28, July 2, 2014; February 5, 20, July 15, 2015; January 7, 2016.

Emporia (Kansas) Weekly News. Chronicling America: Historic American Newspapers, Library of Congress. www.chroniclingamerica.loc.gov, accessed March 18, 2016. Newspapers.com Historical Newspaper Archive. www.newspapers.com, accessed October 16, 2016.

Enid (Oklahoma) Daily Eagle. Grace Armantrout Museum, George West, Texas.

Enid (Oklahoma) Events. Grace Armantrout Museum, George West, Texas.

Evansville (Indiana) Daily Journal. Chronicling America: Historic American Newspapers, Library of Congress. www.chroniclingamerica.loc.gov, accessed October 16, 2016.

Fayette County (Ohio) Herald. Chronicling America: Historic American Newspapers, Library of Congress. www.chroniclingamerica.loc.gov, accessed July 15, 2015.

Fort Worth Daily Gazette. Chronicling America: Historic American Newspapers, Library of Congress. www.chroniclingamerica.loc.gov, accessed October 17, 2012; June 23, 2014; March 18, 2016.

Fort Worth Star Telegram. Fort Worth Public Library, Newsbank, Inc., America's GenealogyBank. www.infoweb.newsbank.com, accessed December 5, 2014; May 12, 2015.

Frontier Echo (Jacksboro, Texas). University of North Texas Libraries, Portal to Texas History, crediting Dolph Briscoe Center for American History, Austin, Texas. www.texashistory.unt.edu, accessed February 20, 2015.

Galveston Daily News. University of North Texas Libraries, Portal to Texas History, crediting Abilene Library Consortium, Abilene, Texas. www.texashistory.unt.edu, accessed September 17, 2014; February 3, August 21, 2015; January 20, March 18, 2016.

Galveston Weekly News. Barker Texas History Center, University of Texas at Austin.

Georgetown (Texas) Watchman. University of North Texas Libraries, Portal to Texas History, crediting Dolph Briscoe Center for American History, Austin, Texas. www.texashistory.unt.edu, accessed March 8, 2014.

Golden Era (Lincoln, New Mexico). Chronicling America: Historic American Newspapers, Library of Congress. www.chroniclingamerica.loc.gov, accessed November 3, 2015.

Grand Forks Evening Times. Chronicling America: Historic American Newspapers, Library of Congress. www.chroniclingamerica.loc.gov, accessed May 10, 2015.

Harrisonburg (Louisiana) Independent. Chronicling America: Historic American Newspapers, Library of Congress. www.chroniclingamerica.loc.gov, accessed February 5, 2014.

Highland Weekly News (Hillsborough [Hillsboro], Ohio). Chronicling America: Historic American Newspapers, Library of Congress. www.chroniclingamerica.loc.gov, accessed January 7, 19, 2016.

Houston Chronicle. www.chron.com, accessed December 5, 2014.

Houston Daily Post. Chronicling America: Historic American Newspapers, Library of Congress. www.chroniclingamerica.loc.gov, accessed May 10, 2015.

Houston Telegraph. Portal to Texas History, University of North Texas Libraries, crediting Dolph Briscoe Center for American History, Austin, Texas. www.texashistory.unt.edu, accessed December 12, 2015.

Houston Telegraph and Texas Register. University of North Texas Libraries, Portal to Texas History, crediting Dolph Briscoe Center for American History, Austin. www.texashistory.unt.edu, accessed May 6, 2013; February 5, 2014.

Indian Chieftain (Vinita, Indian Territory). Chronicling America: Historic American Newspapers, Library of Congress. www.chroniclingamerica.loc.gov, accessed November 3, 2015, March 18, 2016.

Indian Journal (Muskogee, Indian Territory). Newspapers.com Historical Newspaper Archives. www.newspapers.com, accessed March 18, 2016.

Junction City (Kansas) Weekly Union.

Kansas City Star. Fort Worth Public Library, Newsbank, Inc., America's GenealogyBank. www.infoweb.newsbank.com, accessed May 12, 2015.

Kansas Daily Commonwealth (Topeka).

Kansas Herald of Freedom (Wakarusa, Kansas Territory). Chronicling America: Historic American Newspapers. www.chroniclingamerica.loc.gov, accessed September 17, 2015.

Leavenworth Daily Conservative.

Leavenworth Times. Newspapers.com Historical Newspaper Archive. www.newspapers.com, accessed April 14, 2016.

Leavenworth Weekly Times. Chronicling America: Historic American Newspapers, Library of Congress. www.chroniclingamerica.loc.gov, accessed June 7, 24, July 2, 2014; July 15, 2015.

Los Angeles Daily Herald. Chronicling America: Historic American Newspapers, Library of Congress. www.chroniclingamerica.loc.gov, accessed August 5, 2015.

Lubbock Morning Avalanche. Newspapers.com Historical Newspaper Archive. www.newspapers.com, accessed April 23, May 14, 2015.

Medford (Oklahoma) Patriot. Grace Armantrout Museum, George West, Texas.

Miami (Oklahoma) Daily News-Record. Newspapers.com Historical Newspaper Archive. www.newspapers.com, accessed July 16, 2016.

Milan (Tennessee) Exchange. Chronicling America: Historic American Newspapers, Library of Congress. www.chroniclingamerica.loc.gov, accessed June 7, 2014; January 19, 2016.

Milwaukee Journal. Google Newspaper Archive. https://news.google.com /newspapers, accessed May 12, 2015.

Muskogee Daily Phoenix. Grace Armantrout Museum, George West, Texas.

Nebraska Advertiser (Brownsville, Nebraska). Chronicling America: Historic American Newspapers, Library of Congress. www .chroniclingamerica.loc.gov, accessed June 28, 2014.

New North-west (Deer Lodge, Montana). Chronicling America: Historic American Newspapers, Library of Congress. www.chroniclingamerica .loc.gov, accessed January 7, 2016.

New Orleans Bulletin. Chronicling America: Historic American Newspapers, Library of Congress. www.chroniclingamerica.loc.gov, accessed January 7, 2016.

New Orleans Daily Crescent. Chronicling America: Historic American Newspapers, Library of Congress. www.chroniclingamerica.loc.gov, accessed May 5, 2013; February 5, 2014.

New Orleans Democrat. Chronicling America: Historic American Newspapers, Library of Congress. www.chroniclingamerica.loc.gov, accessed January 7, 2016.

New Orleans Republican. Chronicling America: Historic American Newspapers, Library of Congress. www.chroniclingamerica.loc.gov, accessed April 20, 2013.

New York Daily Tribune.

New York Sun. Chronicling America: Historic American Newspapers, Library of Congress. www.chroniclingamerica.loc.gov, accessed May 10, 2015.

New York Times.

Northern Standard (Clarksville, Texas). University of North Texas Libraries, Portal to Texas History, crediting Dolph Briscoe Center for American History, Austin. www.texashistory.unt.edu, accessed March 21, 2014.

Norton's Union Intelligencer (Dallas, Texas). University of North Texas Libraries, Portal to Texas History, crediting Abilene Library Consortium, Abilene, Texas. www.texashistory.unt.edu, accessed March 18, 2016.

Oakland (California) Tribune. Newspapers.com Historical Newspaper Archive. www.newspapers.com, accessed December 8, 2016.

Oklahoma City Evening Free Press. Grace Armantrout Museum, George West, Texas.

Omaha Daily Bee. Chronicling America: Historic American Newspapers, Library of Congress. www.chroniclingamerica.loc.gov, accessed October 16, 2012; November 3, 2014.

Pampa Daily News. Newspapers.com Historical Newspaper Archive. www
.newspapers.com, accessed April 23, May 14, 2015.

Peoples Press (El Reno, Oklahoma). Grace Armantrout Museum, George
West, Texas.

Perry (Oklahoma) Journal. Newspapers.com Historical Newspaper Archive.
www.newspapers.com, accessed July 16, 2016.

Phillipsburg (Kansas) Herald. Chronicling America: Historic American
Newspapers, Library of Congress. www.chroniclingamerica.loc.gov,
accessed January 7, 2016.

Pulaski (Tennessee) Citizen. Chronicling America: Historic American
Newspapers, Library of Congress. www.chroniclingamerica.loc.gov,
accessed June 7, 2014.

Rock Island (Illinois) Daily Argus. Chronicling America: Historic American
Newspapers, Library of Congress. www.chroniclingamerica.loc.gov,
accessed January 19, 2016.

Saint Johns (Arizona Territory) Herald. Chronicling America: Historic
American Newspapers, Library of Congress. www.chroniclingamerica
.loc.gov, accessed June 7, 2014.

Saint Landry Democrat (Opelousas, Louisiana). Chronicling America: Historic American Newspapers, Library of Congress. www
.chroniclingamerica.loc.gov, accessed January 7, 2016.

Saline County Journal (Salina, Kansas). Chronicling America: Historic
American Newspapers, Library of Congress. www.chroniclingamerica
.loc.gov, accessed July 15, 2015.

San Angelo Press. Chronicling America: Historic American Newspapers,
Library of Congress. www.chroniclingamerica.loc.gov, accessed
May 10, 2015.

San Antonio Express. National Archives at Fort Worth, NewspaperArchive
.com. www.newspaperarchive.com, accessed March 26, 2015.

San Antonio Light. University of North Texas Libraries, Portal to Texas
History, crediting UNT Libraries, Denton, Texas. www.texashistory
.unt.edu, accessed June 23, 2014; March 18, 2016. Chronicling America: Historic American Newspapers, Library of Congress. www
.chroniclingamerica.loc.gov, accessed July 2, 2014. National Archives
at Fort Worth, NewspaperArchive.com. www.newspaperarchive.com,
accessed April 10, 2015.

Sandusky (Ohio) Register. Newspapers.com Historical Newspaper Archive.
www.newspapers.com, accessed December 8, 2016.

Shiner (Texas) Gazette. Chronicling America: Historic American Newspapers, Library of Congress. www.chroniclingamerica.loc.gov,
accessed May 10, 2015.

Shreveport (Louisiana) South-Western. Chronicling America: Historic American Newspapers, Library of Congress. www.chroniclingamerica.loc
.gov, accessed July 15, 2015.

Southern Sentinel (Plaquemine, Louisiana). Chronicling America: Historic American Newspapers, Library of Congress. www.chroniclingamerica.loc.gov, accessed February 5, 2014.

Stark County Democrat (Canton, Ohio). Chronicling America: Historic American Newspapers, Library of Congress. www.chroniclingamerica.loc.gov, accessed April 20, 2013.

Sun River (Montana) Sun. Chronicling America: Historic American Newspapers, Library of Congress. www.chroniclingamerica.loc.gov, accessed October 17, 2012.

Thibodaux Minerva. Chronicling America: Historic American Newspapers, Library of Congress. www.chroniclingamerica.loc.gov, accessed February 5, 2014.

Topeka State Journal. Chronicling America: Historic American Newspapers, Library of Congress. www.chroniclingamerica.loc.gov, accessed April 25, 2014; May 10, 2015.

True American (New Orleans, Louisiana). Chronicling America: Historic American Newspapers, Library of Congress. www.chroniclingamerica.loc.gov, accessed October 11, 2016.

Tulsa Daily World. Chronicling America: Historic American Newspapers, Library of Congress. www.chroniclingamerica.loc.gov, accessed May 10, 2015.

Vernon (Texas) Daily Record. Newspapers.com Historical Newspaper Archive. www.newspapers.com, accessed April 23, 2015.

Waco Daily Examiner. Chronicling America: Historic American Newspapers, Library of Congress. www.chroniclingamerica.loc.gov, accessed June 20, 23, 2014. University of North Texas Libraries, Portal to Texas History, crediting UNT Libraries, Denton, Texas. www.texashistory.unt.edu, accessed June 20, 23, 2014.

Western Reserve Chronicle (Warren, Ohio). Chronicling America: Historic American Newspapers, Library of Congress. www.chroniclingamerica.loc.gov, accessed July 15, 2015.

White Cloud Kansas Chief. Chronicling America: Historic American Newspapers, Library of Congress. www.chroniclingamerica.loc.gov, accessed June 23, 28, 2014.

Wichita City Eagle. Chronicling America: Historic American Newspapers, Library of Congress. www.chroniclingamerica.loc.gov, accessed April 24, June 7, 23, July 29, 2014; January 7, 2016.

Wichita Daily Eagle. Chronicling America: Historic American Newspapers, Library of Congress. www.chroniclingamerica.loc.gov, accessed June 25, 2012; April 24, June 7, 2014; January 19, 2016.

Wichita Eagle. Newspapers.com Historical Newspaper Archive. www.newspapers.com, accessed April 23, 2015. Chronicling America: Historic American Newspapers, Library of Congress. www.chroniclingamerica.loc.gov, January 19, 2016.

Index

Smith, Theobald, 32

Smoky Hill/David Butterfield Overland Dispatch Stage Trail, 183

Smoky Hill River, 133, 145

Somervell County, TX, 98

South Concho River. *See* Concho River

South Dakota, 55

Southern Crioulo, 12

South Platte River, 29, 33, 111

Southwell Company: 237n10

Southwestern Historical Quarterly, 67

Spain, 12, 51

Spanish fever. *See* Texas fever

Spanish Fort Bend, 88–89, 222n13

splenic fever. *See* Texas fever

St. Denis, Louis Juchereau de, 14

Stamford, TX, 147, 199

stampede, 22, 26, 36, 40, 43, 45–47, 54, 100

Standard Oil Company, 230n7

Star Telegram, 185. *See also* Fort Worth Star Telegram

Starr County, TX, 211n22

state highway commission. *See* Texas State Highway Commission

Steen, G. N., 221n8

Stephen F. Austin's Texas Colony, 55

Stephens County, OK, 92, 143, 198

Stephens County, TX, 101

Sterling, CO, 111

Stevens, Enoch, 221n5

Stinking Creek, 92

Stockmen's Association, 187. *See also* Texas Stockmen's Association

Stonewall County, TX, 27

Story of Old Fort Worth, The, 163, 238n3

Sugg, W. W., 84, 134

Sumner County, KS, 93, 95

Sweetwater, TX, 122

tailing, 37

Tamaulipas, 14

Tarrant County, TX, 2, 87–88, 202n5, n13, 215n2

Tascosa, TX, 27

Taylor County, TX, 101–102, 112

Taylor, TX, 42

Tebo and Neosho Railroad Company, 21

Tehuacana Creek councils, 72, 215n2

Tejas Indians, 14

Teller, Henry M., 120, 122

Tennant, H. S., 160–161, 182, 228n23

Tennessee, 23, 71, 97

Terán, Domingo de los Ríos, 14

Texas: cattle trailing era, 1–131; Chisholm Trail controversy, 132–189

Texas cattle disease. *See* Texas fever

Texas Cattle Trail, 63, 95, 115, 132, 143, 160, 168–70, 185

Texas Country Reporter, 237n10

Texas Department of Transportation, 184, 246n21, 247n22

Texas Emigrant Road, 55

Texas fever, 6, 7, 15, 79, 82, 104, 117, 192, 196, 197; cause, symptoms and effects of, 21–33, 82–84, 110–11, 124–30

Texas Fever District, 32–33

Texas Gulf Coast, 10, 25, 167

Texas Highway Commission, 148–52, 154, 157, 181, 184, 199, 200, 246n21. *See also* Texas State Highway Commission

Texas Historical Commission, 183, 237n10, 246n21